THE DECLINE OF THE
AMERICAN
ECONOMY

Clement Onyemelukwe

A STRUCTURAL ANALYSIS OF THE U.S. ECONOMY

Library of Congress Control Number:		2016916225
ISBN:	Hardcover	978-1-5245-3634-3
	Softcover	978-1-5245-3633-6
	eBook	978-1-5245-3632-9

Print information available on the last page.

Rev. date: 11/11/2019

To order additional copies of this book, contact:
Xlibris
1-888-795-4274
www.Xlibris.com
Orders@Xlibris.com
746679

THE DECLINE OF THE
AMERICAN
ECONOMY

Clement Onyemelukwe
Engineer, Economist
Group Chairman, Colechurch Internationald

ALSO BY CLEMENT ONYEMELUKWE

Economic Underdevelopment: An Inside View

*The Science of Economic Development and Growth:
The Theory of Factor Proportions*

Acknowledgment

I want to pay my respect and convey my love to my wife of fifty-five years, Catherine, for her support in my writing this book. Many times, she argued and challenged my arguments and ideas in this book.

Contents

Preface

Structural Economic Science

The Decline of the American Economy is intended to tell Americans that their country's economy, which fed American power and buoyed up Western civilization in the past two hundred years, is declining. American leaders and politicians however refuse to admit that there is a problem. Part of the cause of the problem is politics: a country in which we are seeing the ugly side of democracy in which nothing gets done because of partisan politics. To my mind, however, the greater part of the problem is the failure of US economists to understand and diagnose the country's basic economic structure and the far reaching effect it has on the country's economic history and future prospects.

Conventional economics in the US and indeed the West is increasingly unable to deal with a world that is getting more technologically complicated. For most conventional economists today American economy is all about finance: interest rate, inflation, Wall Street indexes, globalization, trade, economic indexes, financial reserves etc. For those of them who still think analytically, production is made up of only labor and capital, and omitting material, quite oblivious that one cannot produce anything without materials. They continue in the path of increasingly *squeezing* labor out of production in the name of productivity. These are the basic errors of capitalism. US economists equate capital invested in US dollars as the measure of US economic growth achieved through financial management in furtherance of capitalism.

Conventional economics' error is in not including the factor material as a production factor and increasingly playing down labor in economic analysis. Strctural economics, on the other hand, has progressed and it is now possible to analyze any economy in three-dimensional terms of labor, material and capital (production aid). The basic difference between conventional economics and structural economics science is that structural science is concerned about how a country can make the best, efficient use of its endowed natural resources of labor material and production factor (capital) and not how—as conventionally, one can manipulate and maximize finance in the expectation that this will maximize economic growth.

It is not surprising that the conventional economics in the United States lacks the necessary tools with which to analyze and understand what has structurally increasingly gone wrong with the US economy. This book is a (scientific) structural economic analysis of the American economy based on the general economic science that I established in my 2005 book: *The Science of Economic Development and Growth: the Theory of Factor Proportions.*

I have been disillusioned with conventional economics since I gained my engineering degree at the University of Leeds in the United Kingdom in 1956 and my economics degree at the University of London in 1960. With my scientific engineering background, I found much of what I was taught in conventional economics to be false, inconsistent, and unscientific. I've been working as an economist and a scientist over the past over fifty-five years to strcturally update conventional economics, for which I had earlier written two books: *Underdevelopment: An Inside View* in 1974, and *The Science of Economic Development and Growth: The Theory of Factor Proportions* in 2005. I became a US citizen in 2007.

I have tried my best to keep this book simple, even though the topic is complicated and a lot more research into economic science is required that now needs to be taken up in universities. I wanted economists and non-economists to come away from reading this book realizing that we in the United States are facing the biggest national crisis today: an economic decline. I hope that many people who read it will put their hands up to ask those who run our affairs to sit up and do something about the structurally collapsing US economy and that US conventional economists will take up structural economic science.

Part 1

Structural Deficiencies of the US Economy

Chapter 1

America's Structural Economic Imbalance

The 2007–2009 American recession officially began in December 2007, lasting eighteen months until its official conclusion in June 2008. It was longer than the previous three recessions in 1973–1975, 1981–1982, and 2000–2001, and it was the deepest recession since the Great Depression.

More than eleven years after this recession was supposed to be officially over, economic growth was a struggling about 3 percent compared to 7.7 percent a year post the 1982 recession and 6.2 percent a year after the 1975 recession. As of 2019, the US economic growth has not recovered to its prerecession level.

The 2007 recession took American policy makers and their economic advisers by surprise. The Chairman of Fed at the time, Ben Bernanke, was telling Congress on July 18, 2007 that: "Overall the US economy appears likely to expand at a moderate pace the second half of 2007 with growth strengthening a bit in 2008 close to the economy's underlying trend."[1] He got it all wrong because very shortly after his speech the United States went into recession. President Bush at the State of the Union Speech to Congress in the same year said, "We are now in the forty-first month of job growth and recovery that has created 7.2 million new jobs so far. Unemployment is low, inflation low, and wages rising." Bernanke and the President were, therefore, taken unawares by the recession. The economic profession was unable to predict the recession

1

despite masses of conventional statistical data, academic research, and models because they did not understand the structural structure of the economy they were dealing with.

If a friend who has been healthy and strong over the years, plays tennis every day and regularly sees his doctor suddenly collapsed I do not need anyone to tell me that my friend must have an inner structural ailment that his doctor was unable to diagnose. A reasonable conclusion from this analogy is that the US economy is structurally ill and collapsed suddenly in 2007. Another reasonable conclusion is that whatever caused the recession is also outside the knowledge of conventional economists represented by Bernanke at the time. A third conclusion, considering the fact that the immediate previous recessions were mild compared with the 2007–2009 recession, is that the US economy has a cyclically irregular and unpredictable behavior. That means that what is driving the US economy must have a large component of cyclical irregularity.

If the US economy has cyclical irregularity, it means that it is (technically) structurally unbalanced. Every six or ten years or so, the US economy slips into some kind of recession whose behavior can never be predicted. If the economic cycle suffers an unexpected bigger gyration, as it did in 2007–2009, it means that it is unavoidable that US will have many more recessions in the future and that some of them may be worse than the 2007–2009 great recession and there are prospects for possible depressions. Scientists associate irregular cyclical behavior with what they call dynamic imbalance. They will say that the US economic structure is dynamically unbalanced.

Describing the American economy as structurally unbalanced may come as a surprise to many Americans because American policy makers and our conventional economic experts have told us that we have the best economy in the world. Having pointed at the gravity of the American structural economic imbalance, I needed, as an engineer and economist, to put this imbalance in perspective to show how this is causing trouble for the US economy, and how structural economic science is needed if we can save US long-term economic prospects.

An economy is a dynamic structure because it is perpetually 'moving' and changing. The structural law of dynamics is that any moving object (including us, human beings) needs to maintain a dynamic balance in order to achieve normal movement. A car in motion must maintain a dynamic balance at all times. A car consists of many components that must operate as a coordinated whole. An out-of-balance condition in the wheels of a car can cause increased wear on the ball joints and the deterioration of the shock absorbers and other suspension components. Dynamic imbalance can cause side-to-side swings of a car while in motion. It is the job of the designer of the car to ensure that the car is built with only components that are necessary in the con text of the dynamic balanced movement of the car. Deadweight, that is weight that has no task to perform, disturbs the dynamic balance and causes high gas consumption.

A car in dynamic balance moves effortlessly and effortlessly achieves maximum speed. A car that is dynamically unbalanced cannot easily achieve maximum speed because the car is contending with many out-of-phase forces and is gas inefficient. Its unbalanced movement has a cyclical irregularity of motion. The key quality of anything that is structurally and dynamically unbalanced is inefficiency. America's economy because it is structurally unbalanced is inherently inefficient which means that it is increasingly uncompetitive. Conventional economics hasn't got the tools to analyze and understand the American economic structure.

China vs. US Economic Structure

China today is the fastest growing economy in the world. It has not had recessions since 1978. Why has our conventional economics not discovered why the US has continuously had recessions which have increasingly got more violent over time? An Institute of New Economic Thinking was established by grants by George Soros and some others in the midst of the last US/global economic crisis. It was initially claimed by the sponsors of the Institute that the havoc caused by the financial crisis "vividly demonstrated the deficiencies in the outdated current economic theories and the need for new economic thinking". It will help, it was hoped, to stop future recessions in the US. The Institute has so far not succeeded. Most of the key economic theories that led up to the last US great recession are currently doing well and have not been seriouslychallenged by the Institute The Institute has, lacking any structural answers to stop recession, watered down its role by claiming that the Institute is just "a global network of scholars and leaders who are reshaping the role economics play" in the 21st century. They are now supposed to challenge conventional wisdom and to advance new ideas and how economics can serve us in the 21stcentury. While the Institutehas correctly listed what is wrong with present economics in the US as free market fundamentalism, fiscal austerity, financialization and corporate influence on politics, it has not substituted them with serious alternatives.

The difference between the economies of China and the US was described simply by Xu Xiaonian, a Chinese economist once with the China Europe International Business School in China, when he said, in talking about the US recessions that "...so often China and the US are mixed up as being in the same situation. We are told that China is moving to be a capitalist economy just like the US...The truth," he said, "is that the two economies are very different."

Asked why his bank did not watch its interests on a monthly basis as the United States, the governor of the People's Bank of China (the nearest equivalent of the US Fed) Zhou Xiaochuan replied that China was unlikely to follow the lead of the United States and other Western countries in making frequent changes in line with shifting business cycles. He said that from the point of view of interest rates, "we can't even say what cycle we are in"—a politically shrewd way of saying that China has no recessions.

On the eve of an early G20 summit inNovember 15, 2008, the then Chinese Prime Minister Wen Jiabao stated that China continues to take steps to maintain "a balanced and fast-paced economy." He associated their balanced economy with a fast-paced economy.

Structural economics is based on the scientific theory, as stated in my 2005 book, that every economyis endowed with three economic factors of proportion: labor, capital (production aid), and material; and that structural economic balance requires that factor proportions use for all economic production are equal and equal to the factor endowment proportins of the economy. I needed to compare how America and

China use their labor and capital to illustrate US economic structural imbalance first, by analyzing sector capital/labor ratios of the US economy and that of China. Mainly, I focus on the question: What is the proportion of labor and capital used in all its key economic sectors of each economy?

I was able to get the complete set of financial economic statistics for 2006 for both countries, in absence of regular yearly sector quantitative statistics for both countries. 2006 is a year that I also regarded as "normal" economic year for both countries as the US was not in recession. The chart profiles based on figures is shown in table 1.1, covered nineteen identical sectors in each country. Figure 1.1 is the result and shows the Chinese capital/labor ratio profile as a straight line across all the nineteen sectors. This graph shows a balanced economy in China: almost a straight line in which on the scale of the graphs, the capital/labor ratio for the 19 sectors of the economy were for all intents and purposes equal. The US graph, on the other hand, is highly irregular and unbalanced. The sector with the largest capital/labor proportion in China is only about 10 times the lowest proportion compared with 200 in the US.

Table 1.1 (Table 1 Chapter 1)
US/China Capital/Labor Ratio

Industry	Assets (million yuan)	No of employees	Cap/labor ratio ¥	Cap/labor ratio $	Balanced Cap/labor ratio $*2.8	Industry	Assets (billion dollars)	No of employees	Cap/labor ratio $
Wood products	¥78,588	916,200	¥85,776	$10,722		Furniture and related products	$19.9	549,000	$36,248
Apparel, leather, and allied products	¥534,993	6,232,000	¥85,846	$10,731	$30,022	Apparel, leather, and allied products	$17.8	279,000	$63,799
Furniture and related products	¥74,889	838,000	¥89,366	$11,171	$30,046	Wood products	$36.1	565,000	$63,894
Non-metallic mineral products	¥507,497	4,263,900	¥119,022	$14,878	$31,278	Printing and related products	$49.7	635,000	$78,268
Printing and related products	¥95,685	689,700	¥138,734	$17,342	$41,658	Fabricated metal products	$127.4	1,525,000	$83,541
Rubber and plastics	¥396,124	2,835,500	¥139,702	$17,463	$48,557	Rubber and plastics	$77.2	786,000	$98,219
Fabricated metal products	¥364,699	2,482,600	¥146,902	$18,363	$48,896	Motor vehicles	$120.9	1,057,000	$114,380
Paper products	¥222,548	1,347,700	¥165,132	$20,641	$51,416	Electrical equipment	$50.2	429,000	$117,016
Textile mills and textile products	¥1,180,697	6,154,300	¥191,849	$23,981	$57,796	Textile mills and textile products	$41.9	346,000	$121,098
Machinery	¥1,227,015	6,133,900	¥200,038	$25,005	$67,147	Food, beverages, and tobacco	$212.2	1,631,000	$130,104
Electrical equipment	¥875,231	4,039,800	¥216,652	$27,082	$70,013	Non-metallic mineral products	$66.5	506,000	$131,423
Chemical products	¥828,653	3,577,800	¥231,610	$28,951	$75,828	Machinery	$172.6	1,166,000	$148,027
Mining	¥1,484,117	5,965,200	¥247,964	$30,996	$81,063	Computer and electronics products	$280.0	1,289,000	$217,223
Computer and electronics products	¥1,344,163	5,050,700	¥266,134	$33,267	$86,788	Paper products	$101.3	459,000	$220,697
Food, beverages, and tobacco	¥2,052,336	6,994,890	¥293,405	$36,676	$93,147	Primary metals	$129.1	465,000	$283,736
Motor vehicles	¥1,118,866	3,745,800	¥298,699	$37,337	$102,692	Chemical products	$260.7	853,000	$305,627
Primary metals	¥1,418,853	4,329,500	¥327,718	$40,965	$104,545	Mining	$199.4	219,000	$910,502

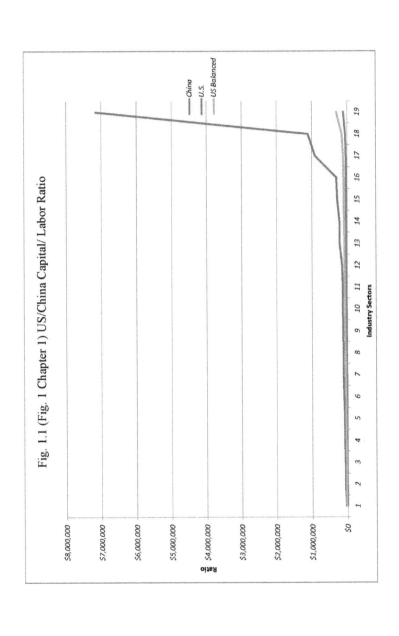

Fig. 1.1 (Fig. 1 Chapter 1) US/China Capital/ Labor Ratio

The left-hand portion of the US economy's graph starts as a slightly upward leaning line comprising of industrial sectors with differing but lower capital/labor ratios (wood products, apparel/leather, furniture printing, rubber/plastics products) and the right hand portion starting from sector number twelve to nineteen (oil/gas extraction, petroleum/ coal, mining, chemicals, primary metals, paper products, computer and electronics, machinery, food, beverages, and tobacco) was developing as we read it to the right into a left leaning nearly vertical line comprising about seven sectors with the third tranche of very large capital/labor ratios vastly larger than those sectors on the left. Broadly speaking, the US graph of its capital/labor ratios can be said to be divided into three broad economic zones: one low level of small capital/labor set of capital/labor ratios on the left distinctly separated from the right-side large capital/labor ratios group on the right divided by a mid-level zone of ratios.

We can, as a broad generalization, describe the US economy, at best, as three distinct economies juxtaposed to each other. The mini-economy on the left of figure 1.1 is practically a third world economy. The very large differences in capital/labor proportions in the United States are staggering, highlighted by the fact that the largest capital/ labor proportion (that of sector nineteen) is, as I stated earlier, nearly 200 times the smallest capital/labor proportion of sector one. The US economy, therefore, has serious capital/labor strutural imbalances.

If the analysis was based on ratio of material and labor or material and capital in place of capital or labor, the imbalance of the US economy will come out much worse than figure 1.1 shows because of the prolific waste of material resources in the United States. Unfortunately, I could not get full statistics on materials for the two countries for 2006. Science tells us that if you can prove that a component of a dynamic element is unbalanced, then you have proved that the whole element is dynamically unbalanced.

The bad message is that the American economy is structurally unbalanced and the structural imbalance of the US economy is getting progressively worse because the capital intensive setor on the right hand side part of the graph is getting larger and larger and more and more capital-intensive as Wall Street expands and that the labor-intensive left is getting more labor-intensive with increasing population and immigration. Except during the short economic respite America had during the New Economy of the 1990s (as I will later describe) and the two World Wars when capital for war prosecution was in short supply and needed to be economized, capital/labor explosion at the right side of the graph has continued to increase. The structural economic imbalance of the US economy is like an advancing cancer that is steadily eating away at America's economic fabric. Recessions are a permanent result of the growing structural imbalance of the US economy.

What Is Capital?

Conventional US economists define production capital in dollars. This is unscientific. In economic science, every economy has an endowed supply of natural resources and manpower. In order to make production possible, every economy from time immemorial must use part of its endowed natural resources (material) in combination with some labor taken out of its manpower endowment to produce capital equipment (production aid), which is used in combination with the remaining manpower and materials to produce goods and services. This is structural economic science. We can call the economic sector concerned with capital equipment production the capital equipment sector, and the sector concerned with the actual production of goods using capital, the remaining material and labor as the production sector. The capital equipment sector is non-productive in that it does not directly produce for consumption. There is, therefore, a continuing choice to be made by each economy on how much of the endowed material and manpower in the economy is to be allocated to the capital equipment sector and how much to the production/consumption sector.

Professor Samuelson's famous pioneering neo-classical economic text was, therefore, correct when it emphasized that there is a choice in every economy. Samuelson however said that the choice was between present consumption without capital investment on the one hand and future larger consumption with capital investment on the other. Samuelson erred scientifically, by claiming that early man produced without capital. Early men used hoes and matchets and looms as his capital to produce. The real continuing choice of every sector, primitive or modern, is scientifically about how much material it uses to create capital and how much to produce goods for consumption. Production whether in the primitive or modern society cannot, contrary to Samuelson's claims, occur without capital: production aid (whether as arrow or knife or grinder) just as we in the twenty first century need machines (capital) to undertake the production process.

There is, therefore, a basic universal structural economic "science" irrespective of the state of civilization. It is the act of conversion of material into a final or semifinal good that constitutes the creation of economic wealth. Because US conventional economic's principal objective is to maximize capital, the US has not maintained a balance— the correct balance—between how much material and labor to assign to the creation of production aid (capital) and how much to use for production of goods. Excessive capital equipment use (what is known as capital-intensive 'technology' as we see fully displayed in figure 1.1 for the US) not only displaces/minimises labor in production but only denies the economy the quantity of materials that could have been used to produce a larger quantity of consumable goods but used to create capital equipment.

The meaning from figure 1.1 is that US is wasting its materials and labor resources by creating an excessive capital-intensive economy compared with China that uses less material for capital creation and therefore, has more material available to produce goods and does not displace labor from production. The whole position is relative depending on the relative natural resource endowment of China and the United States. The US economy comparatively has an inefficient and wasteful use of its material resources. The US economy is too capital-intensive for its good. It is a case of what I will call 'structural uncompetitiveness,' a reflection of the present underlying structural inefficiency of the US economy. The US economy is structurally unbalanced as Fig.11 shows compared to China's economy. I will say that the bulk of USpresent and past economic problems derive basically from its growing structural imbalance.

I decided to put the overall position in perspective of what I have been saying to show in figure 1.1 what US capital/labor profile will look like if the US economy were to be balanced (like China) using China's balanced economy as a basis. The current total natural resources of the US and China (in $billions), including their energy resources are $11,750 and $7,120 respectively.[2] The populations of US and China are 330 million and 1.3 billion respectively. Using proportionality, which is the basis of my theory of factor proportions(to be discussed later), and using the balanced economy of China as in fig 1.1) as a basis, the United States should on the basis of its population, (which is about one fourth that of China) and with a 65 percent greater natural resources base than China, I arrived at the conclusion that a balanced US economy should have capital/labor ratio of only 280 percent times that of China instead of its current over a thousand times. Put it in another way, US economy will be a balanced economy if it substantially reduced its capital input in its operating economy by as much as 4 to 5 times. This issue should be borne in mind as the economic rivalry between the US and China is being discussed.

This structurally balanced economy profile of China is shown in figure 1.1. It is a horizontally displayed line under that of the U.S. graph. That there is enormous waste of resources in the US economy even in "the third world" part of the US economy (i.e. the sub-economy to the left of figure 1.1) is evidenced by the fact that, as shown in that figure, America's actual capital/labor ratios in its three sub-economies are far higher than the capital/labor ratio that America will have if its economy were to be balanced). The main obstacle to solving the US structural imbalance is capitalism supported by its present entrenched political structure as summarized earlier by the Institute of New Economic Thinking.

The US average capital/labor ratio from table 1.1 is $234,260 compared to China's capital/labor average of $28,032, a mere 11 percent of the US capital/labor ratio. The estimated annual manufacturing of the United States at the time was $1.83 trillion versus $1.73 trillion for China. Considering the real present value of the dollar and the yen and that US figures contain a lot of outsourced components, it is clear from this pattern that China had long since then overtaken the US in manufacturing. China manufacturing overtook the US in manufacturing since 2000.

China, therefore, has far greater manufacturing output than the US with less capital and less material use and inherently cheaper costs. Prevalent views in the US accusing China of cheating should realize the inherent structural advantages it has over the US. The enormous waste of material resources in the US economy is, therefore, evident from our analysis: at a time when material commodity is getting scarce and expensive. The excessive material we use in the US for capital formation could be converted into more goods as well as provide more employment by reduced capital displacement of labor.

Between 2000 and 2006, capital invested in industry in the United States increased by about 30 percent while the capital/ labor ratio increased by a staggering 73 percent. The 30 percent increase in capital investment contributed only 24 percent to the GDP while nearly 5 million industrial jobs were lost. This pattern of waste of materials and simultaneous in-built joblessness in the US economy constitute the basic structural foundation of US present basic uncompetitiveness and its growing dependence on imports. The United States finds itself in a vicious spiral because when American companies are faced with high costs arising from their structurally unbalanced economy, they engage in more capital intensive activities in the belief as shown in latter chapters that that is the way to reduce cost of production. Americans have a fixation with capital intensive technology and consequent disastrous factor proportions.

American Dualistic/ Triplistic Economy

In order to understand in greater depth America's economic structural imbalance, figure1.2 presents the US economy, for simplicity, as a relatively labor-intensive sector (the left-hand side of figure 1.1) for the United States juxtaposed with a capital intensive sector (on the right of figure 1.2). That is an economic dualistic position—typical of most underdeveloped economies. They have a third sector lying in between referred loosely as the middle class economy in the US

In figure 1.2, the labor-intensive sector has labor content 1 OL L and capital content OLC L. The capital-intensive sector initially 1 1 1 1 1 had capital OC C C and labor OC L C. When capital OCOC was added to the capital-intensive sector (as is continuously happening in the United States), the result is that the resource allocation point moves from 1 to 2.

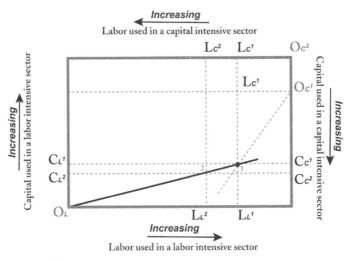

Fig.1.2 *TITLE:*
Factor struggle in US Economy

The unfortunate net effect of this is that the labor for the labor intensive sector equal to LL^1 LL^2 is taken by the capital intensive sector equal to LC1 LC1. The capital intensive sector additionally C takes capital from the labor-intensive sector CL1 CL2 equal to C1 C2 C1 C2. Previous factor grab by the capital-intensive sector has led to the near elimination of the middle class economy in the US An increase in capital intensity OC OC results in a disproportionate increase in production of goods in capital-intensive sectors at the expense of the labor-intensive sector. Conventional economists call this a biased expansion of production possibilities.

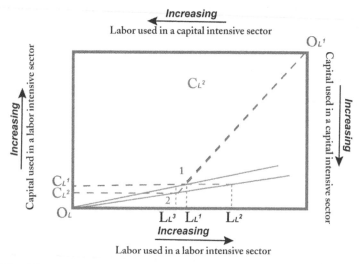

Fig.1.3 *TITLE:*
Additional effect on factor struggle due to inflation

Another condition that causes factor changes in the US economy is population change and immigration. The last US census data from the Census Bureau confirmed that as Jed Koiko stated in a *New York Times* report of April 18,2019 that migration is keeping US population growth above water. We know that the new immigrants are largely professionals bolstering urban cities and likely to end in the capital sector of the US economy—a major factor in the US factor allocation at present and in future.

This time, due to say immigration increase, labor L1 L2 is added to the labor intensive sector. It is seen that a new position in figure 1.3 is reached whereby the capital intensive sector again stole labor up to L3 and capital C1 C2 from the labor intensive sector. The net effect is that as new capital is added in the economy and labor increase flows into the economy, the capital-intensive is constantly squeezing the labor-intensive sector in a constant struggle for factors of production.

Here then is the clear indication that the American economic structure is unstable as there is inside it constant "poaching" and struggle for factors of production between sectors. That is part of what I mean by saying throughout this book that the American economy is structurally and dynamically unbalanced.

Figure 1.1 graph for America in actual fact portrays a triplistic US economy, from which one can see that the United States has a more serious unstable economic structure than figure 1.2 and figure 1.3 depict when material as a factor is inclded. That is why, as we go along in this book, I will want to show that US conventional economists have no idea what the structure of the US macro-economy is like and that most of what is currently written and taught by US conventional economists about the US micro-economy and by inference about the macro-economic structure of the United States is misleading.

These 'structural' struggles for factors of production caused by movements in the capital-intensive sector coupled with the structural instability caused by the material factor waste in the US economy all work together to create a beast of an economy that is structurally unstable and inefficient in the use of the country's resources and uncompetive. It is clear that because figure 1.1 shows that the US economy is in fact three economies in one constantly fighting for factors of production, it is one in which the high capital sector on the right always tends to be the winner.

What I have described in figure 1.1 is the structural relationship of labor and capital (production aid). The total structural picture of the American economy will additionally, as I have already pointed out, require for completeness additional labor/material and material/capital studies in the context of a three dimensional structure of the economy. The graphs for labor/ material and material/capital for the United States will present a as I have hinted a much worse picture of the structure of the US economy knowing the waste of material resources which characterizes the US economy. The structural imbalances of the US economy are worse than what I have just described in figures 1.2 and 1.3 because the structural struggles are not just between one labor intensive sector (sub-economy) and a capital intensive sector (sub-economy), but a struggle among three factors: labor, capital, and material. If we take into account that the actual situation is not just capital/labor, but also capital/ material and labor/material (a three-dimension) economic structure, the structural chaos in the American economic structure because of its imbalance is easy to imagine. The United States, therefore, structurally has an economy worse in some respects than a third-world economy, which some conventional economists disdainfully describe as economic dualism. I will in future chapters show that US President's Council of Economic Advisers, reading their year to year reports and all agencies public and private in the US involved in economic forecasting lack knowledge of the changing basic structure of the economy and don't know at each point what underlying factors that will determine the structural future of the economy.

I think that I have in this chapter unraveled the underlying deep causes of America's broken and unbalanced economy, which I will bring into life in the coming chapters as I talk of America's increasing uncompetitiveness. It is, therefore, false for conventional economists and US policy makers and planners to claim that the small business sector (labor-intensive sector on the left of figure 1.1) in the United States is lying structurally peacefully side by side with, and cooperating with the large capital-intensive sector on the right an arrangement in which we are told that all the sectors of the triplist economy have mutually agreed that the sector to the left is given the assignment of producing the bulk of job growth for the economy, while the one on the right is assigned the task of producing the economy's wealth while the middle is acting as buffer between them. In fact it is the struggle for factors as I just described that causes the continual squeezing out and the disappearance of the middle economy which we associate with the middle class.

The statistical error in **all** published conventional private and public economics statistics in the United States is clear because they are all based on the wrong assumption that the US economy is balanced and that the arithmetic sum total of its micro-economic activities is equal to its macro-economy.

Early Development Economists

The primary importance of a balanced economic structure, as a necessary part of sustainable economic growth, was recognized by early development economists in the United States in the 1950s. These pioneers were in effect seeking to upturn the ideas of the early economists like Keynes and wanted to replace them with something more scientific. Classical economics, and indeed our monetary and financial system in the US up to the recent Great Recession, *believed* that capitalist market economies were always self-correcting and when disturbed will return to full employment in relatively short order. Keynes's economics was a challenge of classical economics. His claim was that there were circumstances in which the self-equilibrium mechanism became dysfunctional creating an *under-employment equilibrium.*

Early development economics was a search in structural economics, asking the basic question: what structure of the economy is best created conditions for a maximum economic growth. Those development economists concluded quite correctly that maximum economic growth required a structural dynamic balance of the economy. The real debate was between those who argued that maximum economic development results from planning and operating the economy as a balanced structural economy and those thinking that maximum economic development was through deliberate unbalance, as the economy that tends to a dynamic balance.

Prof. Ragnar Nurske, after whom an economics professorship is named in Columbia University, concluded in a book titled *Problems of Capital Formation in Underdeveloped Countries* in 1953 that rapid economic development requires a frontal attack...a wave of capital investments in a number of industries each of which is complementary to the other in what he called 'balanced growth.' A balanced development was required, according to him, "to avoid the social consequences of uneven development," as we have today in the US—increasing inequality and poverty. Professor R.S. Eckaus considered what he titled "Factor Proportion Problem in Underdeveloped Areas" in an article in *American Economic Review* in September 1955. This is the first time the term "factor proportion" was used in economics which was the basis of my book on the "Science of Economic Development and Growth." To the opposing group amongst early development economists, balanced growth is not as a static phenomenon but as a dynamic event. The famous Harvard and Yale economist Prof. Albert Hirschmann contended in his 1958 book *The Strategy of Economic Growth* that a deliberate unbalancing of the economy, in accordance with some predetermined strategy, will act as incentives and pressures to move the economy forward as the economy seeks to attain as an ever shifting state of dynamic balance.

In the end, it is clear that the opposing groups among these pioneers were arguing for the same thing from opposite ends.

They, in fact, all agreed on the need for a balanced economic structure. While one side was seeking the balance as a static balance, the other was seeking the balance in a dynamic context.

I did not see the point in the argument between these two early development pioneers. As an engineer, I know that you can not achieve dynamic balance without static balance. The main thing is that these early development economists realized that dynamic structurally-balanced economy was a *sine qua non* for economic development. We have seen that today that America's economy is structurally unbalanced. The problem that these early economists faced is that, having realized the need for a balanced economic structure, they lacked the knowledge how to analyze investments in a way to show how structural economic balance can be built up and maintained. In particular, they were unable to realize that structural economics was comprised of three factors: labor, production aid (generally called capital) and material. They erred by regarding production as made up of only capital and labor as conventional economics currently persist incorrectly to assume. The result was that the early development economists could not advance their analysis and ended up in a dead end after their peak in the 1950s. I have called this the era of structural development economics.

The 1980s saw a brief revival of interest in structural development economics in what the proponents called "New Growth Theory (Endogenous Growth Theory)." Professor Aghion and Howitt prominently in their book *Endogenous Growth Theory* (1998) stated that endogenous growth theory was intended to "open up technological progress and innovation to systematic analysis and study their effort on growth." They saw capital accumulation and innovation as two aspects of the process of economic growth. They claimed that technology is a kind of capital good. They claimed that technology can be stored over time because it does not get completely used up and can be accumulated through R& D and "other knowledge–creation activities." It was clear that new growth theory could not get anywhere because technology and innovation are generalized concepts with no defined structure. With the death of development economics, *conventional economics today has abandoned development economics and has no structure.*

I needed to overcome the dead end which early 1950s and 1980s development economists faced with my own theory of factor proportions. The two prominent operating words in the work of the 1950s early development economists were (a) structural balance (b) factor proportions. The central theme in their work was structural balance. One of them Professor Eckaus, as we saw, described the problem as one of factor proportions in the title of his 1955 article. My theory of factor proportions and structural balance is my scientific economic/development growth theory following from the work of early development economists, stating that for sustainable growth the factor proportions of all production activities in the economy must be structurally *equal* and *equal* to the economy's endowed factor proportions.

The fact that we buy the factors of production : raw materials, machinery, and labor with dollars and that we measure economic growth in dollars does not mean that the economic growth process is a dollar (monetary) process. Finance is a shadow of economic activities, not the substance. A shadow is never a correct picture of the object. Economic development/ growth is a technology process, governed by scientific laws—a point conventional monetary and financial economics ignores. Tooday in the US economics is simply dollars, a situation which the Institute of New Econimic Thinking called financialization of the economy.

The Nobel Prize winner Robert Solow acknowledged the error of conventional monetary and financial economists that capital is the key to economic growth. At his Nobel Prize acceptance speech, he told the world:

> "In the beginning (that is the beginning of his research), I was surprised at the relatively minor part the model ascribed to capital formation—the result seems contrary to common

sense. The fact that the steady–state growth is independent of investment quotation was easy to understand. It was harder to feel comfortable with the conclusion that even in the shorter run, increased investment would do very little for transitory growth. There is a major factor other than capital that is responsible for economic growth. The fact of the unknown factor was a measure of the [conventional] economist's ignorance."

No conventional economist has to date told us what the *unknown factor* is. Sometimes this unknown was called in ignorance the *residual factor*. In truth it admits the ignorance of conventional economics. The unknown/residual factor is actually the material factor.

Law of Factor Proportions

Figure 1.1 is the first time I tested my theory spelt out initially in my 1974 book, *Underdevelopment: An Inside View* (with a graphical illustration) and restated in my 2005 book *The Science of Economic Development and Growth: The Theory of Factor Proportions*. The law of *factor proportions* is a general structural/scientific economics law that states that maximum sustainable economic growth can only be attained *by any economy* if the proportions between the three factors in all economic production activities are *equal* and *equal* to the endowed factor proportions of the economy. It is a scientific attempt to put the three natural factors of production into a general scientific theory of production.

China, shown in figure 1.1, has maximum sustainable growth because it has balanced factor proportions (i.e. balanced economic structure). This general growth economic law, and its structural implications will feature prominently in this book as we discuss the US economic illness and the centrality of the US unbalanced economic structure. It fills the void in conventional economics, which as of today does not have a structural statement on how to achieve maximum economic growth after the failures of many of its conventional economic growth theories some of which were Nobel Prize winning theories in the name of economic science.

In the remaining part of this chapter, I intend to take up a number of major economic topics which eludes US conventional economics because it lacks a structural knowledge of the US economy.

Inequality in the US: A Structural Economic Problem

Inequality is a topic about which all economists in the US show a great deal of ignorance. The structural imbalance of the United States economy is the cause of its worsening inequality. The structural capital/labor figure 1.1 for the United States is a clear mirror image of US inequality profile. Because of ignorance about America's structural economic problems and that its structural imbalance is the cause of inequality, American economists and politicians have incorrect political, financial, and social explanations of it.

Prof. Robert Lieberman of Columbia University wrote an article in *Foreign Affairs* January/February 2011 titled "Why the Rich Are Getting Richer." He claimed incorrectly that inequal ity in the United States is "the result of public policies that have concentrated and amplified the effects of economic transformation and directed its gains exclusively toward the wealthy." His case was that since the late 1970s, "Congress has cut tax rates for high income repeatedly and relaxed the tax treatment of capital gains and other investment income, resulting in windfall profits for wealthiest Americans." False claims were made by Professor Stiglitz in the *New York Times*, "Inequality is not inevitable," (June 26, 2014) in which he accused politicians of causing inequality, diverted hundreds of billions of dollars in bailouts to banks. He stated that the American political system is overrun by money. Economic inequality translates to political inequality yields increasing economic input.

In a 2015 report the IMF ignorantly claimed the "neoliberal policies increase inequality which produces further economic norms in a 'trade-off' between growth and inequality." Prof. Paul Krugman also made inequality in the US a political issue, as he claimed, caused by the

Republicans. In 2006, he published what was intended to be an attack on the Republicans especially President G.W. Bush on the growing inequality in the United States.[3] He claimed that since the 1970s, inequality in the United States began rising again. He admitted that the gap between rich and poor started growing before President Ronald Reagan and continued to widen through President Clinton's years.

He however claimed that what was happening under George W. Bush was an entirely "unprecedented" rise in inequality. While he also admitted that America has never been an egalitarian society and that inequality is not new in the United States, he failed to say when inequality started in the United States. Instead, he pulled out a statement by two economic historians Claudia Goldind and Robert Margo that said that in that period between 1933 and 1945 'The Great Compression' happened. As a result of the compression, so he claimed, the rich in the United States got dramatically poorer, and workers got considerably richer.

According to Krugman, Americans, as a result of the Great Compression, found themselves sharing similar lifestyles in a way not seen since before the Civil War. The inequality under George W. Bush was, in his view, extraordinary. In *New York Times* of May 9, 2014, Krugman now said that: "The vast gulf that now exists between the upper-middle class and the rich didn't emerge until the Reagan years." It does not matter who Krugman wants to accuse provided he is a Republican. Yet in *NY Times* January 16, 2016, he claimed that inequality is caused by (a) differing productivity of people (b) luck (c) access to power. He claimed wrongly that inequality is inevitable but not inequality without telling us what vast inequality is.

Krugman's knowledge of economic history either failed him, or he failed it. He did not know that inequality has a long history in the US. It intensified after the United States wrenched economic leadership from Britain in the late nineteenth century.

The well-known economic history book by Douglas North and Robert Fogell (two Nobel laureates in economics) has this to say about income distribution:

We see them (the wealthy in the 1920s) as self-satisfied and self-indulgent...Some historians have seen a direct link between the growing concentration of income during the 1920s was going to the rich, who were not spending it fast enough to maintain aggregate demand.

This is the same thing is happening in the US today. Some early economic publications and politicians even claim that the Great Depression in the 1930s was principally caused by income inequality. The well-known economic historians Walton and Rockoff observed that the long-term trend toward income inequality in the United States was interrupted by World War I. North and Fogel further quoted from the work of the historian Kuznets who orian Charles Holt concluded that all of the increases in real income in the 1920s went to the upper income groups.[5] A 1934 Brookings Institute study reported that by 1929, approximately 24,000 families in the United States had a combined income as large as that shared by 11.5 million families in the United States. The study reported that between 1920 and 1929, per capita disposable income for all Americans rose by 9 percent but that the top 1 percent enjoyed a whopping 75 percent of this increase. It stated that: "There has been a tendency at least during the last decade or so for the inequality in the distribution of income to be accentuated."[6]

Contrary to the inference which Krugman was seeking to make from what Goldin and Margo said, the reality is that just as the World War I 'interrupted' the growing inequality in the United States and resumed after the World War I, World War II, also only interrupted the growing inequality in the United States. In my book on factor proportions, I analyzed the World War II economy in detail and showed how structurally balanced it was and how it reduced income inequality at the time.

The French professor Thomas Piketty's pioneering book on inequality titled *Capital in the Twentieth Century* published 2014 was a sensation in the world of conventional economists. Here for the first time, a conventional economist was telling his fellow conventional economists that income inequality has a very long structural history. Professor Krugman called the book a "bona fide phenomenon" in *New*

York Times of April 25, 2014. Piketty's book contained well researched financial statistics of "after-tax rate of return Vs growth rate at the world level from antiquity until 2100." For those making politics out of inequality, he had this to say in very simple terms: inequality is intrinsic to capitalism and if not combatted will reach levels that threaten our democracy. In a speech at the Economic Policy Institute May 2014, he declared that "Wealth inequality has been rising at 6 to 7 percent per year— three times faster than the world economy. *Nobody knows where this will stop."* He was acknowledging without knowing it that inequality was a structuralist capital issue as in figure 1.1.

Piketty's solution was a worldwide progressive tax system on the wealthy, not because that will stop inequality, but to *preserve the elements of democracy.* As a conventional economist, Piketty only had his financial figures but could not say what in capitalism causes inequality. Economic science is in a position to say what structurally causes inequality.

American economy is, as we have seen in figure 1.1, divided broadly into three economies with a structural shape that mirrors the inequality profile of the United States. The activities on the right of the structural graph in the economy covers capital-intensive activities on the right. These activities have very large capital content per unit of output and low labor per unit of output. Total income 'r' received by the businesses in ultra-capital-intensive category will, all things being equal, be high as it is this sector that dominates the capitalist economy's output. Those who own capital will receive the bulk of this very large income, leading to high financial returns to capital 'r' because their capital contributes a very high proportion of the country's total output. As the economy grows at the rate 'g' dominance of the capital sector and 'r' all the time grow. As the economy grows 'g' and as the capital-intensive sector increases, the economy is more unbalanced with lower and lower 'g'. As Piketty says r>g is a historical fact and will continue in a capitalistic economy. Income to labor in this capital-intensive sector (made up of high class trained skilled labor) is small in size but very high compared to labor income in the other sectors. Labor supply on the left side of figure 1.1, the labor-intensive sector is very large in size, but its output in the economy is comparatively very small. So the return to labor (wages) on the left is small and continues to decrease. This is what happens also in third world economies.

The size of middle class in the middle of structural map is bound to be getting smaller as the capital-intensive sector gets more and more capital intensive. This is because I have shown earlier in figures 1.2 and 1.3 how the capital-intensive sector continues to invade the labor-intensive sector and increase its dominance of the economy either as more capital from into in it (figure 1.2) or as more labor flows into the labor-intensive sector on the left of figure 1.1 and figure 1.3) by way of unemployment or immigration or increase in population. The middle class, as US history demonstrates, is being squeezed out from both sides.

It is therefore easy from all this to see how the middle class in the US is shrinking. It is clear that middle class economic strategy announced by Obama as President in his time intended to revive the middle class on a stand-alone basis cannot succeed because the middle class "problem" is a structural problem. From all this, we reach a conclusion of great economic and political importance that the structural problems of the US economy are long-persisting. We have seen that it is the capital-intensive sector which continually increases its domination of the economy either through actions depicted in figure 1.2 or figure 1.3 not only leading to greater returns to capital intensive sector but at the same time reducing the economic growth of the economy due to increased structural imbalance of the economy and so increasing income inequality. Income inequality is a structural defect of a capitalist economy. It is therefore incorrect to accuse those who benefit from income inequality of causing income inequality.

The capital-intensive sector which causes increased inequality is made up of, among others, US large corporations and Wall Street. These large corporations are exulted by the American government as carrying the American flag in the world. Paul Krugman once praised them as purveyors of monopolistic international trade, while Professor Stiglitz called them the purveyors of American technology that promote globalization.

America can only solve its inequality through structural rebalancing of the economy and because the country's structural economic imbalance is getting worse, its income inequality has historically been on the increase. All capitalist economies of the West have unbalanced structural characteristics similar to fig.1.1.

US Productivity Paradox

The US economic policy makers have always claimed that the US economy is far ahead of many countries in its productivity. Conventional US economists worship at the altar of productivity. The economics Nobel Prize winner, Michael Spence, incorrectly put it this way: "Innovators create technologies that substitute capital for more expensive labor. The value added per worker rises and the displaced workers do other activities where their added value is also higher, activities that require judgment and analysis."[7]

A flawed assumption in this statement is that there is always an alternative job for the displaced worker. The professor gave the erroneous impression that substitution of labor with capital has no economic structural consequence. The professor forgot that what he called capital is basically a large amount of material combined with some labor. Therefore, productivity is not free lunch. You get productivity by substituting labor with material. In conventional economics, conventional economists like Professor Spence forget the existence of material and think productivity is free and invoving efficienicies achieved by good internal organization.

A McKinsey Global Institution report concluded that higher productivity destroys jobs only in the very short term and concluded that in the United States every ten-year rolling period since 1929 has seen increases both in US productivity and employment. It further stated that since 2000, the largest productivity gains have been in the sector that has seen a large employment reduction.[8] The report asserted that even on a rolling annual basis, 69 percent of the periods have delivered both productivity and jobs. The Economic Report to the President in 2013, on the other hand, says that productivity growth appears to have slowed down after the 1990s.[9] The 2017 report confirmed that US productivity has stalled.

The question for McKinsey and other conventional productivity experts is if the United States had been so very successful in productivity growth over these years even since the Great Recession, why has US manufacturing now declined behind that of China? The answer is that productivity is a dangerous booby trap. Productivity, as presently practiced, is the attempt to increase output per worker by using more and more excessive materials and labor (that is capital) out of the country's material resources to create capital. This adds to the economy's already bad structural imbalance as we see in figs 1.0. 1.1 and 1.2.

Increased productivity is not the result of American ingenuity or 'innovation' but the deployment of more and more capital. As prices of material commodities in the world are set on an increasing trend, the US increasing productivity is, therefore, obtained at a very high "price" to the economy and at increased economic structural imbalance of the economy adding to the economy's uncompetitiveness. The push to increase productivity will come to the end as it now seems to be only 1.9%, fifth in the world.

To bring the discussion to full cycle, I say that the drive for higher productivity adds to America's waste of its material resources (which could have been used in boosting production of needed goods) used to drive capital intensity which adds to the capital intensive sector of the economy, which in turn adds to the country's structural imbalance. By throwing people out of jobs and turning them into idle production factor resources through claimed resultant efficiencies we also worsen US economic structural imbalance. Increased productivity in the United States therefore adds to the country's macroeconomic uncompetitiveness.

The US Bureau of Labor Statistics is the principal US government agency charged with measuring productivity. In its quarterly publications usually titled *Overview of BLS Productivity Statistic*, the bureau makes it clear that its published productivity and related cost data are designed for "use in economic analysis and for public and private policy planning in the United States."[10] BLS data are widely used officially to forecast and analyze changes in prices, wages, and income. BLS data are used by academics, research institutes, Wall Street, and government agencies. BLS statistics are the most authoritative set of statistics with regard to matters like productivity.

The BLS publications explain that there are two primary types of productivity statistics: labor productivity and multifactor productivity. It does not mention materials. It defined labor productivity as data on output per hour and unit labor cost. It defined what it vaguely called multifactor productivity as a measure of output per unit of combined inputs. BLS defined multifactor productivity as *'consists of labor and capital and in some cases, intermediate inputs such as fuel".* "Intermediate inputs" is an expression of BLS ignorance—remember the ignorance Professor Solow expressed in his Nobel Prize ceremony speech. *Combined inputs* is a cover-up by the BLS for its ignorance and the country's neglect of materials as a key input in conventional economics. After its vague explanation of what combined inputs involve labor and capital means, BLS did not know what the third input is. That is why BLS knowing that there is an unknown third input openly guessed that the third unknown factor may be what it called *intermediate input such as fuel.* In fact in a 3D scientific economic analysis, that third input is material. The BLS cannot be blamed for its ignorance because conventional economists ignorantly currently hold that only capital and labor make up economics production.

Policy makers and conventional economists in the US don't realize that output per unit of material may in some instances be more important to the economy than output per unit of labor or unit of capital and that sometimes depending on the economy, economizing/saving on materials as a national policy may be more important to the economy than economizing on labor (productivity). Solow said the "residual" is more important for growth than capital.

There is, therefore, an undefined private and public policy conspiracy/ignorance in the US to drive up labor productivity in the United States in the fixated drive to keep labor cost low either by reducing wage rates or sacking staff and holding trade unions in check. There is a basic discrimination and prejudice against labor in the United States to the serious detriment of the US economy. Here is how the *Labor Department Report* June 2009 once described this retrograde conspiracy claiming increase in productivity in United States: "Productivity rose in the first quarter (of 2009) as US firms slashed their workforce outpacing the drop in output."[11] The Department reported 2009—in the midst of the most severe recession since the Great Depression—that US labor productivity in the second quarter rose at an annualized rate of 5.5 percent, the largest since 2003. In the third quarter, while the recession was raging, US productivity increased 9.5 percent annualized rate, the fastest in six years. Compared with 2008, productivity was up 4.3 percent, the biggest twelve-month rise in the history of a first series first calculated in 1948. America is soaring in productivity is causing an increasing imbalance of its economy. Focused productivity is in truth economic growth retarding. Current labor-based productivity currently in the US is at its lowest of about 1.9% p.a. Robby Jindal, a former Governor of Louisiana in the Wall Steet Journal of March 12,2019, talked of "Years of wage stagnation" and diminished economic prospects that have soured many Americans on the system that made the U.S. the world largest economy" in an article titled "American Capitalism is Fine, thank you. In the article, he reminded us that President Trump has stated that capitalism generates prosperity abroad at the expense of American workers.

Negligent and indifferent wasteful attitude to natural resources in the United States, as I had earlier discussed, has led to a type of economic profligacy in the country through the pursuit of labor productivity using capital intensive production, based on an illusion of natural resource inexhaustibility, a near belief that America could always find technical solutions raw materials. American politicians and economists have behaved as if the country has moved away from the scientific study and preservation of natural resources to a political and economic decision to exploit its material resources with abandon, a trend now belatedly being checked by new feeble outcries about the environment. Capitalism is the unscientific result of (a) ignoring material as a factor of production and (b) pressing productivity so as to reduce the role of labor in production and making it out that production (wealth-creation) is essentially capital formation.

Structural Economics and Unemployment

From structural economic science, we see unemployment differently. Conventional economists regard some level of unemployment as both desirable and necessary, so as to prevent a growing economy from, what they used to call "overheating NAIRU" (Non Accelerating Inflation Rate of Unemployment). In structural economic science, full employment is the aim of all economics. Overall poor employment history of the United States is the result of a mismatch in factor proportions. The second and third mini-economies of the US, namely two sections of figure 1.1 in the middle and on the right side of the US profile are not contributing to employment in any significant extent.

The small-business labor-intensive sector confined to the extreme left of US figure 1.1 contributes nearly 53 percent of the total US employment despite its relatively low contribution to output. It is the small start-ups in that small section of figure 1.1 to the right that contributes over 65 percent of the new jobs in the United States. The Kaufman Index of Entrepreneurial Activity 2010 stated that the startup rate in 2010 was the highest in fifteen years consisting of a little higher than half a million new businesses as the poor economy and high employment led individuals to want to start their own business. The rate reduced 20 percent in 2011 and by similar figure in 2012 and 2013 all contributing to increasing US unemployment and decreasing entrepreneurship. The rate increase however rose in year 2016, third year in a row, indicates that small business growth has recovered from its Great Recession slump, but as the producers of index commented, "entrepreneurial growth in the US is today largely down from the levels in the 80s and 90s. New small business start-ups survival tracked by the Bureau of Labor Statistics have been on the decline since the peak of the Great Recession.

Most of the new businesses were not industrial, ranging from construction on one side to services like health careon the other. Over 99 percent of employing organizations in the United States are therefore small labor-intensive businesses, which are out of line with the natural factor proportions of the United States. It is clear that the great bulk of the US economy (i.e. the bulk of the US economy from the middle to the extreme right of figure 1) makes little contribution to US employment.

As new capital is continually injected into the ultra-capital intensive sector of the United States, right of figure 1.1, as I have shown from figure1.2, the capital-intensive sector of the United States continually invades the less capital intensive sector further reducing its employment capacity. The long-term prospect of employment of the United States is not bright as the structural struggles for factors between the sectors of the US economy intensify as more capital is injected into the right of figure 1.1 causing the economy's increased biased production behavior. Conventional economists cannot explain the low employment character of the US economy.

Engineers structurally design a car or jet plane to carry only those basic weights that are absolutely necessary to maintain road movement/ flight dynamic balance. If the weight of a car or plane is excessive, it will tell adversely on the car/plane's ability to achieve dynamic balance. The weights of the passengers, and seats, and the cargo are calculated into the designs as active and necessary weights that must be taken into account in the quest for dynamic balance. Unemployed labor, though a full part of an economy, is a deadweight on the economy that does not perform any economic action. As a deadweight on the economy, unemployed labor actively adds to the structural imbalance of the economy, which increases uncompetitiveness.

Conventional economics, that says that an optimum level of unemployment is required in an economy, is erroneous. In economic structural terms, the concept of a safety net by which unemployed labor is maintained by grants and other social benefits is a great source of American structural uncompetitiveness. Unemployment is a deadweight on the economy. A safety net is an admission of failure of economic management and structural evidence that the economy is unbalanced.

Deplorable State and Collapse of Current Conventional Financial/Monetary Economics: The Search for Viable Macroeconomic Theory

(Economic Intellectuctualism)

Intellectualism is based on the belief that some gifted people have the ability to think out revolutionary ideas that move knowledge forward. Conventional economics is all about economic intellectualism. Economic intellectualism is based on the notion that economists have the intellectual powers to analyze and to solve all economic issues, helped at times by research. As a philosophical exercise, economists come with their differing backgrounds, experiences, politics and biases, which leads to arguments and differences in conclusions. Conventional economics is not a discipline and cannot be a science.

Thomas Friedman in his Nobel Lecture helped lay the foundation of economic intellectualism in 1977 when he tried to distinguish between what he called 'exact sciences' and economics which he called a branch of philosophy because "they (economics) deal with human behavior." Friedman was wrong that economics deals with human behavior. In arguing that there is no difference between the way social sciences and exact sciences behave or should be treated, he tried to argue that there is no "certain" substantive knowledge, and in both exact science and economics, there are *only tentative hypotheses that can never be "proved", but can only fail to be rejected.* Friedman was wrong that there is no "substantive" knowledge because he incorrectly believed that all knowledge and its extension depend on our (human) knowledge which progresses by waiting until someone suggests a "new hypothesis." This is intellectualism, the belief that all knowledge derive from our intellectualism coming from gifted intellectuals. Friedman had an exaggerated view of human intelligence (intellectualism). Human intellect is prescribed by nature. Our intellectualism is our attempt at differing explanations of the mystery of nature. There is vast human ignorance to compare with that the vast bulk of knowledge nature has in place even before man showed up on earth and which everyday we are "discovering'. If nature put natural resources and humans on earth, why can man not accept that nature would have set up rules or natural law how these endowments are to used so to achieve maximum economic returns. Intellectualism or controlled experiments may not help in identifying those rules (natural law). It is a matter of discovery. Intellectualism is not an essential requirement for "discovering" natural laws.

Conventional US economists like the idea that they are economic scientists. We have currently two Economic Science Associations: one is the NY University Economic Science Association and the North American Association. There is a journal titled *Journal of Economic Science*. All of them claim that economic science is a science because they deal with economic issues that are ordinarily difficult to examine by using "naturally occurring data." They claim they use "controlled experiments" to advance economics science ideas. But their stand is itself unscientific. Science is about natural matters and naturally occurring data. It is not clear what controlled experiments mean. They will like to call such experiments scientific. A matter is not scientific merely because one used a scientific method to study it.

A number of US faculties of economics are called Faculties of Economic Science on the same basis as the Economic Science Association. These faculties additionally engage some esoteric type of research activities and research into some emerging technologies. But these do not make them economic science.

It was Martin Wolf, the chief economist of the Financial Times at the time, who once said that if all (conventional) economists in the world were laid end to end, they would not reach a conclusion. He said that "The first law of (conventional) economics is: For every economist, there exists an equal and opposite economist."[12] On September 10, 2013, Oliver Blanchard Chief Economist of IMF confessed that "The economic crisis has put into question many of our (conventional) beliefs." Until economics becomes a scientific discipline, conventional economics will continue being a fleeting intellectualism. Blanchard said that economists needed to accept (new) *intellectual challenges.* Mr. Blanchard got it right that conventional economics is made up of economic beliefs, no different from religions with their beliefs. In view of the questions raised on these beliefs, because of the unexpected recession of 2007, Mr. Blanchard said that the profession faced new intellectual changes. He did not suggest science but called for new intellectual challenges. Current macro-economics has unfortunately been built on the towering intellectualism of two towering charismatic economists: Keynes and Milton Friedman. Other intellectuals have come and gone. There are current intellectuals usually professors who we respect whatever they say because they said it. Mr. Blanchard accepted in effect that the intellectualism of Keynes and Friedman have failed. We are now at a dead-end in conventional economics because there are no more towering, charismatic economic intellectuals to be celebrated and copied to get us out of the present economic impasse in the US.

I find the columnist Daniel Altman's write-up in the *New York Times* of Sunday, May 4, 2007, 'Economic View' intriguing when he decided to put President Bush's tax cuts claims to a large group of 177 economists as to what factor was responsible for the mid-2003 to 2006 economic growth. He decided to test the former president Bush's claim on US economists that Bush's 2001–2003 tax cuts were responsible for the growth that occurred in the US from mid-2003. He offered them five possible responses to choose from (a) The tax cuts signed by the President Pent-up demand following the recession of 2001, the corporate scandals, and the invasion of Iraq. (c) Both a and b (d) neither a nor b was important: the growth was part of the regular business cycle (e) There was no way to tell.

Among the 49 who answered, according to Altman, were many of the best known names in the field. Of these, Altman said, five, including two Nobel laureates, known for their conservative views, said tax cuts were the most important factor. Three economists chose (b). Three chose (c). The majority of 30 answered (d) or supplied an answer not listed.

Under (d) one said that the growth was part of normal business cycle by which recovery follows recession. Most of the others volunteered answers ranging from (1) they claimed the growth was due to unprecedented period of low, short-term interest (2) productivity growth (3) innovation (d) the growth was not real growth only an inventory correction (4) pent-up demand following a recession (5) tax cut hurt, not helped the economy (6) mili tary spending in Iraq spurred the growth. To complete the package, a senior economist and policy adviser in a Federal Reserve Bank was said to have voted (d) but, for good measure, added "if we hold ourselves to the highest standards of scholarly rigor, we could not answer anything but(e)," namely that there is no way to tell.

Early in 2008, a commission made up of twenty-one best (intellectual) brains in development work including two Nobel Prize winners, was set up by the World Bank to fashion out the best economic tool for achieving economic development released its report. That means that despite pretenses to the contrary, the World Bank acknowledges that conventional economics has no clear idea how to achieve sustainable economic development which it claims is its primary function. At the inception of the commission, its chairman, the Nobel Prize winner Michael Spence said, "Our goal is to assemble the best insights (intellectualism) from economic analysis and practice that lead to actions, policies, and investments at national and international level to support growth." The commission was looking for a framework for economic development preferably wrapped in an overarching theory. After two years, the commission report told the world that there is no enveloping theory to economic development. The commission concluded that what is needed is that economic policy makers need to customize and *experiment* with policies rather than follow any set of guidelines. Conventional economics can therefore not be a science.

A disappointed US professor, William Easterly, stated in an article in the *Financial Times* on May 28, 2008, that his students could have reached the same conclusion as the commission for less than $4 million that the World Bank spent. Since the 1950s conventional economists have crowded the world with empirical financial economic development theories that have no general application. American economic "experts," because America is supposed to be the most successful economy in the world, have flooded the world with worthless economic theories and in the process have been misadvising and misleading third world countries in the process. Professor Easterly rightly said that there are seven billion economic experts in the world because the world population is seven billion. So far as Western conventional economics continue unchanged it is bound to bring Western economies down with it.

John Kay, the well-known British economist and one time visiting professor at the London School of Economics put the position nicely when he stated that "Economics (that is the current brand of economics) may be dismal, but it is not a science." Paul Krugman in the *New York Times* on October 22, 2012 boldly stated that economics isn't as much a science as we would like.

Expressing the early need for science in economics, the famous Austrian-British economist Friedrich Hayek (1899-1992) asked, "Why should we, however, in economics have to plead ignorance of the sort of facts, on what to plead ignorance of the sort of facts, on what in the case of physical theory, a scientist would certainly be expected to give precise in information."

The Death of Conventional Macroeconomic Theory

The unexpected severity and depth of the 2007–2009 recession and ensuing financial disaster of 2008 finally exposed the total uselessness of all the existing financial and monetary macro-economic theories. Central banks in the major advanced economies of the West had earlier been in the business of constructing misleading and expensive macroeconomic models, like their counterpart in the United States before the collapse in 2008. They convinced themselves they controlled their economies with these models. It was part of the conventional economist's attempt to be scientific. For example, in 2007, after the August liquidity crisis started, Frederic Mishkin, a distinguished academic and then a governor of the Fed, gave an assuring talk at the Federal Reserve Bank of Kansas City annual symposium. He presented the results of simulations of the economy from the Fed's FRB/US model on the US macro economy. Even as house prices fell by a fifth in the two years, he assured his audience from the model that the slump will only knock off only 0.25 percent from the Gross Domestic Product (GDP) and only a tenth of a percent point in employment. The reason was that, according to him, the Fed would respond *aggressively* to house price drops by which he meant a cut in Federal funds of one-percentage point. The Fed had to cut interest not by 1 percent as Mushin had said but by five times that to a low present rate of mere 0.25 percent. Even after this unprecedented rate cut, the problem escalated in size and complexity far more than everyone ever feared. What is worse is that because of infighting and ignorance of structural macroeconomics in the Fed, the people in the Fed were horribly divided about what was to be done about this unexpected development. The bottom finally dropped from the US economy later in 2007 when the recession started. The Bank of England in 2010 discarded its multimillion pound sterling financial economic model when recession suddenly descended on the United Kingdom without any hint from their model.

Financial models mushroomed in conventional economics, in an attempt of making conventional economics a science. Greenspan has correctly told us in his book, *The Map and the Territory*, that models are by their nature vast simplifications of a complex reality. He told us that there are literally millions of relationships that interact every day to create aggregate GDP even for a relatively simple market economy. Greenspan told us that because only a small fraction of these interactions can be represented in any model, economists are continually seeking sets of equations that while few in number, nonetheless are *presumed* to capture the fundamental forces that drive modern economies." They were seeking how to define the structure of the economy only that they were doing this in financial terms and seeking to turn that finance into a science. But finance is not a science. He further added that "Finance has always been the most difficult component of an economy to model." It is hoped that when structural economic science is fully studied and established, it will be possible to apply artificial intelligence to produce machines that will provide solutions to the most intricate economic problems serving the need, which conventional economist unsuccessfully sought to meet with economic models.

Greenspan put the failure of conventional economics this way in his book: "The degree of certainty with which the so-called hard sciences are able to identify the metrics of the physical world appears to be out of reach of the economic disciplines." Structural economic science as proposed in this book is the "hard" science which Greenspan was seeking. In the "hard" sciences, throughout history, battles usually ended in decisive victories, with true science ousting intellectually inspired claims and mysteries. In conventional economics, laced with guesses and intellectualism the battles have been interminable. 'Temporary defeats' were often followed by the regrouping of the defeated group for a new assault in a continuing circulation of counterclaims. The non-scientific nature of current economics profession is responsible for its inconclusive and ongoing battles.

But then, in the shifting tide of non-science intellectual economic battles, as memories of the Great Depression faded, the 1950s saw a revival of the old classical economics and Keynes was shoved aside. Even the disciples of Keynes, now called New Keynesians, came to accept that the financial market gets it right much of the time and did not need the kind of intervention Keynes preached. Much of the past decades in the United States, therefore, witnessed the triumph of advocacy of the efficiency and rationality of the financial market through arguments that often lacked any structural analysis. Neoclassical economics returned in fury against Keynesian ideas as the charismatic Friedman condemned Keynes claims and asserted that only in special circumstances should a government exercise limited role in the economy by keeping the money supply in the economy growing, the so-called theory of monetarism. If this had been done in the late 20s, according to the Friedman, the 1930 Depression could have been avoided. Friedman claimed that governments should not push unemployment below 4.8 percent, otherwise the economy risked overheating, the forerunner of the now dead NAIRU. Today disciples who came after Friedman, pushed the sanctity of a free market beyond any limit Friedman would have imagined. The old romance of classical economics once more blossomed as we were now told that we are rational economic individuals interacting in a perfectly rational financial market that was baptized as a science supported by fancy mathematics and equations. So long as mild recessions came and went, those in charge thought that it was thought their mastery of monetary techniques that solved the recessions to the point some economists thought they had found the key to eliminating recession altogether. Keynesians were silenced, or so it was thought until 2007 when the tremor of a never witnessed deep recession since the Great Depression sent the economy into a mental and bodily relapse. When the Fed searched its Friedman cupboard of medicines to cure the illness, as it had apparently done successfully before, it found that the medicines it had all along were this time ineffective. Interest rate with which the Fed played its monetary games was almost at zero. An economic tsunami was on its way. Keynes was back after years in the wilderness. (Financial) stimulus became the tool of politicians who had no idea how to deal with the economic relapse in front of them. Monetary economic theory had gone round its vicious circle. Today after Obama's romance with economic stimulus in 2010 and 2011, "it is time," according to Jeffrey Sachs in an arti cle in the *Financial Times* on June 8, 2010, "to plan for the post-Keynesian era. Stimulus has not worked." Mainstream Keynesian economics had faced its end but the diehards among them have not surrendered.

The truth is that neither Friedman nor his latter-day followers nor Keynesians and his successors got it right. Their theories are not scientific economic theories. They have not faced the structural imbalance of the US economy. They are financial theories falsely claiming to tell us how to manage the real economy. Financial people, beginning in the 1970s, got mesmerized with what they thought were their entry into science. They too wanted be addressed as economic scientists with their new foray into mathematics. Matt Nolan, a well-known economist, argued in the context as if *neoclassical finance is about building bridges and railroads.* The general argument is that relativistic and quantum revolutions of the twentieth century backed by Einstein's relativity theory have shown that much of Newton physics to be wrong, yet engineers still design buildings and bridges following Newton's laws and the overwhelming majority of the buildings and bridges don't fall down. The argument of some core financial experts is, therefore, that the errors in neoclassical finance don't fault its basic 'scientific' status. But they are wrong. The argument is false 'technical' analogy. Nobel Prize in economics was at one time freely awarded for pioneering work in the theory of financial economics. In an article in *Wall Street Journal* titled "En-Nobelling Financial Economics," Gregg Jarrel, professor at the University of Rochester, imploded that the choice of Nobel Economic Prize winners "finally acknowledged that the field of financial economics is a genuine science, in the same league with physics and mathematics."[13] The implosion of the financial market in 2008 put to rest the wild claims that finance is a science. The fact that you apply scientific methods of analysis, as I earlier remarked, does not make what you are studying a science just as Professor Chetty in an article in the New York Times of October 21, 2013 titled "Yes, Economics Is a Science" incorrectly argued that because economists are "developing tools that *approximate* scientific experiments to obtain compelling answers to specific policy questions," economics is a science.

The truth is that monetary and financial theories that I have just discussed cannot truthfully be described as macroeconomic theories because they do not have anything to say about the nature and structure of the macro economy.

As *The Economist* belatedly discovered—after years of wor-shipping financial theorists—that "Finance is a veil, obscuring what really matters."[14] Financial macro-economics treats the real economy as a black box because its proponents don't understand what is inside the box. In his belated turnaround criticism in May 2009 of the management of the US economy, Greenspan poured scorn on himself and others from the 1950s and throughout his reign as Fed's chairman, who adored what was regarded as the extraordinary intellectualism of the famous charismatic economist Professor Markowitz. The professor's writings were for a long time acclaimed to have produced insights in what was called 'economic risk-management.'

Greenspan told us that Markowitz's writings were widely embraced by academia and financial professionals, and global regulators. A number of economists, who borrowed from Markowitz's intellectualism, went on to win several Nobel prizes in economics. Greenspan now admitted that Markowitz's risk management structure was discredited leaving a trail of financial and economic havoc. Dick Parson, Chairman of Citigroup, in an interview in May 2009 confessed that what he called 'the financial engineering technology' that ruled Wall Street and the economy in the pre-2008 recession was a mass delusion.

The veneer of respect surrounding the conventional economics profession tore at the seams as the shock of the 2007 through 2009 reces sion began to be felt. The titans of the profession in 2009 publicly and privately and for the first time since the Great Depression, admitted their foolery. In a seven-page *New York Times Magazine* article September 2009 titled "How Did Economists Get It So Wrong," Paul Krugman told us that "the fault lines in the economics profession have yawned wider than ever." America has wasted the last seventy years. Krugman worried that, "It is much harder to say where economics profession goes from here." The truth is that, as this book goes to print in 2019, 'economics' is still where it was in 2009.

Yet less than two years after, Krugman was now telling us how the US economy can be managed. Robert Lucas, once acclaimed as one of the greatest macroeconomists of his generation was recently accused of "making ancient and basic analytical errors all over the place." Another acclaimed towering figure in macroeconomics, Robert Barrow of Harvard has recently been described as "making truly boneheaded arguments." Brad DeLong of the University of California Berkeley summed up the position by saying that "To outsiders, the cacophony (between opposing camps in macroeconomics) underlines the profession (that is economist)'s uselessness."[15]

In an LSE Lionel lecture June 10, 2009, Krugman said that most of macroeconomics of the past thirty years was "spectacularly useless at best and positively harmful at worst." He said that we are living through the Dark Age of macroeconomics. *The Economist* concluded that "The past 30 years of macroeconomic training at American and British universities were a 'costly waste of time'."[16] One will think that thereafter, Krugman will be at the front of a search for economic science.

Professor Paul De Grauwe of the University of Leuven concluded, after a review of the sorry state of macroeconomics in a *Financial Times* article called 'Warring Economists,' July 22, 2009, that "We need a new science of macroeconomics."

He further said that "The basic error of 'modern' microeconomics is the belief that the economy is simply the mathematical sum of microeconomic decisions of rational agents." But, he said, "The economy is more than that. The interactions of these decisions create collective movements that are not visible in the micro... It will be difficult to model these collective movements."[17] In an article I earlier quoted by

Professor Raj Chetty of Harvard titled "Yes, Economics Is a Science" of October 21, 2013, he correctly admitted that "It is true that the answers to *many* "big picture" macro-economic questions—like the causes of recessions or determinants of maximum growth—remain elusive." The two questions happen to be the most important question in economics for the US. The Fed's lack of answers to these big questions is the reason why in chapter 8, I showed that the Fed is part of US economic's problem for feigning erroneous answers that are contributing to US economic decline.

Case Study: "Forensic Science"

Criminal justice was at one time, a case of an accuser stating his/her case through a defense counsel and the prosecutor stating the case against the defendant. It was up to the judge or jury to decide, on the weight of evidence who they believed. Bias, prejudice and simple ignorance made it that injustices were common and people sent to the gallows for crimes they did not commit.

Forensic Science came into the scene in the 1980s with the science of DNA. DNA profiling became the order of today. Forensic science transformed and modernized the criminal justice system throughout the world. Economics could do a similar transformation with the application of economic science. Conventional economics is opinions of its participants.

General Ignorance about Recession and Depression: Financial/Market Macroeconomics to the Dust bin

Professor Raj Chatty correctly called the cause of recession "an elusive big picture question." Krugman, on the other hand, told us in his economic depression book that "There's more or less unanimous agreement among economic historians that the banking crisis is what turned a nasty recession into the Great Depression in 1930."[18] Elsewhere, he said that the Great Depression was the result not only of lax regulations in Washington and reckless risk-taking on Wall Street but also of faulty (financial) theorizing in academia. Further backing his banking explanation of recessions, Krugman once claimed that "Vulnerability to business cycle may have little or nothing to do with your more fundamental eco nomic strengths and weaknesses: bad things can happen to good economics."[19] The Great Depression, according to him, was all caused in Washington and Wall Street. According to Krugman, recessions and depressions are all a financial problem. From my review of the state of macroeconomics, Krugman was wrong especially when he himself admitted earlier that macroeconomics for the last 70 years has got it wrong.

Just listen to what the *New York Times* of November 1, 1929 had to say barely a month after the Wall Street crash of September 29, 1929 that contradicts Krugman's claim: "Trade reports show that as yet the stock market collapse has had little effect on business." So it cannot be claimed that the cause of the depression was financial.

Julius Klein, assistant secretary for Commerce and a close confidant of President Hoover, declared on the radio that business was sound and that the crash was not a *major barometer of business.* Many other newspapers picked up the theme, as detailed by Maury Klein in his remarkable book, *The Crash of 1929.* "The sagging of stocks" stated the *New York Daily News*, "has not destroyed a single factory, wiped out a single farm or city lot or real estate development, decreased the productive powers of a single workman or machine in the United States."

An editorial of the *Times* found a useful solace in the crash by stating that: "Painful as the experience has been, the longer result of it will be restoration of the community's mental health and vision." The well-known engineer and economist at the time, Stuart Chase, wrapping up what Maury Klein called in his book "A six-month survey on the structure of American survey," dismissed the crash as a factor in the broader business picture, and told a reporter that "we probably have three more years of prosperity ahead of us before we enter the cyclic tailspin which has occurred in the eleventh year of each of the four great previous periods of commercial prosperity."[20]

The economist/engineer was in effect saying that they had regularly had recessions in the eleventh year of each of the four great previous periods of commercial prosperity before the 1929 Wall Street crash, and that at the time of the crash, the depression (high recession) was being expected as part of a cycle. But in classrooms all over the United States today, students are told that the Wall Street stock market crash of October 29, 1929 (Black Tuesday) was the worst thing that engineered the depression. Some other economists disagree and say it is the financial action of Reserve Bank that took the US further down the depression, not that it caused the recession. Others say, no, it is mismanagement of banks that caused the problem. There was a run on the banks they claim, just as a run on banks almost gathered momentum in the 2007 through the 2009 recession.

Authorities (State and Federal) were blamed during the Depression that closed banks and reopened them in an uncoordinated haphazard staggered manner. Some say that the Depression was fueled by Hoover's attempt to balance the budget. Other economists, persisting with the financial theme, tell us that what they call the bad state of international trade at the time caused by the US Smoot-Hawley tariff or further worsened the depression. A professional money manager, Liaquat Ahamed the Pulitzer-winning author of the book, *Lords of Finance,* claimed that the Depression was caused by what he called "the misguided restoration of the gold standard in the 1920s and the massive inter-governmental debts, including German reparation, resulting from World War I."

He accused four men of engineering the perverse policies that caused the Depression: the then Governor of the Bank of England Montagu Norman, the then head of the New York Federal Reserve Benjamin Strong, Head of the Banque de France Emile Moreau, and Head of German's Reichsbank, Hjlmar Schat.[21]

Krugman has written so many times on depressions and recessions that he can be called an expert on the subject. In his latest book on the topic, *The Return of Depression Economics and the Crisis of 2008,* he sought to explain recessions, their causes and cures. He defined recessions as "insufficient private spending to make use of the available productive capacity." In further explaining this version of recession, Krugman told us of his now famous Sweeney story of the 150 family baby-sitting coops. The professor proceeded to say that in the real economy, recession is caused because of shortage of cash in the economy and because the public as a whole is accumulating or hoarding cash. The professor said that the coupon issuer in modern economy is the Fed and that it is the job of the Fed, as the central bank, to add or subtract cash as needed to prevent recession.

He claimed quite surprisingly that recessions could be cured with *surprising ease* by the Fed printing more money. If Krugman is right that recession is people saving money, the 2007 recession would not have taken place at a time between 2007and 2008 when consumption had climbed to 70 percent of GNP. House savings had gone from 10 percent of disposable income in 1980 to near zero in 2007. In the follow-up to the 2007 through 2009 recession, the Fed had fed money to trillions to the US economy through Quantitative Easing that made no immediate change to the economy. The economy was not revived with any *surprising ease.*

The average family in the United States at the time was $80,000 in debt, giving a total debt of $2 trillion including mortgage, facilitated by easy credit and car leasing facilities. Household savings rate had gone from 10 percent of disposable income in 1980 to near zero in 2007. The Fed could not easily deal with the longest recession of 2007 despite the huge sums it wasted in the attempt to stop it.

Krugman further told us that in 1987, the US stock market crashed with a one-day fall that was as bad as the first day's fall of the 1929 crash. He told us that the Fed pumped so much money into the system that the real economy did not experience a recession. He claimed that the Savings and Loans collapse led to a credit crunch, which he said was one major cause of the 1990 through 1991 recession. According to him, the hedge-fund firm LTCM's failure which caused a runaway panic in 1999 did not cause a recession because of the immediate intervention by the Fed.

Here is Zhou Xiachuan, Governor of the People's Bank of China at the time, in a speech said:

> While many kinds of instability or turbulences afflict financial systems, only a minority is created by the financial system itself." The majority reflects problems

in the real economy—the so-called 'mirror image' in the financial sector. The real economy and financial system mirror each other just as NPL problem usually reflects troubles with firms in the real economy...One characteristic of the modern economy is that the financial system is a barometer of the entire economy; troubles in the real economy are often first broken out in the financial system. Problems in the financial system, however, are not caused by the financial system alone.

This is a correct structural economic distillation of the facts. Finance, according to Zhou Xiachuan, is a mirror image of the economy. Being a mirror image means that finance is not the real economy. Finance is only a barometer of the real economy but not the real economy. According to Xiachuan, only a minority of problems in the financial system is caused by the financial system itself. The majority of problems in the financial system are caused by problems in the real economy. Xiachuan will, therefore, say that problems in the financial system cannot cause a recession, but problems in the real economy can cause recession. This is a point American and Western conventional economists, in this regard Krugman on recessions and the Great Depression have consistently failed to get.

Krugman also talked about the recession that shook East Asia in 1997, which he called a financial meltdown. I was, therefore, most surprised that in his book, Krugman sought to give a non-financial interpretation to the same 1997 East Asian recession. He correctly claimed that prior to 1997, these countries witnessed an economic boom. He told us that as the boom got underway, they replaced handsaw with a lathe, another way of saying that the countries increasingly adopted more capital intensive technologies. He claimed that once workers in East Asia had state of the art machines, subsequent Asian economy growth up to 1997 began to look like those of the developed world. Profits were high, according to him, when capital can be employed with skilled and cheap labor. He observed however that as capital to labor ratio continued to rise, the rate of profit began to fall. The economic gains resulting from injecting more and more capital in these economies, according to him, became less and less. It appeared that, according to him, it was this reduction in the growth pattern in the East Asians that led to recession as profits slowed.

He argued that once slower growth rates began to appear, investors began to dump East Asian stocks, which, according to him led in turn to capital market and currency problems. It appeared to me here that this time Krugman was saying that the East Asian recession was caused by structural economic imbalance not financial crisis, which was a mere consequence of structural imbalance.

But as one will expect in this undisciplined profession, there was no shortage of economists who will say that Krugman's views on depression/recession are incorrect. One group of economists claims that general lack of sufficient demand is not a good explanation for recession because prices always move to match supply and demand. What can I say? They have a point. Appearances, they claim, can make things look as if there is general lack of demand. They are not, however, right that supply and demand *always* match. Another group of economists protests that recessions are no more than temporary *confusion* among workers and companies as they try to sort out unusual changes taking place in their particular businesses. At the other extreme are economists who say that price fluctuations and changes in demand have nothing to do with business cycles. Rather they say that changes in demand have to do with technological changes, which can make affected workers voluntarily decide not to work. Therefore, the unemployment during a recession, according to this group of economists is because workers decide voluntarily not to go to work.

Financial economists added another word to the profession's double talk dictionary: 'bubbles', similar to another of the profession's double talk word: 'shock/s'. We are told that financial bubbles can cause a recession. We are told that the dot-com bubble caused the short 2001 recession. The term 'house price bubble' has been with the profession ever since the Asian crisis, and the Japanese economic downturn when some economists claimed that house price bubble contributed or caused the financial crisis which in turn caused the recessions in these countries. It is not clear what causes an economic bubble. Economists call it a bubble because it can burst any time, for a reason and for no reason. With the recession that started in the United States in 2007, we are told that it was the house price bubble that started the recession. Professor Robert Shiller, Mr. Bubble, acquired quite a reputation in the profession because he succeeded where others failed. Although like others, he was trying to make a financial model from historical statistics. He was able to make 'science' by correlating historical data from 1934 and 1953 and made a forecast in 2005 that US house prices will burst by as much as 40 percent and throw the United States into a recession. The recession came in late 2007. Shiller, overnight became an economic guru. It was not however the drop in house prices that threw the United States into recession. He has since won a Nobel Prize in 2013 on his ability to value "assets."

Even as economists are giving us divergent views of recession, others in this undisciplined and unscientific profession offer diametrically different views and attitudes to recessions. The Nobel economics laureate Professor Solow in a Channel 13 interview with Paul Solman on November 21, 2008, said that recession is caused when people drop consumption. More importantly, he said that recessions "can come for purely psychological reasons." In a *Financial Time* article in 2008, Greenspan attributed "our economic despair" (recession) to human nature's propensity to sway from fear to euphoria and back, a condition, according to him, that no economic paradigm has proved capable of suppressing without severe hardship.[22]

Some early economic philosophers had also weighed in to tell us that recessions are not only necessary but cleansingly refreshing. The well-known Australian legendary economist Professor Joseph Schumpeter and some disciples after him celebrated capitalism. Capitalism is the embodiment of the entrepreneur, who drove technology forward and followed it by periods of economic retrenchment and recuperation. Recessions, according to Schumpeter and his followers, are creative destruction, inevitable for progress. Recession was capitalism re-invigorating itself, they were telling us.

It is clear that the conventional economics profession and the Fed do not agree what causes recessions/depressions. If you don't know the cause of a problem, then you cannot know how to solve it.

Why Recessions Are the Direct Consequences of Structural Imbalance: No Financial Action Can Stop/Slow a Recession

In this chapter we have come full circle. I have shown why the economic structure of the US is unbalanced. Our unbalanced economy has an irregular cyclical pattern so that every seven to ten years we have to find ourselves back to square one (another recession).

History is clear that it is a drop in demand is what we notice to tell us that recession has started. Great Depression is full of evidence of drops in demand heralding the depression. *Iron Age,* the equivalent of the *Wall Street Journal* in the 1920s, stated in March 1929 that "Mass production after acquiring great momentum under the spur of ever increasing costs and constantly expanding sales has run into the stone wall of saturated demand."[23] The error is that conversely conventional economists think that the way to stop recession is to increase demand.

The 1930s economist A. Adams pointed out that unemployment in those days was due to the closing of industries, "itself a result of an excess of goods in the markets which in turn is due to shortage of purchasing power of American consumers."[24] On September 20, 1929, the president of the Standard Oil Company of Ohio told the National Petroleum Association at its twenty-seventh annual convention that the fluctuations of prices that had been occurring in the industry for a long time indicated *fundamentally unbalanced economic conditions. Price cutting in our industry has a peculiar significance.* Since it cannot stimulate the total demand, it tends toward industrial self-destruction. About the same time, the executive director of the American Institute of Steel Construction stated that: "We are at a stage of industrial development where it is much easier to produce than to sell." He observed that "There are some industries where demand is declining or where it is impossible to increase it to any extent."

The US Department of Commerce's statement in September 1929 on the production of motor vehicles announced that in terms of factor sales, the month of August reflected "accurately the dip in demand for new cars which developed after the turn of the half year." Peter Temin, that well-known economic historian, believed that there was a collapse in consumer spending and attributed the Depression primarily to this "unanticipated" and "unexplained" decline in consumption. "The fall in aggregate demand spread throughout the economy."

Temin stated that, "Time has not been kind to the school of thought that blames the Depression on the stock market crash." He concluded that "The stock market crash is not a big enough event on its own to cause a depression," but added, 'This is not to say that the crash had no effect."[25]

It is clear from all this that fall in demand in the whole US economy started well before the stock market crash. By early 1929, well before the stock market crash, the ratio of total industrial employment to the population was lower than what it was between 1910 and 1920. In regard to housing, the economists Atack and Passell noted that, "In each year of the years between 1924 and 1927, the ratio of real residential construction to GNP was at record level—in excess of 8 percent of GNP and represented about half of gross domestic investment—by 1929 residential construction was less than half its mid-decade peak." They added significantly, "In part, the decrease stemmed from declining demand for housing."[26]

We have reached the conclusion that US and similar recessions are caused by structural economic imbalances. Rather than tackle structural imbalances, financial experts have taken over telling us they are seeking for ways either detect the start of recessions or what to do to ameliorate its effects thinking that in cyclical economic conditions, recessions will over time readjust the economy out of recession.

I want similarly to talk about another recession that ushered in one of the biggest international financial crisis: the 1997 East Asian financial crisis. Henderson attributed the large monthly current-account deficit in late 1996 in East Asia as due "not to (poor) export growth but to a collapse in imports as domestic demand slowed."[27]

In Thailand, the Economic Intelligence Unit noted that as the country entered the third quarter of 1996, it was becoming eve cause loss in demand is the result not the cause of recession. It means that neither stimulus nor Fed's change in interests or other financial measures can solve recession. A recession/depression will go away on its own time only when the cycle of unbalanced structure of the economy allows it. The only way to stop recessions/depression is to re-structure the economy.

It is wrong for conventional economists to explain the Great Depression simply by reading the economic history of the 1930s without searching what economists or economic leaders who lived the experience of Depression thought were the causes of the Depression. A summary of these will show that economists during the Depression analyzed the Depression in structural terms not in financial terms.

The 1930s saw a lot of interest in what was called the "under consumption/overproduction" explanation of the Depression. President Roosevelt, in his 1933 fireside chats attributed the economic collapse to "over speculation and overproduction of practically every article or instrument used by man...millions of people had been put to work, but the products of their hands had exceeded the purchasing power of their pocketbooks," he said. He observed, "Under the inexorable law of supply and demand, supplies so overran demand which would pay that the production had to stop. Unemployment and closed factories resulted." In frustration, the President stated the whys of the depression:

> "In so far as we have a general overproduction situation
> in industry in the United States, it was brought about by
> diverting too large a percentage of the national money
> income in making new capital equipment and too small a
> percentage of the national money income into purchasing
> finished consumers' goods.[29]

He was, in effect, seeing the problem in terms of the structure of the economy, saying that Americans had gone too capital-intensive and diverted too much of its limited material production factor resources into capital equipment creation and reducing natural resources available for goods production. Adams described the supply-demand problem at the time as one in which "profits have been too high and real wages slow or where prices have not been adjusted to the lower cost of production during economic progress." He complained that the monopolistic price controls in operation between 1922 and 1929 kept prices from being lowered as rapidly as the cost of production was dropping. What he called the "displacement of labor by automatic machinery" between 1922 and 1929, according to him, resulted in surplus labor, which stopped wages from increasing as rapidly as did profits. Reading these comments of Adams is a repeat of my analysis in this chapter about present day craze in the US to automate and apply increasingly capital-intensive strategies and relative loss by the lower income sector as profits jump and the income gap increases and surplus labor pool increase.

Robert McElvaine in his book *The Great Depression 1929–1941* stated that no cause of the Great Depression was of larger importance than the growing maldistribution of income in the 1920s America. He stated that "any interpretation of the origins of the Depression that places significant emphasis on maldistribution must account for the peaceful coexistence of prosper ity with maldistribution in the years preceding the Crash."[30] He was talking of the imbalance in the economic structure at the time, like the United States of today. The economists Walton and Rockoff 's theme on the Great Depression that "something drastic and unexplained" needed to happen to explain the setting in of the depression agrees with Temin's view that something "unanticipated" and "unexplained" (structural collapse) resulted in a decline in demand and caused the Depression. They were referring to the unanticipated and unexplained out-of-phase demand behavior of the economy.[31] Professor Hairault, and his colleagues Professors Henin and Portier described the position as a *shock* to demand. In my book *The Science of Economic Development and Growth*, I described the Great Depression in the following words:

> The Great Depression was basically an economic hemorrhage. The capital-intensive sector of the economy at the time was juxtaposed with the low-capital-using sector at a time when the American population was growing substantially.

It is therefore clear that neither recessions nor depressions have financial causes. Conventional economists tell us incorrectly that the 2007–2009 recession was caused by a financial crisis that started in 2008! Ignorance continues as people refuse to accept the recessions are structural and not financial, even though it often has vast financial consequences. This ignorance is confirmed recently in the 2017 Report of the Prsidential Economics Council of 2017 which stated that 'steps should be taken to protect against future recession and another Great Recession, in particular by modifying what it called the design of automatic stabilizers like unemployment insurance that can be expanded or extended during down turn which would provide better countercyclical support for the economy during recession and combine short run fiscal expansion with medium and long run fiscal consolidation to maintain fiscal discipline and curb entitlements. It is clear that the authors regretfully accept recessions as part of the US economic structucture.

How I Discovered the Economic Law of Factor Proportions

As an engineer, I quickly concluded when I enrolled in the economic faculty of London University in 1958 that the natural resource of raw materials and manpower were the tools nature made available to humans from time immemorial by nature in order that they can eke out a living and grow. That still remains the case today and forever. When humans arrived on earth, they realized that they were not strong enough, tall enough, and could not stand old or heat. They constructed various capital equipment devices and tools using some of the raw materials in order to make up for their limited strength or heights and their inability to deal with heat and cold I called all these devices production aid (capital). Thus, for their economic production, humans had three factors of production endowed by nature to enable them to undertake their economic activities. This position has not changed and will not ever change despite the $20^{th}/21^{st}$ centuryhuman : 21st century claimed intellectualism and financial prodigy. Capital equipment today by way of plant and machinery is production aid essential ingredients of production because humans don't have the physical ability, as I stated earlier to undertake all economic production by hand.

Each country in the world has different endowed ratios of factors. In using the factors of production, the actual ratios of usage may differ from the country's endowed ratios. The proposition is that it is best for balanced economic growth (remember the early development economists) that all economic activities in an economy use factor proportions that are the same (equal) as the economy's endowed factors of production.

Since there are three factors of production: materials, labor, and production aid (capital). I quickly realized the position after studying Professor Eckhaus's article of September 1955 in what for the first time factor proportions was mentioned when the professor affirmed need for balanced economic development through factor proportions.

If the operating factor proportions are to be the same as an economy's endowed factor proportions, it quickly occurred to me from my engineering studies at the university that I was in familiar territory. In my engineering, I was involved in mathematical calculus of derivatives which is all about rate of relative change between two items say 'x' and 'y' and how from a study of this to determine how action in which the items change can attain the highest output speed. With three factors of production x, y, z, we have the following calculus differential equations (where dx, dy, dz represent differential changes in the value of x, y, and z):

$$\frac{dx}{dy} > 0_1 \quad \frac{dy}{dz} > 0_1 \quad \frac{dz}{dx} > 0.$$

The changes need to tend (>) to zero (0) because relevant changes in the proportions among the three factors should not occur since the proportions are supposed to remain equal to the endowed natural factor proportions of the economy. A dynamic balance between changes in factors of productions is supposed to result in the fastest dynamic speed of economic growth of which the three factors of production are the engine. Dynamic balance is the only condition that enables the achievement of the highest speed in all movements: airplane, ships, cars, propulsion, including the economy.

I next studied the research of Professor Everett Hagen in his book *Economics of Development* (Richard D. Irwin Inc. Illinois) 1974. The professor successfully debunked previously held opinion (which is still prevalent in the US) that capital intensive pattern of development maximizes output. At other times, this false conclusion from conventional economics is arrived at assumed gains in productivity that are expected to result when a given unit of labor is associated with more and more capital. The professor showed that under certain conditions, capital intensive development can lead to less than optimum capital-labor allocation indifferent sectors and lead up to an overall loss of output. The professor produced two graphs fig.1.3 and fig. 1.4 representing two sectors—manufacturing and agriculture from which he showed that capital intensity can lead to a loss of output by an economy.

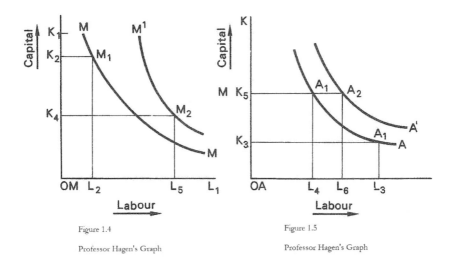

Figure 1.4

Professor Hagen's Graph

Figure 1.5

Professor Hagen's Graph

Professor Hagen's pioneering work only had one deficiency. In his time and as of now conventional economists, as I had earlier pointed out, think that growth solely as a function of labor and capital. He also wrongly thought of capital in terms of money. If Professor Hagen had realized that production is made up of three factors—labor, material, production aid (capital)— he would have reached similar conclusions like me that equality of operating factor proportions to a country to the economy factor proportions will ensure that maximum economic growth and not a capital-intensive economy. What I have is therefore is an economic law of factor proportions.

Chapter 2

Structural Economic Ignorance
and Arrogance in the US

The US economy is structurally unbalanced. It is facing what looks like a long- time terminal illness. As I write this, I cannot make up my mind whether the ongoing deterioration of the US structural economy is part of the recurring pattern in human history in which empires rise and fall. If it is, then what we are seeing may be part of an inevitable course of history that the United States as a world economic power has had its day.

In this chapter, I will characterize the key economic policy makers in the United States as ignorant, arrogant, complacent, highly-politicized, short-term oriented, and one-worldist.

Structural Economic Ignorance

The danger we face today in the United States is that, in absence of an enveloping structural macroeconomic theory, economists in the United States lack a scientific structural knowledge of the US economy and exhibit considerable ignorance of what the economy is facing.

While there is an increasing volume of empirical research and investigations, it is research and investigations based on conventional economics, often location and time bound. Oftentimes the research has a political bias.

What strikes me, therefore, is the profound level of structural economic ignorance among those in whose hands the fate of our economy has been entrusted. For nineteen years from 1987 to 2006, one person dominated the economy of this country as Treasury Secretaries came and went. That man is Alan Greenspan. His words were revered. He was an economic maestro. On October 4, 2008, long after he left office, Greenspan was at Capitol Hill to discuss the crisis that had overtaken the United States. After asking Greenspan some questions, Henry Waxman, House Committee chairman on Government Oversight and Reform, said to Greenspan, "In other words, you found that your view of the world, your ideology was not right. It was not working." Greenspan in his characteristic straight manner replied, "Precisely. That's precisely the reason I was shocked. I have been going for forty years or more with very considerable evidence that it was working exceptionally well."

Greenspan's ideology that financial markets knew best how to run the economy was widely shared in Wall Street and that manufacturing is not part of a modern (ideas) economy, a view shared in various degrees by eminent economists like Professor Stiglitz. They claimed ignorantly that the New Economy of the 1900s heralded a replacement of material used in manufacturing with ideas. In order words, they wrongly regarded the New Economy of the 1990s as the logical end to manufacturing era of the United State and its replacement by digital-controlled economy. They convinced themselves that manufacturing was a mid-era activity as economies mature into digital-based service economies. They failed to realize that digital technology is manufacturing.

Professor Picketty, the well-publicized and known economist who at the age of 22 started his journey into poverty and who at the age of 42 came out with what conventional economists acclaim as a major contribution to their knowledge of inequality had this to say about academics in economics in the US. He said: "What I found quite surprising when I was in MIT was that there was a level of arrogance (in economics) with respect to other disciplines in social sciences, which was incredible." He said: "In the case of income distribution which I was interested, we had almost no historical facts about which we knew anything I found the gap between the self-confidence of the profession and the actual achievement of the profession quite astonishing." Or as Branko Milanovic, senior scholar at the Luxembourg Income Study at the Graduate Centre of the City University of New York told Emily Eakin of *The Chronicle of Higher Education* that "Economics (in the US) has lost its taste to address big issues." This is because conventional economics lost its way in macro-economics. According to Dr. Milanovic, economics in the US has "gone into tiny issues, the extreme of which is *Freakeconomics,* which addresses the behavior of sumo wrestlers and why drug dealers live with their mothers."

I will next illustrate the long persisting structural ignorance about the US economy among US economic policy makers by discussing the periods when US economy took a sudden 'abnormal' turn either by way of recessions or an unexpected high growth. It is the time when a machine behaves abnormally that you know whether the machine mechanic knows his machine. I will discuss (a) recessions in the United States from factual reference to the Great Recession of 2007, 2008, and 2009 when the US economy declined 'abnormally' and (b) the New Economy of the 1990s, periods when the US economy grew 'abnormally'.

2007–2009 Great "Recession"

I had in chapter 1 mentioned that as the 2008 recession was already on, Paulson and Bernanke were incorrectly assuring Congress that there would be no recession. Bernanke's Fed was in fact forecasting a growth rate of 1.8 percent for the US economy in 2008, not recession. Bernanke's famed research, as an economics professor on the Great Depression, set him aside as an international expert on recessions and depressions. It was the same Bernanke and a former economics Nobel Prize winner Robert Lucas who told us in 2003 and 2004 that the United States will not have any more major recessions because US modern monetary management strategy has solved the problem. Bernanke and Paulson had no idea how to stop the recession when it started late in 2007.

Before Paulson's interview of November 2007, Paulson told us in February 2008 that with the recent rate cuts and planned stimulus, he and Bernanke expect to avoid a recession even as the recession had started. In March 14, 2008, Paulson said to NPR 'All Things Considered' program, when the recession had already started, that the global economy was as strong as he had seen it in his thirty year business career. Less than six months after the clean bill he gave to global economy, the global economy was on the point of total collapse. What was Paulson's view on financial rescues? The same Henry Paulson on November 13, 2008 in an interview with Jim Lahre was telling us that, "The situation we've confronted is the kind of thing that happens once or twice every hundred years." He now told us that the US economy was facing challenges that will last for some time, so will the financial markets. In 2007, he told us that a very strong global economy should insure continuing growth. He told us that players damaged by being too heavily involved in risky mortgage securities should not be insulated against losses. He said that "One of the natural consequences of excesses is that some entities will cease to exist."

He said that credit crunch is a "reassessment or re-pricing of risk" that shouldn't surprise anyone, and might even be a helpful corrective.[32] Shortly after, Paulson led the *too-big-to-fail* movement. When the financial crisis arrived in 2008, it was the same Paulson who rushed to Congress to propose a hurried TARP bill of $785 billion to rescue the same institutions who took on toxic assets from risky mortgage and who he earlier said should be left to cease to exist. Members of Congress were like hostages. In a bill only three pages long prepared by Paulson, they were in effect being told by Paulson that if they did not pass his bill, they would be responsible for the damage that would come to the financial system. The improvisational nature of Paulson and Bernanke's actions turned President Bush and Congressional Democrats into virtual bystanders, uncertain about what was to come next and left to wonder about the new power dynamics that was playing out in front of them.

After Paulson received Congress's approval for the $785 billion TARP money, he suddenly changed his mind. He realized he did not know how to value the toxic assets he wanted to buy because he hadn't thought through what he was doing. He then decided, on the urging of the socialist Labor government of Britain, which was also experimenting, that what was needed instead was to pump money direct into the banks by buying into their preferential shares. This was so that they can lend out the money in the mistaken belief that the credit flow to Wall Street banks was what was needed in order get the economy going.

As he settled on investing in banks, Paulson and his team suddenly realized that a large bulk of the credit in the real economy was coming, not from the banks he wanted to bail out, but from non-bank sources and it was necessary also to pump money into those non-bank financial institutions. Later in December, Bernanke woke up to another discovery that while he was preoccupied with his fund pumping into the big banks, the mortgage casualties at the ground level needed urgent relief.

John Gapper of the *Financial Times* on the December 12, 2000 called the whole disaster a matter of "improvising our way out of trouble." 'Improvising our way' is a common and continuing style of economic management in the United States, as many instances of combined ignorance and appearance of expertise will be discussed in this book because policy people are dealing with important issues of which they only have a financial guess about.

The frustration of Congress with incompetence and ignorance of economic policy makers burst into the open in 2008 in the House Financial Services Committee, which were a few months later on December 10, 2008. To most questions posed to the Treasury representatives by members on how funds pumped into the banks flowed in the real economy they got the answer that that "none of us knows the answers." A member told the Treasury representatives that it appeared they were lied to or bamboozled because Treasury was equally ignorant like the members and was not really sure how to restore the economy. Another member decried lack of an industrial policy in the United States. Treasury's lack of a plan and lack of knowledge about the real economy cannot surprise anyone. Another member lamented that after Congress had been pressured by its leaders to pass the bailout bill, and after they discovered that the Treasury and Fed had no control of the situation, they now realize that the bailout money, whether from Treasury and Fed, is going to be spent *wrongly, incorrectly, and wastefully* and that they were bamboozled into passing the $700 billion bill and that Treasury had no plan.

Asked in an interview why only a few conventional economists foresaw recession and the financial meltdown that followed in 2008 and what that says about the brand of economics that claims it is a science, Professor James K. Galbraith agreed: "It is an enormous blot on the reputation of the profession. There are thousands of economists. Most of them teach. And most of them teach a theoretical framework that has been shown to be fundamentally useless."[33]

> Because of the growing complexity of our society, it is intrinsic, it is not accidental, it is unavoidable, it is not a failure of preparation or learning that elected and appointed officials cannot know what to do. But where will we find officials…who are ready to acknowledge that they do not and cannot know what to do.
>
> Joseph Coates 1993

The recipe for perpetual ignorance is: "Be satisfied with your opinions and content with your knowledge" (Elbert Hubbard 1856–1915).

Dr. Ron Paul, the mesmeric member of US Congress and a two time Republican Presidential candidate in an article published March 27, 2006, well before he entered the Presidential race in 2008, in his 'Ron Paul Archives' wrote: "I believe one of the greatest threats facing this nation is the willful economic ignorance of the political class. Many of our elected officials at every level have no understanding of economics whatsoever, yet they wield tremendous power over our economy…"

It is regretful that the US

Ignorance About Industry and Manufacturing

In a speech in March 2007 to the Economic Club of Washington, Henry Paulson set out to prove that US manufacturing was in good health. He stated that, "Today, we have 21 million manufacturing jobs in the country—highest in US history. The manufacturing represented in the 50s represented 30 percent of the workforce. Today it represents 10 percent." Paulson then poured scorn on people who regard this statistics as a decline in US manufacturing. But to him, "America is the world's number one manufacturer, accounting for 20 percent of worldwide manufacturing value added that is more than Japan, twice as that of Germany and more than 2.6 times that of China." He continued:

> We manufacture more today than we ever have in our history—seven times as much real output in 1950 with about the same number of workers. And a greater share of manufacturing jobs than before is highly skilled and high paying. Competition has pushed businesses to invest in technological investment that allow workers to be more productive and earn higher wages.

Paulson like many Treasury Secretaries before and after him was fully out of depth in his analysis because he was viewing manufacturing with financial/treasury glasses. He, thus, missed structural consequences of the manufacturing problems facing the United States. So far as the 'financial' index of manufacturing and statistics on productivity were edging up, Paulson was happy. Mr. Paulson began this particular speech with what he told his audience he was the happiest about "the radical transformation of the US industrial companies and manufacturing." He told his audience that over the past three decades he has seen a radical transformation of the US manufacturing industry led by "technology and automation. "He told his audience, "In the 70s as I walked through factory floor or assembly lines, workers were everywhere. Today, you are struck by the degree and sophistication of automation." He added, "The increases in productivity are startling."

This self-congratulatory posture, which permeated US policy thinking at the time, demonstrated a basic lack of understanding of the place of technology choice in economic development. US economic policy makers like Paulson were probably looking to the day when robots will do everything and everyone will stay home having fun. It did not occur to Paulson that job creation is a basic need of any successful economy. US manufacturing output needs at the time were far greater than the sevenfold increase Paulson boasted about. Today, we are now second to China in manufacturing. The manufacturing decline of the United States stares all of us in the face as the country's chronic and growing trade deficit grows. Mr. Trump was well aware of these deficiencies when he came to into office and needed to protect the detoriating US manufacturing by raising tariffs and wanting to stop car imports and entering into a forced trade negotiations with China. Trump has wanted to bar the Chinese company Huawei, a leading Chinese telecommunication producer from building its next generation computer and phone networks in Europe and the US. Since he came into office, Trump has embarked on a stealthy, occasionally threatening global campaign to stop Huawei and other Chinese firms from participating in the most dramatic remaking of the plumbing that controls the internet, an original US production. There is a waning confidence of lifting the manufacturing sector in the United States to the top position.

Professor Stiglitz put the current incorrect theme on US manufacturing in perspective when he said:

> Just as the eighteenth and nineteenth centuries marked a change from agricultural to an industrial economy, and the first quarters of the twentieth century marked a movement from a manufacturing to a service economy, the end of the twentieth century marked a movement to the weightless economy, the knowledge economy.[34]

This is wrong and misleading. Greenspan, for his part, scorned people who worry about US's "loss of traditional manufacturing jobs" because he said that they regard the loss as "a worrisome hollowing out of the US economy." He said it was not. "On the contrary", he claimed that, "The shift of manufacturing jobs in steel, autos, and textiles... to their modern equivalents in computers, telecommunication, and information technology is a plus, not a minus, to American standard of living."

He concluded rather shockingly: "Traditional manufacturing companies are no longer the symbol of cutting-edge technologies; their roots lie deep in the nineteenth century or earlier."[35]

In a farewell speech at the National Economic Council in Washington on December 13, 2010, Larry Summers stated Obama administration's bias against manufacturing when he said:

> We are moving toward a knowledge and service economy—
> You don't succeed by producing exactly the same thing
> that other people are producing in the same way just at a
> lower cost—there is no going back to the past. Technology
> is accelerating productivity to the point where even China
> has seen manufacturing jobs decline…The argument that
> it's okay for the United States to be losing manufacturing
> jobs because even China is losing them has been used by
> free-market economists for the past eight years to justify
> the de-industrialization of America."

The assertion that China lost manufacturing jobs was not true. In 2007, world steel production increased by 6.2 percent at the same time as American steel production decreased by 3.6 percent. Today, US imports steel mainly from China followed by Canada. Continued growth of Chinese imports of steel into the United States has all but eliminated domestic US steel industry. It is clear that the technical error of analysts of financial conventional economists like Stiglitz, Paulson, Greenspan, and Summers that have 'encouraged' the demise of US manufacturing.

Economy Watch June 2, 2016 reported that manufacturing in the US turned significantly weaker, hitting its lowest point since 2009.

The New Economy of the 1990s

The 1990s was a period of unprecedented post World War II economic growth. It wiped away the US national debt. Economist called the phenomenon New Economy. The period further exposed the ignorance of those running the US economy. While 2007 and 2008 were years of economic decline, the 1990s was a period of unprecedented sustained growth. What happened during the New Economy decade went against everything American economic student taught at undergraduate and graduate classes in the United States. What happened took US economists and those managing the US economy by surprise. That is why they called it New Economy.

In discussing the New Economy, the 2001 Economic Report to the President admitted that "the remarkable economic trends of the

1990s took many by surprise." This is because they did not know or understand the structural changes taking place in the US economy. Alan Greenspan, in a speech in 1998 about the New Economy, asked, "Whether there has been a profound and fundamental alteration in the way our economy works that creates discontinuity from the past and promises significantly higher path of growth than had been experienced in recent decades." He could not explain what he was seeing.

On another occasion Greenspan declared:

> "We policy makers have engaged in a lot of on-the-job training in recent years. The remarkable American economy whose roots are still not conclusively known and the Asian crisis that caught us by surprise, among other humbling experiences particularly sensitive, as to how fast the world can shift under our feet."[36]

Early in 2000, Greenspan again said:

> "It has become increasingly difficult to deny that something profoundly different from the typical postwar business cycle has emerged...Analysts are struggling to create a credible conceptual framework to fit a pattern of interrelationships that have defied conventional wisdom based on our economic history of the past half century...It may take years before we fully understand the nature of the rapid changes currently confronting our economy."[37]

The truth is that American economic policy makers and US economists did not and never as of to date understood what happened in the New Economy because they lacked the structural analytical knowledge of the economy. They were looking at the events through the dark glasses of their neoclassical financial/ monetary conventional economics.

Greenspan and others made valiant unsuccessful attempts to explain the 'unusual' simultaneous occurrence of high economic growth/ demand, low inflation and low unemployment which reinforced the label the New Economy. As usual in such circumstances, conventional economists start guessing and intellectualizing standing on their feet. They coined new words like Greenspan's "wealth effect", "weightless economy", and "knowledge economy" to describe what they could not understand. Expressions like "weightless" and "knowledge economy" helped Americans believe that the collapse of their manufacturing sector is the step in the right direction for America because "weight" is associated in a derogatory tone with manufacturing that uses materials. Relying on conventional capitalist economics, which insists that capital investment is key to economic growth, US conventional economists unsuccessfully tried to show that the New Economy was caused by increased and unprecedented level of capital investment in the US when a detailed analysis, as detailed in my book *The Science of Economic Development and Growth* showed instead that US productive capital/labor ratio growth trend declined during the New Economy.

At the heart of another issue that bewildered these economists during the New Economy is the neoclassical article of faith called NAIRU (Non-Acceleration Inflation Unemployment). Conventional economics, which Greenspan ignorantly equated with what he called "conventional wisdom", and based on what he said formed the core of "our economic history of the past half century," states as an article of faith that rising economic growth leads to 'overheating' of the economy. This brand of economics believes that this overheating generates inflation as employment increases in the economy's attempt to meet increased demand. The answer, according to them, is that a bout of unemployment is required in order to cool the economy by raising the interest.

According to conventional economics, the economy must always maintain a certain level of unemployment in order to keep inflation under control. NAIRU was therefore at the center of US conventional economics teaching. As the New Economy in the 1990s gathered speed, conventional economists were, therefore, aghast that as unemployment was dropping, growth was gathering speed, and yet inflation was not increasing. At first the Economic Report to the President said that "The new, higher trend of productivity since 1995 has temporarily lowered the NAIRU." But as NAIRU started to disappear altogether, there was consternation among economists and policy makers. In a 1999 paper for the Federal Reserve Bank of Boston, a certain Roger Banner practically made a laughing stock of himself and the economic policy makers to say that NAIRU was not dead but "was merely sleeping." During a congressional testimony in July 2000, Greenspan courageously sounded what the *New York Times* called "an epitaph" to NAIRU. Greenspan told the members that, "My forecast is that NAIRU, which has served as a useful statistical procedure to evaluate how the economy was behaving, like so many types of temporary models which worked, is probably going to fail in the years ahead as a useful indicator." If NAIRU died, as it was turning out at the time, there would have been no need for the country to have a Federal Reserve Bank, whose main function is supposed to be to control inflation through a "monetary policy." The *New York Times* article correctly stated that if NAIRU was dead, it made the next interest increase by the Fed harder to justify. This is because at the time as the New Economy got under way the claimed connection between unemployment and inflation collapsed. Indeed, at the time, Professor Roger Bootle stated that the prime difficulty facing macro-policy makers since 1970 has been the containment of inflation. He added:

> "The collapse of this enemy (inflation) (which took place in the New Economy) left policy makers a bit like the West's defense establishment after the collapse of the Soviet Union and the end of the Cold War—still possessing old equipment (that is missiles) but not sure where to point it."[38]

Monetary policy was at a dead end. Ignorance wrapped in NAIRU claims and monetarism was exposed. Since the 1990s, NAIRU has disappeared from US conventional economics literature. Many years later, the Fed needed conjuring the fear of inflation at any corner to justify its continued existence.

Curiously in the same speech in early 2000 as vintage Greenspan did not know what hit him, he still said:

> I do not say we are in a new era, because I have expe-
> rienced too many alleged new eras in my lifetime that

have come and gone. We are far more likely, instead, to be experiencing a structural shift similar to those that that have visited our economy from time to time in the past. These shifts can have pronounced effects, often overriding conventional economic pattern for a number of years, before these patterns begin to show through again over the longer term.

Greenspan was right that the US experienced a structural economic shift, but could not understand it. Greenspan did not understand the New Economy of the late 1990s but was wishing that the new situation he did not understand will soon end not because the new situation is not wanted but that a return to normal will bring him(Fed) back in control in familiar territory. The situation finally came to normal as Greenspan hoped when the New Economy collapsed following, at the behest of Wall Street, the factor-proportions of IT, the cause of the New Economy became increasingly capital-intensive : the IT burst.

President Bill Clinton's Council of Economic Advisers for its part also asserted in its 2000 report that, "It will be a grave error to assume that the economy (that is the New Economy) has been so transformed that basic rules of economy no longer applied."

All these people did not understand the seismic structural changes taking place at the time in the US, details which are in my book *The Science of Economic Development and Growth: The Theory of Factor Proportions (2005)*. Despite the prevalent ignorance about the New Economy, Greenspan and Rubin never hesitated to take credit for the New Economy. Bob Woodward's bestselling book titled *Maestro: Greenspan's Fed and American Boom*, which called the New Economy a Greenspan phenomenon! President Clinton claimed the economic growth of the time was due to his own economic ingenuity.

Professor Stiglitz, who was the Chairman of the Council of Economic Advisers, during the New Economy, had since written a 379 page book about the New Economy: *The Roaring Nineties*. I would have expected that he would, at least, from his vantage position in the White House economic team give us details of the special structural economic and technological factors that caused the New Economy. He could not. All he did in his book was to denounce what he considered were the deceitful myths, created by his fellow neoclassical economists, which surrounded the success of the New Economy. He simply claimed incorrectly and surprisingly that the 1990s boom was artificially created. He went back to his usual theme of regulation and the markets and imperfect market information, for which he got his Nobel Prize, to say incorrectly that the boom was caused by excessive de-regulation.

On page 4 of his book, he said that the New Economy was a shift from the production of goods to what he vaguely described as the production of ideas—(IT)-entailing the processing of information, not of people or inventories. He was, in effect, incorrect saying that the New Economy was not due to manufacturing strategy but what he called ideas. On pages 50 and 51, he referred vaguely to 'technological innovations' as "making it attractive to invest in America." He did not tell us what he meant by innovation, the same vagueness that pervades the writings of most US conventional economists that write about the topic. As a conventional economist, Stiglitz and others got it wrong by not realizing that the New Economy was in fact rooted in change in manufacturing and factor proportions structural change and not on "ideas."

The unfortunate thing, as I already regretted, is that the "New Economy" ended without US economic policy makers and conventional economists understanding it. Krugman, not to be outdone, will only admit that during the New Economy, "it turned out that something had, in fact, changed in the (US) economy." Instead of admitting he did not know, he said in his updated book on depression economics, some nearly ten years after the New Economy, that economists are still arguing what changed during the New Economy.[39]

It is not true that economists are currently arguing what changed during the New Economy. They have since conveniently forgotten the New Economy. Krugman admitted that "Unemployment fell to levels not seen in decades, yet inflation remained quiescent," as the US witnessed a sense of prosperity it had not experienced since World War II. Despite his not knowing ab what changed and the relationship between inflation and unemployment during the New Economy of unprecedented economic growth, Krugman in his 2008 book still insisted that the way to manage the economy in the context of the New Economy is to increase unemployment in order to reduce inflation through NAIRU. The question for these economists is if you found out that NAIRU and the related claims about NAIRU's connection with inflation and unemployment did not work when the economy was passing through it's the fastest and sustainable growth since World War II, why did you not officially discard NAIRU and go for a balanced economy as there was during the New Economy. As late as November 2013 at the nomination hearing of Janet Yellen as Fed Chairman, it was clear that all those discussing the ability of the country to balance its budget during Clinton's New Economy at the hearing did not understand the economic structural reasons responsible for the budget balance, including Yellen.

Economic Arrogance

Capitalism is an ideology that ostensibly gave the United States economic dominance. Capitalism is the foundation of conven tional US economics. Capitalism is rooted in the belief that capital is the prime mover of economic power. 'Capitalist triumphalism' has dominated American economic thinking. Greenspan once called the American economy "the most competitive large economy in the world." Professor Thomas Piketty has shown us that capitalism is the source of inequality. This chapter will say that in an increasingly scientific and technologically driven world, capitalism, like all other ideologies, has become an obstacle to economic competitiveness. Capitalism is drowning America.

> "As I see it now, today's capitalism is an empty ideology and intellectually impoverished. Most economists and political thinkers (in the US) are hanging on to obsolete categories, harking to beliefs as old as the Republic."
> Joseph Coates 2006

Arrogance is not pride. There is nothing wrong with pride in one's achievement, and there is a lot the US should be proud about. Arrogance is different. When one believes he knows better than anyone else and does not care to listen to others or learn from them he is arrogant. It is worse when arrogance is combined with ignorance as is typically the case in the US.

Arrogance by US economic leadership has long been coming. In the late nineteenth century, the US successfully took over the economic leadership of the world from its colonial master England and was instrumental in the defeat of Nazism. After World War II, the US became the undisputed economic leader of the Free World. I have read many accounts by historical economists seeking to explain why America overtook England at that material time. Much of the literature on this lacks depth. While some economic historians will say that the abundance of natural resources in the new country was the key to America's success, the bulk of the literature concentrates somewhat arrogantly on how industrious the early Americans were, how they left behind the feudalism of Europe and embraced individualism and entrepreneurship. John Chamberlain rephrased this sentiment when he claimed that America's success story owes much to "its selective inheritance from the old world" and that:

> "In offering protection for the individual in all his rights, the Founders recognized that economic and political liberties stand together or fall together…the stress was on the individual…and the individual tended to make his own decisions if only because he could walk off into the forest if unsatisfied."[40] This self-praise still persists.

After World II, the United States faced the Soviet Union in a long battle for economic and military supremacy, the Cold War. The Soviet Union promoted ambitious industrial plans of basic and heavy industries of chemicals, iron, cement, and numerous electric-powered large industrial enterprises using its abundance of raw material endowment. By 1960, the Soviet Union had 12.5 percent of world's industrial and agricultural production as against 25.9 percent of the United States. Such was Russia's rising growth that the Soviet Premier, Nikita Khrushchev, in 1960 boasted that the Soviet Union will "bury" the US economically within twenty years.

Soon, however, the Soviet economy started to disintegrate as its economy started to collapse while its agriculture was also failing. The economy finally collapsed in 1991 under its own weight. It was a centrally planned socialist economy. America felt it had triumphed over the Soviet Union because of the triumph of capitalism and freedom over totalitarianism.

The United States next faced the economic challenge from Japan. By 1980s, Japan could look back on three decades of steady growth at 6.5 percent and was leading in electronics, semiconductors, and automobiles. Japan's problems were not long in coming. Here is a country whose mainstay initially was light industries and whose factor proportions fitted a country with little raw material source and, therefore, poor capital base. It achieved rapid growth in exports rising annually in the 1960s by 18.4 percent and with an increasing balance of payment surplus. By 1968, its economy rose above all European countries and was second to that of the United States. The Japanese were sure they would soon overtake the United States. Japan, unfortunately, changed from a low materials factor propotions country to pursue a highly material abundant capital-intensive, structurally damaging economy. Under government control through the centralized and powerful Ministry of International Trade and Industry (MITI), Japanese banks funded large new conglomerates in iron and steel, shipbuilding, motor vehicles, machine tools even as small/medium industries were relegated, all of which heralded an unbalanced economic structure. By 1988 and 1989, Japan's fate turned sour. By 1990, the Japanese economy collapsed. Japan is as of today still not on its feet because it has a structural economic imbalance and used factor proportions that did not fit its factor proportions? It can never prosper as long as it maintains its present operating factor proportions. It can, therefore, be said that through its history, America has so far seen off many challenges to its economic position.

President Bush in his State of The Union message in 1992 said that the Cold War didn't just end; it was won (by the United States). Reagan called America the magic of free market. Asked by Spiegel March 2006 if US public opinion might not be turning against globalization and open markets, Henry Paulson arrogantly replied, "As a matter of fact, during the last century people were always coming up with alternatives to capitalism, and they were broadly either communism or socialism." Asked further on another occasion if there were no alternatives to capitalism, he said there were none.[41]

Krugman said in his 2008 book on Depression *Economics* that the great enemies of capitalism have always been war and depression. It did not occur to him that depression is a structural characteristic of capitalism which is within the control of Americans. Arrogance rooted in ignorance is and continues to be the Achilles' heel of US economic problems. Drawing from Paulson's remark that there is no alternative to capitalism, Greenspan will probably say that globalization is capitalism. In his book, *The Age of Turbulence,* Greenspan talked about capitalism and globalization as being the same thing.

It is useful here to quote that Bill Christison, a former political analyst, in an article titled "The Disastrous Foreign Policies of the United States" in *Counter Punch Magazine*, May 28, 2002. He said that "The all-out campaign of the US to impose on the world its own version of big-corporation, free trade globalization is every bit as damaging to international peace and justice...."

Nowhere else is US arrogance more evident as attempts by some US economists and economic policy makers to lecture the Chinese on how to run their economy. Americans had all along deceived themselves into believing that China's economic growth is because China is turning itself into a free market capitalist economy. American economic leaders regard it as their uninvited responsibility to guide the Chinese in that process. In 2007, before the recession came on, Greenspan said that China is in dire need of financial expertise, presumably from the United States. Listen to Paulson again:

> "Without question, the nation (China) must modernize its financial sector, open up its capital account, and move to a more consumption-based model of growth. A competitive, well-regulated financial system and free flow of capital will help reduce the extraordinary high levels of precautionary savings and allocate capital to its most efficient use, which will help productivity and living

standards. China must also pursue fiscal and regulatory policies that address the investment/savings imbalance."

He continued:

"China faces several critical, immediate challenges. The first is the pressing need to put in place widely-accepted, market-based tools to keep its economy from veering out of control. A much more flexible, market-driven exchange rate along with a more nimble, self-determined monetary policy are key ingredients to stable and sustainable, non-inflationary growth."

Even as recent as March 15, 2013 while his own country's economy was still in a semi-coma, Paulson was still advising China in a similar tone in an article in FT. Before he left the World Bank, Robert Zoellick wanted to impress us with his World Bank publication on China titled "China 2030" in which, like Paulson, he wanted China to open its financial market to international private financial market, to liberalize banking; otherwise China's 9 percent growth will peter out to about 5 percent by 2030.

I have a direct experience of the arrogance of the US economists. My book, *The Science of Economic Development and Growth: The Theory of Factor Proportions* (412 pages) was published in 2005. The cold shoulder I received from US academics and the established economic research institutions in the US, which either did not understand what the book was saying or did not want to know, was a shock. I e-mailed over fifty professors to tell them about the book and what it was trying to say. There were no takers. A professor, to whom I sent an advance chapter synopsis, condescendingly e-mailed me to say that my work could not be accepted as a book, that maybe a journal will take an article from me. A professor at a university economic research institute, whose primary research is on economic growth, read the book and replied: "It (the book) certainly focused on fundamental and important questions. I think it is important that these questions be considered…until testable hypotheses can be formulated, I'm going to remain skeptical."

He said that his work is "focused on more narrow microeconomic issues, and so he won't be able to make suggestions." My book dealt extensively with micro and macroeconomic issues and the connection between the two. The professor was looking for an excuse. That the professor said that until more testable hypotheses can be formulated he will remain skeptical was troubling. Here was a book bristling with testable hypothesis, which he could take up research in. I could not make up my mind if the professor did not understand the science in the book or did not want to understand it. Other professors said they were too busy to read or review the book or never acknowledged me.

The book was sent to major conventional economic journals for possible review. There were no takers. Only one professor in the United States Challaly Talele made an effort to read and understand the book. Here is his review:

> Mr. Onyemelukwe, a project management professional and lecturer (I am not a lecturer), has written a work of distinction. Challenging the traditional two-factor scheme of labor and capital in economic growth theories, he proposes a three factor scheme of labor, capital and material/natural resources. Material resource is not just a convenient, malleable complement in production as traditional economic theory treats it but exists as a factor of production in its own right. Economic development/ growth, which is identical for the author, is the interplay of proportionality among the three factors of production. Onyemelukwe contends that countries harnessing their economic resources in accordance with their factor proportions have developed; those that have not have failed to develop. To the author, economic development in accordance with factor proportions is a law of nature. Onyemelukwe also applies his theory with distinction to a spectrum of related topics spanning trade and growth, international factor mobility, globalization, and the new economy. His analysis of economic history in terms of factor proportions is illuminating. In presenting his case for the three factor scheme, he deftly weaves his argument

with logic, historical illustrations, and facts and figures. The profession should take notice of this important contribution. Summing Up: Highly recommended. Upper-division undergraduate through professional collections.

On the whole, I missed the opportunity to have more conventional economists to discuss 'The science of economic development and growth.' I had the feeling that economists, economic journals, and intellectual chat radio, and TV stations like Book TV did not want to know what I was saying, as I am neither a professor nor a research fellow in one of US prestigious institutions or from Wall Street but an unknown black. In any case some of these people in their arrogance did not see what science has to do with economic development and economic growth.

With this present book, I also sent excerpts of it to 30 professors of conventional economics claiming to be specialized in macroeconomics and offered to send the full manuscript when it is ready. I had not even one response. Yet many of them claim in their CV that their research specialty is in macroeconomics. The newspapers like the *New York Times* active in conventional economics have no time for economic science. The Institute of New Economic Thinking did not make comments on receiving my manuscript despite its stated mission.

The arrogance of US conventional economics is intended to keep economists safe and protected in a rarified atmosphere that is their own. The arrogance has the effect of making ordinary Americans think that US economists see what they cannot see. It has discouraged ordinary Americans from discussing economics and from actively questioning the many economic contradictions and unanswered questions that dominate US economic life. Americans lack the courage to say to their economic and political leaders 'we feel you are taking us down the wrong route. You are taking us for a ride'

How can one explain the fact of Bernanke? Here is a professor, who is reputed to be the top expert on the Great Depression and researched extensively on what he says were the errors committed by the leaders who caused the Depression in the 1930s. While as a member of the Federal Reserve in 2002, he heralded the triumph of understanding the apparent mysteries of the Great Depression in a speech marking the ninetieth birthday of Friedman who himself had boasted that he could have stopped the Great Depression. In 2004, Bernanke celebrated the Great Moderation in economic performance (which included the claimed control of economic cycles) due to what he regarded as improved economic policy making in February. By 2007, he was forecasting a growth for 2008. When the 2007 through 2009 recession came, Bernanke, now Fed Chairman did not know what to do because he suddenly found that the normal tools he thought he had faiiled.

Bernanke and his colleague in 2009 later turned up to boast that they pulled the US economy and the financial market from the brink and prevented what could have been a depression and that we should be grateful to them. They held the position because we were lucky to have ended up only with a Great Recession. Bernanke was immediately rewarded with a confirmation for a second term as the Chairman of the Fed.

If a bridge had collapsed killing a few people, engineers would be called out to an official inquiry to be castigated and disciplined and even imprisoned for professional neglect. The BP Gulf of Mexico spillage, a technical failure that killed eleven people and damaged much of the Gulf, was followed by the stiffest penalty and an inquiry. A 9/11 Commission was set up, among other things, to investigate into the US intelligence's prepared ness for what happened and to investigate on their response. Blames and punishment were meted out by the 9/11 Commission Report, published with fanfare. The negligence, incompetence, and ignorance of our economic intelligentsia had put the country in enormous hardship and suffering, causing deaths and human suffering, but no one could hold them to account.

Barry Ritholtz summarized the position aptly when he said:

"While the republic burns due to unsavory combination of incompetence, radical ideology, and casino capitalism, the clowns seem ever determined to avoid any and all personal responsibility for the damage they have wrought. Instead, they flail about blindly, blaming everything and everyone, except their own horrific negligence."[42]

Complacency

There is a basic refusal by US economic policy makers to admit that the US is facing chronic structural problems and that they have no answers for solving them. The official attitude is that the US economy is so big and so successful that nothing can dethrone America from its preeminent economic position. Even as the US economy was imploding in 2008, the official feeling was that America will soon renew itself on the path to economic strength. To day in 2019, at a growth rate of a mere 3%, the Federal Reserve was in a speech by its Vice Chairman Richard January 10, 2019 congratulating the Fed at 3% growth for the US as "the fastest annual growth recorded in 13 years" and "the longest in recorded US history" when China has maintained a growth of 6.5 to 7% over the past many years attempting soon to make the US a second world economic power Kevin Phillips opened his book, *Bad Money, by* telling us that "The most worrying thing about the vulnerability of the US economy circa 2008 is the extent of official understatement and misstatement; the preference for minimizing how many problems there are and how interconnected they are." One is reminded of Bertram Russell, "There is no nonsense so arrant that it cannot be made the creed of the vast majority by adequate government action."

In an act of complacency, arrogance, and ignorance, however, US economic leaders over time want Americans to believe that there is no problem beyond their ability to solve it. Paulson once told Americans:

> "We run a trade deficit because of our vibrant and growing economy creates a strong demand for imports, including imports of manufactured inputs and capital goods as well as consumer goods, while our trading partners do not have the same growth and/or have economies with relatively low consumption. Moreover, the US has strong invest ment opportunities, but Americans do not save enough to finance all worthwhile projects in our country. Foreign capital helps increase our capital stock and improve labor productivity, resulting in higher wages for our workers. Other countries save far more than they invest and excess liquidity comes to the United States because our strong

economy offers attractive opportunities. The trade deficit and associated capital flows are fundamentally a reflection of our own and other countries' economic choices."[43]

This is arrogant nonsense. On another occasion, Paulson, at his best complacent self, said that trade imbalances normally take care of themselves by currency adjustments or as increased growth occurs.[44] On yet another occasion, Paulson has sought to downplay Chinese and Japanese hold over the US national $1 trillion debt by saying that the debt amounts to only two days of US treasury trading.

Paulson in his time and others after him put up an arrogant bold face that United States is too big to face a dollar crisis even though United States had before faced a dollar crisis on a smaller manageable level in 1970. Greenspan scornfully told us that we who bother about trade deficit are rooted "in the obsession of mercantilists of the early eighteenth century to achieve a surplus in their balance of payments…."[45]

To a question on the same theme, during a WNYC radio interview on May 21, 2010, Krugman sought to say that US debt was not serious. He reckoned that US deficit was only about 3 percent to 4 percent GDP high. Complacently, he told his listeners that if the country reined in its health care costs, then it would have no long-term debt problem. The debt has since gone out of control even though in the interview he said that the 3 percent to 4 percent GDP could be taken care of by (a) reduction in costs especially the military that could shave off 1 percent (b) Hoped-for-growth recovery will ensure revenue exceeded costs. By 2019, the debt has risen to about 8.8 % of GDP. Robert Simpson in his *Newsweek* article earlier on September 3, 2007 titled "The Catch-22 of Economics" gave his twist to American complacency. He stated:

> "The reality…is that the economy follows its own Catch-22: by taking prosperity for granted, people perversely subvert prosperity. The more we—business managers, investors, consumers—think that economic growth is guaranteed and that the risk and uncertainty are receding, the more we act in ways that raise risk, magnify uncertainty, and threaten economic growth. Prosperity destabilizes itself."

He claimed that his insight explained "why terms like 'the business cycles' and 'boom and bust' survive." To some Americans including many in policy positions they regard tales of American economy crisis as really not true or vastly exaggerated. Many in our Congress, who voted the frightening figures, did not really believe that the country cannot afford them until the Tea Party landed on the public stage due to popular agitation against the management of the country's funds. Perhaps hopefully popular action can highlight the ignorance and arrogance of our eco nomic experts. The Tea Party did one thing good for the United States. They helped to let people know that resources are not inexhaustible. The Great Recession, unexpected as it was, helped to reduce American complacency still there in large measures as the US faces the new challenge from China.

Resiliency Gimmick

The American claim of resiliency is a branch of its complacency and arrogance. Claims about resiliency atarted early. In a 2001 Annual Report titled "A Resilient Economy" the Federal Reserve Bank of Dallas boasted:

> Every day, 135 million Americans report to work, striving to improve their living standards. Every day, 285 million US consumers determine the pattern of employment and production through their spending on goods and services. Americans make up just 5 percent of the world's population, but our $10 trillion economy accounts for a quarter of global output. We own, consume, and make more of nearly everything...We're the world leaders in every cutting-edge technology. We're the world's greatest trading nation—the biggest importer and the top exporter...It is foolhardy to pick a fight with a rich nation. The greater the economic power, the more a nation can sacrifice to fight its enemies while still attending to the need and wants of its population...The US economy had a per capita income of $33,996 in 2000. In 1940s, the nation fought and

won World War II, against a powerful enemy, with just
a third of today's economic power—$11,724 per person,
as measured in constant dollars. Fighting the war against
terrorism will cost billions of dollars. But with its huge
economy, the United States can afford the tab.

Greenspan subscribed to the claim about the resilience of the
American economy backed by his academic theorizing. In a testimony
before the Senate Committee on Banking, Housing and Urban Affairs
on September 20, 2001 just after 9/11, he argued that the 9/11 terrorism
will have a significant effect on the US economy over a short term and
long term. He claimed that the American economy will recover. He
claimed that over the past couple of decades, the economy has become
increasingly resilient to 'shocks'. Former Republican House member
stated that: "No other economy in the history of the world could take
the setbacks that we have endured and respond with such amazing
resilience...We have successfully met every challenge presented to us
in this new, young century, just as we did in the last."[46]

After what he witnessed in the New Economy, Greenspan believed
that the ingenuity of Americans will continue the rapid technological
advance and associated with faster productivity growth needed for the
US to attain unchallenged levels of resilience. In February 2002, in a
House presentation, Greenspan further elaborated on this concept of US
economic resilience. He believed that because the economic slowdown
that started in 2001 lasted shorter than "the long history of business
cycles would have led us to expect" the character of the US had changed.
He asked what has changed in the US economy in recent decades that
provides "such resilience and whether such changes will persist in
future." He again claimed, "Doubtless, the substantial improvement
in the access of business decision makers to real-time information has
played a part." Six years later, we had the worst recession.

President G.W. Bush has also used the resiliency claim to buttress
his special economic leadership. In his State of the Economy Report,
January 2007, he said:

I was here in October 2001. I recognized then our economy had been hit hard and there was great uncertainty
about the future. It was a tough time for the country. Many
people were out of work. By mid-December, nearly a million jobs had been lost. The collapse of the Twin Towers
had left dangerous cracks in this building's foundations. I
said I was optimistic that our economy will recover from
these attacks. But if I'd told you that we would also make
the recession one of the shortest on record, that we'd have
confronted corporate scandals, absorb a tripling in the
price of oil, fight global war, and help a whole region of
our country recover from a hurricane, you might have
been a little skeptical...When people across the world look
at America's economy what they see are low inflation, low
unemployment and the fastest growth of any major industrialized nation. The entrepreneurial spirit is alive and well
in the United States. There is one undisputed leader in the
world in terms of economy, and that's the United States of
America. (Applause).

It is not only politicians and economic mandarins that boost
the resiliency rhetoric. Our opinion framers are also in the game.
Kenny Soward of AC Associated Content News, writing on the 2007
through 2009 recession, stated that after the downturn—a euphemism
Americans conveniently adopt to avoid using the word "recession"—
"the willingness of Americans to depend on themselves is becoming
stronger day by day." He claimed that: "By next year, Americans
will look to themselves to turn things round." He then made a mental
leap of arrogance that "With immigration levels remaining high and
unemployment the highest it has been for years, America will have a
labor force ready and willing to do things as cheaply as other sources
of labor such as in India, China and Mexico."

President Obama was also guilty of this arrogance. In a speech to
the US Chamber of Commerce January 7, 2011, he said, "We still have,
by far, the world's largest and most vibrant economy. We have the most
productive workers, the finest universities and the freest market." He
told the meeting of President's Export Council September 10, 2010 that,

"Because the best way we know how to compete and win in the global marketplace is by doing what we know best: harnessing the talents and ingenuity of our people to lead the world in new industries." In his 2011 State of the Union Address, with the same arrogance and boast, he said:

> For all the naysayers predicting our decline, America still has the largest, most prosperous economy in the world. (Applause) No workers, no workers are more productive than ours. No country has more successful companies or granted more patents to investors and entrepreneurs. We're home to the world's best colleges and universities, where more students come to study than any place on earth.

Obama on a visit to a transmission plant in Indianapolis in May 2011 even as the US economy was almost down and out told the workers that "The fact is that we are still making progress. And that proves how resilient the American economy is."

In a major outburst in W News of January 3,2019, Todd Wood had this to say: "There is a historic truth about the American economy—it is deep, wide and resilient. Even in the face of misguided and maligned influence, the American economy bounces back." The unfortunate resiliency mentality has closed the mind of many Americans on the dangers facing the continued long-term viability of the economy. The resiliency claim by all these commentators has its structural foundation in the fact that the US has recessions and has always been, it seems to many, able to "recover" each time. (Exlibris staff insert Chart 2.1 here). The fact that a person has heart attacks from which he usually "recovers" each time does not mean the he is healthy. To people like Todd Wood, the ideological angle will say that the American economic resilience is because it is a free-market economy which it is claimed continually renews itself.

Politicization of Economics

There is nothing which I dread so much as a division of
the republic into two great parties, each arranged...and
concerting measures in opposition to other.

John Adams, 1735–1826

US politicians see their need to score a political point as more
important than the economic fate of the country. The politicization
of economics in the US has sharpened in the last few decades, partly
because a difficult economy gives more room for passing blame and if
you score a political point you are putting yourself well placed for the
next election. There is what Lou Dobbs years earlier called *political,
ideological schism* which paralyses economic debate in the United
States. Much of the political, ideological schism in economics is fuelled
by alarming ignorance of economic fundamentals as to how to end
structural deficiencies of the economy. Therefore, there has to be two
economics in the United States, one for the underlins and the other
for people at the top. There was a time it was a clash of Reagonomics
vs. Rubinomics, each of which was full of contradictions and misread
history. Reagonomics was that economic growth will maximize by
cutting taxes that will enable people to save, invest, and take risks.
In truth, Reagan, behind the scenes, raised taxes under many guises.
Rubinomics was the claim that a balanced budget and reduction of
long-term interest were the best way to achieve maximum economic
growth alluding to the New Economy growth of the 1990s, but the
truth is the rapid growth of the New Economy arose not from Rubin but
from structural changes in the economy. After two decades of battle,
Rubinomics and Reagonomics came to a stop but behind it all is the
persisting economic ideological differences between the two parties
deriving from them.

What worsens the already bad situation is that some influential
US economic academicians have clear ideological leanings and are
identified with political parties. When an economist openly panders to
a political party, he or she further muddies the profession, more so when

we are saying that the economic profession in the US should find its way to turn the profession into a science, if the US economy is to survive.

Economic prescriptions in the US therefore change as the political ideology of outgoing and incoming administration changes. Political appointment of economic policy advisers are drawn from the pool of economists that are party members and sympathizers who are expected, if necessary, to bend their economic actions and utterances to support prescribed political economic ideology.

There is a gridlock of ideas. Governments and opposition have each become very good at massaging economic data and sometimes almost deliberately seeking to misinform Americans. Clive Crook complained in an article in the *Financial Times* of February 9, 2009 that economics in the US outside the academics has become the continuation of politics. According to him if you wish to know what Krugman (or for that matter Professor Robert Barro on the other side of the political spectrum) thinks on any policy question do not read their scholarly writing. In his September 18, 2015 NY Times column, Paul Krugman stated that "Bill Clinton's tax hike was followed by a huge economy, that George W. Bush tax cuts by a weak recovery that ended in financial collapse." These political statements by Krugman are patently false and misleading. The only way out of this economic mess is to develop economic science to act as a benchmark. Crook observed that politics and economics are always difficult to keep apart. He said that his earlier confidence that economists are not wasting their own and everybody's time is diminishing. It is a conspiracy in which politicians seek to turn economics into their tool and there are willing economists to help them do just that.

In his 2007 State of the Economy report, George W. Bush, supported by his Council of Economic Advisers, indulged in political cherry-picking of figures and misrepresentation. The Council ended up laying a false claim to solid economic achievements arising from Bush's tax cuts under what they called the *pro-growth* policy of the President that was supposed to have csame claim ascribed by Reagonomics. A look at the effect of the tax cuts on investment between 2001 and 2007 with G.W. Bush did not show any significant increase in business investment. In fact, business investment declined in 2001 and 2002. It declined by almost 12 percent in 2006. The decline rolled into 2007 followed by a recession. The increases in GDP cited by Bush lasted for only three to four years followed by a disastrous 1 percent growth in the first quarter of 2007. Even then the growth was not in the productive sector but that in services. Bush stated that, "We're now in the forty first month of uninterrupted job growth in a recovery that created 7.2 million jobs. So far unemployment is low, inflation is low, and wages are rising."

But the quoted employment number of jobs clearly did not factor in the growing population of the United States from natural growth and immigration all of which act as a weight on the economy. The job creation was taking place as the US manufacturing was losing jobs because of an embarrassingly bourgeoning service sector. Nor was it correct to talk of wage increases when, adjusted for inflation, the wage earner was no better off. On the other side, even as he knew that China's economy had just overtaken that of the US on a pp basis in order for Obama to look good, the Treasury Secretary Jack Lew without qualification falsely claimed on NPR evening news on October 15, 2014, that America was the largest economic engine in the world.

In the same political posturing as G.W. Bush, President Obama in his 2016 State of the Union Speech claimed that "We're in the middle of the longest streak of job creation in history. More than 14 million jobs, the strongest two years of growth since the 90s, an unemployment rate cut in half...." Obama was talking of recovery from a long recession. Recovery from a long economic sickness is not the same thing as long-term expanding growth of the US economy. At less than 2.4 percent growth in the past few years, a percentage much less than before the recession, President Obama cannot claim that US economy is strong as he sought to claim in the speech. But he was also telling some people what they wanted to hear. In September 2018, Summers characeristically claimed that "Trump exaggerated economic progress and tax credit he did not deserve." March 5, 2019 on the other hand still discussing Trump's tax cuts in a Wall Street Journal article titled "Tax Reform Unleashed the US Economy", Phil Gramm and Michael Solon, claimed that because of Trump's tax cuts not only did the economy grow higher than the 2% projected by the CBO but also caused a wind fall of $4740 of GDP for every family of four and prompted the CBO increase federal revenue projection for the next decade by $1.2 trillion. They ended with a slight to Democrats that, "It is a great paradox of modern America that those who support more government programs generally espouse economic policies that impede growth....." Democrats and Rebulicans alike should always remember that if your income comes from milking the cow, you need to keep the cow healthy."

Short-Termism

There is nothing more ignorant than to think all that matters is today: Leave tomorrow to itself. This is particularly dangerous for an economy like the United States with its. The term 'short-termism' became widly popular when Wall Street watchers began, not long before the 2008 financial meltdown, to notice the unsavory trends in Wall Street that finally precipitated to the worst financial crisis in sixty years. Short-termism also applies to the entire management of the US economy. If you are running a business, it is good from time to time to clear your table and ask yourself what you are doing, where you going, and what do you do today to assist you to get there. That is what the Chinese do with their five-year plans. We don't have any such thing in the United States.

Wall Street is the nerve center of short-termism in the United States. The management of companies quoted on Wall Street emphasize on short-term goals that enhance their share price. Corporate leaders, investors, and analysts focus on quarterly earnings and results. It is called *fast management*. Company presentations by quoted companies emphasize short-term quarterly results and lack attention to long-term strategy, fundamentals and long-term value creation.

Many quoted US companies will pass up profitable long-term opportunities that will have a short-term adverse effect on their immediate earnings. Companies downplay research because it does reduce short-term returns. In the space of twenty five years, quarterly earnings are said to have gone from being a mere requirement to an obsession in Wall Street. If you produce quarterly earnings forecast and exceed it, you are a hero and your shares will get a boost. Instead of developing a new business, why don't you acquire an existing one is the attitude? Remuneration of chief executives and the top of quoted companies have been based on short-term results fuelling greed. All this has led to cooking the books, restatements, and some well publicized scandals. Some Wall Street proposals intended to deal with the problem of short-termism before the 2009 crisis were: (a) to do away with quarterly "earnings guidance" (b) to peg executive compensation to long-term strategic and value creating goals instead of short-term goals (c) companies to communicate to Wall Street more frequently on long-term strategies. None of these proposals saw the light of day because they were out of tune with Wall Street culture.

An often quoted example of short-termism is the US car industry before its last meltdown and revival. While US car makers were losing markets to Toyota and Hyundai over the years, they were permanently hooked to the low hanging fruit in the shape of hot truck and SUV sales while the Japanese rivals focused on longer goals of fuel efficiency and potentially longer term demand for environmentally compliant vehicles. Their hot sales of trucks and SUVs pleased Wall Street. They were reluctant investors in new hybrid car technology and high energy efficiency cars to their eventual detriment. When the chips came down, the so called big three of the United States were reeling and finally collapsed. It is worth noting that these big three once complained not long before to President George W. Bush that they were losing market to their Japanese competitors at the time because of, you know what, Japan was manipulating its currency: sounds familiar.

Keynes' characterization of Wall Street, even in those early days, not merely as casinos but as the childhood games of Snap, Old Maid, or Musical chairs is still true today and more so. I will say, as Charles Munger said in April 2010, that Wall Street is one sophisticated gambling 'casino'. Its operators need a state of short-term induced constant change because the greater the speed and intensity of change, the more they profit.

They back actual changes with rumors, speculations, and expectations. 'Volatility' is supposed to mean that many changing factors have not played out yet. 'Fear factor' is part of the game in creating change. It is difficult to see how Wall Street, no matter the regulation, can get its customers—the companies—to switch away from short-termism when its core fabric is woven in short-termism.

A key cause of short-termism is structural, namely US recessions. There is now increasing sophistication in recession forecasting which acts as a constant reminder to the investor to get what he/she can while the going is good. Short-termism disease has eaten deep into the American psyche: Dows watching. Adam Sternberrgh the *New York Times* Magazine Editor at large sought to prescribe a tonic for this disease. In an article in November 2008 titled "Ignore the Dow" he asked people to desist from Dow watching. He called it "emotional gambling." For quite a sizeable proportion of Americans, the Dow determines their daily mood. They have come incorrectly to believe that the changing Dow Index tells us the state of the US economy, acting much like an instant people's meter of the economy. Gerald Loeb said, "Market values are fixed only in part by balance sheets and income statements; much more by hopes and fears of humanity; by greed, ambition, acts of God invention, financial strain, weather, discovery, fashion and numberless other causes to be listed without omission."[47]

The problem of short-termism is so deep that June 6, 2018 Jaime Dimon and E. Warren issued out a joint statement concluding that: "Every generation of Americans has a responsibility to leave a stronger more prosperous society than the one if found." Nothing has been done or can be done to bring in the necessary reforms when the basic structure of the US economy is not known.

A cartoonist correctly described the Dow Jones Industrial Average as a temporary relief from economic reality. For all its little use as a real indicator of the US economy, the Dow is a key holder of US short-termism watched even by most powerful policy makers in Washington. The Democrats are supposed to be the party that is not so warm about Wall Street. But imagine what happened the evening after the Senate defeated the bail out bill for Detroit car manufactures in 2009. Harry Reed the Democrat Senate Leader at the time went on TV to tell the press that he was appalled that the Republicans blocked the bill. He told reporters, "I dread looking at Wall Street tomorrow (Dow). It is not going to be a pleasant sight."

US Short-Term Economic Governance

Economic governance in the United States is opportunistic and short-termistic. Two factors contribute to short-termism in US economic governance. There is a general aversion to planning. The American regards word planning as a socialist word, reserved for planned and regimented systems. Free market enthusiasts prefer that no one is in charge. Free market enthusiasts, the champions of capitalism, don't want the government in the way. There is a vicious circle here because the other reason why there is no planning is because it is difficult to plan for an economy with irregular cyclical character caused by its structural imbalances. A key effort in the past decades was the discipline of model-based economic forecasting sometimes called econometrics, using a vast array of mathematical tools. Greenspan, in his book *The Map and the Territory,* said that his initial fascination with econometrics was over the years tempered with skepticism about its relevance to a world in which a state of seemingly unmodelable animal spirit is so critical a factor in economic outcomes. The Chinese have their five-year plans that derive from their science-driven economic strategy as I will discuss in a future chapter but the US economy drifts as it hits crisis andcontinuing cycles of reces sions. When a country has no acknowledged tools with which to plan and forecast, it has to resort to beating out fires and short-termism. The economic unpredictability and unmanageability of the US economy can be gleaned from Chairman Bernanke's testimony at the semiannual monetary report to Congress on February 14, 2007. Speaking on monetary policy he said:

> Monetary policy affects spending and inflation with long and variable lags…At the same time, because economic forecasting [in the US] is an uncertain enterprise, policy makers must be prepared to respond flexibly to developments in the economy when those developments lead to a re-assessment of the outlook.

Bernanke's approach in his time was essentially short-term because he could not predict medium or long-term and there was no reliable medium and long-term macroeconomic data available and he knew it was subject recession cycles. When in June 2013, Bernanke announced the possibility of the Fed closing QE3 in 2014; the announcement was couched in terms that showed that the future shape of the economy was a clear guess. After all, the main basis on which Bernanke chose to be optimistic about the economy was the 'reported' improvement in the housing market, which was only a microeconomic data. Microeconomic data, in this case improvement in the housing market, was not a basis for forecasting the macro-economy.

This short-termism is not only, as I have tris evident when the Council of Economic Advisers in their 1988 report stated:

> Because policy operates with a lag and the economy is hard to forecast, some misjudgments are unavoidable. The administration's principle of systematic and credible fiscal and monetary policy is designed to minimize these policy mistakes by not changing policies frequently on the basis of economic conditions of the moment or any short-term forecasts. To do so would invite and perhaps generate costly error.

Here is Professor Stiglitz describing his work as the chairman of the Council of Economic Advisers under Clinton:

> It was part of my day to day responsibilities not just to monitor what was going on, but to think about what might go wrong, and to fix it before it was apparent that it was broken. I could see the American economy from a variety of perspectives seldom available…while we talked to all the leading economists in business, government, and academia, seeking out their different interpretations of what was going on, I also had the opportunity to talk to labor leaders as well as CEOs, to venture capitalists as well as Wall Street financiers. Part of my job was to listen to concerns and explain what we are doing, and these frequent forays put me in touch with grassroots in a way that academics seldom are.[48]

This is disappointing for an economy whose structural foundation, as we have seen in Chapter 1, is very weak and increasingly spinning out of balance, and yet our finan cial/monetary economic policyholders in the Council of Economic Advisors did not acknowledge there was a problem.

The Chairman was, in his own description, in effect acting as plumber to fix leaks. There was nothing in Stiglitz's description of his job that talked of long-term planning, structural research or strategy.

In many ways, our economic policy makers are simply fire fighters just as Stiglitz portrayed it. Paulson summarized this short-termism by saying that "Rather than trying to forecast or project where a problem may come, what we do is just make sure we're ready if one does happen to come."[49] A corporation that adopted this approach will collapse in no time.

US Economic Management: White House Economic Management

October 27, 2007 was the date when Ratgan Dylan of CNBC organized what was called the "CNBC White House Economic Summit" with President Bush's Economic Team made up of Commerce Secretary Carlos Gutierrez, Chairman of Council of Economic Advisors Edward Lazear, Director of National Economic Council Allan Hubbard, and Director of Office of Management and Budget Jim Nussle. The summit covered a wide range of issues. All those present at this economic summit who were the top brass of Bush's 'economic' team were guessing about where the economy was going interpreting through what they called economic indicators, essentially published statistics.

October 2007 was about two to three months from the start of the 2007 to 2009 recession in December 2007. Mr. Dylan asked how confident they were that the housing problem will not tip the economy into recession. Lazear stated that the third quarter looked "actually pretty strong" but could not give a clear answer to Mr. Dylan's question.

[Housing was actually said to have caused the recession.] One of those in the meeting mentioned that the CEOs of FedEx, YRC Trucking, and Rydar had noticed a drop in traffic. These CEOs were the ones hinting to the President's Economic Team of possible slowdown in the economy. In fact, the econ omists in the White House use FedEx and UPS to "take the pulse of the economy" (in absence of scientific ways of judging the state and structure of the economy).[50] The recession of 2007 took the President's Economic Team by surprise.

Asked where the economy is heading in view of the poor sales in housing, Hubbard could not answer only to say that Bernanke and Paulson told them that the housing will not have a quick turnaround—which it never did. He then took the chance to reel off his President's chest beating praise of Bush's economy: job growth over the past forty-nine months and employment currently at 4.7 percent and increase in exports of 12 percent and only 2 percent for imports. He concluded, in answer to the question that "we feel positive about the economy and obviously concerned about housing." Two/three months from statement, the 2007-2009 reces sion started.

So it was clear that the White House Economic team had nothing in preparation for the recession and did not know the economic position of the US, a theme I will expand on in chapter 8. The President's Economic Team at this Economic Summit took pride that consumer sales, wage growth, hours at work, productivity were all increasing on the eve of the 2007 recession. Exports were up 12 percent over the past year they reported and imports only 2 percent to 3 percent higher. Asked clearly if recession was likely, they all said no. Indeed the members sang praises of the economy, which they attributed to good economic policies of their boss President Bush. They praised the economy as a resilient economy. Lazear talked of substitutions that make it possible for effects, for example, of higher oil prices not to have too much effect on the economy. He observed that residential housing was declining but said that commercial property was substituting residential decline by increases in it. Gutierrez enthused and told Mr. Daglan that "The President, from the beginning, believed in the power of free enterprise, the power of freedom, the power of ownership, the power of letting entrepreneurs be entrepreneurs."

Lazear and Gutierrez endorsed the claim that America has open, flexible markets, "our capital moves quickly, our labor moves quickly, our businesses move quickly." They concluded that it is "important to keep the environment that way so that business can move freely. That is one of our tremendous advantages..." The group told Mr. Daglan that America continues to have the most productive countries in the world. "We are seeing that in small businesses and large businesses... We're becoming a lot more efficient," they claimed. So here was the country's highest organ of economic policy and strategy that claimed the economy was strong and was very happy with an economy that was almost in a recession.

I took a look at the 2008 Economic Report of the President prepared by the Council of Economic Advisers to President Bush with Professor Edward Lazear as chairman. The economic advisers are supposed to research, to collect data of the American economic growth and trends and advice on economic policy. Their Economic Reports were to be thing for an in-depth analysis of the US economy. It is noteworthy that at the date of the 2008 report (February 2008) the country was already in a recession that started around the end of 2007. Yet, the report incorrectly claimed that "the expansion of the US economy continued for the sixth consecutive year in 2007." It continued that "Economic growth was solid at 2 percent–5 percent during the four quarters of the year, slightly below the pace during 2006."[51]

The Report contained 116 tables and some 45 graphs and charts, almost all of which were about financial or financially-based data. A few of the tables were head counts statistics of such data as population, employment, mortality and number of vehicles, etc. The entire report was essentially a financial report with no structural in depth economic data from which economic strategy and direction can be distilled. The President's letter forwarding the report to Congress proudly claimed that over the past six years, "the American economy has proven its strength and resilience." It claimed that "The economy is built on a strong foundation, with deep and sophisticated capital market." This was untrue as the economy was already in recession, followed by a capital market financial crisis. In the letter, the President listed six issues of economic policy he wanted Congress to pay attention to from the report. First was the need to keep taxes low because these Republican-appointed economic experts told us in the report that Bush's cutting of tax spurred economic growth. Second, the president wanted Congress to help Americans with increased homeownership—again a financial action. Third, he urged Congress to continue opening new markets for trade and investment, issues I considered in chapters 5, 6 and 7 and concluded that US pattern of trade and investments was not doing the economy much good. Fourth, the President said healthcare should be made more financially affordable for which he said he had proposed changes in tax code. We are back again to tax and finance. Fifth the President urged Congress to increase energy security and confront climate change. Sixth, the President urged Congress to press for a strong and vibrant education system. For a country whose economy is in decline, the President's list of six issues he wanted top attention showed that the President was not aware the country's economic illness and was not aware that economic structure of the country is disintegrating.

President Obama at one time had quite a diverse set of economic advisers. Larry Summers, the Director of the President's NEC Council, Paul Volcker, Chairman of a National Economic Recovery Advisory Board, with many members drawn from the private sector and the universities; and then Mrs. Romer, Chairperson of the Council of Economic Advisers. The financial crisis brought the Fed and the Treasury and White House closer than before. Geithner and Bernanke had taken credit for solving the financial crisis. Rahm Emmanuel the President's Chief of Staff enthused that "Tim Geithner helped steer the financial sector and *the entire economy* through the worst crisis since the Great Depression." Geithner in turn said he couldn't have done it without Bernanke. He told us that:

> He (Bernanke)'s done a remarkable job of helping steer this economy out of the Great Recession. And I think he'll play a very important role in helping in the success of our efforts to try to make sure we are bringing this economy back to durable growth.

In turn, Bernanke told the Washington Post that he couldn't have done anything without Geithner, that he was his rock and complements him, almost coming to tears. It was congratulations all around for taking the country through the worst recession in history, while a country like China has never had a recession for over a quarter of a century. Thomas Friedman correctly pointed out that Obama's team is "heavily staffed by academics, lawyers and political types."[52]

Friedman should have added that the key members of the economic team are Wall Street bred and financial economists. Friedman said there is no senior person in Obama's team who has run a large company or built and sold globally a new innovative product. Friedman said that that is partly the reason why the administration has been mainly interested in pushing taxes, social spending, and regulation—(financial matters)—not pushing trade expansion, competitiveness, and new company formation. He should have added that none had a structural knowledge of the US economy.

Economic advisers have principally been picked from famous financial/monetary professors or public figures that are intended primarily to give legitimacy and prestige to the presidents' programs. Friedman was basically complaining that Obama has no comprehensive economic strategy and does not have the support expertise to undertake a comprehensive economic strategy. Friedman pointed out that even though Obama has many innovation ideas, they, as I will put it, don't flow from a comprehensive economic strategy. Picking, as Obama did, renewable energy, fast speed rail transport and shovel ready projects as Federal government economic priorities is not a structural economic strategy. After they did not succeed with their initial confident assertion that they could help the President see the back of the recession, the members of this claimed elite economic team quietly quit.

That the need for government to focus attention on planning the economy and developing a detailed, long-term comprehensive structural strategy needed to organically grow the economy's competitiveness was never in Obama's mind can be discerned from his statement to reporters on April 29, 2009. He said:

> "I don't want to run auto companies. I don't want to run banks. If you could tell me right now that, when I walked into this office that banks were humming, the autos

were selling and that all you have to worry about is Iraq, Afghanistan, North Korea, getting health care passed, figuring out how to deal with energy independence, deal with Iran, and a pandemic flu, I will take that deal."

Obama is not different from past presidents. Many presidents in US history will regard their principle role in economic management as fiscal management but not to get into specific in-depth issues of economic structure and strategies. The trouble is that no one in the US is doing it.

I needed to make reference to the Economic Report to the President of 2013 to further show considerable detachment between White House economic establishment and the true economy of the United States. As most people bother about the slow growth of the US economy, it was quite a great disappointment that the report, while acknowledging the slowing growth of the US economy, said that it was because of the changing demography in the United States, that the US working population is set to decline and that the country was also facing slower productivity and thirdly that research shows that economies take time to recover after a financial crisis. This is rubbish. It was an excuse for ignorance.

The implied claim of the report that a declining rate of population growth means lower economic growth is a structurally incorrect claim. The idea that it is increased immigration, as was being suggested in the report, that was needed to solve the country's slowing economic growth is also incorrect. The factor proportions stipulation of the theory of factor proportions in structural economics is supposed to take care of changes in factor availability/ demography. In effect, the 2013 Council of Economic Advisers was acknowledging America's economic decline but was telling us that the US has no immediate solution to it because, according to the report "the long-term trend of rising participation (of labor in economic activity) appears to be coming to an end and that the decline may be greater after 2008 which is the year the first baby boomers reach early-retirement age of sixty two."[53] These statements portray ignorance of structural economics.

The report, even with the bleak picture it painted about US economic decline, still stated the administration was working to build a stronger, fairer, and more resilient economy. It had nothing to back up its claim. The report claimed that many of the problems that caused the financial crisis and the recession were built over the decades and that the nation will not have a durable economy until the underlying fundamental issues are addressed. The report stated that the intention was to focus on a number of underlying structural problems many of which developed over the course of decades and consisted by reference to structural problems only of financial matters.

When I read this, I was hoping that these leading economists would address the litany of the structural economic problems of the US economy. They did not. It turned out regrettably that the *stronger, fairer and more resilient economy* and the *strengthening the foundation of growth* that the report talked about were only wishes only to do with the Democrat's concern about the disappearing middle class and their concern about an aging population. So Obama's statement in the report, to which these economists enthusiastically subscribed, was that the President wanted to start dealing with rebuilding the US economy "from the middle class" not "from the top wealthy." It was political posturing because the so-called middle class problem cannot in truth be solved in isolation but only in the context of a structural reform of the whole US economy as I earlier pointed out.

The report claimed that the American Tax Relief Act rolled back *some* of the immediate financial inequality. This has not stopped the continued increase in inequality in the US that has started engaging the interest of everybody. I have dealt with inequality in Chapter 1. Resilience, which the report talked about, in the context of the administration's climate change initiative and education that we were told will assist in advancing lagging productivity was a clear indication of confused thinking. True resiliency of the US economy can only be achieved by making the economy recession free. In totality, the economic advisers to the president in 2013 did not seem to be aware of the very serious structural economic problems facing their country and that the economy was and is actually in decline.

The report stated that the American Recovery and Reinvestment Act of 2009 was "the boldest counter cyclical stimulus in US history". This is false. The recession from 2008 was the longest since the Depression. The report speculated about what it considered "the success of Recovery Act in raising employment and stimulating growth" was a false assumption. Ten years after ARRA, as this book goes to press, the American economy is only able to achieve a growth rate of 3 %. Here as usual, in the absence of a scientific macroeconomics, these conventional economists in the Council at the time resorted to models. One model was used to 'demonstrate' that Obama's stimulus changed the economy by comparing the economy with what the economy would have been if there was no Recovery Act. Another model was to use State variations in ARRA spending and then extrapolate the total spending for the whole economy and the unsubstantiated claim that this arithmetic sum is the relationship between the stimulus spending and the claimed growth and employment in the economy. We have earlier discussed the uselessness of economic models, especially when one knows what they want the model to "prove." Greenspan himself turned round later to condemn economic models.

I have used examples of two past Economic Reports to the President 2008 and 2013 to show that revolving Councils of Economic Advisers in the US have no understanding of the serious structural economic imbalance facing the US economy. The US National Economic Council, a more political body than the Economic Advisers also in the White House, is charged with advising the President on economic policy and to see that the President's economic policies are implemented.

The NEC is also not equipped to understand the structure of the economy. Like the Council of Economic Advisers it exists to sing the praise of its boss: the President. President Obama and the NEC talked a lot about innovation with no effect. NEC argued that in an increasingly interconnected and globally competitive world, unleashing innovation is an essential component of a comprehensive economic strategy. The Council stated that, as globalization erodes the return to traditional practices, the key to more jobs and more prosperity is to create and deploy new products and processes. Put another way, the statement of the NEC is that the greatest job and value creators of the future will be activities, jobs and even industries that don't exist today. This is all parly correct and obvious but does not deal with the basic problem. While you are preparing for tomorrow, ensure that you have a good hold of today. The US lost its industrial base when it allowed its basic industries of those days to move to Asia because it believed that, with its technology, it will triumph with its innovative industries based on the wrong belief that US technology and innovation are superior. Innovation will not bring future economic growth to the US because much of our innovations is not in line with the country's factor proportions because they are essentially capital-intensive. Technology is not synonemous with capital-intensive practice.

As Davey Maney stated, a President has multiple layers of economic voices and opinions contending for his or her attention, and there is a lot of economic horsepower whispering in the president's ear—but if that horsepower has been ideologically filtered, there is a problem as well as adversely the President's core philosophy.[54] A basic central problem, as Obama's statement earlier cited, is that political presidents will not be able and/or interested to lead in *technicalities* of changing the much needed economic restructuring of the US.

The US Treasury Economic Growth"Management"

The US Treasury is supposed to be the only 'executive' US government agency charged with promoting 'economic growth'. Its mission is to "serve the American people and strengthen national security by managing the US government's finances effectively, promoting economic and financial stability, and ensuring the safety, soundness, and security of US and international financial systems." In this context, the department is responsible for a wide range of activities such as advising the president on economic and financial issues, encouraging sustainable economic growth, and fostering improved governance in financial institutions. To undertake this role in economic growth, the department has an Assistant Secretary manning the Office of Economic Policy. He is responsible for *analyzing and reporting on current and prospective economic development and world economies and assist in the determination of appropriate economic policies.* The Assistant Secretary for Economic Policy is responsible for review and analysis of both domestic and international issues and development in financial market. The Office participates along with the Council of Economic Advisers and Office of Management and Budget in preparing of the administration's budget. In particular, the office states that it "conducts research and assists in the formulation and articulation of public policies and positions of the Treasury Department on a wide range of microeconomic issues." Its publication stated that recent examples of the microeconomic issues the office has handled included—wait for this: terror risk insurance, financial disclosure, and auditing, stock option, parallel imports, health insurance, retirement income security, and long-term care. If this list is what is in the US economic growth program of the Treasury, it is clear that the office is doing nothing about economic policy and strategy.

Financial rescue occupied much of Paulson's tenure as Treasury Secretary, which was marked by inefficiency indicative of lack of real initiatives to change the economic structure of the United States. Here was a man who was in no doubt what his responsibilities were. He told us he was the chief economic policy adviser charged with advising the President on economic and policy matters and to promote a strong economy as he said in his book, *On the Brink*. Yet in his whole time at the US Treasury, there was nothing by his account in his book that he did on the broad economic front to promote a strong economy. His total time was devoted almost exclusively to rescue of the financial market, in his incorrect belief that a 'healthy' financial market means a healthy economy. He did nothing about the real economy that was already in full swing of recession throughout most of his time as Treasury secretary. Paulson was not alone in the belief of official Washington and most economic academia in the United States that all economic problems in the United States have financial answers, monetary or fiscal.

In his strong focus of the money market, Paulson told us in his book that one of his first acts as Treasury secretary was to build a "Markets Room" at the Treasury "to monitor independently and in real time what was happening on Wall Street and around the world." If he was in charge of advising economic policy, why not an Economics Room that will enable him to monitor independently and in real time what was happening on the real economy.

Paulson said the Markets Room was often his first stop in the Treasury in the mornings. In his zealous pursuit of Wall Street rescue, he told us he resuscitated the almost moribund President's Working Group on Financial Markets (PWG), which was set up after the 1987 financial market crash "to make policy recommendations" but had only functioned ceremonially. The PWG included the Fed chairman, chair of SEC, and chair of the Commodity Futures Trading Commission. He co-opted Tim Geithner of the New York Fed and John Dugan of the OCC, all Wall Street types. They never, going by Paulson's account in his book, discussed anything strategic about the real economy.

Since the White House and the Treasury are the two locations in the Federal government where US economic policy and strategy are housed, it is clear from my review that the country lacks a strategic structural economic plan.

One-Worldism

One-worldism, as the US economic policy drifted, was fully brought to the notice of the US public by Greenspan in his famous *Oasis of prosperity* speech of 2000. It was at a time when Americans were basking in the 1990s New Economy economic boom. In contrast, the world economy at the same time was getting into turmoil as the financial market disruptions were hitting some countries. Greenspan in the speech to business scholars at the University of California Berkeley jolted his contented listeners who were basking in the New Economy prosperity that "It is just not credible that the United States can remain an oasis of prosperity unaffected by a world that is experiencing greatly increased stress." He told the audience that the standard of living in every nation the US did business with should be a matter of concern to them. He claimed that: "We could never gain the full benefit of the technology revolution unless the world shared in the growth."[55] This is "one-worldism" as Greenspan confirmed a major policy shift in the US.

One-worldism is a piece of US economic principle marked by the subordination of America's economic problems to the problems of the 'global economy' because US internal economy was becoming an unsolved problem. Henry Paulson spelt out US one-worldist policy when he said, "Our prosperity is linked to the strength of foreign economies. And we are adversely affected by their economic declines and financial shocks. There are no islands of economic stability in today's world."

Paulson elaborated by saying that: "In today's interdependent world, US exports and US employment opportunities are affected by how well our major trading partners are doing."[56] One-worldism is a different world view from what motivated Americans throughout their early history. It is a sea change in US economic policy, philosophy and psychology, in contrast to what US was as is evident in the following statement of the Economic Report to the president of 1962:

> The recovery and growth of the US economy are not important for the United States alone. The vigor of our economy depends in large measure on the strength and stamina of the free world and the standing of freedom in the minds of men everywhere. Leadership in the world requires the support of a growing and dynamic (US) economy using to the full its vast productive capacity.

It is clear that present US global economic position, articulated and initiated by Greenspan and Paulson, is different from what the 1962 report was describing. Nathan Gardels, Editor of the *New Perspective Quarterly and Global Viewpoint* in his January 24, 2007 edition summarized the change in US global position very simply that "America no longer owns globalization". America's loss of its ownership of globalization gave birth to one-worldism.

Today, American one-worldism is a surrender of the American economy to the world economy in which the United States looks at its economic problems in the context of being a member of the global economy. Compared with the stance of the 1962 statement in the 1962 report to the president, one-worldism marked a loss of confidence by us economic leaders. With their one-worldist economic policy, the

American economic leaders also tended to lose concentration on the American economy.

In an earlier speech at the Council on Foreign Relations in New York March 2005, Greenspan demonstrated the gradual loss of US concentration on the US economy. He observed that recently, the United States had been incurring "ever-larger trade deficits," yet as he observed, "the dollar's real exchange value, despite its recent decline, remains above its 1995 low." At the same time, he observed that the United States just moved from budget surplus in 2000 to a deficit that is projected to be around 31.25 percent of GDP that year. He then asked whether anything fundamental happened to the US economy that "enables us to disregard all the time tested criteria for assessing when economic imbalances become worrisome."

He answered that it is because "We do seem to be undergoing what is likely, in the end, to be a one-shift in the degree of globalization." He indicated that globalization had enabled the US "to disregard all time tested criteria for assessing when economic imbalance (in the US) becomes worrisome." Globalization made US policy makers to drop checks on the US economy, namely that globalization has overshadowed the US economy.

Ben Bernanke in lectures in 2005 and 2007 set out to answer why the United States, which was lending in 1962, was now borrowing heavily in the context of what he called *global-saving glut*. He set out to prove that the deterioration in the current account of the US was not primarily due to its economic policies and other economic developments in the United States. He was convinced that the correct answer lies in a "global perspective that takes into account events outside of the United States." He concluded that over the past decade, *a combination of diverse forces* created a global savings glut. He then argued that there has been "a remarkable reversal in the flow of credit to developing and emerging market economies that transformed those economies from borrowers on international capital markets to large net lenders." He regarded US trade imbalance as *the tail of the dog*. He stated that today when all economies are open and with well-developed international markets, savers lend to those who wish to make capital investments. He did not, therefore, see what is wrong with the fact that the US is now a borrower country. He, therefore, concluded that some of the key reasons for the large US current account deficit are external, claiming that "purely inward-looking policies are unlikely to resolve the issue." He sought to give comfort for US trade imbalance instead of looking for solution for this economic illness.

One-worldism has permeated the full fabric of US economic policy. Substantial numbers of policy makers in the United States believe that the solutions to US economic problems drive largely from the state of the global economy. Having helped to drive globalization, American policy holders now complain about the problems it brought. Trump arrived to change this global pyschlogy and policy—somewhat late. America first is Trump policy, coming at a time globalization had taken over US policy. Professor Krugman, a strong Democrat confirmed America's one-worldism in a short NY Times article January 25th 2019 titled "Trump, Trade and the Advantage of Autocrats" when he vigourosly, with party and personal antagonism against Trump, attacked Trump on his trade war with China when he incorrectly claimed that there was no constituency demand for protectionism in the US and suggested that the Chinese were offering Trump "a personal political payoff."

Chapter 3

An Economy of Contradictions

Webster's dictionary defines contradiction as "a situation in which inherent factors, actions or propositions are inconsistent or contradictory to one another." Like a yacht in light winds, no sooner than the US economy catches a breeze from one direction than a gust comes from another direction as it struggles to move forward because its structural economic structure is unbalanced.

Unemployment in the US

America was supposed all this time to be the largest economy in the world, but it cannot always guarantee full employment and higher income for its working population. The United States by the beginning of 2019 had unemployment of a little less than 4 percent of the population. All these emphasize the cyclical nature of the US economy and its structural problems. The bulk of people we claim as employed in the US are in the non-productive sector (services): restaurants, health services, etc not in manufacturing.

Unemployment has continued to fluctuate widely and unpredictably over its history because of the economy's cyclical characteristics. America's population in 1990 was 248 million. By 2010, it had increased to 310 million. By 2018, it was estimated at 327million. The Census Bureau estimates that by 2050 it will have topped 439 million. To put matters in perspective, it is useful to state that US population in 1900 was only 76.1 million. The growth of population is 60 percent due to natural growth and the rest by immigration makes the US one of the fastest growing populations among industrialized countries. America has never achieved full employment. Between 2000 and 2005, the population of the United States increased by nearly 15 mil lion while there was a job growth of about 2 million only. By 2018, unemployment was about 3% lowest since the mid-1990s. Instead of the United States becoming more labor-intensive to absorb the large increases in its population in line with its factor proportions, the economy, as we have seen in chapters 1 and 2 is instead getting more and more capital intensive and more structurally unbalanced wasting the country's natural resource endowment, all of which makes the US economy increasingly less competitive.

A 2010 Brooking Institute study by Michael Elsby and his collaborators confirmed that the deterioration of the US job market during the 2008 recession was the worst for more than sixty years, a clear confirmation that US economic imbalance is steadily worsening as part of the cyclical character of the economy. The study noted that in some ways, earlier patterns of unemployment have not only been replicated but were scaled up. The study noted US employment structural problems. The country was suffering a kind of hysteresis in which lengthening spells of unemployment were becoming self-perpetuating as skills eroded or grew irrelevant. The study further noted that there is a growing structural mismatch between the workers' skills available and what workers' companies will need.[57]

US policy makers tell us that it is to the small business sector they look to create employment in the United States. In its belief that it is the small businesses that create the employment United States needs, Congress for example in September 2010, passed Obama's sponsored bill to vote $30 billion to be passed to banks for onward lending to small businesses. SBA is up and doing. Much of this is politicking. Small businesses are what they are: small. There is no way US small businesses can produce the volume of the employment that matches the needs of an economy of which they, the small businesses, only constitute a small part.

The actual unemployment in the US is far worse than official published figures claim.[58] Unfortunately, the two political parties in the United States like to play politics with unemployment. There is an implied accusation that whichever party is in power was influencing the figures. In the process, people unfairly impugn the professionalism of public servants charged with preparing these figures. The underestimation of unemployment in the United States is not an issue with the officials but an issue about the structural weaknesses of the system they were given to work with. The US Bureau of Labor Statistics itself implies an acknowledgement that an official quoted: US unemployment rates are grossly understated because the bureau itself provides a series which it calls 'alternative unemployment measures'. The Bureau's alternative unemployment measures show that if hidden unemployment factors: involuntary part-timers and people discouraged from seeking new jobs are taken into account, the unemployment rate for January 2007 will, for example, be 8.2 percent instead of the official rate of 4.5 percent. By December 2008, this alternative would have been revised to 15 percent. By the end of 2009, we will be at the 20 percent mark. Longtime unemployed in Sept 2009 rose to 5.4 million, fourfold since start of recession. The 9.2 million working part-time nearly doubled since the start of the recession according to Keith Hall, Commissioner of the Bureau of Labor Statistics in testimony to the Joint Economic Committee of Congress Friday Oct 2, 2009.

Unemployment in the US is both short-term and long-term. It may arise because someone's skills are no longer required. It may be *frictional*: namely unemployment caused by change between jobs. Official statistics can blur the difference between long-term and short-term unemployment. A dynamic balanced economy ought to be responsive to these changing employment needs of an economy. This is not the case in the United States.

Recent independent studies have focused on determining the actual unemployment rate of the United States by looking at many areas of unemployment, which official figures statutorily ignore. Total official unemployment is the number of jobless people who have actively looked for work during the past four weeks. This measure understates unemployment in a number of respects. It excludes involuntary part-timers, namely people who want a full-time job but have to settle for part-time or spilt-week schedules. Estimates of the studies are that this category can add up to 1.5 percent to the unemployment rate of the United States. The official rate also excludes those who have searched for work, got discouraged, and stopped looking as well as those who are seeking work but have not looked for work in the four weeks before the official count of unemployment. These two categories are estimated to add another 1.4 percent to the US unemployed- mint rate. Unemployment ought to include people temporarily out of work, like those on sick leave or who took an early retirement, or who are disabled can work. Estimates of this group can add a whopping 4.2 percent to the unemployment rate.

There are a substantial number of unemployed people, who are covered by government assistance programs. Some economists claim these government sponsored interventionist programs increase unemployment rather than reduce it because the people registered do not really want to work. They also argue that these programs compel people who would otherwise not register as part of the labor force to register as if they are part of it. These economists also regard the involvement of unions as interventionist because they argue that unions help increase unemployment by seeking for uncompetitive wages. Estimates by these economists range from 1 percent to 1.3 percent attributed to what are called interventionist contribution to unemployment rate.

The core conservative economists in the United States believe that many unemployed persons are inherently lazy and that many of them frankly prefer not to work. In their view, persons who have no job in the United States each deserve their fate. If I, for the sake of argument, partially grant the conservatives their argument that up to one-third of the people registered as unemployed under these interventionist schemes are lazy, the contribution of interventionist programs to US unemployment will be lowered to a figure still as high as 0.3 percent and 0.87 percent, say 0.58 percent.

Another source of hidden unemployment, not reflected in official statistics, is the large number of people who declare themselves as 'self-employed' after failing to find a job but would have preferred a full employment. Many new businesses collapse within three years because the economy is basically unstable. I have not attempted to give an estimate of this hidden source of unemployment, but it is substantial.

A true assessment of unemployment, according to many independent experts, ought also to include prison and jail populations because they are no different from people covered by government interventionist programs. The Pew Center on the States estimated the number of people in prison, probation, and parole in the United States as about 7.3 million, or about 3.1 percent of the adult population. The US has the highest prison population in the world including the most repressive states.

When we add the contributions of these hidden sources of unemployment less the contribution of 0.87 percent to existing official rate due to 'interventionist' factors, it is clear that United States actual unemployment is at least 8 percent to 10 percent higher than official published figures state. In 2009, the true unemployment rate in the United States is nearer 20 percent instead of the official 10.2 percent. By 2010, official unemployment remained above 9.6 percent and down to a little over 9 percent in 2011, despite the fact that the recession was supposed to have ended in early 2009. For all this, the true unemployment should be nearer to double at 19 percent to 20 percent. Even at an official claim of 5 percent, the real unemployment is about 13 percent to 15 percent.

Unemployment in the United States is a very serious economic and social problem. It is the number one visible cyclical economic challenge of the US. We waste labor. Not so visible but equally devastating is the waste of material resources. American economy is creating a group of people who will find it difficult to ever get back into the work force. The economic part of the problem is that while US technical economic structural imbalance causes unemployment, unemployment itself constitutes idle factor resources, which in turn make the technical structural imbalance even worse.

The problem is that, because of the political importance of employment, most Americans wrongly think that a President can do a lot in the present setup to change the employment position in the United States. Presidents, in return, try to behave as if they can. The Fed also tries to make people believe it can create employment. When the official unemployment reached 10.2 percent in 2009 (despite the fact that the original Obama administration's economic guru team boasted that they could quickly drop unemployment to 6 percent out of the recession), there was widespread anger. In a *New York Times* article of November 23, 2009 titled "The Phantom Menace", Krugman took up the issue. But like many others, Krugman wrongly thought (as I earlier pointed out in chapter 1) that during a recession or slow growth, increasing employment required increasing the already large financial stimulus that had already been put in place which, according to him may require increasing the deficit. In the article, Krugman castigated Republicans who did not want the deficit to increase. Krugman later in another *New York Times* article October 7, 2012 titled "Truth About Jobs," claimed that if Congress had approved Obama's American Jobs Act, a substantial improvement in employment would have occurred since summer 2011. He was also sure that job prospects in the US were bright because the number of aging baby boomers, the fraction of Americans in their prime working lives was falling fast. He also saw the declining consumer debt, and a housing revival as all factors which pointed to a recovery and higher employment. He was sure, therefore, that the country was on its road back to full employment and recovery. He was dead wrong. Years after Krugman's forecast, recovery from the Great recession is still out of reach. Employment increased only because of the aging of baby boomers, not because of structural economic reasons.

In another *New York Times'* article from May 30, 2011, Krugman admitted that "a consensus has emerged among movers and shakers that nothing can or should be done about jobs." This is because those people realize the recession and its follow-up is a structural problem which they don't understand and have no answers. Nobody can "create" employment. It is a good economy that creates employment.

Krugman criticized the Organization for Economic Cooperation and Development (OECD) for conceding that it lacked an overall lack of knowledge on how to solve the unemployment dilemma. The OECD stated truthfully and correctly that "The room for macroeconomic policies to address these com plex issues is largely exhausted." The OECD correctly suggested that countries to "go structural" in order to seek for solutions, a wise realization by OECD that the problem of unemployment and other economic ills were nothing that can be solved by financial tinkering with the economy because they are structural problems. Krugman took exception to this because he thought that structural reform would take time to realize and therefore "would have little impact on the current employment situation." That was incorrect.

Krugman, instead, said he had his immediate solution to the problem of unemployment, which he said was unorthodox. He focused this time on what he called private debt by individuals. What was needed, according to him, was to get individuals to do anything that will give them money; and, thereby, establish increased demand in the economy. He suggested (a) a WPA program and (b) mortgage modification, intended to reduce debt—again financial—which he said was acting as a drag on the economy. It is all financial tinkering to what is basically a structural problem. It could not work.

Krugman's ideas on stimulus—the Keynes style—are wrong, as I discussed in chapter 1, namely that his assertion if low demand is the immediate ate consequence of recession that one can eliminate recession by creating demand by spending money. There are no such quick fixes to structural economic problems as Krugman was suggesting. That is why time is running out on the United States to start basic fixing of its structural imbalance. The Fed and the political class in the US like to claim credit when the economy inevitably recovers cyclically from recession. Obama in his last State of the Union speech 2016 claimed that the US was growing and creating jobs at the fastest pace since 1999. This politicking with the economy unfortunately is the style of US Presidents and the US Fed.

America's actual active working population has not benefited from the economy. Wages in the last thirty years, even before the 2007 recession, have not kept pace with the achieved growth of the economy. Discussing this issue in a speech on February 2007, Ben Bernanke stated that since 1947, the real hourly compen sation of US workers in non-farm business increased by more than 200 percent after adjusting for inflation. He concluded that the "real reward for an hour of work has more than tripled over the past sixty years." Over the same period, he said that real disposable income per capita has increased almost 270 percent; real consumption per capita has increased almost 280 percent.

Bernanke ought to have put his figures in context. Two hundred percent, 270 percent, and 280 percent, don't mean anything unless they are set against a benchmark. We know from examining published historical trends in inflation that the US gross domestic product, adjusted for inflation, increased by a figure of more than 500 percent since 1947 (the year Bernanke chose as his reference year). If the GDP has increased by 500 percent since 1947, it is clear that, contrary to Bernanke's claim, workers in the United States have not benefited favorably from US economy. Workers' share of the GDP has fallen over the years.

To make the contradiction in Bernanke's analysis worse it needs to be pointed out that the wage per hour which Bernanke used is an average. Higher wages are earned by the shrinking group of workers employed in the manufacturing sector. We now know that white collar service sector workers who 'replace' jobs lost in manufacturing earn on the average 20 percent less. So as manufacturing continues to shed jobs, the average wage of US workers as a whole will continue to deteriorate farther.

While these average figures represent a snapshot of the position, they are worsened by the unpredictable variation in job security due to cyclical economic swings of the US economy. The Great Recession greatly worsened workers' fate in the United States. Given these factors, it is not surprising that yearly fluctuations and the gap between the highs and lows in individual earnings and family income have increased sharply since 1970. Among families, seeing declines in income, the size of the typical loss has increased. For example, the chances that an American family will see a 50 percent drop in its yearly income has more than doubled since the early 1970s rising to about one in six families in recent years. Involuntary displacement of labor, down sizing or outsourcing in both manufacturing and services, and the recession has further decreased job security. By 2009, 17 million US households cannot feed themselves, which is about 14.7 percent of US households. One third of people in this group skips meals and sometimes don't eat. The International Human Rights Clinic of NYU Law School estimates that by 2013, the number of families in this position has increased to 50 million.

At the other end of the scale are the very poor wage earners, earning below average and protected through the establishment of the minimum wage. The first minimum wage was set up in 1938 (as a reaction to the 1933 depression) at $0.25/hour to the current $5.15. The minimum wage has never been able to afford a family of four to live above the poverty level. Calculated in real 2006 dollars, the 1968 minimum hourly wage of $9.27 was the highest minimum wage in US history when it ranked about 90 percent of the poverty level. The real dollar minimum wage rises and falls because of periodic adjustments. The period 1997 to 2007 was the longest that minimum wage was not adjusted. The House in January 2007 raised the Federal minimum wage to take effect in three installments and six months after the measure becomes law at a real value of $5.85 and $6.85 in 2008 and $7.29 in 2009. Over 13 million workers (about 10 percent of the US workforce) were expected to benefit from the 2007 increase. In 2013, the President unsuccessfully tried to raise Federal minimum wage which now stands at $7.25. The share of all workers earning poverty-level wage has not substantially changed hovering between 30 percent and 23 percent over the past quarter of a century.[60] States are responsible for setting minimum wage on the basis that minimum wage is to take account local costs and conditions. As of 2018/9, 29 states have minimum wage higher than the Federal government.19 In comparison of wages in relation to age of workers, America ranks at the bottom along with Japan. In general, minimum wage does not pretend to be a living wage.

By 2019, the US economy had fully recovered from the Great Recession not due to the Fed and the US employment scene changed. In the words of Richard Claridan, Vice Chairman of the Fed at a NABE Conference February 28,2019, in a paper titled "US Economic Outlook and Monetary Policy, "The unemployment is near the lowest in 50 years and average monthly gains have continued to well outpace the increases over the longer run to provide for new entrants to the labor force. Most increases of nominal wage growth are running at or somewhat above the 3% pace and recent gains are rising at or somewhat the 3% pace and recent gains have been strongest for low-skilled workers and has encouraged people to join the labor force and others who might have left to continue working." With unemployment at historic low, one would think that US workers were at the point where they will command a greater share of the US national income.

In an article dated February 25, 2019 titled "Workers Claim a Shrinking Slice of the Pie" in the Wall Street Journal, Paul Kierman showed graphical and other evidence that despite all the gains in low employment and higher wages stated, the working class of the US is faced with the prospect of receiving a ever shrinking part of the US national income. Paul assembled explanations by conventional economists for this which are all speculative and wrong. The true explanation is structural. Fig 1.2 shows to the correct structural explanation, namely that in the structural imbalance of the US economy, the capital-intensive sector dominates the US economy by continual "stealing" labor and capital from the labor-intensive sector which itself accounts for the bulk of US labor. The capital-intensive sector benefits from what in the first chapter was called "biased expansion of production possibilities." I also indicated in chaper1 that Piketty also found that poverty (which the Professor correctly ascribed to the labor-intesive sector of a capitalistic economy) will ensure that returns to capitalistic economy keeps a pace ahead of the overall growth rate of the economy because a capitalistic economy uses capital to grow. The prospects, to answer Paul Kierman's puzzle are that with a large capitalistic economy like the US total labour is bound to receive a continuing reduction from a growing national income.

US Poverty

The problem of US 'low' wages takes us to the problem of poverty itself. The 2005 census told us there are an estimated 37 million Americans currently living in poverty. The US Census Bureau data from September 2011 showed that as of 2010 the number had gone up to 46.2 million, the largest figure in the fifty-one years since poverty figures were available, up from 43.2 million in 2010. Poverty in the US is a growing prospect. Between 2005 and 2007, the percentage living at half-level income increased by 26 percent. People living with income less than 50 percent of their poverty threshold increased from

5.6 percent to 6.3 percent from 2008 to 2009. The US Census Bureau data released in September 2011 says that America's urban, suburban, and rural communities are also all witness to the growth of what adds up to "abject poor." The abject poor in the US are individuals living on $5,250 a year. For a family of three, two adults and a child, it is $6,922 and a family of four it is $10,222 a year.

Then we turn to poverty among American children. Children represent 34.9 percent of America's poor. The 2011 Census showed that children living in families below poverty level increased from 15.6 percent in 2001 to 22 percent in 2011, marking a decade of increases in child poverty in the United States. Currently 22 percent of all children in the United States live in families with incomes below poverty level, and it is expected that this figure will soon go up to 25 percent, the largest in a generation. One does not need any further proof that US poverty/income inequality is getting progressively worse.

American economists and policy makers don't understand the factor proportions structural causes of poverty. Idle human resources are economic deadweight. The deadweight worsens the imbalance of an already unbalanced economy. Child poverty her alds a growing third world underclass in the United States.

Politicians and leaders in the United States prefer to play politics with poverty. Their political orientation will push them to argue whether poverty figures are overstating or understating the problem. A conservative blog, for example, as far back as 2004 claimed that:

a. 46 percent of poor people in the United States as of 2004 have their own homes (should have 'owe mortgage');
b. 64 percent of poor people in the United States have air conditioners;
c. only 6 percent have crowded homes;
d. 75 percent of poor households have a car, 30 percent have two cars;
e. 97 percent have color TV and over half has two or more TVs;
f. 78 percent have VCR or DVD player while 62 percent have cable or satellite TV reception;

g. 73 percent have microwave ovens, more than 33 percent have stereo and another 33 percent has dish washer.

It concluded at the time that most American poor live in material conditions that would have been regarded as well-off a few generations ago. It asserted from the figures it presented that there are relatively few poor persons remaining in the United States. As an afterthought it also claimed the living conditions of the average poor person (which it apparently wanted to describe with the above figures) should not be taken to mean that all poor Americans live without hardship. Alongside this blog which was from two staffers in Heritage Foundation was a plea: "Help support Heritage's efforts to spread conservative ideas."

A former New York Mayor in a similar vein had said that the disadvantaged in the US live in dwellings with flush toilets, color TV and refrigerators and have cell phones.

There has been a lot of political posturing on poverty. There are those who, to cover their ignorance and arrogance regard poverty as a necessary consequence of free market capitalism. The poor are said to be the losers of the system. Some describe poor people as lazy people. The well-known Irving Kristol, sometimes called the father of neo-conservatism, said that if the poor were given handouts, it encouraged dependency, and if they were given preferential programs, they ceased to strive. Mitt Romney made similar comments during his Presidential campaign in 2012.

Many people, on the other hand, have through time said that what is needed is to provide 'safety nets' for the poor, so as to limit how far down they fall off from the economy. They refuse to endorse the view that poverty and income inequality are a contradiction of what true structural economic development is. The liberal class refuses to accept legitimate accusation by the right of 'big government' as often each government subsidy for the poor establishes a new government bureaucracy. Obamacare is a good example.

There has not been any shortage of ideas among liberals and progressives on how to wipe out poverty in the United States. 'The War on Poverty' is the name of the legislation first introduced by Lyndon Johnson in his State of the Union address January 8, 1964, which led

Congress to pass the 'Economic Opportunity Act' of 1964. Johnson said that the Act was not intended merely to expand old programs or improve what is already being done. It strikes at the causes, not just the consequences of poverty."[61]

The Act initiated many programs: head start, food stamps, work study, Medicare, Medicaid, and so on. The Act was mainly focused on giving half a million underprivileged Americans help to develop skills, continue education, to find useful work, and to give each community the opportunity to develop a comprehensive plan to fight poverty and help carry out the plans. Volunteers in their thousands were to be recruited to serve the needs of the poor, including retired as well as young volunteers. New programs of loans and guarantees were created to provide incentives to those who will employ the unemployed. For all this, Johnson created an Office of Economic Opportunity in the Executive Office of the President. Johnson's Job Corps trained disadvantaged and at risk youth and provided more than two million disadvantaged young people with integrated academic, vocational and social skills they needed.

Johnson introduced the War on Poverty program at a time of economic recovery when poverty had fallen from 22.4 percent in 1959 to 19 percent in 1964. So it is not clear how much of Johnson's program contributed in a drop from 23 percent below eighteen years poverty group in 1964 up and down to 16 percent as well as a dramatic decrease in poverty among Americans over 65 from 28.5 percent in 1966 to about 10.1 percent currently.

For all his best efforts, Johnson could not end poverty in the United States. Today poverty/inequality in the United States is alive and doing very well and getting bigger because of the US increasing factor proportions crisis. The President incorrectly identified "the streets of our cities and farms of our countryside" as the 'source' of poverty. He, therefore, thought that the attack on poverty has to be undertaken in the local communities. The source of poverty, he failed to realize, is the economic structure of the United States.

A blitz on poverty came from former Senator John Edward, a 2008 presidential candidate, who campaigned on the platform that he wished by his plans as president to abolish poverty altogether in the United

States by the year 2036. In 1968 Bobby Kennedy was on a similar campaign message. Edward proposed a number of changes which he argued were needed to achieve poverty eradication in the United States. For a start, he would embrace a plan for universal health care by which he, as President, will compel uninsured Americans to buy health insurance from a pool of private plans, although there will be option to buy into a government program modeled after Medicare—reminds one of Obamacare.

Under Edward, employers will either have to offer health packages to their workers or pay into a national fund for the uninsured. He would triple the earned income tax credit to cover low income workers with children to those without children. To promote savings among the poor, he will create *work bonds*, in which the government would match the first $500 in saved wages each year. He will create a million "stepping stone jobs" to draw more poor adults into the workforce presumably along a New Deal style of creating government projects. He wanted making the first year of public college free for students below a certain level of income who agree to work ten hours a week. He will give vouchers to families who currently live in public housing, which they can use to rent affordable apartments in other neighborhoods.

Edward's plan was to cost about $290 billion annually. While President Johnson's poverty plan aimed to fight poverty at the source but could not identify the source, Edward's plan did not seek to identify the source of poverty. What he mistakenly wanted was to attack the consequences of poverty but not the cause. He wanted to throw the money at the problem as it were. Edwards, Kennedy, and Johnson all assumed that the solution to poverty lies with employers and the government committing themselves to bankroll social programs. Most poverty programs today in the US follow the same path.

The UN following Trump's withdrawal from the UN human rights agencies attacked poverty in the US in a report in 2019. The report stated: The United States is a land of contrasts. It is one of the world's wealthiest societies, a global leader in many areas and a land of unsurpassed technological and other forms of innovation. Its corporations are global trendsetters........But its immense wealth and expertise stand in shocking contrast with the conditions in which vast numbers of its citizens live. About 40 million live in poverty, 18.5 miilion in extreme poverty, and 5.3 million live in Third World conditions of absolute poverty......The United States has the highest rate of income equality among Western Countries. The report pointed that the Standford Center on Inequality and Poverty ranked the US 18th out of 21 wealthy countries. The Report mentioned that in 2018 that the US had over 25% of the world's 2,208 billioneers. It pointed out American citizens "live shorter and sicker lives compared to those in all other rich democracies. It claimed that there is dramatic contrast between the immense wealth of the few and the squalor and deprivation in which vast numbers of Americans exist. The Report significantly pointed out at Trump's $1.5 trillion tax cut in December 2017 which according to it benefitted the wealthy and worsened inequality. The Report blamed Trump but stated that that Trump only inheritesd the position but made things worse and that terms like "trickle down" correctly describe the US economy.

The UN Report did not fully get the point, namely that US economy almost from its inception is a structurally unbalanced economy in which the structural balance is steadily worse. Each President comes in to work with this structural weakness. I don't think Trump meant to increase inequality in the US.

Inequality Again

I have shown in Chapter 1 that our conventional economists in their ignorance of the nature and causes of inequality in America have made inequality a political matter. Recently in a NY Times article of June 29, 2014, Professor Stieglitz claimed that inequality in the US is caused by politicians and that the American political system is overrun by money. He claimed that economic inequality translates into political inequality and inequality yields increasing economic inequality. In his book *Freefall*, he claimed foolishly that the problem with inequality is that the top 1 percent wants it that way.

Piketty has correctly concluded from his financial studies that in a capitalist system, the rate of return to capital 'r' will continue to outpace the growth 'g' of the economy as a historical fact. The structural scientific explanation of all this is by reference to Figs. 1.1., 1.2. 1.3 in Chapter 1. As the capital-intensive sector—at the extreme right side of Fig. 1.1 – expands, it increases the size of capital-intensive sector and reduces the size of the right-hand sectors, thus further increasing the structural imbalance of the economy which in turn continues to reduce the economy's growth rate 'g'. The continuous growth of the capital intensive sector enables it to account for an increasing total of the economy. The rate of return to investment 'r' continues to increase as a result. This is the cause of inequality and rising poverty. It shows that the contradiction between democracy and capitalism is set to increase.

Inequality and poverty in the United States are rising and currently at their highest over the past 100 years. Since the 1970s, the portion of national income attributed to the US super rich, the top one-tenth of 1 percent of Americans, has increased to over 20 percent. It is partly that the poor are getting poorer but that at the same time the rich are getting astronomically richer all the time. In 2004, according to Congressional Budget Office's official analysis, households in the lowest quartile were making only 2 percent more (adjusted for inflation) than they did in 1979. The minuscule gain was not because of higher wages but because people were working longer hours. Those in the next quartile managed only a 11 percent rise. The middle group was up by 15 percent. The fourth quartile rose by 23 percent. It is when you get to the top quartile that the real big gain is—63 percent. The 400 richest Americans in 2006 had a collective net worth of $1.25 trillion, an increase of $120 billion from the year before. By 2010, the figure went up to $1.37 trillion. The figures are "at least" figures. The United States has the greatest disparity of wealth in the entire industrialized world, as the World Bank stated. The CBO report in 2011 showed that 1 percent of households have gained about 275 percent after federal taxes and income transfers over the period 1979 and 2007. According to the Fed, while the average income of the top 5 percent of households rose 38 percent between 1989 and 2013. Adjusted for inflation that figure is 50 percent lower than in 1989. Average real net worth of families in the country's top 5 percent had surged 89 percent between 1989 and 2013. The *Economist* of September 21, 2013 has reported that 95 percent of the gains from the recent recovery has gone to the richest 1 percent, whose share of the overall income is once again close to its highest level in a century. However, as can be expected in a politically contradictory country, people on the far right, the so-called trickle-down conservative economists as the World Bank Report mentioned, see it differently and honestly hold up the claim that markets work at maximum efficiency when left undisturbed, enabling some of the funds flowing to Wall Street and corporations to trickle down to the middle class and the poor through investment and spending.

Up to the time of the Great Recession, the official attitude to inequality was positive. In February 2007, for example Ben Bernanke made the following statements (a) "Although we Americans strive to provide equality of economic opportunity, we do not guarantee equality of economic outcomes, nor should we." (b) "We also believe that no one should be allowed to slip too far down the economic ladder, especially for reasons beyond his or her control." (c) "Economic opportunity should be as widely distributed and as equal as possible; that economic outcomes need not be equal but should be linked to the contribution each person makes to the economy."[63] Bernanke said that the difficult question was:

> How to balance the need for maintaining strong market-based incentives, which support economic growth and efficiency but may be associated with greater inequality of results, against the goal of insuring individuals against the most adverse outcomes, which may reduce inequality but also tends to diminish the strength of incentives.

Bernanke finished his speech by suggesting that "a better approach to policy" was to "allow growth—enhancing forces and to try to cushion the effects of any resulting dislocation" He listed a whole package of safety net measures, which included training and retraining workers and national investment in education. Bernanke did not get it.

In January 1977, President Bush stated that the United States has inequality because "We have an economy that rewards education, and skills because of that education." On the left of the continuum are populist Democrats who want to use the tools of government to divert money from the wealthiest Americans. Unfortunately, the Obama administration has this label. Taxing the rich will not stop the on-going structural process of inequality. The excessive and growing cost of safety nets in the United States is bound to increase.

Before the 2007 recession, inequality was beginning to rattle people in the United States, even some so-called conservatives. While admitting that inequality in the United States is a problem, President G.W. Bush thought that excessive CEO salaries and compensations was a matter for company shareholders to deal with. To him, inequality was not a matter for the administration or Congress.

The swelling concern about inequality finally caught up with some Democrats who are Wall Street types at the time. Most notable was Robert Rubin, the former Treasury secretary, a man whose great virtue is said to be free of ideology and an ardent builder of the free market economy. His 'conservative' approach of balancing the budget and promoting free trade, otherwise known as *Rubinomics* when he was at the Treasury were not exactly things that endeared him to the liberals in the Democratic Party. In his publication *The Nation* called *Born-again Rubinomics*, Rubin began talking about inequality as a *deeply troubling fact of American life* that threatens the trading system, even the stability of the *capitalist, democratic society.* He admitted what a lot of free trade opponents have been saying for a long time that globalization has helped generate the thirty year stagnation of US wages, squeezing middle class and below and directing wealth to the upper brackets. He launched the so-called *Hamilton Project*, a policy group of like-minded economists to develop ameliorative measures to aid the threatened workforce and other less privileged in the society. In a policy strategy paper co-authored by Rubin, the problem was stated thus: "Prosperity has neither trickled down nor rippled outward." In an interview, he explains the fear that:

> "Where there's a great deal of insecurity, where median real wages are, roughly speaking stagnant, and where a recent Pew poll showed 55 percent of the American people think that their kids will be worse off than they are, I think there is a real danger of heightened difficulty around issues that are already difficult, like trade."

It was however disturbing that Rubin seemed more motivated by the need to create a political constituency to assuage the poor levels of the American society. He was more intent on how to defend trade and global/ Wall Street system against possible popular backlash. Rubin's intention seemed to be how to avoid disturbing the fundamentals of the global system by addressing its economic disparities. Lawrence Summers, former Treasury secretary and a former economic adviser to Obama jumped in more explicitly by saying (in an attempt to protect the status quo):

> "The challenge is…to protect a basic market system based on open trade and globalization, to make it one that works for everyone or for almost everyone, at a time when market forces are often producing outcomes that seem increasingly problematic to middle-class families."

Mr. Rubin and Professor Summers are wrong because they failed to realize that globalization and free trade cause/add to structural imbalance that causes inequality. In a preamble to a planned discussion in July 2007 titled "A New Social Contract" the Hamilton group put out the following statement:

> In the decade after World War II, the United States developed an implicitly social contract that business, government, and individuals would play a role in ensuring the health, retirement, and other benefits that families need. That social contract is breaking as firms retreat from their role as provider of social benefits and as demographic trends strain our social insurance programs. In a global economy marked by rapid technological change, global labor markets, and mobile capital, a new model is needed to provide American families with economic security and to keep the American economy productive.

These were mere wishes with no supportive structural data. Today Hamilton has been abandoned by its founders and now turned into mini studies, generally social in character, as to how to help the poor and underprivileged in the US

Janet Yellen had been outstanding for her concern for the less privileged. Even before she became the Federal Chairman, she had been concerned with low employment in the US economy. Then in February 2014, she added economic inequality to her concerns. She told Congress that inequality was "one of the most disturbing [economic] trends facing the nation." Coming from the Economist-in-Chief of the US, not partisan, it means that the US has taken a major turn to repair inequality as a problem in its economy and not a necessary component of a free-enterprise economy.

The problem Yellen has is that in her position as Fed Chairman, she and the Fed have no expertise to solve the country's unemployment (which I will deal with in Chapter 8) or inequality. In a speech October 17, 2014 carefully titled "Perspectives on Inequality, and Opportunity from the Survey of Consumer Finance" at the conference on Economic Opportunity and Inequality by the Federal Reserve Bank of Boston, she expressed her great concern at the growing inequality in the US. It was all politically self-serving.

Yellen specified in her speech what she described as "building blocks of opportunity" in the US—early childhood, education, affordable higher education, business ownership and inheritance. It is difficult to see what one can do with Yellen's building blocks, because if every citizen in the US had equal access to these building blocks, that in itself would not stop economic inequality. Inequality, as I have stressed, is a technical structural problem arising from the unbalanced structure of the American economy as shown in Figure 1.1.

The contradiction is that all functions of the Fed are unfortunately geared to promoting economic inequality. To the extent that the Fed superintends and supports Wall Street, it is promoting inequality as I have detailed in Chapter 9. Apart from the growth of inequality which arises from the growing structural imbalance of the economy, the Fed also in other ways adds to inequality. The Q.E. was a massive boost to US inequality. The lower mortgage rates following the 2007-9 recession, for example, helped people who already own homes or have credit enough to buy homes. As Sy Harding in "Investing" October 17, 2014 commented: Those recurring cycles of bull and bear markets in stocks and bonds, the blowing of bubbles and their bursting in real estate and other assets (bonds and stocks, etc...) are hugely profitable for the top 5 percent because they make it their business to understand what is going on, so they can buy low and sell high."

It is therefore difficult for Yellen to put into practice her wishes on inequality. She instead makes inequality worse because the Fed is tied to the wrong structural macroeconomics.

Hollowing Out of US Manufacturing

I had earlier talked of the time human beings appeared on earth. They had to comply with the natural law that the only way for them to supply their economic needs and grow their economic wealth, is to convert the natural resources (materials) around them to desired economic products. They did this by applying human labor in combination with production aids (capital) comprising of various tools and aids produced from the materias. We call the tools production aids. The aids were necessary because humans don't have the necessary stamina, height, or the ability to stand the heat/cold that may be needed to undertake the various material conversion pro cesses that they needed. The modern man will call this capital.

The law of production is that economic wealth is the result of the combination of (three factors of production) material, capital (production aid), and labor. The basic structure of any economy is, therefore, three dimensional (3D). Primitive man later devised some materials as coins as a means of exchange—coins and later finance. By appropriate combination of these: material, labor and capital, economic wealth was created facilitated by an agreed means of exchange. Finance from age-old times existed merely to service wealth creation process but was not economic wealth itself. Today, contrary to natural economic laws, we now want finance and services to be the economic wealth instead of the endowed material resources and the human resources in action using ca.

Material processing is at the root of economic wealth creation. Nature established six types of material processing: casting, forming/

shaping, machining, joining, finishing, chemical conversion from time immemorial. As clever as our scientists and intellectual economists are through all history, they have not added to these six fundamental categories. When a country decides to neglect manufacturing and not to give it priority, as America does, it is reducing its ability to create economic wealth. The famous former United Kingdom minister, Sir Keith Joseph, in a lecture titled "Monetarism is not enough' stated that an economy declines when its wealth producing sector (manufacture) begins to shrink."[64]

The US increasing relative decline or neglect of manufacturing, now second to China, means that the country's raw material endowment (required for conversion into economic wealth) is not strategically utilized and/or also wasted in excessive capital-intensive manufacturing. There is a growing culture within the elites in our political parties together with our conventional financial economists and Wall Street that manufacturing is not a priority, and that the United States does not need an industrial plan and strategy. Our policy makers are more worried that Dow Jones or NASDAQ indexes were falling than that manufacturing index was falling.

Paul Craig Roberts of 'Counterpunch' (a US Newsletter) once described America as a *has-been economy* in which manufacturing has declined and one in which US corporations outsourced manufacturing to other countries and creating economic wealth for those countries because that is where the material processing is conducted.

The start of the deteriorating US manufacturing base is confirmed in the result of a comprehensive study by the US Business and Industry released in early 2007 just before the Great Recession, trends have continued practically unabated. Its survey in 2007 showed that 111 of 114 key US-based industrial sectors lost domestic market share to foreign-produced goods between 1997 and 2005 alone. Import penetration rose to 83 of these and fell only for 31. The survey emphasized that the industries affected are the kind of high-value and capital-intensive manufactures that some people would class as the backbone of any world-class national manufacturing base: the so called 'high-tech' industries.

These are the kind of *high-technology* manufactures that US policy makers say are the future of US industrial preeminence (innovation). The labor-intensive sectors of the United States already decimated by imports were not included in the survey. US textiles, for example, just before 1997 posted record shipments and near record profits, invested in new textile plants and equipment and record export. The Asian devaluation, following the Asian financial crisis, decimated the industry. By 2000, it posted an annual loss of over $350 million. US foundry, the key to all industrial fabrication, has similarly collapsed. *Products from foundries are used to make 90% of all manufactured goods.* Over the past twenty years, over 1000 foundries in the US have disappeared. Two of the largest car parts foundries have in 2015 filed for bankruptcy. Six out of every ten foundries filed for bankruptcy protection since 2013. About fifty foundries are closing in the United States every year at the time of the study. Over the past twenty years, more than one thousand foundries where material processing were conducted have therefore disappeared, a contraction to just 2,380 foundries. Charles Kurtt, President of American Foundry Society said that US foundry industry is "in deep trouble." There are over 30,000 foundries in China employing two million people. China's current yearly foundry output is valued at about $44,500,000 billion compared to US $12,250,000 billion. US now imports foundry materials from China.

Home market over the period shrank by 50 percent or more for many industries, some of due to imports. These include pharmaceuticals, computers, telecoms, hardware, navigation and guidance equipment, broadcasting and wireless communication, motor power train, and transmission equipment. Eight more manufacturing areas, notably tires, electrical switchgear and switchboard, commercial and service industry machinery lost nearly 50 percent. Of those where imports have captured between 60 percent and 69 percent are autos, environmental controls, aircraft engines and engine parts. In six manufacturing areas including machine tools and imports penetration, it is more than 70 percent.

Between 1990 and the beginning of 2006, US manufacturing output grew from $1,040 billion to $1,493 billion, still the largest in the world, but by 2012/3, Chinese manufacturing output of $2.9 trillion had comfortably overtaken that of US at $2.43 trillion. The value of actual net US-based manufacture is much less than this considering the increasing US outsourcing of US manufactures. For example Boeing, one of the most prominent manufacturers of the United States has up to 60 percent of its components manufactured outside the United States. Yet all this outside manufactures are recorded as Boeing manufacturing output.

In January 2007, the manufacturer's inventories contracted by its fastest rate of 8.6 percent over December 2006 when seasonally adjusted. According to the US Institute of Supply Management, this was the largest decrease since 1984 when the index dropped from 57.8 percent to 49.1 percent. Recession in 2007 has decimated the US industrial position. By the beginning of 2009, as US recession was underway, manufacturing in the US was at its lowest in twenty years at $1.73 trillion. New orders by January 2009 were the lowest since 1948, when it will be remembered that manufacturing was a higher percentage of GDP than now. The percentage of GDP attributed to manufacturing has declined from twenty seven in 1950 to twenty-three in 1970, to fourteen in 2000 and to twelve in 2009, and slightly increased to 12.8 percent in 2013 compared to 30.5 percent for China as far back as 2011 and output just up to $2.09 trillion.

On the employment front, the news is also disappointing. Between 2001 and 2003 alone, the US manufacturing sector lost three million jobs. Between 2000 and 2009, it lost 9 million manufacturing jobs. By 2010 the total loss was 11.5 million. In chapter 2, I drew attention to Paulson's statement that while real output of US manufacturing increased seven times since 1950, it did so with the same number of workers. The acceleration in the decline in manufacturing jobs has accelerated since 2000. By mid 2016, US manufacturing had only 12.1 million jobs, far below the already diminished prerecession level. Faced with global competition and unable to raise prices US manufacturing companies, as we have noted, tend to eliminate labor by moving to capital-intensive operations in the erroneous belief that the only way to fight price competition is to reduce labor (productivity). The Manufacturing Institute and Brookings estimate that by 2020, there will be 2 million jobs unfulfilled manufacturing jobs in the US.

In 2006, Professor Goolsbea, a top Obama economic adviser and recently head of CEA, said that the long-term decline in manufacturing jobs did not worry him while Greg Mankin, a Harvard economist who once headed President G.W. Bush's Council of Economic Advisers once justified the fall in employment in manufacturing by saying it was an inescapable consequence of rapid productivity growth. I have in chapter 1 described the country's productivity mirage and how the US rabid drive for productivity is instead making the US more structurally uncompetitive. These economists lacked a technical structural knowledge of the economy. They see everything too simplistically as labor versus capital in what is essentially a three-dimensional economic system.

Capital-intensive operation is not flexible because of high fixed costs. Capital intensive operations are, therefore, particularly vulnerable to the swings of recessions and recoveries of the US economy. So US manufacturing has increasingly boxed itself in a complex competitive world market. Of the eight recessions since 1950, real US GDP has declined on the average of 2 percent but the manufacturing output has declined 7 percent. By the standard of overall output, the recession of 2001 was mild. However it hit the manufacturing sector hard. The manufacturing output declined by about 6 percent from fourth quarter of 2000 to the third quarter, during which time, GDP fell by 0.5 percent. Capital-intensive manufacturers also find it hard to recover after a recession. That is one of the reasons many of them move overseas to China which has no recessions. In the first two years after the 2001 recession during which GDP was supposed to increase by 6 percent, manufacturing declined slightly and by mid-2003 was still down some 4 percent below its previous peak in mid-2000. The recession up to 2009 caused a decline of about 12 percent in US manufacturing compared with a GDP fall of 2.9 percent. The capital-intensive manufacturing, which US manufacturing uses as its answer to increasingly cheap, imported, manufactured competition, finds itself unlike in China, boxed in America's cyclical economy. Capital-intensive manufacture requires continued and high steady demand to survive because of its high overheads. It lacks the flexible ability to deal with low and swinging demand caused in part by structural seasonal changes.

The error of US economists of equating economic growth with capital investment can be illustrated by economic structural analysis that shows that China's annual economic growth of up to 9 percent to11percent during much of the last two decades has been achieved with an average capital/labor ratio that is about 5 percent of that of the United States. From this perspective, it can be seen that a sevenfold increase in capital/labor ratio in US manufacturing between from 1950 today is excessive and impedes its macroeconomic growth potentials. The failure of US manufacturing to grow is undeniable when it is noted that China has surpassed the United States as the world's highest rising manufacturer of goods with less capital (and material). At one time the US manufacturing sector was double that of China.

The contradiction is that US economists judge the health and *vitality of the country's manufacturing sector by reading the US manufacturing(financial) index.* What matters has to do instead with structure of manufacturing and how it is able to adapt to changing competitive conditions. It is clear that present US manufacturing strategy is not contributing significantly to the growth of the country's macro economy because it is capital—investing itself out of existence in the name of new *technology* and *productivity.* In a 2016 paper titled "US Economic Policy," Andrew Smithers confirmed this incorrect policy posture. In looking to the future how US can can increase its low GDP, he claimed that "Any significant and sustained improvement in the rate of growth is likely to require a *marked acceleration* in the growth of the net capital stock. There is the related bizarre idea among economists and political leaders in the US as we have seen in chapters 1 and 2 that productivity is a free gift that you will get if you are clever and resourceful and more capital-intensive when, in fact, productivity and high capital use are indica tive of a wasteful and inappropriate use of the country's mate rial resources.

The problem is that there is no shortage of Americans like Paulson and others who feel that US manufacturing is first-class. Dr. Thomas Duesterberg was the President and CEO of the Manufacturers Alliance/MAPI. He is as the President of the Institute for Technological Advancement, an affiliate of the Manufacturers Alliance, a member of the Board of Directors of the Manufacturing Institute, an affiliate of the National Association of Manufacturers, a former assistant secretary of Commerce for International Economic Policy and an author. He should, therefore, know. In a publication in August 2009 titled "MAPI's View on US Manufacturing," he listed ten salient points based on which he believed the US manufacturing is strong and healthy. I will comment on his main claims. The first main claim is that the quantity of manufactured goods produced in the United States has kept pace with US overall growth for the last ninety years. Since 1947, for example, he pointed out that manufacturing value added has increased sevenfold, same as the US GDP. He stated that while employment in manufacturing has steadily declined, and that currently one in six private sector jobs are still in or directly tied to manufacturing. While he conceded secondly that when measured in value-added production that manufacturing has gone down from 27 percent of GDP in 1950s to 12 percent in 2009, he attributes this to the higher productivity of the sector, low prices of manufactured goods, and the rapid growth of the US service sector.

He observed that between 1987 and 2008, the US manufacturing productivity has gone up by 103 percent. He claimed that US manufacturing is doing well in the global competition and global trade because of enhanced labor productivity by which unit labor in the United States have declined 40 percent relative to 14 percent average only of fourteen other principal industrial countries since 1986. He boasted that 57 percent of all US exports are home manufactures. On the other hand, according to him, US manufacturing provides premium wages and benefits, about $32 per hour, which is 9 percent higher than the US economy wide average. US manufacturing accounts for more than one fifth of all energy in the United States and energy efficiency have increased by 43 percent since 1987 alone and better than 33 percent for other sectors. He argued that the tax burden on US manufacturing is more onerous than in other major competing countries except Japan. He also claims that US manufacturing is a source of innovation and suffers from recession fluctuations. US manufacturing declined by an estimated 12 percent in 2009, better than 20 percent during depression but worse than the GDP decline of 2.9 percent in 2009.

Dr. Duesterberg's complacency can be infectious because of his position in the industry and his experience in government, and people expect that he knows. But has he considered that maybe the sevenfold increase in US manufactured quantity may not be enough? He takes the sevenfold increase in US GDP from 1947 as a benchmark. China, which came on the scene in 1975, has overtaken US manufacturing. US GDP record and its manufacturing are not as good as Dr. Duesterberg wants us to believe.

Regrettably, much of Dr. Duesterberg's satisfaction with US manufacturing is based on productivity claims. US manufacturing is able to pay what the author called "premium wages and benefits" because it had indiscriminately opted for high capital-intensive operations with a smaller number of employees and got rid of the bulk of its labor. Capital-intensive operations invariably require high energy consumption. If the United States adopted less capital-intensive manufacturing, it will reduce its energy consumption much more than at present. He beat his chest that 57 percent of the total US exports are manufactured goods. Dr. Duesterberg's boast is empty as US trade imbalance is not going to reduce anytime soon. He should be told that some of the fastest-growing exports from the US to China, for example, are cagricultural commodities—cotton, oil seed, pulp, as well as chemicals and metals, which often come back to the United States as finished manufactured goods. US export to China has grown almost six times since China (for selfish reasons) joined the WTO in 2001. Still, as of today, the US has serious trade imbalance with China which engaged the urgent attention of Trump. The US National Association of Manufacturers contended in a report that in 2008 the United States's share of Chinese import of manufactured goods was only 8.2 percent, far behind Japan 17 percent, EU 15.6 percent, South Korea 12.4 percent, and Taiwan 12.1 percent.

Overrated US Service Sector

The US service sector is by far the largest and fastest growing sector of the United States economy. The service sector is sometimes called the non-goods producing sector. This has been rising since 1950 and presently employs over 80% of private sector employment in the United States. The US service sector is not a productive economy with

10 occupations with the largest projected growth between 2008-2018 are in the service sector. A major component of the sector is the finance. By 2008, 77.2 percent of jobs in the US were in the service sector and according to the US Department of Labor, by 2018 this will rise to 78.8 percent. While the US financial sector contributes little to the country's GDP, it is the main origin of the economy's structural imbalance.

Domestic American financial sector profits accounted for 13 percent of US pretax profits in 1980. In 2007, it jumped to 27 percent. In 2009, the figure was 41 percent. Eighty-five percent of all corporate earnings in the United States can be attributed to the financial sector. It is responsible for only 8.4 percent of GDP. In 2014 business services and consumer-related businesses attracted the majority if US private equity investment (PEGCC). The US productive sector was in effect in relative decline adding to the country's structural imbalance by encouraging more capital into its capital-intensive sector. As capital intensiveness allowed financial firms to do more with less people, paychecks and financial perks in the financial sector have continued to rise. The United States is, therefore, a 'footless economy' because, as we have seen, it is not growing its productive sector at any rate near the service sector. The US fast growing service sector, without a growing manufacturing sector to support it, has constituted a permanent and growing source of demand for imported manufactures as the country seeks life supply support to meet its financial wealth consuming needs.

The intangible nature of the service sector in the past made people look down on it. It was originally viewed as low 'productivity' and inability to 'innovate': restaurants, barber shops, health workers, and cleaners. It was characterized by low-paying jobs, low education requirements and poor institutional organizations. In recent years, there has been a rapid change of attitude to the service sector—a service sector revival spurred on by the incursion of the new vistas and revolution in IT into the service sector. Analysts now see service as a growing dynamic component of the economy, characterized by large absorption of new *technologies* and human capital. In March 2007, a new organization was formed by universities and tech companies called *Service Research and Innovation Initiative* to innovate *digital* into the service sector with a view to further improve *productivity* and growth in the service sector, which now wants to develop what the group calls *service science*. *Service, Education, Research and Innovation* (SERI) another group is to provide a forum to those who have special interest in services. This grand view of services has tended to shift the attention of policy makers further away from production to services and has also moved international trade policy to shift to international export of services.

It is now also widely accepted that a significant share of research and development (R&D) conducted in the manufacturing industries can support the provision of the services provided by the non-manufacturing sectors. Today, some service activities incorporate as much research into their *products* and services as manufacturing industries. With manufacturing industries outsourcing much of their research and development to the service sector, the profile of the burgeoning service sector continues to increase. Many service firms now find that their research and development result in increased speed and efficiency in their services to their customers who are sometimes intermediate suppliers to both manufacturing and non-manufacturing businesses. For example, R&D conducted in IT by service-sector firms has greatly increased the flexibility of manufacturers helping them to adjust their products to customer needs and to make their products more user-friendly in their sales.

The telecommunication service is one beneficiary of new technology. It is said that telecommunication has facilitated the *death of distance*, enabling service providers and users to conduct business without regard to geographical location. Information and communication service technology have become an inseparable component of any business.

Service innovation has lowered transaction costs and increased reliability and security. The telecoms services consist of a broad range of about two thousand firms operating in providing access to facilities for the transmission of voice, data, and full motion picture/video between network termination points and telecom reselling. In 2008, total annual revenue in communications exceeded $350 billion with employment of approximately 1.13 million (about 0.73 percent of the total US employment). By 2012, revenue had jumped to $985 billion.

In 2007, the total revenue of the financial services organizations was $1.9 trillion, employing approximately 4.3 million. The recession ending in 2009 has hit these revenues and employment significantly, but as of 2010, financial services account for 5.77 million employees in the United States. For all its *power* in a growing service sector in the United States, the financial industry faces a tough future. In 2009, the United States exported $70 billion in financial services but had a deficit of $1.6 billion in financial services and insurance trade. Non-US financial markets—more than three quarters of the world's GDP, about two thirds of the world's equity market capitalization, about two thirds of the world's debt, and 95 percent of the world's consumers—are outside the United States. The BRICS countries (Brazil, Russia, India, China and South Africa) alone are expected to account for 50 percent of the global GDP by 2050. The US financial industry will increasingly move outside the United States where the busi ness is.

With United States's initial lead in IT, it was expected that the Americans will maintain their lead in IT technology and innovation with which they expect to dominate the world with new high-tech products and services. As will be expected, the United States has been losing out even on this last outpost.

A *Business Week* survey described the position in an article titled "Outsourcing Innovation" in March 20, 2005. US companies, according to the survey, were outsourcing science and technology as well as innovation and the manufacture. When US companies began farming out IT manufacturing in the '80s and '90s, they said all the important research and development will remain at home. Today that pledge has evaporated. Today, companies like Dell. Microsoft, Apple, Google, and others are largely manufacturing overseas. Some IT firms are buying complete designs of some digital devices from Asian developers. In the end, many of these companies are basically service companies in the United States. Global electronics contract (outsourcing) manufacturing reached $360 billion in 2011 and is expected to reach $426 billion by 2015. A Deloitte 2018 survey confirms that the growing strength of outsourcing particular I cloud and automation. Chinese manufacturing companies generally receive 20 percent or less of the revenue from exporting outsourced goods to the United States, according to a US economist who testified to Congress. So while our US companies receive large financial wealth returns and savings from selling the outsourced goods with which they strengthen their balance sheets and profits (dividends), the United States relatively has lost economic wealth and technical innovation to the outsourced countries. More worrisome earlier in 2014 were the data of the US National Science Foundation (NSF) is that the other countries, especially, China, Korea, and Taiwan are making their research investment at a faster rate and turning out a greater number of scientists and engineers than the United States.

US manufacturing companies are becoming increasingly service/ assembly companies as they outsource their manufacturing overseas. In February 2004, Boeing announced it was planning to collaborate with India's HCL Technologies to develop software for everything from navigations systems and landing gear to cockpit controls for the new 7E7 Dreamliner jet. This trend has strengthened. With its latest plane the 787, Boeing has outsourced nearly 70 percent of the plane's manufactures restricting its Seattle plant as an assembly plant—bolting together modules designed and produced elsewhere. Boeing responds that its suppliers have provided their own development, designs and manufacturing funds. Pharmaceuticals like GlaxoSmithKline have been teaming up with Asian biotech research companies to bring out new drugs. By 2010, Procter & Gamble was to have half of its new product ideas to be created from outside up from 20 percent. China has pressured firms like GE to establish research facilities in China in order to secure lucrative contracts and concessions. Much of the outsourcing is dictated by the basic uncompetitiveness of the US economy in which supplies can be obtained cheaper outside the US. Apple and Microsoft outsource most of their manufacture.

> The bad message is that innovation and research alone don't create economic wealth. Economic wealth only occurs only if and when natural material or semi-processed materials are processed to make a product. Innovation and research for which Americans beat their chest that they excel in are useful actions that can enhance material processing, but they don't by themselves constitute economic wealth creation. When Boeing outsources its manufacturing,

retaining mainly the function of conceptual design and integration of the plane's systems, the economic wealth is not created in the United States but in those countries where the manufacture and fabrication are transferred to. Listing the table of nations in ranking of their research and development (R&D) expenditure as percentage of GDP, Israel is first. US is seventh and China thirty-ninth. But today China has overtaken the United States in manufacturing and wealth creation.

Living Beyond Our Means

America was supposed to be the richest country, but it is the world's largest debtor. We have taken on things that are beyond our means. America has continued as the self-appointed world sheriff. The Iraq and Afghanistan wars were big drains on US finances. We are positioning troops and our naval presence worldwide. We have devoted a growing part our resources especially since 9/11 in protecting ourselves and the world against terrorism. As the economy breeds poverty, we have continued to create a socialist dependent economy as the structural imbalance of the economy creates increasing poverty: a vicious circle. What we have is a national overreach.

David Brooks in a *New York Times* article titled "The Ecstasy of Fiscal Policy" on Friday, April 2, 2010 said that Americans have grown complacent and careless. For two hundred years before, he said, Americans lived precarious lives. There were booms and busts, economic cycles, devastating epidemics, and natural disasters that came without a warning. "These conditions," he said, "instilled a sense of prudence among Americans through time. The thought of running excessive debt, living beyond your means, filled them with horror."

He told us that in the 1960s a politician would have been voted out of the office if he had allowed the federal debt to double in a decade. The difference between the 1960s and now is that, as I have shown, the US economy is now more unbalanced since the 1960s—poverty is increasing, and available resources are getting smaller as the economic growth is slowing and the deficit has become a growing permanent feature of the US economy. In earlier times, it was also thought that national debt caused inflation but when it came to be known that that was not true, the spending spigots got turned on. Keynes's *spend your way* rhetoric that started with Obama's stimulus added to the debt G.W. Bush left. Financial stimulus could not stop a recession. Trump's stimulus only made caused a little murmur in growth. because the recessions and depressions are structural problems. Eliminating national debt, therefore, cannot grow the economy since national debt is the result and not the cause of a poor economy. Neither the adoption of fiscal measures intended to increase *investments* (for example by stimulus or tax), nor artificially creating *demand* can on their own rectify the structural imbalance that caused the recession in the first place. A recession can only stop when the economic structural cycle allows it.

Greenspan in his despair about US economy's future stated in his new 2013 book *The Map and the Territory*:

> "Unless the upward momentum of entitlement spending (in the US) is contained and turned around, the erosion of gross domestic savings will almost surely continue to suppress capital spending, productivity and growth in standard of living, as it has done incrementally for nearly a century. Net domestic savings is now approaching zero and gross domestic savings is headed in that direction.... We can continue to pawn or sell the nation's capital assets to fund growing social benefit consumption, at least for a while... there is a limit to accumulation of foreign borrowings."

This problem of living above our means was the theme of Bernanke as Fed chairman in a testimony titled "Long-term Fiscal Challenges and the Economy" before the Committee on Budget of the House February 28, 2007. He correctly described CBO's revised gloomy 2007 forecast of the deficit as "the calm before the storm." He pointed out that federal spending for Social Security, Medicare, and Medicaid together totaled 40 percent of federal expenditure in 2006 (8½ percent of GDP). According to Bernanke, the most likely outcomes of this scenario involve increasing federal debt to unprecedented levels.

Bernanke also speculated on the effect this will have on the US economy. According to him, rapidly increasing government debt and deficits will drain funds away from private capital formation and further slow economic growth. Bernanke often advised Congress, the administration, and the American peo ple to confront America's fiscal problems—what he regards as about how large a share of the nation's resources are devoted federal government programs. He believed that Congress and the administration should set tax rates that can achieve appropriate balance of spending and revenues in the long run. Bernanke advised the need for monitoring current and long-term levels of government outlays relative to GDP. Following these remarks on April 7, 2010, the *New York Times* the next day told us that it was a rare foray by Bernanke into the realm of fiscal policy. That was not quite true.

Since 1997, Bernanke came out many times providing what on the surface were brilliant insights into the country's fiscal problems. He quite often lectured Congress on it. His theme was always the same. He often told his listeners that the aging American population posed a fiscal challenge for the United States. He spoke about the budget pressure posed by Social Security and Medicare.

He said on April 2, 2010 that, "The arithmetic is, unfortunately, quite clear." He advised: "To avoid large and sustainable budget deficits, the nation has to choose among higher taxes, moderation to entitlement programs, such as Social Security and Medicare, less spending on everything else from education to defense, or some combination of the above." He further said on that occasion "These choices are difficult and it always seems easier to put them off…until the day they cannot be put off any more." "A sharp near-term reduction in our fiscal deficit is probably neither practical nor advisable but a long-term plan for fiscal sustainability could help lower interest rates and borrowing costs, and even stimulate economic growth," he advised.

He was wrong to imply that *better* fiscal management alone will stimulate economic growth. But this was the Fed's way at the time of deflecting attention from its inability to live up to its claim that it can grow the economy. The Fed had kept interest at some ridiculously low level for years since 1999 without a whisper of a strong economic growth in the United States. Many people unfortunately regard the reduction of deficit as a means of how to grow the US economy. The 2010 Bi-partisan Commission held up the hope that lowering the deficit will "—help our economy grow, keep us globally competitive and make it easier for businesses to create jobs."[65] This is misleading.

Representative Rhyan stated that in the House Budget Committee March 2013 that "By tackling the debt, this budget will help grow our economy and ensure the next generation inherits a stronger, more prosperous America." Unfortunately, many US leaders, politicians, and economists, see the reigning in of the debt as what is needed to put the United States back on the path to rapid economic growth. The Republican Party broadly argues that cutting government costs and cutting taxes will stimulate private investments that will promote economic growth. The Democrats, on the other hand, believe that taxing the wealthy and providing for the not-wealthy will help increase demand which will stimulate economic growth in a typical Keynesian style. These two apparently opposite fiscal (financial) prescriptions for economic growth lack structural economic merit.

Krugman, for some time, has argued that debt was not a problem. Others look at balancing the budget as necessary, so as to increase confidence of US creditors and encourage investments. All these different and often opposing and wrong prescriptions, comfortably aligned with each political party's political ideology, create a confusion arising from conflicting politically framed conventional economic concepts—one believes that it is increased demand that will solve a recession, the other that it is new investments from the well-offs in the system. Krugman was trying to draw our attention by overstating the problem in his wrong belief that it is demand that creates economic growth. I refer to a paper I mentioned earlier by Andrew Smithers titled "US Economic Policy" in which he correctly pointed out that both major parties, despite their apparent differences, jointly claim that economic growth derives from fiscal stimulus. Andrew Smither was suggesting that both party might be wrong going by the experience of the well-known Mervyn King, former Governor of the Bank of England for over for over ten years and currently professor at both New York University and the London of Economics and who personally was involved in managing the 2009 global financial crisis who in his popular book

The End of Alchemy—Money, Banking and the Future of the Global Economy told us that the UK 's National Plan 2013-2015 failed even though it was based on the plan that the UK economy will grow through stimulation of demand.

The deficit fell to $483 billion in the fiscal year 2014, a reduction of nearly one third from $680 billion in 2013 and about 2.8 percent GDP. The Treasury Secretary Jack Lew called it "the most rapid reduction in budget deficit since the World War II."

The reduction at the time was due to a number of factors (a) Growth in revenue of about 99 percent in fiscal revenue to $3.02 trillion due to an increase individual and corporate tax receipts both to better tax collection, to normal recession cycle and 31 percent increase in Federal Reserve earnings due to Q.E. (b) There was a drop in healthcare costs and a drop due to budget pact between the parties. Obama imposed some taxes in 2013 that added to revenue. (c) There was substantial reduction in costs because of the sharp reduction in oil imports and reduced imports of oil.

It is therefore clear that the improvement in the deficit was not due to any strategic improvement in US economic growth prospects. One thing is clear: the prospects of solving US long-term deficit are not bright so long as the long-term source of revenue (the economy) is not robust and so long as the structural economic imbalance of the economy continues to worsen. Growing interest on debt will become the US third largest problem—crowding out investments in US central programs— like education and infrastructure. As of June 2016, the debt was $19.3 trillion. In 2019, it is $22 trillion

As James Bacon in 2010 concluded in the face of the International Monetary Fund's (IMF) continuing downgrading of US growth prospects over the next ten years, "US policy makers will find themselves in a fiscal and monetary straitjacket, with less and less room to maneuver. Interest payments on national debt will consume an ever-growing percentage of the economy."

He observed:

> "As recent World Bank research shows, the US has prob-
> ably passed a tipping point—when the national debt

exceeds 77 percent of the Gross Domestic Product—at which each percentage point increase in debt/GDP ratio erodes annual economic growth by nearly one-fifth of one percentage point.". Mr. Bacon's warning is still relevant today.

Chapter 4

China's Economic Growth Strategy

There is a large measure of ignorance about the Chinese economy fueled by the average American's belief that Chinese economy is moving to a market economy. In 1974, I published a book titled, *Economic Underdevelopment: an Inside View*. It was the forerunner to my 2005 book, *The Science of Economic Development and Growth: The Theory of Factor Proportions*. The 1974 book was my attempt as an engineer and economist to study the inside structure of underdevelopment. In the book, I postulated on the basic scientific fact that economic development involves the correct use of labor, material, and production aid (capital). I said that the science has not changed since man appeared on the surface of the earth. I called the three items factors of production as I have done in this book. I then asked in the book if there is any science as to how to maximize economic success in the use and application of these three factors of production. I realized that the proportions between these factors are the things that distinguish one economy from another. I stated that the factors of production—capital, labor, and natural resources available in any economy comprise the tools with which its economic development can be undertaken. It is the different proportions between these three basic factors that give each economy what I called in the book its distinct *economic personality*.

From these statements, I made three general statements about economic development in the book. The first is that maximum economic development occurs when the operating factor proportions of all economic production activities in the economy are equal and equal to the endowed factor proportions of that economy. That is a balanced economy-which US is not. I stated the position in a different way by saying that maximum sustainable economic growth (which I called *big push* in the book) requires that an economy makes maximum use of its least scarce factor. I further stated, "It is only when all available supplies of the least scarce resource are operating together with the other resources that one can ensure that the whole economy is geared into full economic activity through the full use of all productive resources." I stated on page 19 of the book that "maximum economic growth occurs when development is *balanced*." I further stated "the balance lies in ensuring that factor proportions in all sectors are not out of line with one another or with the factor proportion endowment of the particular economy." In page 26 of the book, I said that when we talk of the control of factor proportion, we are immediately dealing with technological essence of development. I said that technology is the science of factor proportions. I concluded by saying that "The essence of economic development is the correct combination of factors that suit the factor proportions of a given area." As early as 1974, therefore, I had recognized in the book that there is a 'science' of economics. I now call this in this book as a law of economics. In 2005, I wrote a follow-up book on economic development titled, *The Science of Economic Development and Growth: The Theory of Factor Proportions.* The third generalization I made in the 1974 book about economic development is that "—development cannot truly get underway until it is indigenized and participated in by the mass of the people themselves." My point in the 1974 book is that an underdeveloped economy cannot achieve strong sustainable economic growth without indigenization of its technology. I wrote the 2005 book when I realized that the economic growth theory I put forward in the 1974 book applied equally to developed as well as to underdeveloped economies and, therefore, a general theory/economic law. it I labeled factor relationships in mathematical terms between the three factor endowments of an economy Pn, which I called the "natural factor proportions" of the total economy. According to the two books, maximum economic growth occurs when P1, P2, P3 = Pn, where 1, 2,

3, etc. are the economic sectors. I used appropriate graphs in the 1974 book to prove my general theory of economic growth.

Over thirty years after publishing my 1974 book, I was very surprised that the Chinese Prof. Wu Jinglian—standing committee member of the Chinese People's Political Consultative Conference and described by Wikipedia as one of China's preeminent economists specializing in economic policy—had this to say in his 2004 publication: "The basic characteristics of China resource endowments are abundant human resources, scarce natural resources, capital resources in short supply, and vulnerable ecological resources."[67] He was in effect examining the natural factor proportions of China. He wrote that, "Given these resource endowments of China, China's economic structure should be toward activities low in energy and resource inputs and capable of capitalizing on China's advantage in its supply of human resources...." He was in effect saying that all activities (sectors) in China should ally with Chinese natural factor proportions, of which human resources is the least scarce and low material use which is relatively scarce. He concluded that "Only under such circumstances can minimum resources generate maximum value." That is what my book was saying 30 years earlier!!

Referring to the old Chinese industrialization approach which China inherited from the Soviets and China's initial dash for foreign investment, the Chinese professor said following the old Soviet approach could have finally tumbled China into "the pitfall of taking advantage of weaknesses, while avoiding strengths, whereby certain sectors or localities may achieve some growth and gains at the expense of serious welfare losses on the part of society as a whole." That is what the US financial sector is doing.

The Chinese professor in effect wanted China to avoid resource and capital-intensive activities and go for a balanced growth strategy based on China's factor availability. He described capital as "a very valuable, scarce resource that needs to be highly cherished and effecployed." He noted that, in line with another important Chinese economist, Prof. Zhang Jun, that over the initial twenty years, China's economic growth path was one of what he called *overinvestment* because China's share of capital investment in China's GDP rose steadily from 25 percent to over 40 percent in 2003. It was a hand-over from the Soviet era. US is currently on the path of overinvestment.

Professor Jinglian regarded overinvestment as a source of economic instability in China in the immediate early era of present China. He next argued that overinvestment causes "income among low-income groups to rise only slowly resulting in increasing income inequality between rich and poor." I extensively dwelt on these themes in chapters 1 and 2 of this book, where I repeated that that excessive capital investment in the United States leads to structural economic illnesses of the United States the cause high unemployment, and inequality and economic growth decline in the US.

Professor Jinglian's views and those of other Chinese economists coming thirty years or so after my 1974 book were literally a reproduction of my 1974 general theory. Being an economic theory linking labor, material, and production aid makes it a scientific economic theory because science is only concerned with matter (things with physical existence) not things without physical existence like finance. As I proceed to describe and analyze the present Chinese economic success, it will be clear that present Chinese basic economic strategy is in line with what I said in my 1974 book. I support it not as an angry black American but because it is scientific. I am still interested to find out whether the Chinese read my 1974 book for ideas and motivation.

It needs to be stressed here that China's economy from 1952, well before the early West's foreign investment came into China, was a robust economy in terms of GDP. There are conflicting accounts of the extent of this robustness. An OECD study by Angus Maddison in 1998 claimed that from 1952 to 1978 GDP in China, by measuring purchasing power, was multiplied by 3 while per capita income rose by 80 percent, industry rose from 10 percent to 30 percent of GDP. China's official documents claim that from 1952 growth topped figures like 21.3 percent in 1958,19.4 percent in 1970, 18.3 percent in 1964, 17.0 percent in 1965,16.9 percent in 1969, 15.6 percent in 1953, 15.0 percent in 1956. At the same time there were severe recessions: -0.3 percent in 1960, -27.3 percent in 1961, and -5.6 percent in 1962, -5.7 percent in 1967, -4.1 percent in 1968, and -1.6 percent in 1976. Westerners have, as to be expected, cast doubt on these figures. Some Westerners claim that the Chinese figures on its early economic growth vary, depending on who was doing the analysis. Some others claim that officials of centrally planned economies tended to exaggerate output. Others state that the figures are exaggerated because Chinese central planners worked under the concept of gross social output which excluded many segments of the economy under GNP. The pre-1978 Chinese economic growth cannot safely be described as any lower than after 1978 when China broke off from Soviet control The main point I want to make from all this is that pre 1978 Chinese growth was not sustainable growth and had many ups and downs with a number of recessions. The question is, going forward, what did the Chinese do to stop recessions in their economy from 1978 to date, but which the US has so far not been able to do?

Continuous Balancing and Rebalancing

The Chinese present economic success is the result of continuing experimentation and adjustments and readjustment over the years of trying to improve and fine-tune the structural balance of the economy. The prospects for the Chinese economy are, aretherefore, one of increasing strength over time. In a book by Wu Xiaobo in 2008 titled, *China Emerging*, the author said that "macroeconomic adjustments had become a special norm in Chinese vocabulary." The Chinese were continually adjusting the proportions towards equality.

Wu Xiaobo said that the adjustments now occur with regularity every three to five years. "In a certain sense" he said," the thirty years of Chinese economic miracle has represented the victory of the purest (scientific) experimentation, of a very practical and concrete approach to events."[68] This contrasts with the US that has a fixed financial/monetary ideology based on a free market. Quoting Den Xiaoping, the Chinese modern economic founder who urged Chinese that "feeling for the rocks with your feet as you cross the river" and that "it did not matter whether the cat was black or white." Wu Xiaobo said that "So long as people could feel for the stones with their feet as they crossed the river, so long as they knew that irrespective of whether you are a white cat or black cat, so long as you catch the mice, you know you were a good cat, they could face any setbacks."

Xiaoping reference to white or black was in regard to the need to avoid ideology in economic strategy, a plea to be scientific. The one strategy of the presentChinese economy has no political ideology. The ideology only involves what to do with the wealth created by scientific economic management. Balancing and rebalancing is an essential part of economic science because the endowed factor proportions keep changing dependent on how the endowed factors are being used and conservation practices. Rebalancing is not always successful and sometimes the Chinese have not been successful, resulting in the drop in economic growth trend which we have seen recently. The continuous scientific balancing and rebalancing is the hallmark of Chinese economic strategy and management

The Role of the State

The first issue that China tackled early in its economic experimentation after departing from the Sovets was the role of the state in economic development. Despite the intense resistance that one will expect on this matter coming from the so called hardliners, who did not want change, and the *progressives,* who wanted an overthrow of the communist control of the economy, the First Session of 7th National People's Congress in April 1988 passed an amendment to the Constitution that permitted "the private sector to exist and develop within the limits of the law as a supplement to the socialist public sector." After this, the need for further expansion of the private sector was debated on four fronts. The first were those, who argued that whether a country has the character of socialism, they were not determined by the share of the state sector in the economy but that what mattered was whether the party has correct policies that prevent polarization between rich and poor. The second group argued that there are different ways for implementing public ownership such as various funds and foundations, cooperatives, and community ownerships; and that it is wrong to confine public ownership to state ownership or to consider state ownership *as the supreme form of public ownership and the essential goal for socialist to pursue.* The third group argued that modern scientific and technological revolution requires that since the role of human capital and creativity is so important, the guiding principle of socialism should allow diverse ownership to develop side by side. The fourth group adopted the pragmatic argument that there is a limit of what state capital can support, and, therefore, it is necessary for the state sector to reduce its scope and allow non-state sector to take up the financial slack. It can be seen that these arguments basically diversified the structure of the Chinese macroeconomy while on paper claiming socialism as the epitome of economic strategy.

For example, in 1978 household savings in China accounted for 3.4 percent of the total Chinese savings while the state owned 1.6 percent. In 1990, the ownership structure of China's savings had changed in which 83 percent of the total savings from households, while the state owned 17 percent.[69] The continuing withdrawal of the state and increasing role of the non-state sector (sometimes loosely called private sector) saved China from the unbalanced growth that its mentor Russia suffered.

The Soviet Union finally collapsed by adopting large capital intensive state-owned industries. China, therefore, overnight eliminated the possibility of having the American type right-hand side highly capital-intensive sub-sector of figure 1.1 in chapter 1. Ignorance about the real economic position in China by Americans has left Americans with the impression that China's economy is run exclusively by the state. On the contrary, China has had an increasing non-State run economy since 1988. It has made another push to private sector economy in 2013. In Chapter 8, I tried to state that US monopolistic private economy is no more 'liberating' as a state run monopoly. If China started with state-owned companies, it needed time to reduce/adjust them.

It can be seen that the transition from state ownership in China was accompanied by a new definition of socialism as not the ownership of *resources but the adoption of policies that prevent the polarization between rich and poor and allow diverse ownership to develop side by side.* The next years, after the 7th National Peoples' Congress in 1988, were about taking up with discussions and arguments in China about the structure of the macro economy. In an overall assessment of what happened in China, Prof. Jinglian Wu described the period between 1980 and 1994 as that of four rounds of changes in macroeconomic policies. They were structural changes.

Continuous Testing the Ground Experimenting

The stage for economic experimentation in China was set from 1978, following China's break with the Soviet Union in 1957. The *Great Leap Forward* in 1978 was an attempt at economic planning when the 10 Year Outline for Development of National Economy 1976 to 1985 Plan was adopted based on constructing or expanding 120 large projects and building 14 large bases of heavy industry supposed to fetch average industrial growth of 10 percent or more which included nine large chemical imported plants.

The Great Leap was a failure and was described as *new sufferings to the body on the sick bed* marked by high inflations. Between 1979 and 1981, action was taken in reverse to scale down on these large investments of the Great Leap Forward, which in turn brought inflation down and turned the balance of trade from deficit to surplus.

The Cultural Revolution that followed was a disastrous effort intended at instiling the need to bring development into rural China and reverse the drift to the urban areas at the time. This, therefore, destroys Soviet-style rapid large industrialization. It was in his last year before his death in 1975 that Chou En Lai, premier under Chairman Mao, finally proposed a new direction for building a socialism based on Chinese experience away from the Soviet Union. Deng Xiaoping and a small handful of persons, who survived the political repression of the Cultural Revolution under Chou's protection, created a new direction for economic development at a conference in 1978 to build *Socialism with Chinese Characteristics* (not Communism). Deng and his like-minded reformers adopted policies to open the Chinese economy towards market policies and foreign influence. The policies included efforts to expand rural income and reduce central planning. The most visible reform was the creation of special economic zones. Foreign investors in Free Zones—primarily from Hong Kong, Taiwan, and other East Asian nations—were given exemptions from all taxes and from regulations that normally hampered regular business. While initial investments were modest, the zones grew very rapidly. In addition to the special zones that they established, these leaders reformed land ownership, so that farms rather than being cooperatives were effectively privatized. Direct foreign investment increased from $916 million in 1983 to $3.5 billion in 1990. The imbalance, however, led to price rises that manifested itself in the uprising in Tiananmen Square.

Prof. Chun Chang at the University of Minnesota said that while Westerners tended to perceive the uprising in the Square in 1989 as student-led push for political reform and democracy, "the true popular support for the uprising had more to do with the general Chinese public's dissatisfaction over the adverse consequences of the economic reforms...." By 1992, Deng approached Jiang Zemin, Mayor of Shanghai who brought the Shanghai group into the central leadership to continue Deng's ideas just before his death. The objective of Jiang and Deng was to confirm the Eastern and Southern coastal areas of China as the industrial base of the country. All these Deng-inspired changes in development tactics re-shaped the economic structure of China. It was what I call spatial development, which was later to be things that later strategies were to correct, as we will see.

It is necessary to disabuse the mind of Americans who say that all Deng did was introduce capitalism in China. On the central role which manpower (labor as a factor of production) was to play, Deng said: "We often say that man is the most active production force. Man refers to people who possess a certain amount of scientific knowledge and experience in production and skill in the use of tools to create material wealth."

Deng emphasized the role of man in Chinese economic development, which is in contrast to the US where capital (quantum of financial investment) and productivity are the key to economic growth.

Of the role of market forces which Deng unleashed, he countered by saying:

Planning and market forces are not the essential difference between socialism and capitalism. A planned economy is not the definition of socialism, because there is planning under capitalism, the market economy also happens under socialism. Planning and market forces are ways of controlling economic activity. Deng's reform actually heralded the introduction of the planned management of the macroeconomist by Chinese-qualified technically professional bureaucrats instead of intellectual ideologues like the Adam Smiths, Keynes, and Friedman of America who propagated economic ideologies of free market and capitalism. Deng's reforms were in a way a bottom-up approach, as he was seeking contacts with Chinese municipal authorities from his exalted position of Chinese top leader in contrast to perestroika by the Soviets.

Deng's initiatives would later pave the way for the Chinese to prepare their five-year development plans. The result of this bottom-up approach, part of balancing the economy, is that many years later some Westerners anxious to get into business in China were to complain that the provinces in China hold too much economic power. Accusations about corruption among these local authorities were to feature in the Western press.

"Westerners want," according to John Gapper, a writer at *Financial Times* in 2009, "—getting the municipalities that control corporate investment in local enterprises to step back and let liberalized financial sector to take over." Mr. Gapper is ignorant because he fails to realize that these local enterprises are part of China's de-centralized structural strategy to maintain a balanced economy. He ignorantly asserts that "municipalities encourage local communities to expand by directing capital to them."

"Bureaucrats," he further claimed, "have incentives to fund growth rather than achieve higher margins and pay workers well." This is stupid. When does high margin ally with high wages?

The Deng initiative to introduce large participation of foreign investment in a spatial type of development strategy brought its own set of economic problems. Foreign investment even though it helped to increase GDP and introduce foreign technology, was unable to absorb the developing working class. It also resulted in incredible increases in income in the East and South, doubling four to six times from 1980 to 2002, while, as will be expected, from a lack of spatial development strategy, only pockets of areas among the peasants in the West and North saw any increase in income and living standards. Income inequality in the US today is the result of over concentration of capital as in figure 1 in chapter 1. Professor Jinglian called it American "overinvestment."

Between 2001 and 2003, there were fifty-eight thousand riots and demonstrations by workers and peasantry arising in China from resulting low living standards due to foreign overinvestment in the East and South of China and poverty elsewhere. The change of regime, with the ascension Hu Jintao and Wen J i b a o the fourth generation leaders faced a country with sharp divisions in income and unemployment. This is because while the continuing influx of foreign private capital, and joint ven tures stimulated growth and created jobs, the jobs were too little and tended to flow into particular sectors out of proportion to the economy as a whole—a problem we are all currently familiar with in the United States. The resultant threatening fears about characteristics of economic cycles that affect the West in free market societies that were beginning to occur in China at that time were widely reported then in Western newspapers. The Chinese needed to further experiment again between 2002 and 2003 with a new economic structure, as they realized that free flow of capital investment from outside could lead to structural economic instability.

Post-Deng Economic Strategy

At this point, the new regime between 2002 and 2003 undertook a study of the world economy and its tendencies to economic cycles and what to do to avoid getting China's economy enmeshed in it. The new Chinese leaders realized that, despite Deng's market-oriented reforms, the regime had to decide to pull back a bit on market economy creation of the West, exercise its authority to interjecting regulations, control the movement of capital, and maintain the overall balance of all the sectors of the economy. It was like reading from my 1974 book about balance of factor proportion of the economy. The Chinese government realized that it has a right to government income from taxes to use them as allocations to different sectors to create economic balance and accordingly to reinvest such income in *areas which did not attract private capital.* In short, it was the role of government to correct structural/spatial imbalances that will result if everything was left to the private investors as we have currently in the US. The new Chinese regime between 2002 and 2009, therefore, set out to intervene in investment flows *based on macroeconomic plan for regulations and control of capital investment as well as the appropriation of capital funds away from the concentration on economic growth in the East and South* caused by Deng's spatial development initiatives.

The study was initiated by the new leadership and culminated in a national conference on December 1, 2003. The conference was officially described as representing "a massive board of directors for the economy planning the use and investment of all forces of production in its capability, the human labor force, farm, factories, and service as well as the capital investment in plant technology and science."

17th National Congress

These Chinese experimentations in economic management were guided by a scientific outlook on development. The Chinese *documents of the 17th National Congress of the Communist Party of China* stated that the Congress emphasized the need *to thoroughly apply the scientific outlook on development.* The Congress resolved that scientific outlook on development be hereby *incorporated in the Party's constitution.* This formal adoption of scientific approach by China was a major watershed in development economics tied up to my declaration in my 1974 book. The documents of the 17th National Congress said that scientific outlook on development meant putting people first at its core. The documents stated: "We must pursue a comprehensive, balanced and sustainable development."[70] The documents stressed the need to *harmonize economic growth with population, resources, and environment.* This is the basic theme of my 1974 and 2005 books on economic development and growth. In March 1978, Xiaoping convened a *National Science Conference* in which the concept of science as a productive force was adopted and the long march toward the creation of a modern socialism by year 2000 was announced. On May 11, 1978, the Communist Party organ, the *People's Daily,* published a text that stated that "Any theory that supersedes reality and declares itself inviolable and not open to question is not scientific...Instead, it is obscurantism, blind idealism, and cultural authoritarianism."[71]

It took some years for this scientific approach to be stamped on the Chinese economic strategy. The documents of the 17th National Congress 2007 fully declared that: "The Scientific outlook on development takes development as its essence, putting people first as its core, comprehensive, balanced and sustainable development as its basic requirement, and overall consideration as its fundamental approach."[72] Elsewhere, the Congress document stated that "Scientific development and social harmony are integral to each other and neither is possible without the other."[73]

This was the Communist Party's final official acknowledgement that balanced factor proportions is the essence of good economic strategy. Deng Xiaoping from the early days urged Chinese to "cast off the shackles that bind our spirit. We need to bring about a great emancipation in our way of thinking." That is exactly what this book is telling Americans. Deng was urging the Chinese to cast out ideology in economic development and stick to the science of economic development. Americans still stick to capitalism and free enterprise ideology which lacks a scientific base in economic strategy. The situation is further muddied in that in every Western democracy the free enterprise ideology in economic development is muddied by partisan politics.

Central Committee of the Chinese Communist Party

A review of the Politburo of 2011 the Central Committee of the Chinese Communist Party of China, which is the highest organ of the Congress of the Communist Party, charged with, among other things with economic development is important. As the party's highest organ on economy, the qualifications and background of the Politbro are is revealing. The membership was changed late in 2012 to make way for the new Politburo that took over in 2012 and so on and on till today.

Here are the committee members:

1. Hu Jintao—secretary of the Central Committee and president of the People's Republic of China, Water Conservancy Engineering graduate specializing on hub hydropower at Tsinghua University, Water Conservancy Department postgraduate and instructor, technician and secretary of Sub-Bureau, Fourth Engineering Bureau, Ministry of Water Conservancy.

2. Wu Bangguo—Radio and Electronics graduate specializing in electronic vacuum devices at the Tsinghua University, former deputy chief and chief of Shanghai Electronic Tube Factory, and former secretary of the CPC Shanghai Municipal Committee in charge of science and technology.

3. Wen Jiabao—Geology major at the Department of Geology and Minerals at the Beijing Institute of Geology, former director general of the Policy and Law Research Office of the Ministry of Geology, and prime minister of China.

4. Jia Qinglin—Industrial Enterprise Planning stu dent of Shijizhuang Industrial Management School, Electric Power major of Hebel College, former direc tor China National Machinery and Equipment Import and Export Corporation, and director of Taiyuan Heavy Machinery Plant.

5. Li Changchun—Electric Machinery major at Harbin Institute of Technology, former deputy director of Shenyang Bureau of Mechanical and Electrical Industry.

6. Xi Jinping—chemical engineering graduate of Tsinghua University, doctor of laws graduate of Tsinghua University where he studied Marxist theory and ideological education availing of an on-the-job postgraduate program at the university's School of Humanities and Social Science.

7. Li Keqiang—Law graduate of Peking University, Master and Doctor of Economics degree holder at the Peking University, premier of China in 2012.

8. He Guoqiang—*Inorganic Chemical Engineering graduate of Beijing Institute of Chemical Engineering, and former technical director of of Lu'nan Chemical Fertilizer Plant Shandong Province.*

9. Zhen Yungkang—*Geophysical Exploration graduate of Beijing Petroleum Institute, and former general manager of China National Petroleum and Natural Resources Corporation.*

10. Wang Gang—*Philosophy graduate of Jilin University, and former clerk of the Publicity Section of No. 8 Company of the 7th Bureau, Ministry of Construction.*

11. Wang Lequan—Educated in social sciences in Jiaonan County, Shandon Province; former secretary of the Xiajing Uygur Autonomous Regional Committee, and first political commissar of the Xinjiang Production and Construction Corp.

12. Wang Zhaoguo—*Power Generating Machinery major at Harbin Institute of Technology, former deputy director of the Second Automotive Works, and former director of Taiwan Affairs Office of the State Council.*

13. Wang Qishan—History and Economics graduate of Northwest University, former deputy director at the Rural Policy Research Office at the CPC Central Committee and Rural Development Research Center under the State Council, and director of the National Office for Pilot Areas of Rural Reform.

14. Hui Liangyu—Agriculture graduate of the Agriculture School of Jilin Province, former deputy director general of Jilin Provincial Agricultural Bureau, head of the Rural Policy Research Office and Rural Work Department of the CPC Jilin Provincial Committee.

15. Liu Qi—a graduate from the Metallurgical Department of Beijing Institute of Iron and Steel Engineering, majoring in iron smelting, senior engineer in the Institute with rank of a professor, manager of Wuhan Iron and Steel Company, minister and secretary of the Leading Party Members' Group of the

Ministry of Metallurgical Industry. Note: Here's an alternative rewrite of Qi's qualifications—Metallurgical Engineering graduate and Iron Smelting major at the Beijing Institute, senior engineer with rank of professor at the Beijing Institute, Minister and Secretary of the Leading Party Members' Group of the Ministry of Metallurgical Industry.

16. Liu Yunshan—Education graduate of Party School of the CPC central Committee, member of the Political Bureau and Secretariat of the CPC Central Committee, and head of the Publicity Department of the CPC Central Committee.

17. Liu Yandong—Engineering and Chemistry graduate of Tsinghua University, engineer at Beijing Chemical Experiment Plant, former head of the United Front World Department of the CPC Central Committee.

18. Li Yuanchao—Doctor of Law from the Central Party School, Master of Economics from the School of Economic Management of Peking University, former Vice Minister of the Ministry of Culture.

19. Wang Yang—Master of Science degree holder from the Party School of the CPC Central Committee, workshop director of food factory in Suxian Prefecture Anhui Province, engineering graduate with a master's degree in engineering, and vice minister of State Development and Planning Commission.

20. Zhang Gaoli—Economics major in planning and statistics graduate of Xiamen University, Guangdong Maoming Petroleum Company under the Ministry of Petroleum Industry employee, former director of the Ministry of Petroleum Industry Planning Division.

21. Zhang Dejiang—Economics graduate of Kim Il Sung University Korea (DPRK), former vice minister of Civil Affairs Ministry of Civil Affairs.

22. Yu Zhengsheng—Engineering graduate major in automatic control of ballistic missiles of the Missile Engineering Institute, deputy director of Research Institute for Promotion and Application of Electronic Technology in the ministry of Electronics Industry, assistant chief engineer and head

of the Department of Microcomputer Management of the Administration for Computer Industry, minister of construction.

23. Xu Caihou—Electronics Engineering graduate of Harbin Institute of Military Engineering, former director of the Political Department of the 16th Group Army of the Ground Force, and Political Commissar of the Ji'nan Military Area Command.

24. Guo Boxiong—PLA Military Academy graduate, former chief of staff of the 55th Division of the 19th Army of the Ground Force, former commander of the Lannzhou Military Area Command, member of the CPC Central Military Commission.

25. Bo Xilai—Chinese Academy of Social Sciences major in International Journalism graduate, former deputy secretary of the Party Committee of Dalian Economic and Technological Development, former minister of Commerce and leading Party Members' Group of the Ministry of Commerce.

26. He Yong—Engineering graduate major in precision instruments and machinery at the Tianjin University, factory director, chief of the political division of the State No. 238 Factory, member of the Standing Committee of the Party Committee of the Factory, director general of the Office of Science and Industry for National Defense.

27. Ling Jihua—MBA graduate with postgraduate education in political science from Hunan University, director general of the Publicity Department of the CYYLC Central Committee and editor in chief of the Youth League Journal, former deputy director general of the Research Office of the General Office of the CPC Central Committee.

28. Wang Hunin—Fudan University graduate major in international politics, did postgraduate studies in Education, doctor of law degree holder, professor and dean of Fudan University Law School.

It is this committee that submits the economic reports/plans that the National Congress of the Party examines and decides on. The committee directs on a day-to-day basis the entire work of the party of which economic development is primary. The fact that the current president and prime minister, all technocrats in 2011 were members of the committee shows the highest importance China attaches to economics and science. To be president in China you need years in technology and economics. Since the National Congress generally meets once in five years and not in session, the committee is in full-time con trol. The committee in effect directs and formulates the economic strategy of China. The National People's Congress is the highest organ. of state power under the People's congress system. The president and his "deputy" are not full-blooded politicians as in the US. They are in fact technocrats first and foremost.

Out of the twenty-eight members in this list, fourteen are engineers, including the Chinese president and the prime minister at the time. The current present president (an experienced engineer) and now life President and four members are economists, three are qualified in education, one has a journalist background, one has a combined mathematics, economics, and law background, one has an education and law background, one is in history and one in philosophy leaning on Marxism and the last is from humanities and social science.

I decided to put out this list in order to contrast between the US and China on the issue of economic management to show that economic development is a far more serious topic in China than in the US. In chapter 2, I reviewed the very flimsy arrangement—or non-arrangement— the United States has made for its economic management through a Council of Economic Advisers, a handful of (financial) conventional economists, mainly academicians with no business/technological/ scientific experience chosen from those who share the political leaning of the current president's political party and National Economic Council, all under the effective control of the President, who is primarily a politician who appoints them and all supposed to be advising him. The President of the US is US Chief Economist of the US. At the US Treasury, as I showed, there are pretenses that economic management is professional and comprehensive. The economic management of the US varies with changing party politics of changing Presidents. The Treasury Secretary mostly drawn from Wall Street usually has no direct economics or technical skills, even though a Treasury secretary is also supposed to be an economic adviser to the president. A Treasury

Secretary and his assistant secretary on economic matters participate with other secretaries of state as necessary in economic matters with the president and with the director of budget as a member in the US National Economic Council.

These highly financial/Wall Street/political groups and financial-based economic professors contrast with the list I have given of Central Committee in China, not dominated by theoretical *economists* but by experienced professional in all relevant economic fields with the emphasis on science, engineering and economics to pursue scientific balanced economic structure on an ongoing basis overlooking the work of the National Development and Reform Commission charged with economic planning and strategy. The basis of present day Chinese economy is the need for a plan and strategy of all sectors usually by the NDRC underlying the whole economy and the whole future economic system. These future actions are fully studied by the NDRC (and published nationally to get input from the public) before their submission as official plans. Because Westerners are not happy with the very idea of planning, they miss out on understanding how the planning of the structure of the Chinese economy is underlined by economic science. Many Westerners in the context have reasons not only for not understanding the inevitability of NDRC in this basic task to plan the Chinese economy in its present or different form but also for their wishing for the death of the Commission.

There is no way the US can in its leisurely approach to economic strategy expect to achieve a stronger economy than China given the arrangements China has made to plan and scientifically manage its economy. Our US financial/market economists will tell you that economics has nothing to do with science as I pointed out in Chapter 1.

12th Five-Year Plan

China embarked on its 12th Five-Year Plan for 2011 to 2015. The Central Committee met October 15 to 18, 2010 for the plan just as it met October 2005 for the 11th Five-Year Plan. The plan was intended to strengthen the structural balancing of the economy as a continuation of the 11th Five-Year Plan. The plan was geared to further reduce the income disparity between rural and urban, between coastal region and the North and Western outlying areas. The thrust was to further reduce spatial differences in poverty, and to increase wages, and curtail exports. The plan stated that rural modernization will be a major task in China over the plan's period. With the deepening of industrialization and urbanization, it stated that rural modernization should be pursued. It should be evident that there was as a result a fundamental shift that has greatly reduced rural-urban migration as well as reduced itinerant labor. The effectiveness of the Chinese rural balancing strategy is clear. For example, a *Wall Street Journal* of February 5, 2019 titled "In China, Rural Consumers grow faster than the Urbanites" described the result of spatial balancing of the economy, contrast with the US continuing declining and growing abandoned rural areas. The Premier Keqiang presided over the meeting on the compiling of the 13th five-year plan (2016-2020) which is targeted mainly towards outpacing the US economy.

Chinese Study of Western Business Cycles and How to Avoid Economic Cycles in China

China has not had a recession since 1978. I find it difficult to understand why American economists who regard themselves as experts on China have not found out what China is doing that America is not doing that causes America to suffer this chronic economic disease. The conference of December 1, 2003 in China was intended also to study the cyclical characteristics of the world economy. The government report of this study stated that "At present, the descriptions and explanations about various [Western] cycles are not entirely accurate and scientific..." In effect, the Chinese were saying that explanations of economic cycles by American economists who say that economic cycles have financial causes are incorrect just as I said in chapter 1. The Chinese were, therefore, saying that the West does not know the causes of the most serious economic sickness they suffer—recession and depression. The report further ominously stated that understanding of the scientific laws of the world economy "is extremely important to the rapid, sustainable, and healthy development of China's economy." It said:

> It is necessary to regard China's economy and the world economy as a whole to understand and master, comprehensively examine the external conditions of China's economic development, promptly discover the latest tendencies and situations in the world economy, and scientifically foresee the basic tendency of the world economic development. It is necessary to pay attention to the impact of China's economy on the world economy as well as the impact of the world economy on China's economy and master the two-way interactive relationship between the two.

The report said that mastering the operational law of the world economy will enable China *to fulfill pursuing advantages and avoiding damages.* It does not readily occur to many that the Chinese have studied and continue to study the world economy (globalization) and how to take advantage of it. When policy makers in the West make demands on China to meet what they regard as shared global responsibilities, they forget that they are dealing with a country that is angry and silently resentful and seeking advantages. The Silk Road project has a very long origin. Wilson summarized the posi tion in his short history of China and the West as follows:

> "Many of the causes for China's failed state in the early twentieth century [from which it is trying to recover from] had their roots in China's disadvantageous relationship with the West. The fall of China in early 20th century was largely the result of unremitting series of body blows by the West [at the time] directed at crippling the prestige, sovereignty, military power, and economic well-being of the Chinese empire."

Wilson concluded by saying, "This is the historical memory that dominates the national conscience of contemporary Chinese."[74] China is basically seeking to revenge the wrongs of the past and to take advantage of globalization, not to be part of it. America's one-worldism is the opposite posture, which among other things enables China to take strategic economic advantage of the US. China therefore has studied the world economy and the recessions in the West and have devised how to take advantages of the West economic vulnerability. While the US expects China to maintain a code of international good practice in its economic behavior, that is not China's main preoccupation. The truth is that while a country like Iran is belligerent against the US for the humiliation it suffered during the Shah's regime, China is seeking revenge through planned quiet long-term economic domination of the world.

Economic Efficiency

Writing in 1982 in a paper titled, "Money and Banking in the People's Republic of China: Recent Developments", a Chinese economist stated that drastic changes in Chinese developmental objectives and the basic economic structure were taking place. The writer stated that: "The national objectives are no longer high industrialization and socialization at all costs—as Deng wanted—but an increase in economic efficiency and a rise in people's standard of living."

In terms of strategies, the economist said that "China is shifting from a policy of unbalanced growth to a more balanced approach." He said, "In other words, heavy industry no longer receives an overwhelming large share of the state investments, now light industry and agriculture are given their fair share."

The author concluded that under these circumstances, it is inevitable that the role of money and banking would be affected. His statement about the role of money and banking is significant. In the United States, the role of the banks is not determined by the structural change needs of the economy, as I will show in chapters 8 and 9. Banking in China is the lubricant, not the engine. The banks and financial institutions in the United States are a law to themselves under the overall leadership of the Fed. Main Street is an appendage of Wall Street.

In October 2005, the 16th Central Working Committee of the Communist Party examined and approved proposals for the 11th Five-Year Plan (2006–2010). The plan upturned what it called Deng's "getting rich first theory." The plan examined Deng Xiaoping's theory in the 1970s and complained that it was intended to allow some of the people to get rich first. In upturning Deng's ideology, the plan ushered in what it called *common prosperity* intended to bridge the growing gap between the rich and poor and *avoid the polarization of society*. The plan said that this will represent a historic adjustment to the pattern of Chinese five-year plans since China began its market-oriented reforms in 1970. An expert on macroeconomics at Qinghua University at the time said, "It (The plan) shows that the CPC will give special attention to the construction of a balanced market economy." The 11th Five-Year Plan further explained that Deng proposed the principle of allowing some regions and people to get rich first was to be changed. It stated that the idea departed from Chinese *egalitarianism* even though in Deng's time it managed to energize the country. Li Chong'an, an NPC deputy and vice chairman of NPC Law Committee described the 11th Five-Year Plan changes as "a major shift in economic policy from urban development and heavy investment in billion dollar projects to boosting rural and sciencetech investment for sustainable development." He called it "putting more emphasis on economic efficiency."

Dr. Ding Yuanzhu of the MacroEconomic Research Institute of the National Development Reform Commission (NDRC) said while putting emphasis on economic efficiency, that "China will stress social equity by narrowing the gap between the rich and poor." Chinese experts historically recognize that gap between rich and poor is economic inefficiency because in line with my 1974 and 2005 books, the gap creates idle resources in the economy. Great strides have been made in the last few years to create development and industrial growth in Chinese rural areas, greatly curtailing the rural migration that was heavy some years ago. Chinese government had greatly restricted rural migration in the plan that the development will grow into the rural area as part of its balanced economic strategy. The strategy is to maintain, as a basis for economic growth, structural balance in the whole economy as in fig 1.1.

In a World Bank Research Paper, September 7, 2007, Jianum He and Louis Kuijs estimated that rebalancing the Chinese economy as contemplated by the 11th Five-Year Plan will rreduce the share of urban per capita income in China as a percentage of the economy's capita income by 30 percent and reduce Gini coefficient from 0.46 in 2002 to 0.41 in 2034. The 17th National Congress of the Communist Party affirmed the factor proportion principle when it resolved that the party "will improve the distribution system to allow factors of production such as labor, capital, technology, and managerial expertise to have a rightful share according to their respective contribution." I have in chapter 3 talked about the need to tackle the US economic structural imbalance to scientifically tackle its worsening income inequality.

The 11th Five-Year Plan envisaged, in the continuing fine-tuning of the economy, a smaller growth rate of 8 percent in 2006 and 7.5 percent over the five years to 2010 emphasizing the Chinese's continued step back from capital-led growth as in the US. It was also a realization that exports might decline, and there's an attempt to take a more-inward looking balanced stance to boost home consumption. Despite this initial effort to curtail growth, because China was immediately hitting 8 percent and over growth.

Uninformed Westerners continued incorrectly at the time to describe the drop to 7.5 percent in growth as a sign of Chinese economic growing weakness.

In 2006, Mr. Kai, Minister of the State Development and Reform Commission, announced that the Chinese people have benefited from the steady and fast economic development. He stated that the SDRC projected that the newly increased job opportunities could pass 10.5 million for 2006, exceeding the nine million his commission planned at the beginning of the year. Unemployment in China in 2006 was put at 4.3 percent; a figure which China is trying to beat. In 2008, China's unemployment went down to about 4 percent. It crept up only to 4.3 percent in 2009 despite the sharp drop in exports as the world economy went into recession. China's projected 8 percent to 9 percent annual growth at the time over the period was to provide from eight million to nine million new jobs a year. Coupled with retirees, this will equate to twelve million job positions a year. Twenty million young people were expected to enter the market between 2006 and 2010. China's 11th Five-Year Plan's focus, as I earlier described, was on a rebalancing of the country's urban-rural development intended to deal with China's migrant labor and rural unemployment (which I call spatial unemployment instead of structural unemployment as in the US). China's spatial unemployment is the result of the country's 'feel the stone under your feet' experimental legacy by which policy makers like Deng started to develop the country first in the eastern coastal areas. But as China moved into 2010, as I have stated, there were signs that the 11th Five-Year Plan of urban-rural balancing is succeeding. Migrant labor was on the decline. A factory owner in Guangdong, a center of Chinese exports, on March 2010 pointed out that "A lot of workers traditionally come from the poorer regions in the western China, but factories are moving out there." He observed that, "Those workers who used to come here can now find work close to home. I don't think we will see many of them moving back here."

The Chinese government has offered rural people who establish small industrial businesses a three-year tax exemption and given the rural sector increasing industrial tempo. Railway expansion has linked China more closely between urban and non-urban areas.

It is clear that by restructuring and continuous rebalancing of its economy, China is through its history poised to achieve sustainable higher employment and more sustainable high growth. By 2012, according to the Chinese plan, GDP growth had dropped by third quarter to 7.4 percent. In his *Financial Times* article, October 19, 2012, Jamil Andrelini correctly observed that "Something has changed in Beijing where far from panicking and doing everything they could to pumping up the growth rate, China's rulers seemed pretty comfortable with their new sub-8 growth." The reason, he correctly stated, was that there were no layoffs in China and that in fact more than ten million jobs were created in China in the first nine months of 2012. Factories making iPhones in Central China complained of labor shortages. Andrelin concluded the long-term sustainable growth was assured. In a *Financial Times* article dated March 21, 2013 titled "China Employers Adapt to Cope with Labor Pains" the reporter told of labor shortages in China versus unemployment in the United States and Europe because of China's vibrant economy. The recent drop of growth rate just below 7 percent in China is part of the balancing process, not the panic, which the West thinks/wishes.

In the spirit in which the Chinese deliberately dropped their GDP growth from 8 percent in the 11th Five Year Plan to 7.5 percent in order to stop what they called "a capital-led growth" the 12th Five Year Plan sought a planned reduction in GDP growth to the present 6.5 percent. The Chinese President said that in 2015 at not less than 6.5 percent annual growth, the Chinese economy was expected to double by 2020. In the West unfortunately these recent reductions in GDP growth rate had given those who are expecting/wishing for Chinese economic collapse something to cheer.

Indigenizing Chinese Economy and Chinese Attitude to Foreign Investment

The expression *people oriented* development, which comes across regularly in Chinese policy documents, also refers to the need to indigenize the economy. I stated in my 1974 book *Economic Underdevelopment:an Inside View* that a core requirement of sustainable economic development in poor countries is the full participation of indigenous populations in the development process. It is this principle that gradually caused the Chinese to change their attitude to foreign investment dominated by the Soviet Union, so that in 2006, China put measures intended to curb foreign investment just as the West was wanting to gate-crash with more foreign investments into China. On August 8, 2006, the Chinese Ministry of Commerce posted in its Web site a new set of "Regulations on the Acquisition of Domestic Enterprises by Foreign Investors" to take effect on December 8, 2006. The new policy towards cross-border mergers and acquisitions was explained in the 11th Five-Year Plan for utilizing foreign investment published by the National Development and Reform Commission. After stating that the state was now giving priority to quality rather quantity of foreign investments, the NDRC stated that emerging monopolies by foreign-invested enterprises were posing a potential threat to China's economic security and that foreign businesses were harming Chinese enterprises' capacity for independent innovation.

The quantity of foreign investments was referring to capital-intensive investments. Capital-intensive activities will upset China's structural economic balance. Today, there are legal and administrative impediments to foreign mergers and acquisitions in China. The 11th Five-Year Chinese Plan also provided for this control and was almost an outright discouragement of foreign investments in view of the structural harm they inflict to the Chinese economy by adding to the country's structural imbalance.

GE, an early West investor, felt the change. As the change was still in its infancy, Jeffrey Immelt of GE in 2008 predicted that GE annual sales in China would reach $10 billion in 2010. As recently as December 2009 before all this, he praised Beijing's economic stewardship in a speech at West Point where he gushed: "Man these guys are good," and for doing "exactly what they say they will do." By June 2010, his tone has changed. "I really worry about China—I am not sure that in the end they want any of us to win or any of us to be successful." June 2016, EU Chamber joined the US Chamber of Commerce to protest what it called "strong arm tactics and unfair" accusations by Chinese regulators against foreign firms. The US Chamber complained that the way China's competition law has been applied is souring the mood of foreign investors after a series of investigations into firms' activities. Chinese failure to deliver on pledges to open market access for foreign investment is said to trigger a "fresh wave of pessimism" among foreign investors. This is at the bottom of Trump's present fight with the Chinese which started in 2017 and in which some Westerners accuse China of seizing technology from Western foreign companies in China.

In my book on Underdevelopment titled *Economic Under-Development*, I emphasized the importance of indigenization, namely that foreign investment in third world must be indigenized not only to align with the factor proportions of poor host countries but also to to involve full indigenous participation. Indigenizing the economy is at the center of Chinese economic policy-which tends to strengthen, in scientific terms, the use of production factors in proportions of endowed factor proportions, has enormous structural economic consequences because it capitalizes on developing indigenous entrepreneurship to spread the economic wealth base through a balanced macroeconomy. Chinese 2006 indigenization policy has made it so so that foreign companies face hard competition from Chinese indigenous companies as well as the requirement to get foreign technology to adapt to Chinese factor proportions. The Chinese companies operate like ants as they tear down the fortified edifice of the foreign large corporations. Chinese companies quickly learn the technology of the foreign investors and then find a cheaper factor-proportionssubstitute to that technology and attempt to cut the competitive base of the foreigner.

For example as early as in late 2010, the quoted price of a K1-level electric cable manufactured by an American company was for example around 10 million yuan per ton. Immediately the Chinese companies developed a substitute selling at 5 million yuan per ton, but in response the American company, the price dropped to 2.8 yuan per ton. At that price for everyone, the US companies was losing money. There were similar price cutting in the mid-end to high-end power equipment manufactured by early Western investors like GE, Siemens, AREVA, and ABB, the top cream of the West in electrical equipment that dominates the world. But after significant cuts, the prices of foreign equipment in China have sometimes dropped well below the prices set by domestic manufacturers, which means trying to maintain market share but with crumbling profits. The China Electrical Equipment Industry Association asserted that "Chinese innovation in the mid and high-end equipment has ended the price setting privi leges of foreign manufacturers. They now find it difficult to charge unreasonably high prices."

The foreign companies that have succeeded in China have concentrated on the higher end of the market but to which Chinese are rapidly coming into. Others have largely faced export, including through outsourcing arrangements, which largely use Chinese labor-intensive technology. Western press and Western economists falsely give the impression that China is very keen on foreign investment or that foreign investment is what China's economy needs to grow. As China faces difficulty in its plans to dominate other economies, it has had to seek to let in foreign investment, for example under a planned Bilateral

Investment Treaty with US that will enable China actively to invest in the US in exchange for investment from the US. You can be sure China has strategized full for this. It is in this light that one can understand China's WTO membership to take advantage of its ability to turn the technology of foreigners into its own. Foreigners are still crashing into China with its very large and increasingly sophisticated market. Early in 2016, and in 2018, China cut down its growth targets generally to 6.5% to 6%. By the beginning of 2017, it had got growth back to 7% by rebalancing the economy. With this 2018, even though rebalancing was not announced it will be assumed that it will be applied as necessary. China in cutting growth rate to 6 to 6.5% in 2018, announced giving foreign companies to enter more sectors in China without Chinese partners, levelling the competition between foreign and Chinese companies, indicating China's success with its indigenization plan that enabled the Chinese to technically operate on equal basis with foreign investment

Climate Change and China

In his analysis of Chinese factor proportions, in absence of absolute measurements of values, Professor Jialing compared Chinese per capita ownership of some Chinese resources with the world average of these per capita ownerships. Chinese percentages of its per capita ownership of world's average worked as follows: farm-land (42 percent), freshwater (27 percent), forests (20 percent), coal (proven and extractable reserves) (53 percent), petroleum (surplus reserves) (11 percent), natural gas (proven and extractable reserves) (3 percent). Chinese government white papers in china.org.cn states that China's per capita average of energy resources endowment is very low. It stated that China per capita average of coal and hydropower resources endowment is 50 percent of world average, per capita endowment for both oil and gas is only about one-fifteenth of the world average, and arable land endowment is 30 percent of world average.

All forms of renewable energy have lower weight by volume than traditional fossil energy. The use of renewable energy, therefore, enables economic activities to operate at factor proportions that are less capital intensive and, therefore, more closely aligned with China's natural factor proportions. Increased use of renewable energy in China will improve its structural balance of the economy. This is the scientific factor proportions' oriented ecomonic strategy behind China's push into renewable energy.

Professor Jialing pointed the resulting strategic error the country China had so far made in overexploiting coal. He noted, for example, that in 2000, China produced 998 million tons of coal. In the first three years of the 10th Five-Year Plan, although, output of raw coal grew at 15 percent on the average, the demand was not met, which, according to him, gave impetus to mines to undertake predatory mining beyond their capacity and encouraged bad safety mining, which resulted in many mining disasters that made headlines in Western press. He pointed past errors in strategy in the development of traditional high-energy consuming, heavy, and chemical industries that are out of line with Chinese natural factor proportions.

He also criticized, for example, Chinese's fast growing aluminum production, which the country encouraged with preferential electricity tariffs. In 2002, China had 119 aluminum smelters, com pared with 53 in 1995. The country produced 3.38 million tons in 2001 compared with 1.68 million tons in 1995. In 2001, eight of these smelters produced over 100,000 tons, nine produced 50,000 tons to 100,000 tons and the rest below 50,000 tons. That rapid escalation in production, in turn, meant consequent substantial and growing Chinese importation of aluminum oxide. China's aluminum industry had been expanding since the introduction of Deng's market reform and further accelerated since its entry in 2001 into the World Trade Organization. No doubt, much of this feverish growth was caused by the escalating internal demand for aluminum in the country.

In 2002, apparent consumption of aluminum was 4.29 million tons, only second to the United States at 8.45 million tons. Forecast is for this consumption in China to grow to 8.8 Mt/y in 2010 and in 2020, the hungry lion is expected to consume 14.3 Mt/y. Despite the substantial foreign exchange earnings from Chinese growing world dominance in the industry, the professor was in effect saying that the industry was not adding to the country's sustainable economic growth capacity because of its unsuitable factor proportions. The adjustment the country is making to increasingly refine its structural economic balance can be seen as emphasis in the 11th Five-Year Plan that started in 2006 away from size, scale—what the Chinese call *high* industry to *quality* activities that provides continuing employment and reduces inequality by de-emphasizing on such heavy energy intensive industry. In 2012, China's demand for steel haddropped. China's demand, which rose 15 percent over the past decade slowed to 4 percent in 2012. As the *Financial Times* reporter Leslie Hook, reported on March 9, 2012, that Nicholas Zhu, a Chinese with ANZ Beijing commented "We are seeing a change of China's growth paradigm as top leaders shift toward greener development." That means de-emphasizing heavy energy intensive industrial activities to accord with Chinese factor proportions

It is clear that apart from environmental and climate change considerations, a major reason the Chinese have for focusing on renewable energy strategy is to restructure their economy, improve its balanced structural economic position in order to further power the already frighteningly powerful Chinese economic engine. This is quietly mentioned in the country's publication titled "China's National Climate Change Program" 2007. Under a section titled "Restructuring the Economy, Promoting Technology Advancement and Improving Energy Efficiency" the publication said:

> Beginning from the late 1980s, the government of China paid more and more attention to the change of economic growth pattern and restructuring of the economy, and integrated the reduction of energy and other resources consumption, the promotion of clean production...The industrial structure has been significantly improved... The breakdown of GDP across the primary, secondary, and tertiary in 1990 is 26.9; 41.3; 31.8 while in 2005, it is 12.6; 47.5; 39.9. The report stated that while the secondary industry has grown slightly, its internal composition has been changed significantly. The proportion of high value-added products has increased due to rapid development in machinery, information technology, and electronic sectors.

Today, the Chinese do not dominate in capital industries because they are not in line with Chinese factor proportions. What the Westerners regard as the Chinese's ability to copy Western manufacturing processes is their ability to adapt Western capital-intensive technologies to Chinese factor proportions which enables the Chinese to maintain a 10-30 percent cost advantage over Western competition in capital goods. The 12th Five-Year China emphasized on reducing material input in production, including reduction in energy consumption of industrial processes. The American will call this top-down management of the economy. US does not have this but loses the economic consequences and competitiveness China has.

Today, in fulfillment of its renewable energy strategy, for example, China is now the world's largest manufacturer of solar panel and wind turbines. From 145,000 MW of hydro, China by 2010, is at 190,000 MW and targeted by 2015, to reach 325,000 MW and 40 GW by 2020. The country expects a six-fold increase in nuclear energy to at least 60 GWE by 2020 and further three to four increase to 120–160 GWE by 2030. A *New York Times* article on July 14, 2009 titled "China Builds High Wall to Guard Energy Industry" captured the current world renewable energy situation by China calling renewable energy a strategic industry, by which China has been trying hard to make sure that its companies dominate globally. China, the article said, is shielding its clean energy sector from foreign companies, while it grows to a point where it is already overtaking the world. In 2018 alone, China added 44GW of solar photovolaic PV and 21GW of wind capacity accounting for half of the world's additions for both technologies and double the capacity of new coal plants it built. Chinese renewable fleet generates enough electricity today to power Germany, the world's fourth largest economy. I will say that the economic structural re-balancing which China is making by its new emphasis on renewable energy is by far more potentially threatening because it makes the whole Chines economic structure more globally competitive and adds to China's long-term structural economic balance and power. At the same time, Chinese control of the renewable energy industry gives it a commanding position (which it has already achieved) to export renewable energy equipment to the United States and other countries. Between 2008 and 2013, China solar panel industry dropped world panel prices by 80%. One thing the Chinese learnt in becoming a manufacturing superpower is that mass-producing a standardized product with full-supply chain support would result in economies of scale and rapid cost reductions. Call this top-down management of the economy which is absent in the US. It is clear from my earlier reference to Chinese Professor Jailing publications that as far back as 2000, the Chinese had realized that replacing coal with renewable energy would restructure and rebalance the economic structure of China and through a rebalanced factor proportions would make the Chinese economy even more competitive and productive. So apart from the reduction of pollution and saving in energy and their dominating the international renewable energy market the Chinese stand to make their economy even more competitive and powerful. The Chinese economy therefore gains from being more structurally balanced from increased renewable energy. That is why they quickly signed the agreement on climate change in 2015.

Do Americans Understand The Economic Revolution Taking Place in China?

There is a frightening ignorance among the US economists and policy makers about China's economy, which has prevented Americans from copying/adapting what they can from China's vast economic success. The reasons are scientific, political, and psychological.

The scientific reason is simple. If Americans don't know that there is a science to economics, they are not likely to want to study Chinese economy and the strategy behind it. They are, therefore, likely to regard any differences they come across in economic strategy in China as strange and bizarre, as we will see in some of the Western comments on China in this chapter.

Americans tend to twist issues on Chinese economy to suit their political needs. The first is the general shared reasoning in the US that the Chinese are winning because they always play foul. Americans have claimed, for example, that its deteriorating trade balance with China is because China's currency is undervalued and manipulated. There was a time when American government and political leaders made sure that any time they meet Chinese leaders this Today no one makes this accusation except that it came up subtly when Trump took up China on trade and an agreement will contain for China to make its foreign exchange transactions available. The claims about Chinese exchange currency being manipulated have been muted in recent years. In July 2005, China revalued the yuan up by 2.1 percent to 8.11 yuan per dollar. The United States ran a trade deficit of $90 billion with China. In the first half of 2008 when the yuan neared its peak value against the dollar, the US trade deficit instead exceeded $115 billion. By the end of 2008, the deficit was now $297 billion. Month by month in 2009 as America was in recession, the trade deficit in February alone was $14.2 billion to increase to $15.6 billion in March. By 2018 US trade deficit with China had climbed to $419 billion.

In a *Tribune* article on January 15, 2005, Keith Bradshaw foresaw the truth when he said, "Many Chinese and foreign exec utives in China say that a revaluation of yuan is unlikely to be a silver bullet for dealing with US deficit." He stated that, "Costs in here (in China) are so low that a revaluation is unlikely to narrow the deficit appreciably and might even increase it." By the end of 2012 the deficit had climbed to $315 billion as the dollar was equal to an appreciation of yuan of 6.21349571. Americans' claim that China is winning because of low wages. Our discussions in earlier chapters about the pursuit of productivity in the US show that productivity this is primarily geared to keeping US wages low. We have just discussed in this chapter local Chinese enormous ingenuity in finding cheaper substitutes to costly Western technology with the same in wages. So it is not just a matter of wages but the inability of America to sort out its over capital-intensive uncompetitiveness of technology as we discussed in earlier chapters.

In this chapter, we saw how a deliberate avoidance of scale and finding "cheaper" substitutes have helped China to build factories and many kinds of equipment at a fraction of the cost of the foreign companies that invest in China.

The claim that wages are kept deliberately low in China is false. The year 2010 was one in which some high profile strikes took place in China, which the Chinese governments either did not intervene or called on employers to raise wages and improve training. The UK *Guardian* reported the position June17, 2010 in an article titled 'Strikes in China Signal End to Era of Low-cost Labor and Cheap Exports." The *People's Daily*, the mouthpiece of the ruling party, warned that the country's wage model was facing a turning point, a day after the Chinese premier Wen Jiabao said that a new generation of migrant workers should be given improved conditions. The Chinese Communists have not forgotten that it was the trade union's Solidarity movement in Poland that overthrew a communist government in Poland. The year 2014 saw a two-week strike by thousands of workers in a company Yen Yuen Indusrial Holdings, a key shoe manufacturing company in Dongguan in the centre of China's export manufacturing zone. The Chinese authorities did not intervene. There are Americans who unfortunately claim that America's long-term strength is in high technology exports to China. This claim is evidenced by an article by VivekWadhawa, in *Foreign Affairs*, titled "The End of Chinese Manufacturing and Re-birth of US Industry," in which he expected Chinese manufacturing to bubble as labor and other Chinese contradictions come to the fore. He was confident that the United States would take advantage of a new set of technologies that were advancing at an what he thought was an "exponential rate and converging to overwhelm the Chinese industry."[77] Similarly, in another article in *Foreign Affairs* May/June 2016 by Professor Daniel Brooks and Daniel Wohlforth, they attempted to show that China's GDP would never catch up with that of the US. They stated that, according to the World Bank data on international payments for intellectual property, the US boasted at the time in 2013 $128 billion in receipts, more than the nearest competitor Japan, with China's less than $1billion. They stated that in 2012, there were nearly 14,000 patents output in the US to about 2000 in China. They stated that since then there had been114 Nobel Prize winners based in the US in physics, chemistry, medicine compared to two in China. They indicated that new statistics about has been called "inclusive wealth" have emerged, attempting, to calculate a country's wealth: (a) manufactured capital (infrastructure, buildings, machines/equipments etc, (b)human capital (skills, education, health) and (c)natural capital (sub-soil, ecosystem etc.). They sought to establish to establishthat the valuation of inclusive wealth was $144 trillion for the US and $32 trillion for China. They argued that the problem is that GDP is like a measure of the flow of goods and services while inclusive wealth measured actual stock which they argued was more important than GDP. However, they were caught in a knot because while the US has more natural resources /inclusive wealth than China, yet China was producing more than the US. The US was not making efficient use of its patents, Nobel Prizes, infrastuctures etc. If the two countries were for sale there can be no comparison between their different sale prices with US worth far more than China.

In May 2006, China announced a plan to become an "innovative country" by 2020 and a global scientific power by 2050. China has planned to double its R&D spending as a percentage of GDP by 2020. But little does the average American know that China had already caught up with the US in so-called high-tech industries and innovation.

The following, however, are the major 'high-tech' industries China planned to undertake: integrated circuits and software, new generation networks for the next-generation internet, national digital TV, advanced computing, biomedicine, civil airplanes, turbines, helicopters and advance aero engines, new satellite systems for thrust augmented carrier rockets, robotics, earth observation and navigation positioning, and new materials for high performance engines. These initiatives are being continued and expanded in the current Chinese 12th Five-Year Plan.

As the Chinese economy and those of some East Asian countries soar, Western policy makers now increasingly complain about large trade deficits with China. It is forecast that deficits in industrialized countries will double from 2014 as EU economic troubles confirm. Now, some people in the US and the West want to make out that correcting international imbalances is a moral obligation dictated by the need to play "accord ing to the rules." Imbalances arose because present debtors like the United States pushed international trade over many years initially with heavily weighted advantages but have finally lost these advantages. Martin Wolf, the well-known *Financial Times* commentator, championed this issue in an article on December 9, 2009 titled "Why China's Exchange Rate Policy is a *Common* Concern." He said that for external deficit countries, the concern is how to lower fiscal deficits without tipping their economies into recession." According to him, "That will be impossible unless they are either able to get their private sectors spending and borrowing as before, or they enjoy rapid expansion in net exports." He continued: "Of the two, the latter is the safer route to health. But that will in turn only happen if the surplus countries expand demand faster than potential output." He concluded that China is the most important player in this game. In other words, he was looking to China to help sort out the world imbalance he complained about!

Martin Wolf is a financial analyst. He is not a structural economist. He and many globalists like him are now making it that China should bail out the US and other debtor countries by producing less and getting Americans to reduce their spend-spend habits. Wolf was writing on behalf of the Western countries, but claimed the problem is of *common* concern.

The former Treasury Secretary Timothy Geithner in 2012 hinted at the desirability of setting targets of surpluses and deficits as percentage of GDP for countries. Angela Merkel, the German Chancellor, a country also with trade surpluses at the time in a *Financial Times* interview on November 9, 2010 titled: "The True Believer" pointed out that "Global imbalances are not just influenced by exchange rates but are also a function of competitiveness." Merkel stated that the competitiveness of countries depends on many more issues than weighing up imports against exports.

She stated that setting up targets for all countries for surpluses and deficits as a percent of GDP was in the opinion of senior German government officials "rubbish" with no"scientific or academic basis." The best advice Mr. Wolf should have given is for countries like the United States and those from Europe to restructure their unbalanced economies so as to improve competitiveness. Wolf in his article also referred us to a 2009 self-serving report by the European Chamber of Commerce titled "Overcapacity in China." The report concluded that China's external surpluses have been a by-product of misguided policy. It claimed that the capital was priced cheaply in China in the 2000s via cheap credit and low taxes on corporate profit, while foreign exchange was deliberately kept too expensive by currency interventions. In the process, according to the report, income was transferred from households to industry. The result was an industry with little job creation. The Chamber claimed that industry in China fell to an extremely low share of GDP, while corporate investments, savings, and current account surplus soared. From what I have earlier said that that the Chinese factor-proportions approach did not provide for a capital-intensive sector, it is clear that the European Chamber of Commerce report was incorrect. Chinese export success is not the result of a capital-intensive sector.

Wolf ended with a fear of possible global depression if indebted countries slashed spending relative to income, while the trading partners determined to sustain their excess capacity over income and exporting the difference. He suggested that it is necessary to pay attention to the impact of China's economy on the world as well as the impact of China's economy, and master the two-way interactive relationship between the two. Wolf did not do his homework. It had not occurred to Wolf that a stable international position will be better achieved if all countries sorted their structural macroeconomic ills rather than playing international financial games. Wolf should know that China's intention is not to cooperate but to master the world economy. The China Conference December 1, 2003 which I referred to earlier, made it clear that the Chinese meant to discover "the latest" and situation in the world economy and *scientifically* force the basic tendency of the world economic development. China wants eventually to master the world.

Wolf wanted to frighten everyone about catching a world recession flu as otherwise, according to him, protectionism will kick in. In structural economics, protectionism is a welcome development because that will allow each country the opportunity to restructure its economy based its factor proportions. It is this idea that the world is one of shared economy that has led economists to formulate false trade theories and globalization, as we will see in later chapters which has brought the present international economic chaos, as I will show in the next few chapters.

A psychological reason why Americans don't want to learn from China is pride. I have described American economic ignorance and pride in chapter 2. As Americans, we feel that we know better than the Chinese because we believe we are still in front technically and that while we have our ups and downs we still believe we are still going to make it and stay in front. We, after all, taught the Chinese the game, and we believe that they are still learning from us. In a *Financial Times* article December 2009 titled "Free Market Ideals Survive the Crunch," Alan Beattie and Geoff Dyer got close to fully admitting that the West made a mess of itself. They referred to a Chinese official who said, following the 2008–2009 recession and collapse of financial markets in the West that, "We used to see the United States as our teacher, but now we realize that our teacher keeps making mistakes, and we have decided to quit the class." The point Beattie and Dyer were making was that, despite the fact that the student stopped coming to classes, he still has a lot to learn. On the whole I think that most Americans omit what makes the Chinese economy to stand out. In her *NY Times* article of March 6,2019 titled "We don't Need State Economic Planning" Veronique de Rugy stated that the difference between the US and China in economic planning is that China's has an authoritian top-bottom planning and control of their economy and that US has a free trade, competitive markets, reasonable regulations and the rule of law. She showed ignorance of the Chinese when she stated that "Central planning is antithetical to innovation, as is already visible in China." She failed to mention what I have in this book regarded as the most important for rapid economic development: namely structurally balanced economy that ensures the full use of resources based on the adoption of the requisite factor proportions with the avoidance of recessions as the Chinese have. She also had no basis to claim, contrary to the whole purpose of this book, that US economy is competitive. With the mental approach of Veronique de Rugy, Americans are being told regretfully that they have nothing to learn from Chinese present success.

In his 2009 book titled, *The Cost of Capitalism*, Robert Barbera enthused that over the past twenty years, capital markets have been the main force driving the globalization of the world economy. He meant American-led capital markets. He claimed:

> "Those against globalization can point to the 2008–2009 global recession as a powerful example of what can go wrong. Nevertheless, the economic facts of global life have accumulated on the ground over the past twenty-five years cannot be ignored. Nearly one billion people in Asia

escaped abject poverty as free-flowing capital financed
development on the scale that dwarfed the World Bank
or aid agencies could have imagined a few decades ago."

He then turned specifically to China to show it was the West that
made China what it is today. He said that "China is the foster child for
the benefits of globalization." According to him, nearly half a billion
Chinese citizens joined the twenty-first century after living in near
feudal circumstances during the reign of Mao. He told us to:

> "Think about infant mortality rates in the many poverty-
> ridden counties of Africa: China's economic circumstances
> were comparable when reforms began in 1979. The four
> hundred million Chinese who escaped abject poverty left
> behind a world of rampant death and disease. The coun-
> try's willingness to link its economy to global trade and
> capital flows, of course, means that its economy now sags
> when recession grips the developed world. But the unprec-
> edented progress of the past twenty-five years should be
> sufficient evidence for the Chinese that the boom and bust
> cycle is worth the ride."

That is sentimental nonsense. Here is ignorance and pride. Barbara
and many people like him in the United States, including the policy
makers, truly believe that China owes its twenty-five years of Chinese
economic success to the West and Western capital and investment. We
are used to children who overtook their parents in life.

There are many Americans who simply think that the Chinese
are simply lucky. They think that the Chinese succeed despite their
incompetence and corruption. International economics professor
of the prestigious university Yale, Gustav Ranis, as early as 2007
characterized China's economy as a capitalist economy suffering a
kind of *Dutch Disease*, a phenomenon that, according to him, happens
"when rapid growth in export can lead to pockets of excessive wealth,
weakening of other industries, and public discontent." China's economic
version, according to him, centers around labor-intensive exports
and massive influx of foreign capital combined with speculation.

According to him, there is warp decision-making at all levels of the Chinese government. Huge amounts of foreign capital, in the presence of a fixed and undervalued exchange rate, he said, encourage "rent-seeking, corruption, and rural unrest." He added that a massive buildup of reserves eliminates incentives to change policy, as Chinese politicians hesitate to anger powerful special interest. Like many people in the United States, Professor Ranis expected the Chinese economy to come crashing down any time as political and social tensions arising from communist control and lack of democracy spread.

Some Americans' problem with China is basically ideological. If you believe that capitalism and democracy are the best thing that has happened to mankind, you are not likely to be searching Chinese literature to find out how they are managing their economy because China is not a democracy. Most of us in the United States have been taught that the most important dividend of democracy is economic growth. Indeed many Americans believe that democracy and free enterprise and market are preconditions for rapid economic development. The failure of the Soviet Union is their best proof that communism or socialism cannot exist together with a successful economy. Many Americans believe that the whole Chinese structure will ultimately crash as ordinary Chinese seek to get democracy. But as Martin Jacques has said, in his book, *When China Rules the World*, "—there is little demand for "democracy" from within China."[78] When people see their standard of living going up and pride in their country rising as outsiders bow to their country's successes, ordinary Chinese are not exactly seek ing for a change.

I have access to two of the most recent Western organized sponsored opinion polls in China. In a 2011 poll by Professor Tony Saich, Professor and Director of the Ash Center for Democratic Governance and Innovation at the Kennedy School of Government, the approval for the Peking government was 96 percent. In 2013, in a major national face-to-face survey published in the *US Political Research Journal*, an extremely high level of public satisfaction was found of about 8 on a 10 scale.

A substantial number of Americans do not like the extent of government involvement in economic planning and management as it is done in China. Even among Democrats in the United States, who are supposed to be the champions of the underprivileged, there is a division about the role of government in economic governance. In a speech June 2016, Obama had to boast, as proof of less government during his tenure and claimed that his governance had the lowest number of civil service servants than at any time recently.

The US economy, as we have seen, is a three structure economy not a unified economy. As a result, it is structurally divided between the haves and the have-nots with a dwindling middle class. Democrats tend to lean towards the have-nots and believe it is the job of government to intervene and bridge the economic gap that gets wider by the day. Republicans basically believe that people make their own bed and that if you are poor while it may or may not be your fault, it is the rich who can help you by investing their money and you should preferably get up and sort yourself out and that there should be no government *hand-outs,* after all, America is a land of opportunity. In a growing technology-dominated world, top-level planning and strategy is a need. There is nothing scientific or structural economics about each movement.

Americans, who oppose major government's role in the economy also do so not only on ideological grounds but also for self- interest: free market capitalism. In his book I earlier referred to, Robert Barbera—he was a Chief Economist of a Wall Street Investment firm now at John Hopkins—called government investment projects "socialized investment." He argued that when companies got it wrong, they pulled out or went bankrupt. But government projects, in his view, face no discipline and are self-perpetuating.

He claimed that "socialized investment" was the strategy of the former Soviet Union and, therefore, was bound to fail in the United States. It is no point arguing with people like Barbera, who are out to protect their Wall Street interests, and only analyze things on the basis of finance and ideology. Yet for people like him, they still want the government to come in when private interests grind the economy to a crisis. He still claimed in his book that government rescue operations are an inescapable cost of capitalism. China for him is, therefore, an anathema.

Economic Development—China's Highest Priority

The 17th National Congress of the Communist Party resolved to take *economic development* as central task of the party, making all other works subordinate to serve this central task. The National Congress Party in China also decided that from October 2007, the Scientific Outlook on Development should be inscribed into the Party's Constitution. The unwillingness of the Chinese to give anything else any higher priority than their own economic development is there to be seen by everyone.

In David Pilling's article in the *Financial Times* in January 2010, titled "China Will Not Be the World's Deputy Sheriff," Pilling correctly concluded that China is not interested in working with the United States in the US self-appointed position as the world's sheriff. There is a wide difference between the United States and China where their priorities are.

Zou Hong, the director of the Institute of European Studies at the Chinese Academy of Social Science, said, "There will for a long time be a big gap between outside expectations [that China will exert more of its influence in world affairs] and China's ability." She says, "China is big, but it is poor. Its preoccupations will still be internal." China however is just beginning to dominate the world on its own terms: a Chinese rival of the World Bank and turning its previous investments in the UN Treasury to spread its investments worldwide.

Obama put a huge store in a joint document signed in November 2009 by the two countries during his visit to China, which laid out a new era of shared responsibility in which the two countries will combine to solve the world's biggest problems. The document received a lukewarm and polite reception from the Chinese. As David Pilling correctly states China's priority is economic growth, because that is how it will recapture its lost glory. China initially preferred to keep a low international political profile and get on with the hard work of building its economy. Their leaders never missed, until recently, the opportunity even recently to tell the world that China is a poor country. This is why what is going on in that country is so scary. The Chinese believed initially that they are still a long way from their economic goal.

Efforts by Obama to wind up this international cooperation with the new Chinese leaders in 2013 did not result in any significant international cooperation.

The sharp contrasts between China and the United States in economic management is clear. First, the United States has no economic planning/science in a world that is getting more technologically complex. In chapter 2, I labeled economic management in the United States as short-termist. Chinese economic management is long-term and broken into five year planning tranches. Second, the United States has no central economic strategy unlike the Chinese, which has a central economic strategy of maintaining a balanced economic structure. All US government economists are merely advisory to a president whose only quality is that he is a "successful" politician. Economic planning in China is a constitutional institution, not directly responsible to the president. The Chinese presidents, as I have shown, are professionals and members of the planning Central Committee of China. Third, economic management in China is concerned with the real economy dominated by scientific thinking. The US *economic* management is an ideology (capitalism) based on financial management concerned mainly with fiscal policy and monetary policy and the financial market run by the Fed that regards the financial market as key to economics, as I will discuss in fuller detail in chapters 8 and 9. I can put this another way by saying that while the focus of economic management in China is the macroeconomic structure, *economic* management in the United States is not aware that there is a US macroeconomic structure that needs study and analysis. The macroeconomic theory in the United States is purely financial market intellectual theorizing. Fourth, the government in China within a common political agenda plays a dominant role in continuing economic reconstruction and rebalancing of the Chinese economic structure. The very high approval ratings that the ordinary Chinese give to their country's economic performance indicates that the environment is conducive to the Chinese government taking a commanding lead in economic management.

The 17th National Congress documents clearly stated that the Communist Party of China "unwaveringly" consolidates and develops the public sector of the economy and unswervingly encourages, supports, and guides the growth/development of the non-public sector." It works to *balance urban and rural development, development among regions, economic and social development—adjusting domestic development— and transform the economic structure.* Spatial balancing is part of structural balancing. Americans don't in general want their government to play a dominant role in the economy. It is a legacy of the Chicago School in Economics that incorrectly insists that there is no need for government to do anything about the economy and that if it did it will do it badly.

The care with which the 11th Five-Year Plan was prepared is worth being described and to show official attempts to involve ordinary Chinese citizens in the planning process. The preparation for the plan took two years. The guidelines were first introduced in 2003 and went through many rounds of development involving various in-depth investigations, feasibility studies, drafting, and expert consulting. A task force, comprised of professionals from various fields was involved in drafting the document. A legion of experts from the central government and local governments were involved. The Transparency Requirement of the Plan required that the general public be consulted at every stage of the development process. Public opinion was sought through the media over a period of sixty days. For the 11th Five-Year plan, over five thousand people submitted ideas and suggestions. In October 2005, the Fifth Session of the Sixteenth CPC Central Committee discussed and passed as "The Proposals for Working on the 11th Five-Year Guidelines for National Economic and Social Development." The State Council finally submitted the 11th Five-Year plan to the fourth session of the 10th National People's Congress for approval. The plan had 48 chapters in 14 articles.

The same wide involvement of Chinese was ensured in embarking with regard to the 12th Five-Year Plan for 2011 to 2015. In order to strengthen the industrial sector, the 12th Five-Year Chinese Plan was intended to further develop know-how intensive and resource-efficient strategic industries. These are planned to add value of 8 percent GDP by 2015 and 15 percent by 2015. These are revealingly the kind of industries: low mate rial/high labor activities. In my 2005 book, *The Science of Economic Development and Growth*, I pointed out that the resource-efficient IT industries were responsible for creating the high growth in the US New Economy in the 1990s. Wall Street has since helped to make them capital-intensive out of step with US factor proportions The Chinese are using these know-how intensive, resource-efficient industries to add further structural balancing to their economy.

As the draft plan was finished, Zhang Ping, Chinese Director of National Directorate and Reform Commission (a prominent division in the State Council of the People's Republic of China) in China, November 2, 2010, publicized the 12th Plan to the Chinese. In an advert, he said, "To fully reflect the will of the people in the 12th Five-Year Plan, advice and suggestions are welcome over the following two weeks." He invited the Chinese to submit memorandum on any aspect of the draft 12th Five-Year Plan.

Chinese Economy Has Already Overtaken the US Economy

China is an economic laboratory. By the time Americans find this out, it may be too late. The IMF in 2011 dropped a bomb in 2012, and no one in America noticed or said anything. For the first time in its history, this international organization set a date when the *Age of America* will end, as Brett Arends of *MarketWatch* called it. The forecast is realistic because it is based on purchasing power basis not the exchange rate basis. Figure 4.1 is the IMF official 2011 forecast of the change of baton as the largest economy in the world from the United States to China by 2016, which is sooner than 2025, which most forecasts a decade ago predicted. The country continues to expand its position economically, taking world market share from Western countries.

Share of World GDP (Purchasing Power Party)

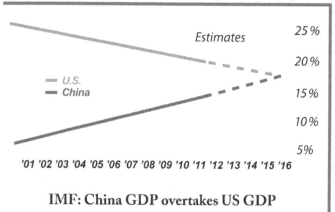

IMF: China GDP overtakes US GDP

Fig.4.1

According to this forecast, Obama will be the last president to preside over the US as the largest world economy on purchasing power parity basis. Looking beyond exchange rates and looking at purchasing power parity, the Chinese economy will expand from $11.2 billion in 2011 to $19 trillion in 2016, while the US whose purchasing power was three times that of China in 2001 will by 2016 rise only to $18.8 trillion in 2016. The simple argument in support of the use of purchasing power parity is that prices of materials are not the same in the world.

A World Bank sponsored report predicted that the Chinese economy will overtake that of the US in 2014 on PPP basis with the IMF expecting China's economy to have grown by 24 percent between 2011 and 2014, while US economy was expected to have to have expanded by only 7.6%. On the basis of real GDP purchasing power parity the Chinese economy overtook that of the US in 2014. The China National Bureau of Statistics, which took part in these studies, surprisingly denied the claim and stated that the IMF report did not reflect the true conditions in the Chinese economy. What this portends at the time is a country, China, that is not yet where it wants to be economically and does wish to make the sacrifices and undertake obligations which being the largest economy can entail. On the other hand on a (financial) market exchange basis, the US is still the world's largest economy. As China's economy gathers strength, its Silk Road programme is an attempt to take on the world as we will review later

The forecasts about America versus China unfortunately give the incorrect impression that when Chinese economy overtakes that of the United States, the United States will now occupy the second place. This is not necessarily true. One thing I have shown in the structural analysis of the United States is that its economy structure is *progressively* getting worse and that its long-term growth rate trend—taking account the ups and downs that will occur as its economic cycles go up and down—is going south. The prospects, as things are presently, are that America might eventually go down to as low as third or fourth place as this century moves on unless something urgent to reconstruct the US economy is done and unless the country admits to its people that it has a problem.

Purchase power parity economics whose principal foundation is that raw materials' price is different in different countries is an attempt to seek a scientific non-financial value of factors of production. It is a neat economic scientific evaluation and confers that the Chinese economy on a scientific valuation is presently the largest in the world.

It is therefore no comfort to America in its claim that it is currently the largest economy in the world on the basis of financial analysis and that it will take China's economy several years before it overtakes that of the US. US current + - 3% growth is not a match for China's 6% if the two economies are in a race.

It is necessary to conclude this chapter to demonstrate the extent which those experts in the West don't know about China, this time Western financial institutions and press. Western financial institutions 2015/2016 forecast the imminent collapse or landing of the Chinese economy.(There is currently one such forecast in 2018/19 that seemed more specifically linked with a slowing global economy). The 2015/16 Western financial institutions'assessment of the Chinese economy in some detail is intended to highlight the basic difference between the economic management in the West (strongly based in the US), and in China. It can be said here, as will be confirmed later by statements by Chinese Central Bank Governors that finance in the West is the engine whereas in China, finance is a lubricant for the engine. Lacking knowledge of this difference, these institutions were sure that the Chinese economy will collapse. The *Economist* of May 7th, 2016 stated: "it is not a question of when or not if real trouble will hit China." It claimed that China required more and more credit to generate less and less growth. Deutsche Global Market Research of June 2016 stated that the cost in terms of unproductive credit growth used for driving up asset prices swelled in China in 2015 with graphs intended to that show that to produce 1% of real growth in China required a debt of $470 billion while additional Social financing of $230 billion (total $600 billion) was required to produce 1% in real growth compared to $370 billion of unproductive credit in the US. The Deutsche Research concluded that Chinese bubble was going to be a larger debt bubble than the US sub-prime bubble of 2009. The *Asia Pacific* Editor Everette Rosenfeld pointed out the fact of what Western financiers see as "easy stimulus money" referring to Chinese households and loss-making companies which he regarded as providing less and less actual stimulus, leading him to conclude that such stimulus was central to a continuing drop in economic growth as the economy continued, according to him, on its way to collapse. Mr. Everette Rosentall of the IMF estimated that potential losses from bad debt in China's corporae sector was equivalent to 7% of China's GDP. Money was said to be flowing from what was described as "opaque channels" outside the regulated banking system, leaving China's economy vulnerable. IMF accused China of "putting a higher priotrity on hitting a growth target than on the quality of the economic output' which it claimed led to the slow-down in the Chinese economy. This in turn, IMF said, caused serious problems for Chinese corporate cash flows and balance sheets, leading to an increase in what a commentator called "zombie firms" in China. It was noted that rising Chinese bond and money-market yields which had touched their highest yields were hunting Western investors with memories of past crises in the US, Japan and East Asia crisis of the 1990s. Some people described the Chinese financial industry as "politics first and profits second" and that political directives were intended primarily to maintain social stability as China's debt soared from 150% to 260% in a decade. It was claimed that when it comes to pumping money into the financial system, China made the Federal Reserve Board and the European Central Bank look almost lackadaisical. China is said to have 70% more money slushing around its economy than the United States. The Bank of International Settlement described China's debt position as "risky trnity": rising leverage ratio, declining productivity and narrowing policy flexibility. Joseph DiStefano of the Bank summarized the position that "The global economic boom from China, the world's only major growth engine since the crash of 2008 in the West is rapidly diminishing and will soon end." Paul Krugman in a *New York Times* opinion of January 8th 2016 titled "When China Stumbles" said that" It has been obvious for a while that China's economy is in trouble. The basic problem," according to the professor, "is that China's economic model involves very high savings and low consumption." It was claimed that China had produced such high amounts of steel, iron and hosts other structural goods that it not know what to do with, amassing additional unprecedented levels of over-capacity, thus making what was estimated as a staggering $2-3 trillion in problem loans, according to Richard Vague in *Democracy Jourrnal 2015*. It was stated that the majority of the debts were owed by state-owned enterprises and property developers The totality of the accusations was the heavy public borrowing for development in urban development and for developing rural areas and new towns, which were described as wasteful and unnecessary

What China was doing that baffled Western financial institutions was it was re-balancing its economy when growth rate slowed by investments needed in the urban sector, in rural areas new towns etc to rebalance the economy. By 2017, the Chinese economy did not collapse as thought in the West. Growth rate climbed up to 7%. Moody which in April 2016 predicted a rapid growth in overall leveraging and growth in shadow banking and had downgraded Chinese sovereign debt the first since 1989 by early 2017, changed from the down-grading to upgrade and now descibed its earlier downgrading as "a warning of past problems rather than a prediction of future risks."

Part 2

US Technical Misunderstandings about International Trade And Globalization

Chapter 5

US Conventional Economic Trade Theories Are False

Allow me to make as many assumptions as I want, and I will prove anything for you.

The most important question from a economic science point of view is: What is the effect of international trade on the US economic factor usage structure? What is the effect of international trade on the US technical economic structure? The intention of this chapter is to show that international trade (and globalization) adversely affect the structural balance of the US. This chapter will, in the process, lay bare the false intellectual and economic theories that have been used to convince and bully governments and politicians in the United States to make free trade a cornerstone of America's economic and foreign policy. I will review in the next chapter the international trade history of the United States. I will show that from early times, the US international trade was discussed as part of US integrated geo-political foreign strategy by early pioneers of the country. This era was followed by a new era, after World War II, when international trade was now seen as a means for the United States to dominate the world through hegemonic diplomacy after—America's World War II victory. By the 1970s and the 1980s, the American advantage in international trade had largely disappeared as the American trade deficit, which first started in 1958, continued to widen as the country's structural imbalance increased with trade and globalization. As American fortunes in international trade dimmed, anti-trade sentiments in the United States grew. Proponents of free trade began to feel the increasing anti-trade sentiment in the US and became convinced that trade prospects in the United States were in danger. So they decided, in desperation, to mount intellectual and academic podium to talk down to the rest of us.

Ricardo's Comparative Advantage of Trade

They dusted off a late eighteenth/early nineteenth century economic treatise by David Ricardo (1772–1823) known as *The Principle of Comparative Advantage*. The theory was a blanket endorsement of free trade as a necessary instrument of economic development for all countries. Since the 1980s, the US economic policy makers and academic theorists have been pushing free trade because they tell us that Ricardo said it was the way to go.

Paul Krugman, in a paper in 1987, declared, "If there were an Economist's Creed, it would surely contain the affirmation, 'I believe in the Principle of Comparative Advantage' and 'I believe in free trade'."[79] The US government drew our attention to its policy to re-affirm and pursue free trade in 2005 when the Economic Report to the President W. Bush declared:

> "The Administration's pursuit of trade liberalization is based upon a long history of intellectual support for free trade. Modern trade theory begins with the nineteenth century's David Ricardo. Ricardo's central insight—his elegant model of comparative advantage—is the starting point from which to explain the gains from trade."

Conventional trade economists are very sure of the superiority of their free trade theory. Alan Greenspan, for example, described those who do not support free trade as *economically uninformed* in his book *The Age of Turbulence*.

Professors Krugman and Obstefeld were so carried away with the theory of comparative advantage that they quoted the iconic Nobel laureate Samuelson as saying that the comparative advantage was the best example of an economic principle that is "undeniably true." Three academics Harry Bowen, Abraham Hollander, and Jean-Marie Viaene in their book, *Applied International Trade Analysis,* called Ricardo's concept *this deepest and most beautiful result in all of economics.* William Poole, a former president of the Federal Reserve Bank of St. Louis, made the following opening remark to an audience in a talk he gave on US International Trade:

> "In fact, there is no issue on which economists are more closely in agreement than the fundamental case for free trade. Economists end to end see eye to eye on this issue, and the two-armed economist does not go through the usual dance "on the one hand, on the other hand when discussing the fundamental case for free trade. There are special cases and temporary exceptions that modify the case for free trade but they do not challenge the basic argument."[80]

Neo-classical and current economists have, therefore, created an aura around the comparative advantage theory. They have consistently labeled those who oppose free trade infamously as protectionists. They charge that 'protectionists' are either motivated by self-interest or totally misguided.

The aura surrounding comparative advantage is, however, undeserved. Comparative advantage is common sense dressed up in academic gown. It says if you are engaged in two activities, one of which you do more efficiently, you should drop the other you are not doing so efficiently and spend all your time on the one you do more efficiently. If you are engaged in two activities inefficiently, one more inefficiently than the other, you should devote all your time on the one you do less inefficiently. The principle is applicable to any other activity of life. That was the common sense Ricardo was saying. But here we are dealing with science. Science is not common sense.

The question is whether this simplistic common sense pre-scrimption of comparative advantage is the key to successful and sustainable economic growth. Turn the claim of comparative advantage to a country. If a country is producing two goods, one more efficiently, it should concentrate on producing the good it is more efficient at and import the other good. Is that all that there is to economic development and growth? What do we mean by efficiently?

Krugman and Obstfeld in their pioneering book: *International Economics: Theory and Policy* declared, "The fundamental reason why trade potentially benefits a country is that it expands the economy's choice." They summarized this by saying, "Trade expands the economy's consumption possibilities." If they mean that trade is about a country expanding its consumption possibilities, then it means that trade is not economic development.

The famous Nobel laureate Samuelson is known for his story of the lawyer and her secretary as depicting the basic principles and logic of comparative advantage. There is a lawyer (a lady) in town who is also the best typist in town. Samuelson asked his readers how the lawyer should best spend her time: whether she should specialize in law and leave the typing to her secretary (a man). Samuelson was of the view that the lawyer should concentrate on legal activities where her relative or comparable skills are more effectively used, even though she has absolutely great skills in both typing and legal work. From the secretary's point of view, Samuelson said that since he is a fine typist, to undertake legal research and write legal brief as typing would be laborious at best and impossible at worst. The secretary is absolutely less efficient than the lawyer in both legal research and typing. The upshot, according to Samuelson, is that the most efficient outcome is for the lawyer to specialize in legal work and the secretary concentrate on typing.

Samuelson's story illustrates some of the more obvious basic weaknesses of comparative advantage theory. Suppose, for example, the lawyer does not have enough legal work to occupy her all the time. It will be wise of her to undertake part or all the typing especially as she is more efficient than the male typist in typing. If a country like the US has unemployment resulting from international trade, it was foolish for it to close American industries that were producing what it now imports in order to encourage imports. If the lady lawyer knows the secretary is privately studying to be a lawyer, it will be equally foolish of her to stop keeping up her typing skills. She may find her law practice in trouble from competition from the budding secretary-lawyer when the former secretary establishes a legal practice, especially if as a former sec retary, the new lawyer, has an in-depth knowledge of her practice and clients.

The United States lady lawyer thought it had comparative advantage in many fields without knowing that its secretary was learning to be a lawyer. Like its former secretary, new countries that were previously not competitors are now out-competing the US lady lawyer. Comparative advantage is a static theory that is unable to keep up with the rapidly changing dynamics of international trade.

Let us go into a more detailed examination of Ricardo's theory. Ricardo chose a very simple case of two countries A and B which are each supposed to be producing two goods—say wine and cloth. The table 5.1 shows the hours it takes each country to produce a barrel of wine and hours to produce a yard of cloth:

		Wine	Cloth
Country	A	80	90
Country	B	120	100

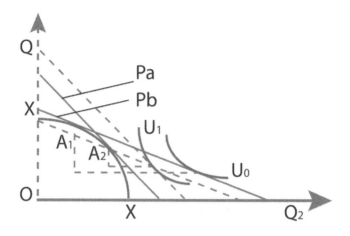

Fig.5.1 *TITLE:*
Concave production possibility

Country A is said to have absolute advantage in the production of both goods, because it produces each good in less time than Country B. Country B is said to have absolute disadvantage in producing the two goods because it takes longer to produce each good. According to Smith who preceded Ricardo, there is no basis for trade between them because Country A has nothing to gain from such a trade. But according to Ricardo, both countries will gain from trade between them because Country A applies less time in producing wine than cloth. And that Country B's relative time disadvantage is smaller in cloth. The relative number of hours needed to produce wine (80 in Country A, 120 in Country B) is less than the relative hours needed to produce cloth (90 in Country A and 100 in Country B. Because of these relative differences, we are told that both countries should trade. Ricardo, it should be noted, ascribed to each good a value equal to the man-hours utilized in producing it. On that basis, it is argued that one barrel of wine should exchange for 6/5 yards of cloth in Country A, while in Country B, one barrel will exchange for only 8/9 yard of cloth. Country A should gain if it specializes in wine and import cloth from Country B at a ratio of one barrel to 6/5 yards or 1W; 6/5C. Country B will benefit by specializing in cloth production and exporting cloth to Country A, where it could receive 9/8 barrels of wine per yard of cloth instead of 5/6 barrel per yard at home.

Ricardo made a lot of *assumptions* to enable him to reach his desired conclusions:

ac. he *assumed* that each country has a fixed endowment of resources and all units of each particular resource in both countries are identical, except for man-hours (labor) in them;

ad. he *assumed* that the factors of production of a country are completely mobile between alternative uses within a country;

ae. he *assumed* that the factors of production are completely immobile between countries;

af. he *assumed* that the relative value of a good is based solely on its relative labor content;

ag. He *assumed* that the level of technology is fixed for each country, although the technology can differ between them;

ah. he *assumed* that 'Costs' of production are constant, namely that labor per unit of production does not change, regardless of quantity and quality of goods produced;

ai. he *assumed* that there is full employment;

aj. he *assumed* that there is perfect competition;

ak. He *assumed* that there are no transportation costs.

Ricardo was based on nine assumptions. It should also be noted that Ricardo did not say that the two countries should exchange goods on the basis of their prices. This point should prove very vital in our discussions later in this chapter.

Current trade economists claim to be engaged in fashioning out 'modern' trade theories initiated by Ricardo. The assumptions Ricardo made in his theory, therefore, need to be assessed in the context of modern day economic conditions. I will briefly comment on these assumptions. It is false, in the first place, to assume that all units of productions are identical in both countries. Cloth in Country A cannot even be identical to cloth in Country B. Cloth is different from wine because different resources namely cotton and grapes are involved in their production. This makes the whole comparative advantage theory incorrect because its assumption implies it is dealing with products, distinguishable as different products (wine and cloth) distinguishable only by the hours used by labor in producing them. Ricardo assumed that factors were not mobile between his two countries. In the current world economic relations, capital, labor, and even raw materials like petroleum and many other commodities are highly mobile between countries. His assumption, therefore, that the relative value of a good is based on its relative labor content is defective. The full employment assumption is inadmissible. Many countries that are being urged to embrace international trade like the United States face varying levels of unemployment. The perfect competition assumption is a fiction in modern day economics. Ricardo's theory of comparative advantage is, therefore, propped up by many false assumptions. You do not create self-serving (wrong) assumptions in order to help you reach a preconceived conclusion.

The sub-title of this chapter stated that if any one of us is allowed to make as many assumptions as we wish, we can prove anything including that heaven is earth. What I wish to do as I go along in this chapter is to, as far as possible, draw attention to the large volume of assumptions and hidden errors that prop up all current theories on international trade.

I will single out one of the fundamentally wrong assumptions in Ricardo for a more detailed discussion—the claim that the value of a good derives solely from its labor content value. Ricardo's theory used differences in labor input as the basis to assert that countries mutually gain from trade.

Most present day conventional economists acknowledge that Ricardo was wrong in his assertion that labor content value is the sole basis for assessing goods. Rather than reject Ricardo's comparative advantage assertions because he used incorrect analysis to arrive at his conclusions, they went ahead to frame their own new additional assumptions while retaining Ricardo's basic conclusions about trade.

For example, they substituted Ricardo's *labor content* valuation with price for no apparent scientific reason. All *modern* trade analyses, without exception, take the supremacy of comparative advantage as given and undertake amusing intellectual exploits and assumptions needed to buttress their case. Their proof invariably involves working from the answer. Once difference in price of goods can be detected between countries through self-serving range of unsubstantiated assumptions and over-simplifications, they then tell us that there are harvests of comparative advantage waiting to be reaped by the countries concerned through trade.

Accordingly, Krugman and Obstefeld simply told us that "For Trade to take place, two countries must differ in the relative price of manufactures that will prevail in the absence of trade."[81] This statement is unfortunate and underlies much that is wrong about current world trade because countries with low costs—however the low cost was achieved (cheap labor, cheap raw materials) permanently can pin other countries with high cost in trade slavery. US is a trading slave.

The Embarrassment of Ricardo

As it became clear to trade academic theorists that Ricardo's theory proposed in the early nineteenth century could not deal with the diversity and complexity of the present international economic and technological world, they were faced with updating and widening the scope of the theory Ricardo. It was an attempted a scientific theory— Ricardo never mentioned price in his theory. He simply concluded that the differences in the production factor: labor between countries should be driving trade between them. Trade theorists now needed to study the economic structure of countries to see how to widen and broaden their knowledge of the economic structures so as to broaden Ricardo's theory and overcome the serious deficiency in it: namely, that the difference between two products in only their labor content. That is where they got into more problems because they were ill-equipped scientifically to understand and analyze structural economics.

Let me set out here some statements in current university textbooks about international trade to illustrate the difficulty current trade economists have in dealing with the scientific structural economic problem that Ricardo left for them.

Professor Appleyard and Field in their textbook, *International Economics,* adopted what they called a new 'framework' to substitute

Ricardo's labor content value. They said that their new framework "provides a means of escaping from the limitations of (Ricardo's) labor theory of value while retaining the comparative advantage conclusions about the basis of trade."[82] Professor Carbaugh in his own textbook stated that his own framework, while retaining the comparative advantage conclusion, was such that "we are no longer using labor to be the only factor input as Ricardo did."[83]

Economists Bowen, Hollander, and Viaene sought to claim that Ricardo's theory of comparative advantage "are effectively theories of related price determination." That is wrong because Ricardo's theory was a comparison of labor content in man-hours only—a scientific quantification, not price.

Even the best Nobel Prize winners in economics cannot predict the price of any good in the international market. Hollander and Viaene further confessed that "External economies are awkward to examine in a well-structured and rigorous analysis since they actually stand for a mixture of dynamic factors." The two struck at the "truth" that international comparison of price determinations is difficult.

The US President's economic advisers had their own say in their Economic Report of 2005 about Ricardo. The report said that critics do not usually argue that Ricardo's theory is incorrect even though the Report accepted that Ricardo omitted key aspects of trade that "undermine the theory's" (Ricardo's) results and alter the consequent policy prescription." The report then said, "Economic models (that means modern models) that take into account of both capital and labor (Ricardo's theory discussed only labor) show that countries as a whole still gain from free trade." They were saying that even though Ricardo's theory is defective, free trade is good!

The advisers then slipped the deadly poison into the drink. They said that (under their modern free trade model) there are differing impacts of trade on different parts of both the economy and the labor force. "Policies aimed at supporting individuals affected by trade are thus vital to ensuring that its gains are widely shared," they claimed.

Using the cover, trade advisers carefully introduced the most vicious poison in current free trade theory, namely that "different sections of the population will receive differing impacts from free trade." This is a subtle acceptance that trade can cause devastation and unemployment in the US alongside claimed benefits to the economy. Trade they admit will adversely the structural balance of a trading country. Trade advisers, therefore, endorse trade-induced inequality and unemployment in America by default because they regard it as inevitable consequence of free trade, contrary to Ricardo's assumption of full employment in each of the trading countries.

As an economic inquiry, Ricardo's comparative theory was his attempt to fashion out a 'scientific' economic theory aimed at achieving maximum sustainable growth through the husbanding of the country's production factor (labor), so that it is fully utilized. Ricardo did not envisage the brutalizing effects of present-day outsourcing of capital and predatory foreign investments that has been hollowing out the US economy.

The secretary and the lawyer analogy assumed that the lawyer and the secretary were fully employed, which is not the case in most international trade situations. Ricardo did not expect the United States to be buying everything from China because everything from China is cheaper. In distancing themselves from Ricardo while endorsing his theory as the best in history, Paul Krugman and Professor Carbaugh each asked in their textbooks whether the Ricardo model was a good fit "for the real world." They further asked whether Ricardo's model could be the basis for an accurate prediction about actual international trade flows. Krugman answered that very few economists believe that Ricardo's prescription is an adequate description of the causes and consequences of world trade, but that he *believed* that Ricardo's comparative advantage probably still mattered in international trade! Carbaugh, on the other hand, said that one should proceed with caution in explaining a country's competitiveness solely on Ricardo's labor productivity. These two professors were in effect saying that Ricardo's theory is basically defective.[84]

Professors Appleyard and Field needed to draw their students' attention to some of the many assumptions of free trade theory. They cautioned their students that some of Ricardo's assumptions did not fit the real world, but then they said that the intent of pointing at these assumptions was "to introduce an element of caution rather than doubt (concerning free trade)." They then made a shameful claim:

"Indeed few principles are so universally accepted by economists as comparative advantage and the gains from international trade. "The two professors were also telling their students on one hand that Ricardo's theory was nothing to be relied upon, but, on the other hand, that they should not dismiss Ricardo because it is not fashionable to do so.[85]

Another author of free trade economics textbooks was bothered about the plethora of assumptions in trade theory. He decided to discuss some of the assumptions of free trade theory, which he said needed to be examined in the context of the *real world*. He told his students in the text that the aim of questioning these assumptions was not to shake their confidence in the advantages of trade. The aim, he said, was merely "to introduce an element of caution rather than doubt concerning neoclassical theory (of free trade)." He said that what mattered was that they have faith in free trade because "few principles are so universally accepted by economists as comparative advantage and the gains from international trade." He was rallying his students to support free trade, irrespective of the criticisms and weaknesses of the concept because economists, whose ranks they will one day join, universally accept trade. Professors Bowen, Hollander, and Viaene in their textbook, *Applied International Trade Analysis*, concluded that the Ricardian model raised more questions about comparative advantage than it answered.

Conventional Economists' Fixation With Price

Attempts by present day conventional economists to reinterpret and recast Ricardo come in all shapes and forms. Professor Bowen and his coauthors in their textbook claimed that "Theories of trade based on principles of comparative advantage, as we have seen, are effectively theories of relative price determination."

They are wrong. Immediately, an economic analysis brings price into an analysis, it ceases to be a scientific analysis. Ricardo never brought price into his analysis even though in his time, economic transactions were transacted on money prices, and there were price differences between countries. It is current free trade economists that have injected money into free trade not Ricardo. Some of them have, therefore, made preposterous claims, for example, that two hours of Ricardo's man-hours is automatically twice as expensive as one employing one hour. Others have claimed that two labor-hours in Ricardo's comparative analysis means that wages to be paid are two-hour rate wages.

Professor Carbaugh muddied the waters further when he sought to inject wages at the heart of comparative advantage theory. He argued that in the United States, Ricardo's man-hour comparative advantage could be nullified by lower hour wages of another competing country. This brings out a point that needs to be emphasized. What may constitute a comparative advantage under Ricardo can be a comparative disadvantage in current free trade analysis when wage rates differ between countries. There is, therefore, a basic contradiction between Ricardo's comparative advantage and what present day economists say is comparative advantage. The truth unfortunately is current trade theories have, in practical terms, long ignored Ricardo. Under Ricardo, America's low man-hour input is itself comparative advantage to the United States. But conventional economists say that the United States has comparative disadvantage because its wages are high.

Professor Carbaugh introduced a comic side to the discussions when he argued that the reason he was introducing price into the trade theory is because "A person at a candy store does not look at Swiss chocolate and US chocolate and say I wonder which nation has the comparative advantage in chocolate production."

The buyer, according to the professor relies on price after allowing for quality differences to tell him which nation has the comparative advantage. Other economists, including Professor Bowen and his coauthors, have claimed that comparative advantage reflects the differences in *opportunity costs*. This assertion is incorrect. The 2005 Economic Report to the President weighed in with its price approach to trade and argued that differences in production technology between a trading partner and home country mean that different prices prevail in the two countries before they open their borders to trade.

Conventional economists are trained only to think of economics in financial and monetary terms, so that they will take the first opportunity available to turn an argument into finance and money because they lack knowledge of economic science. Ricardo's comparative advantage theory was a failed attempt at scientific economic analysis. It was not an exercise in financial analysis. Ricardo defined labor content of a product not in terms of its price but as labor-hours. Conventional economics have continued to date to add financial elements and artistry into the theory of trade: price, costs, wages, exchange rates, transport costs, tariffs, and other cost/financia data with the result that trade theory has lost any pretense it originally had as scientific study.

Professors Appleyard and Field summarized the position (similar to Krugman and Obstefeld earlier) on behalf of all other free trader theorists saying:

> The most important feature to keep in mind (is) that the opening of a country to international trade means exposing the country to a new set of relative prices. When these different prices are available, the home country's producers and consumers will adjust to them by reallocating their production and consumption patterns. The reallocation leads to gains from trade. The ultimate source of gain from international trade is the difference in prices in autarky between countries.

It is clear from these statements that economic growth is not what current free trade is about. It is about obtaining goods cheaper and economic welfare. If it is a matter of buying whatever you want from another country with the lowest price, then the matter is simple. We do not need all this misleading trade theorizing. If international trade is all about getting things at the lowest price from anywhere in the world, then we don't need all the verbiage of trade theory.

It is on basis of price, in which many economists feel comfortable, that most conventional economists based their other claim that trade is 'economically' beneficial to countries. Professor Irwin claimed:

> There is much better, indeed overwhelming, evidence that free trade improves economic performance by increas ing competition in the domestic market. The competition

diminishes the market power of domestic firms and lead to a more efficient economic outcome. The benefit does not arise because foreign competition changes a firm's cost through changes in the scale of output. Rather it comes through a change in pricing behavior of imperfectly competitive domestic firms.[86]

Diminishing the market power of domestic firms is a negation of a country's economic development and affects a country's structural system. The professor like all trade experts regards price of goods as the most important factor. He equates economic performance with price. He also says in line with other economists that lower prices contribute to consumer welfare just as low price imported goods from Asia has added to the welfare of the impoverished American consumer. Professor Irwin is an example of trade theorists who deviate from a macroeconomic analysis to improvised micro-economic analysis, which I will tackle later.

Ricardo Was Dead in the Water From the Beginning

The reason Ricardo's theory, as a scientific inquiry, was dead in the water was because Ricardo omitted to put full value to the product by not including with labor-hours the two other resource inputs, namely capital (production aid) and material in his analysis. I will, however, show that even if he did not omit these two factors, he could never have succeeded in proving comparative advantage, as we know it. Nor is it correct to give the impression, as many conventional economic texts have sought, that Ricardo was not aware of the contribution of capital in production.

In his text on comparative advantage, Ricardo clearly said he assumed that factors were perfectly mobile in a country. If labor was mobile, according to him, it was moving about to meet up with some other factor. Giving Yorkshire and London as examples of locations in England, Ricardo noted that industry was located where the greatest absolute advantage exists and that labor and capital move to the area where productivity and returns are highest. Ricardo was fully aware of capital and price, but he never mentioned them in his theory. I will later take up the issue of the omission by all trade economists of material (3D) as a production factor.

Three new trade theories to replace Ricardo

Trade theorists dumped Ricardo, but, as we see, they never told the world. Most people who have heard of Ricardo still think that he is still relevant as one can see that a 2006 Economic Report to the President reverently referred to Ricardo. Economists have worked hard at finding trade theories to replace Ricardo. So far to date, they have had three unsuccessful attempts that they still insist on teaching students and publishing as textbooks because the myth of international trade as an economic science needs to be maintained, otherwise international trade will lose its base.

The three replacements are called

al. specific factor model of trade;
am. the two-factor model of free trade;
an. economy of scale theory of trade.

Both (a) and (b) were based on rigorous attempts to substitute Ricardo's labor with something dignified and academic. Their failure, as we will see, is because these (conventinal) economists don't understand structural economic science.

Specific Factor Trade Theory

Specific factor theory was developed by Nobel Laureate Paul Samuelson and Ronald Jones in 1971. The model consists of an economy that produces manufactured good and food. Instead of one factor (labor) as Ricardo assumed, there are now, according to the model, three/two factors: land, capital, and labor.

The manufactured good is produced using capital and labor, while food is produced using land as capital and labor. Capital is fixed but labor moves to each of these two capitals. That is to say that capital and land capital are supposed to be specific and permanently fixed to particular sectors of the economy while labor is mobile moving between capital and land. Land has never been labelled a factor of production but Samuelsom and Jones decided to name land as a factor.

As usual with all conventional economists, the authors of the model have no definition of what they mean by capital. Over time after they put up their theory, there was embarrassment about their claim that the capital factors are fixed and immobile. We are now told by trade economists that capital may occur in the long run be mobile even though it may be immobile in the short run. The claim that capital is fixed and immobile for whatever time is structurally unscientific. Today, despite its unscientific base, some trade economists clam that the factor specific theory enables them to evaluate incomes in an economy in which factors are fixed and immobile.

The name "specific factor" refers to the claimed distinguishing feature of this theory/model in which one factor of production is said to be specific to a particular industry. It is assumed to be immobile between industries in response to change in market conditions. A factor may be immobile between industries in response to changes in market conditions. A factor may be immobile between industries for a number of other reasons. Some factors may be specifically designed in case of capital. Robert Carbaugh in his famous book *International Economics* argued that steel capital cannot be used for computer production and vice versa. So each industry has its capital. Some factors are assumed to be immobile/specific for a particular production process. Other factors that have been claimed that could not be transferred in this mad exercise include climate and soil. Jonathon Eaton in a paper titled "A Dynamic Specific-Factor Model of International Trade" in the *Review of Economic Studies* in the *Society for Economic Analysis* 1987 LIV claimed that "savings" is also capital. Labor is assumed to move freely and costlessly mobile between two industries, which in practice is not true. Full employment of labor in the economy is assumed in the theory which implies that the sum of the labor used in each industry equals the labor endowment of the economy. Full employment of sector-specific capital is assumed. The full employment assumption of the theory is not correct, because most countries involved in trade do' not have full employment.

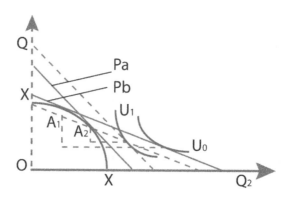

Fig.5.1 *TITLE:*
Concave production possibility

Professor Samuelson and Ronald Jones want to tell us that as far as they are concerned (wrongly though), manufactured good was produced by combination of capital and labor. They omitted material. Despite these analytical errors, the framers of the specific factor model proceeded to make a major false claim, namely that if one draws a graph of quantity of one manufactured product against another manufactured product, and the graph will have a concave shape. They call it production possibility of the economy. The claim is false for two reasons. First, the claim is made with an incorrect assumption, namely that the manufacturing process involves labor and capital one. The authors of the model forget that part of the labor in an economy is used for producing capital and that in scientific analysis of the process capital is both material and labor. So the prosed concave graph they were discussing is not made independent variables.

The second false claim is that manufacture operates under diminishing returns to factors. The claims is based on the claim that as more labor is injected into production, output increases more slowly because there is less capital for additional unit of labor—marginal product of labor is said to reduce labor supply rises. The very idea of diminishing capital being available as labor input increases is structurally unscientific. If capital combining with labor reduces as labor supply increases, it means that the manufacturing products made as labor supply increases have different compositions from those made at the beginning of the production process and are not the same products.

The model assumes that firms will choose output, hence labor usage level such that the market determined wage is equal to the value of the marginal product of the last unit labor. The value of the marginal product is the increment to the revenue that a firm will obtain by adding another unit labor to its production process. There is the assumption that production displays a diminishing return because the fixed stock of capital means that each additional worker has less capital to work on, that is that each additional worker has less capital to work with. This means that each additional unit of labor will add smaller increment to output and since it is assumed that output price is fixed, the value of the marginal product declines as labor usage rises.

The framers of the specific factor theory therefore needed a concave graph of the production function/graph XX—often called *production possibility* (as shown in Figure 5.1)—so as to ensure that line graphs P_a and P_b showing the exact relative prices of the goods Q_1 and Q_2 before and after trade will each only touch the production graph XX at one point A_1 and A_2 each intended to show the exact quantities of the two goods produced at each price as we see in Figure 5.1 If XX was not a concave-shaped curve, it is clear that the claim that trade between two countries exchanging two goods will result in a smooth transfer between A_1 and A_2 and relative price between the two goods smoothly changing P_a to P_b is incorrect. It is clear that the assumptions are technically incorrect and XX was not form a concave graph. These economists cannot proceed with their claims as P_a and P_b may end up in many awkward and unwanted positions. Undaunted, these theorists drew up what called welfare indifference curves measuring what they claim was different levels social happiness U_0 and U_1, intended to make the consistent but unfounded claim that trade invariably increases social welfare which they claim increases economic growth!

Fig. 5.1 TITLE:

The production possibilities it is also claimed, will exhibit increasing opportunities cost because the expansion of one industry can be achieved by transferring labor out of the other, which must contract. Due to claimed diminishing returns to labor, each additional unit of labor switched will have a smaller effect on the expanding industry and larger effect on the contracting industry.

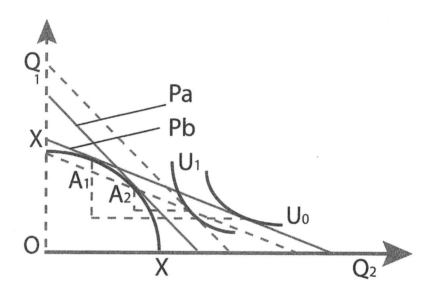

Fig. 5.2 TITLE: Concave production possibility

From these loads of incorrect assumptions, the framers of the factor endowment theory of trade arrived at a concave-shaped production possibility XX in Fig. 5.2 claiming to be the alternative combination of the output of the economy. Trade arises between two countries when they differ in relative price of manufacturers that will prevail in absence of trade. Pa and Pb are the old and the new relative prices arising from trade. A1 and A2 now show the resultant increase of production in the economy.

According to the theory, export from fig 5.2 will have several consequences: not only will output of the particular export sector grow, its price will rise, its profits will rise, wages in it will grow, whole output in the import competing sector will drop, profits will drop, return to capital will drop. Its wages will rise as labor is shifting from it to the export sector. The authors of the specific factor model, despite its false assumtions, do not realize that the center of their theory acknowledges that each of the two trading countries will undergo unplanned and unintended structural changes.

The specific factor model is false. For a start, it is false that it is labor and capital that produce manufactured goods. You cannot produce goods without materials. Production possibility, namely the alternative outputs of the economy, claimed through the numerous false assumptions to be concave, is false. The graphs (fig. 5.1 and fig.5.2)being one of capital versus labor are additionally false because capital and labor are not independent variables. This is because capital is a mixture of material and labor. All the labor in the economy is therefore not available to freely move from one manufacturing sector to another. Some portion of the labor in the economy is required for creating capital. It will be seen that framers of the specific factor model confirm that trade in each trading economy has its winners and losers, a situation which creates and promotes structural imbalance.

As usual, the authors of the model have no definition of what they mean by capital. Over time after the originators of this theory put up their theory, there was embarrassment about their claim that the capital factors are both fixed and mobile. It was a bizarre assertion. We are now told us bizarrely that capital mobility may occur in the long run, even though it may be immobile in the short run.

Two Factor Endowment Theory

The two factor endowment theory, sometimes called factor abundant, was an attempt to correct and amend the specific factor model. It was another attempt to define the factor structure of an economy after the error in the specific model. Krugman understood the problem because he said in his economic text that the two factor model is a "somewhat more difficult" model. Calling it "moredifficult" model, meant a fresh new set of *assumptions* were needed.

The theory of factor abundance hangs on twelve assumptions. The authors: Harry Bowen, Abraham Hollander, and Jean-Marie in their book, *Applied International Trade Analysis,* listed them:

1. Perfect competition in two countries in both commodity and factor markets;
2. Factors of production in the two countries are homogenous in quality and costlessly mobile between industries within each country;
3. The production function for each good is of a neoclassical type and is, in particular, homogenous;
4. Production functions differ between industries;
5. Consumers in the two countries have identical and homogenous preferences;
6. There are no taxes, costs of transport or other impediments to the domestic movement of goods;
7. There are two countries, two goods, and two factors of production;
8. There are no factor intensity reversals;
9. Factors of production are immobile between countries and inelastic;
10. The production function for each good is identical across countries;
11. There are no taxes, costs of transport, or other impediments to the international movement of goods;
12. Consumer preferences are identical across countries.

The sub-title of this chapter is: Allow me to make as many assumptions as possible and I can prove anything to you. In this case, twelve bizzare assumptions were required.

The factor endowment theory is a very daring bold but mistaken trade theory declaration. It claims that comparative trade advan tage is explained exclusively by differences in relative factor endowment differences between economies. In particular, two gentlemen Eli Heckscher and Bertil Ohlin in 1920 formulated this in a theory famously known as the Heckscher-Ohlin theory. The theory highlights the role of nations' factor endowments (according to them labor and capital) as the key supply factors underlying comparative advantage. Notice again that they missed out materials as a factor of production. This time they now claim that the factors of capital and labor (unlike for specific factor model) are all mobile. According to the theory, relative price levels differ among nations because (1) the nations have different relative endowments of factor inputs and (2) different products require that factor inputs be used with different intensities in their production.

According to these gentlemen, given these circumstances, they now, as other theorists before them, turned the theory into a money and price theory when they claimed that a factor is cheaper in an economy where it is in abundance and that such a country will export that commodity for which a large amount of relative *abundant* (cheap) factor input is used. It will import that commodity in the production of which the relative *scarce* (expensive) factor input is used. The theory descended, as expected, into a price theory when the authors were unable to continue analyzing factors in structural economic terms.

The Heckscher-Ohlin theory had a far-reaching impact on the world and its influence in trade thinking over many years was enormous despite the fact that it was false. The theory is the reason why Americans were, for example, told incorrectly to cease local production of textiles because it is believed that America should "profit" instead by importing textiles and exporting capital goods.

The Heckscher-Ohlin theory hangs on the twelve assumptions I have just listed. Hanging on twelve *assumptions,* the factor endowment or abundance theory of international trade is greatly flawed. In the first place, the idea that each product has a prescribed production technology—capital-intensive or labor-intensive—is false. I have already stated that nobody ordained, for example, that a car must be produced by capital intensive production. Nobody ordained that cloth must be produced by labor-intensive production. As I discussed in the last chapter, China is outcompeting the United States in vehicle production with a capital/labor ratio of \$37,337 to \$114,380 for the

United States (see table 1 chapter 1). It is, therefore false to claim that because the United States is supposed to be capital abundant, its capital goods built on its higher capital abundance are cheap and readily exportable.

The trade authors, Bowen, Hollande, and Viaene concluded:

> Faced with weak empirical support for the two-factor model, many analysts sought to resolve the apparent inconsistency between theory and practice by modifyingthe assumption of the model one by one to see what phenomenon might be explained.[87]

Do you see where you prove a theory by modifying your assumptions?

Leontief Paradox

The factor endowment theory of free trade is misleading. For many years after the comparative trade advantage theory was born, economists believed that, as the theory prescribed, the US being classified as a so-called capital abundant country should be exporting goods with high ratio of capital to labor and importing goods of lower capital/labor ratio. In a famous study by Wassily Leontief in 1953, an economist who later won the Nobel Prize in 1973 found that actual US exports were less capital intensive than US imports contrary to the factor abundance trade theory. Trade economists like Krugman correctly called the result the single biggest piece of evidence against the factor-proportions theory of Heckscher-Ohlin. The *Leontief Paradox* was, for some time, part of economic texts.

The paradox confused economists for some time until some economists started having second thoughts about the factor abundance trade theory. As Appleyard and Field put it "Many tests...have suggested that it is necessary to go beyond the two-factor model... because a two-factor test is too restrictive." It was in the end thought that natural resources (material) was needed as a third production factor in determining the correct export trade relationship. This finally solved Leontief paradox.

Bowen, Hollande, and Viaene in their book, *Applied International Trade Analysis,* concluded that, "Factor supply differences alone are not sufficient to explain trade patterns." They said, "Demand and technological differences also appear important." Bowen, Hollande and Viaene are convetional economists and when they don't understand anything, they pass it on as embedded in the lose term: technology. They admitted that "further work is needed to understand the nature of these demand and technological differences and their importance relative to factor supplies in determining trtrade patterns." Elsewhere in their book, they said that the problem with the factor abundance theorem is how to get it to apply to "a world of many countries, many goods, and many factors as well as the ambiguity of concepts such as factor intensity and factor abundance."

Krugman/Obstefeld, for their part, accepted that their findings "do not contradict with the observation that overall the Heckscher-Ohlin model does not seem to work well." They also accepted that Heckscher-Ohlin model has not been successful in explaining international trade. Professor Carbaugh cited a study carried out to test the validity of the theory even after material as a third production factor has been included. He admitted that: "The results (of the test) [still] challenge the predictive accuracy of the factor-endowment theory."[89]

Economy of Scale Model of International Trade

The economy of a scale model of international trade is an empirical theory that took off around the 1980s as Western countries led by the United States sought to dominate international trade by using their enormous capital to create capital intensive investments in regions of the world in order to supply the market in those regions. For example, the US car companies, at the time carved the world into regions where they strategically located their capital intensive manufacturing plants intended to dominate the market for cars in each region. Trade economists, like Krugman, immediately conjured up the economy of scale model in order to encapsulate what they observed. The model was essentially empirical.

Bowen and his coauthors in their book titled, *Applied International Trade Analysis,* stated that while the recognition that imperfect competition and economy of scale are aspects of trade that have long been acknowledged, it is only since the early 1980s that the idea of linking the two into equilibrium models of trade was born.[90] Because what they observed were large economy-of-scale operations, these economists felt (incorrectly) that what they were seeing was different from the two post-Ricardo trade models we have just discussed. For example, Professor Krugman et al wrote:

"Growing discomfort with the incongruity between traditional analysis of international trade, which assumes small producers and pure competition and the reality of huge volumes of exchange involving related products and powerful multinationals sparked off the development of new theories based on economy of scale and atomistic competition."

Here again, Professors Krugman and Obstefeld said:

> "Underlying the application of the monopolistic competition model to trade is the idea that trade increases market size. In industries where there are economies of scale, both the variety of goods that a country can produce and the scale of its production are constrained by the size of the market. By trading with each other, and, therefore, forming an integrated world market that is bigger than any individual national market, nations are able to loosen these constraints. Each country can specialize in producing a narrower range of products than in the absence of trade; yet by buying goods that it does not make from other countries, each nation can simultaneously increase the variety of goods available to its consumers. As a result, trade offers an opportunity for mutual gain even when countries do not differ in their resources or technology."[91]

These statements contain a good number of technical errors. There are no industries in which are inherently economies of scale. The birth of the economy of scale model is the result of the technical misconception initiated by US corporations. It is the corporations who build for economy of scale in whatever industry they want in order to increase sales volume and reduce unit costs with attendant downsides.

The monopolistic competition model is unnecessary because there is nothing structurally different between it and specific and the two factor model. It is incorrect for these trade economists to claim that the specific factor model and the two factor (factor abundant) models are for small industries. Monopolistic competition trade model became obsolete because the character of the world market has since changed and become less monopolistic.

The well-known research by Womack, Jones, and Roos in the US motor industry in 1990 drew attention to a trend which has continued, largely unnoticed by conventional economists in the US and occurring in many other economic sectors—that the motor market in Europe, North America, and Japan was progressively fragmenting, and as the authors described it, "with no end in sight." The report made an observation that also applies to many industrial sectors that "it is possible that we will return full circle to the world of craft production where every buyer was able to custom order a vehicle to his or her needs."[92]

Mass customization is a new paradigm that is increasingly replacing mass production markets. Companies have learned that com peting on the basis of lower price through mass production economy of scale is not a guarantee of success. Bowen et al in their candid comments stated, "There are yet few analyses of relationships between the volume of total trade or intra-industry and characteristics inspired by the monopolistic model." They further told us that: "Existing analyses raise a number of puzzling questions."[93]

The Truth About Trade Theory and Models and US Trade Agreements

Trade theories blossomed in the late 1990's following failure of the early development economists up to the 1980s to conclude a theory development just when international trade was becoming becoming a central issue world issue. The economists at the time, in order to be relevant, had therefore no alternative than to engage in intellectual empirical economics to analyze trade under what they generally called international trade economics. As empirical studies, there was a move to set up economic models supported by changing assumptions and made-up graphs purporting to analyze the micro and macro economics of countries. The enthusiasm in international economics and resultant theories/models finally cooled as it increasingly became clear that changing assumptions and graphs could not fit the complexity of the subject especially because the theories and models tried to analyze trade as exchange based on factors of production in participating countries when structural economics was undeveloped.

The damage however had been done because over the time because the message of comparative advantage of trade has been unfortunately sold and had become the cornerstone of many countries' economic strategy. No further attempts have been made to re-tool or reframe the trade theories/models.

All US Trade Agreements have some form of reciprocity, namely opportunity to export some product and in return to import something. US policy makers have been trained to concentrate on the "gains." They have not been trained to consider the economic sacrifice being made, namely the greater access to US economy by the other country or countries to the Agreement. Having new gainers and losers in the US as a result of each new trade agreement changes/affects the structural character/balance of the economy each time and for an economy that is already structurally unbalanced (fig 1.1) these changes increase the growing decline of the US economy. China, for example, generally imports goods that it does not produce. Those American economists who composed the trade theories have left us a bad legacy because they have left us with the fixed view that international trade brings comparative trade advantage to the US. Trade theories never proved the economic benefits of trade as they all depend on Ricardo's unsubstantiated claims.

Claimed Financial Benefits from International Trade: The P1.3 Trillion/ Year US Trade Bonanza

Following conventional economic profession's failure to scientifically show that foreign trade boosts economic growth, it has resorted to *financial* proofs. For the most ignorant among us, whether or not we understand trade theories, we might readily accept if we are told that free trade has earned the US $1.3 trillion a year backed up by the huge publicity behind trade and globalization in the United States. The US financial market and Wall Street make billions a year from financial transaction connected with trade and globalization. President George W. Bush and the then Treasury secretary Henry Paulson quoted $1.3 trillion figure annual earning for trade to support their case for free trade. This figure was also quoted in a speech by the Chairman of the Fed Bernanke in March 2007.

A group from the Peterson Institute in a major report titled "The Payout to America from Global Integration" in 2006 claimed that US earned US $1.3 trillion a year from trade. The Institute blandly claimed that its claim was because: "Almost all economists advocate trade liberalization as a proven method of increasing national income (by measuring GDP and thereby per capita GDP and GDP per household)" by quoting the very comparative advantage theories and the economy of scale trade theory we have just condemned. By resorting to study claimed micro-economic gains from trade, the Institute sought by arithmetical summation to arrive at the gains for the macro-economy. To do this, they split their micro-economic analysis into (a) import substitution and (b) technological spillovers.

The Institute therefore sought to analyze them using some related studies that were intended to show financial benefits (a) Output elasticity (1950–2003), (b) Product variety (1972–2001), (c) Sifting and sorting (1947–2003). The report also sought from these studies to estimate future economic gains waiting for the United States as international trade is further expanded and as remaining trade barriers are dismantled. Their publication overall estimated an annual gain from trade estimated additional gain in income of $2,800 to $5,000 and additional $7,000 to $12,900 per household. It estimated future gains of $450 billion to

$1.361 trillion per year for the United States. Professors Aghion and Howitt correctly stated: "Overall, our theoretical discussion indicates that it is difficult to identify a priori the effect of trade on income and growth."[94]

The Peterson Institute made a major unsubstantiated claim, when in seeking ways to convince Americans of the huge financial gains from trade it claimed that imports were beneficial to the US economy, a change from conventional trade theory that indicated that those whose industries were closed down because of import substitution "suffered". Peterson's claim was that when analyzing the micro-economy gains, US consumers through import gain access to a larger array of goods from imports (product variety), the economy gains financially, through lower prices and greater choices. The other gain claimed by the Institute was the gain from what it called "technology spillover" namely that import competition, not only can close US businesses but also through competition will increase the efficiency and productivity, innovation, product differentiation of those businesses who survive. On the other hand, Professor Aghion et al argued that trade liberation "will increase the degree of product market competition which is shown to be detrimental to growth"[95]

The Institute failed to acknowledge that closing down sectors of the economy causes structural shocks to the economy and adversely affects the structural balance of the overall economy. The basic analytical deficiency in Peterson's study is that in bringing issues like product variety, sifting and sorting, and technology spillovers into their analysis, its authors were mixing macroeconomics with microeconomics. Because they lack a structural scientific macroeconomic theory to cover the subject, they are studying, they attempted to reach a macro-economic conclusion by treating macro-economics as if it is the arithmetical sum of the microeconomy, the common basic error of conventional economics. Putting it in another way, I will say they thought in a conventional way of thinking that the arithmetical sum of the *gains* and *losses* which they attribute to sifting and sorting and technology spillover will affect individual firms (micro) and will add up and equal to a hoped macroeconomy *gain* (economic growth) of the US economy. I have in this book a number of times pointed out where people have made this mistake. Peterson's Institute financial claims on US trade are, therefore, not correct. Because the Institute claims that *some* businesses will have higher productivity, therefore, the whole economy will witness an economic growth is false because that is a micro assumption. The Institute idea of productivity as I have earlier pointed out in this book consists of the use of capital intensive production methods. That again is a micro-economic assumption.

Peterson, going by the OECD output elasticity study, additionally referred to an assumed statistical correlation between economic growth and a country's exposure (openness) to trade claimed that the US achieves financial gains from the US's large exposure (openness) to trade. Again, Aghion et al, in response, stated that use of country level studies of the link between economic growth and country openness fails to "address the casual relationship between trade policy, trade intensity, and other economic outcomes."[96] Aghion et al added that although it is often convenient to classify countries as either 'open' or 'closed' in practice this conceals a wide variety and extent of interventions. An economist, in a published paper in an UMF conference concluded:

> In many cases, the indicators of 'openness' correlate with other sources of bad economic performance...We find little evidence that open trade policies—in the sense of lower tariff and non-tariff barriers to trade—are significantly associated with economic growth.[97]

Frivolity with Trade Issues

Many people, organizations, and institutions in the United States deliberately talk about trade with a certain amount of frivolity and foolery in order to deflect from the serious economic issues facing trade or to defend their political belief. In the process they raise issues that are either not relevant or are incorrect as a justification for trade. US governments increasingly behave as if those who speak against international trade are either ill-informed or leftists, or trade unions only out to defend their members. The official government attitude to free trade is laced with a large dose of degree of levity and frivolity and a belief that comparative advantage of trade is canon truth. Trade has been seen as a necessary component of foreign policy and spread of democracy.

There are broadly two groups who have vested private interests in the continuation of a pro trade policy in the United States. There are those connected to Wall Street and the large US corporations whose core wealth derives from international trade. The second are conservative groups dedicated to defending capitalism, *economic freedom*, and free enterprise. Free trade is equated with economic freedom and free enterprise. Many Washington Foundations, for example the Cato Institute, the Peterson Institute, and the Heritage Foundation also see the defense of international trade as a major part of their core interest.

The Cato Institute in its Free Trade Bulletin on March 12, 2007 set out to challenge what it called *an almost universal consensus that the record trade deficit of 2006 was a drag on US economic growth*. Like the academic theorists on trade that I discussed earlier in this chapter, the Cato publication was only talking about the prices. The Institute claimed that *evidence from recent decades* (an attempt now to play with statistics) does not support that trade deficit adversely affects growth. It claimed there was a *paradox* in the claims made by various people about trade. It claimed that an alternative explanation in the midst of this paradox is that *an expanding economy promotes rising imports and an expanding current account deficit*. The conclusion, according to the Institute is that *a worsening* trade deficit is associated with faster economic growth while *an improving* deficit is associated with slower growth. By juggling statistics, the Institute finally reached the conclusion it wanted: *that there is no evidence than an expanding current account deficit is associated with slower growth*.[98]

Like the Peterson Institute analysis, these postures are intended to confuse the gullible, of which there are many even in the highest places. The intention by the Cato Institute is to say that it is not proven that trade deficit is associated by slow economic growth. Another Institute, this time the Heritage Foundation came to defend foreign trade with a publication titled, "The Economy Hits Home: International Trade: Why Free Trade Is the Fairest Trade of All."[99] Its approach was not an intellectual exercise. It was a subtle propaganda. Here are a number of the publication's claims:

m. Free trade means no one is forced to trade;
n. It is free and fair when countries with different advantages trade capitalize on those differences;
o. Free nations are more prosperous and have better standards of living;
p. Live free and prosper;
q. International trade has expanded over the last thirty years, income per person and life expectancy has gone up in most countries including those that are poor compared to the US;
r. Free trade is green because a country is allowed if necessary to import climate change equipment;
s. It is productivity growth that causes unemployment not trade;
t. Trade comprises 1/3 of US GDP;
u. Trade is part charity;
v. When new technologies appear, *some* jobs disappear. In particular, certain types of manufacturing jobs can be obsolete. But to view this as a net loss is to see the world economy as static not dynamic;
w. In free economies, the jobs lost through technological advances are replaced by better, more productive jobs that develop from and use the new technology through imports;
x. As more productive jobs replace obsolete jobs, the country's standard of living rises not only because labor becomes more productive, but also by the widespread use of the new technologies;
y. Trade protection causes citizens to pay a higher price and will encourage some local businesses to move into the protected activity, which may mean subsidizing them.

It will be noted that the Heritage publication is meant to give the reader the impression that Ricardo's competitive advantage is alive and doing well. The publication is using academic trade economists' denial that they have not only rejected Ricardo's comparative advantage but also have not been able to replace it, as I showed in this chapter, to make policy makers and other people believe that competitive advantage theory is well and alive. It also gave the impression that the Peterson Institute's claims of trade financial gains were proven. The Heritage's publication made a thing out of the words *free trade* by linking free trade with economic and political freedom to make it that free trade is an act of economic freedom and that economic freedom brings prosperity.

It is, therefore, unfortunate that the issue of trade has been trivialized and corrupted in the United States and that many policy makers unknowingly go along with the foolery. More unfortunate for the United States is that contrary to what our forefathers did when America was the sole world power, United States has since the '60s, as I will show in the next chapter, used trade more and more as an instrument of its international foreign politics. President Reagan, Kennedy, Bush, and Clinton specifically stated in chapter 6 that trade was a means to spread democracy, while President Obama was seeking trade pacts in the Pacific so as to bottle China's political and military strength there as part of spreading US military presence in the region.

The Economic Report to the President in 2013 continued the traditional Economic Adviser's pro Ricardian *comparative advantage* support for international trade. I have shown that theories of trade are a fraud. The Report stated:

> Significant opportunities are available for US firms to expand exports and create jobs, for resources to be allocated to their most productive uses, for innovation to flourish and for consumers to enjoy higher incomes, lower prices and expanded choice. These opportunities, however, have been accompanied by job displacement, downward wage pressures, and other adjustment costs.[100]

This is a wholehearted acceptance by the writers of the Report of free trade propaganda of Wall Street and the Washington Institutes that I have just discussed. On a macroeconomic level, which determines the fate of the whole overall US economy, the authors of the Report accepted that international trade causes higher incomes on one hand as well as job displacements, downward wage pressures and other *negative* adjustments on the other hand. That adds to the structural imbalance of the macroeconomy.

For the first time in 75 years in 2018, the US exported more oil and fuel than it imported, beating most members of OPEC and yet the US trade deficit has been rising. Most US conventional economists now confused, with no scientific explanation of the structural process of international trade—I have reviewed trade theories to show they had no structural foundation—have come to regard trade deficit as mere numbers. If increased oil/gas exports is not enough to slow or reverse US trade deficits these economists should at least admit that the US economy is uncompetitive and increasingly so.

Chapter 6

America's Failed International Trade History

In the last chapter, I have shown that the whole American international trade theory is false and misleading. In part 1 of this book, I have shown how America's basic economic problem is that its economic structure is unbalanced. In this chapter, I intend to undertake a historical review of US international trade to trace the origins of some of America's present economic trade and related economic problems and to show that international trade has added to America's increasing structural economic imbalance.

From as early as the nineteenth century when the American economy topped the global chart, international trade has been the subject of an ongoing debate in America. On one side are the advocates who wanted the United States to shun interna tional involvement in trade. They wanted to protect US businesses from an international attack and help them preserve the economic superstar status it took so long to achieve. At the other end of the spectrum are those, who believed that superstar status means the United States should wield its economic power on the international stage. This first group was originally called nationalists and currently is called protectionists and isolationists. Even at the time, it will be noted that some of the advocates of trade regarded trade mainly as a means to export America's surplus and as necessary to import the raw materials it needed.

In 1889, a US State Department Bureau of Foreign Commerce stated:

> "Every year we shall be confronted with an increasing surplus of goods for sale in foreign markets if American operatives and artisans are to be kept employed the year round. The enlargement of foreign consumption of the products of our mills and workshops has, therefore, been a serious problem of statesmanship as well as commerce."

In 1890, Senator Beveridge said, "American factories are making more than American people can consume. Fate has written our policy; the trade of the world must be ours..." In 1914, Edward Pratt, US Chief of the Bureau of Foreign and Domestic Commerce, said, "We can never hope to realize big prizes in foreign trade until we are prepared to loan capital to foreign nations and foreign enterprises. It is commonly said that trade follows the flag." This hegemony, a kind of economic imperialism, was the running theme of US early trade promoters. It was, unlike today, based on the strength and supremacy of the home US economy.

In a detailed scientific study of the three-factor structure of the US economy over this period in my book, *The Science of Economic Development and Growth: The Theory of Factor Proportions*, I showed how the United States used its *economic and trade isolation* of Britain at the time to overtake Britain economically. The US economy at the time, unlike today, as my detailed study in that book showed, was structurally a balanced economy. I summarized my study of the US/England's relative economic position at the time in the book as follows:

> "All information available points to the fact that the US economy took the world lead in the late ninetieth century. The quantity of goods produced in the forty-five years up to 1860 increased twelvefold. The total value of these goods, a measure retarded by sometimes drastic reductions in their average prices, rose eightfold. Allowing for some roughness in these estimates, the amount of goods available to an average American grew dramatically over the

period, probably about tripling. The demand for manufactured goods between 1815 and the 1849s expanded more
rapidly in America than in Britain in relation to total factor supplies…America, as an economy, was a late starter,
and the only way a late starter can overtake the early
starter is by achieving and maintaining a faster average
speed."

The United States at the time needed its isolation to enable it to
restructure its structural economy in order to achieve high and sustainable growth. America did not triumph because of export but used its
factor proportions in isolation.

Soon after the United States became the number one economy in the
world, the wealth created brought a situation in which some people began
to want to corner the spoils. Trusts emerged. Ted Roosevelt became an
antitrust buster leading to the Sherman Anti-Trust Act of 1890. He did
not make too much success of it. The Woodrow Wilson administration
was pro trade because the US manufacture was increasing from 23
percent in 1870 to 42 percent of total world manufacture in 1926–29
with an annual average trade surplus of $1,380 million between 1919
and 1929. Over the period especially of World War I, during which
Europe lost much of its production base, the United States increased its
export dominance, not trade.

In 1893 there was a relatively mild depression as structural economic
imbalance started for the first time as trusts came to have a hold. From
1908, there were mild recessions in the United States. Woodrow Wilson
was aware that the US economic structure was changing from what it
was when it overtook England as the largest economy toward the end
of the nineteenth century. He stated:

"No one who knows anything about the development of
the industry can have failed to observe that larger kinds
of credit are more difficult to obtain…And that any man
who tries to set himself in competition with any process
of manufacture which has taken place under control of a
large combination of capital will find himself squeezed
out or obliged to sell and allow himself to be absorbed."

President Wilson decided to face monopolies through open international trade (Underwood-Simons Tariff) intended to reduce the monopoly of trusts. He was mistaken because international trade worsens the economic imbalance of an economy. So he in a way through his anti-monoply stance helped the United States on its way to the many recessions that finally blossomed into the Great Depression in 1931. It is regrettable that more than one hundred years later (today), there are politicians and economists, as we have seen in chapter 5 in the US making the same mistake like President Wilson by saying that low price imports improve the US economy, increase productivity, and offer the US customer more choices.

Wilson, like all Presidents after him to date, lacked the political power to deal with the country's structural imbalance head-on. He himself admitted that "there is no use taking away the conditions of monopoly if we do not take away the power to create monopoly." He said that the power to control, guide, and direct the credits of the country is the power to say who shall not build up the industrializing of the country, in which direction they shall be built. He later took some steps aimed at *suppressing* the monopoly of Wall Street through the Federal Reserve Act of 1913 and by setting up the Federal Reserve System (Federal Reserve Act) and Federal Trade Commission of 1914 that was charged with enforcing anti-trust laws and preventing unlawful suppression of competition. These came to nothing as Wall Street and Fed were at the time defending the same interests as they are today, as we will see in chapter 9.

In an important article titled "Technological Change, Monopolistic Competition and Unemployment" in 1931, the well-known economist Professor Robert McCracken contrasted the post-World War I economy of the US with the nineteenth century US economy. He complained that "the industrial system absorbed technical progress without serious difficulty before the war but not since." He said, "But for some reason or the other, the trend was reversed during the war (World War I) with the results that progress did not repair itself nor the technology displaced workers find re-employment during the prosperous years of the twenties."[101] He complained that America had gone into a monopolistic economy, which changed the economy for the worse. He reminded us of the classic conclusions of Adolf Berle and Gardiner Means who carried out an exhaustive study of the growing US corporate structure in 1932. The two authors remarked that "American industrial property, through corporate device was being thrown into a collective hopper where in the individual owner was steadily being lost in the creation of a series of huge oligarchies." The number of trusts in the United States steadily increased at the end of nineteenth century. There were 183 trusts formed between 1899 and 1901. The present structural imbalance of the US economy has a very long history.

When the Republicans next took control of Congress, it was their chance to nullify Wilson's pro trade stance. Already inclined to a pro high tariff stance, they quickly enacted the Emergency Tariff Act of 1921 as a stop gap measure to reverse the Underwood-Simmons Tariff Act. The new Congress, however, adopted a laissez-faire attitude toward business and in effect took a different approach to Wilson's anti-monopoly stance. This gave further impetus to the formation of monopolies (the forerunners of the present US multi-corporations) and set the country farther down its early structural imbalance. The Republicans claimed that the economic prosperity, which occurred during World War I, was due to exports and lack of imports from war-ravaged Europe.

The United States emerged from World War I as a creditor nation with a foreign trade larger than at any other time in its history, with exports at $8.25 billion and imports at $5.75 billion. During the war, it loaned European nations $7 billion and another $3.3 billion after the war for relief and rehabilitation and expected these to be repaid as soon as possible. However the Europeans could not meet the obligations having suffered a gold drain from 1914 to 1917 when they shipped gold to the US to pay for the goods. Germany, which was blamed for starting the war, stopped paying its debts due to a weak economy. European countries complained that without access of their exports to the US, they will not be able to pay their debts. The end of World War I marked the beginning of US hegemony in trade by which the United States wanted to dominate trade through its financial and political power.

The Fordney-McCumber Tariff Act raised tariffs in some cases by 400 percent but the average was about 38 percent. The tariff for raw materials was generally on the low side. The hearings in Congress led to the creation of several new tools of tariff. The first was the *scientific tariff.* The purpose of the scientific tariff was to equalize production costs among countries, so that no country undercut the prices charged by American companies. The difference in production costs was to be calculated by the Tariff Commission. The scientific tariff particularly focused on wages in the exporting country. If wages in an exporting country are low compared to US wages, goods from that country were given a proportionately higher tariff. The second novelty was tariff based on *American Selling Price.* The tariff was linked to the price of American goods. It gave the President, on the recommendation of the Tariff Commission, the basis to calculate duty based on the price of the American good, not the imported good. The scientific tariff was a praiseworthy attempt, even by today's standards, intended to remove price from the international trade which often arises because some countries' costs were lower not because they were structurally more "efficient." In chapter 5, I regretted how present day trade economic theories have degenerated into cost and price affair and have failed to have scientific/structural validity.

Following their failure to convince the United States to lower its tariffs, European and Latin American countries decided to retaliate and raise their duties. Everybody for the first time joined in the affray (trade). Between 1925 and 1929, there were thirty-three general revisions with substantial tariff changes in twenty-six European countries, seventeen revisions and changes in Latin America. In 1927, Australia, Canada, and New Zealand all raised their tariffs in response to the Fordney-McCumber Tariff. America had had its way for so long that it was completely prepared for this torrent of actions from outside the US. The claim by President's Economic Advisers in their Report to the President of 2006 that the trade problems caused by these tariffs war "exacerbated" the Great Depression was a bit of giving a dog a bad name so as to hang it.

I like the words *scientific tariff.* In today's trade, conventional economists regard finance and economics as the same thing. If I produce something at a lower price, conventional economists will say that I am more efficient than someone else who produced the same item at a higher price. But that is not necessarily true. I might have obtained the material from a cheaper supplier. I might have lower labor costs and cheap capital. That does not make me more efficient. If I used the same man-hours and the same weight of material and capital as the other producer, the least that can be said from scientific resources use point of view is that we are equally efficient, despite the price difference. The science of production is interested in resource utilization not prices. If, therefore, one man-hour is used both in China and the US to produce a certain good, then from a scientific point of view, there should be no reason to give price preference to the good from China. If we do, we are penalizing the US worker because he is in an economy that has developed and enabled him to attain a high standard of living. Today, the worker in the advanced economy is being shortchanged and penalized. The US producer is also being penalized in some respects. The *scientific tariff* and American *selling price tariff* were at least serious attempts to apply science of production and factor endowments in the analysis of achieving some kind of science-based trade. Prices in countries are often determined by factors that have no scientific basis. An emerging economy will tend to have lower prices than an advanced economy.

Five years into the Fordney-McCumber Tariff, the US economy was worsening as the depression was gathering steam. It became particularly evident in agriculture where incomes had been declining since 1920. President Hoover came into office with an election promise to raise tariff on agricultural imports. However, the 1928 Republican Party platform had indicated the need for more far-reaching changes and stated:

> "We realize that there are certain industries which cannot
> now successfully compete with foreign producers because
> of lower foreign wages and a lower cost of living abroad,
> and we pledge the next Republican Congress to an exami-
> nation and where necessary a revision of these schedules to
> the end that American labor in these industries may again
> command the home market, may maintain its standard of
> living, and may count upon steady employment."

The Smoot-Hawley Tariff of 1930 further raised tariffs from its 1922 counterpart. Bear in mind that from 1922 to 1930 prices in the United States had dropped considerably because of the recession. A more realistic measure of the increase in tariff rates attributable to the Smoot-Hawley can be found in the study by the US Tariff Commission at the time. According to the commission, the average duties collected under the 1922 law were about 13.8 percent of the value of all imports, both free and dutiable, while the Smoot-Hawley Law will increase this to about 16 percent. The increase in effect was only about 2.2 percent. The commission then compared this with earlier tariff regimes: the McKinley Law (24 percent), the Wilson Law (20.9 percent), the Dingley Law (25.8 percent), the Payne-Aldrich Law (19.3 percent), the Fordney-McCumber (13.83 percent). The proportion of imports, which were to be free of duty under new law, was estimated at between 61 percent and 63 percent, compared with the Wilson Law at 49.4 percent.

From the point of foreign trade, the first question is whether the high tariff and consequent lack of foreign trade caused the depression, as some present day conventional economists claim. This is again another instance in which present trade economists lack the analytical tools and had to resort to disguised forms of guessing. One of them looking back on the era declared:

> "For conservatives, the greatest economic disaster in history needs a villain, and not just any villain…And in this respect, Smooth-Hawley Tariff of 1930 suits their needs perfectly…the Smoot-Hawley Tariff raised taxes on imported goods as high as 60 percent. Not only did this burden the American consumers with another tax, but it effectively killed international trade. Soon all nations were raising tariffs and rushing behind the walls of protectionism. The subsequent collapse of international trade caused the Great Depression."

Others not sure what to say will only say that that the tariff refined what would have been an ordinary recession into a full-blown depression. The Economic Advisers to the President in their valiant effort to promote free trade in their 2006 Report joined this group by declaring, as I indicated before, that "the heightened tariff and non-tariff trade barriers (caused by the Smoot-Hawley Tariff)…exacerbated the Great Depression." These experts provided no scientific reason for their wild claims. The growing economic concentration of the economy was gathering steam. Between 1919 and 1929, some 1,200 mergers had swallowed up more than 6,000 previously independent companies. By 1929, some 200 corporations controlled 50 percent of the economy. The foundations for the present-day structural imbalance of the US were being laid.

In his address accepting the Republican nomination on August 11, 1928, Hoover argued that foreign products raised under lower standards of living were competing in US home markets. In his Boston address on October 15, 1928, he referred the Underwood Tariff of President Wilson as basically seeking the same thing as he is seeking, namely that *the competition which it (Underwood Tariff) provided was competition with foreign wages and standards of living.* The current concept of international division of labor is based on a lack of knowledge of the science of technology. Technology, as I remarked earlier, is a menu of choices, so that no task should be labeled as low technology or high technology. Hoover, contrary to the current concept of international division of labor, correctly stated, "No discrimination against any foreign industry is involved in equalizing the difference in costs of production at home and abroad and thus taking from foreign producers the advantage they derive from paying lower wages to labor."

He was further interested in how costs in the US can be reduced:

> "We have seen a growing realization by labor that the maximum use of machines, of effort and skill is the road to lower production costs and in the end to higher real wages…If we are able by labor-saving devices and reduction of wastes in industry to decrease the cost of production of an article, we know by long experience that a train of consequences of highest importance follows: Wages in that industry rises, prices decrease, consumption increases at home and in our foreign markets…"

The Smoot-Hawley Tariff was not a product of some bigoted protectionists as they are currently made out in the United States. They were politicians trying to deal with what was at the time a first time experience of a phenomenon they had never before come across: Depression, which even today's reigning economists don't understand, judging by their poor 2008 through 2009 mini-depression performance.

The politicians of those days took over a country which prospered enormously from high tariffs and believed, along with President Hoover, that staying the course would help them get over the problems facing them. New tariffs, they said, would take time to yield results. On May 11, 1932, the President vetoed a bill to amend Smoot-Hawley Tariff and declared that "—there never has been a time in history of the United States when tariff protection was more essential to the welfare of American people than at the present."

In the veto, he said:

> "Manufacturers in foreign countries which have abandoned the gold standard are producing goods and paying for raw materials in depreciated currency. They may ship their goods into the United States with great detriment to the American producer and laborer because of the difference in value of money they pay for raw materials and the money they receive for finished goods."

The opposing Democrats never said they wanted free trade. The politicians at the time, like many ordinary Americans, felt the burden which other countries, especially those in Europe, were putting America under. America had been involved in a war it did not want to be involved with and was now owed money by its former allies who said in order to settle their debts they needed to sell to the United States. They wanted to source money from the creditors to pay what they owe the creditor.

The Smoot-Hawley Tariff has conveniently been made a villain by present-day free traders. Listen to US President's Economic advisers in their Economic Report to the President of 2006:

> "(The Smoot-Hawley Tariff) by reducing export markets—the heightened tariff and nontariff trade

barriers—exacerbated the Great Depression. The collapse of world trade from 1929 to 1933, a decline of more than two-thirds in just four years, followed the wake of protectionist policies as countries depreciated their currencies, raised tariffs and imposed quotas. The isolationist policies contributed to a spiraling contraction of world trade and a collapse of domestic demand."[102]

This claim is intellectually misleading. The so-called *collapse of domestic demand* had nothing to do with world trade. The authors of this report were, in effect, saying that the Smoot-Hawley Tariff Act started the depression which is historically incorrect. The drop in demand, as we showed, started from 1928.

Roosevelt was another early President that decried and warned about the early growing structural imbalance of the US economy. He fought his first presidential campaign on the issue of trust *bursting*. In a Commonwealth Club campaign speech September 23, 1932, he told his listeners that a recent careful study showed that six hundred old corporations controlled two thirds of the American industry, while ten million small businesses divided the other third. He told his audience that "it was the role of government to assist the development of an economic constitutional order [balanced economic structure]." He said the United States was pursuing a steady cause toward economic oligarchy "if we are not there already." His fireside chats often kept to this theme. In short, the long-term trend of the US adopting wrong factor proportions and technical structural imbalance of US economy started early. The fight against consolidation and trusts (and technical structural imbalance) in the United States was lost by the famous Supreme Court ruling establishing what it regarded as a difference between *good* trusts and *bad* trusts. Applying what it called *rule of reason*, the court affirmed that a concentration of industrial power was permissible if the method by which a trust got its power and the use it made of the power was reasonable. The Supreme Court did not think of the structural imbalance of the economy unlike China where there are legal and business hindrances to business concentration.

President Roosevelt had the opportunity to transform the US economy. The New Deal was intended, according to economists Douglass North and Robert Fogel in their book *History of the American Economy,* "to reform the economic system to prevent a recurrence of depression and to redress the imbalance between the rich and poor that existed before between the rich and poor that existed even before the contraction." Unfortunately these two problems that started early in the US have not only not been solved but have gotten worse in today's America. It is probably because the importance of task of balancing the economy that at his inaugural address, Roosevelt said, "Our international trade relations, though vastly important, are in point of time and necessity secondary to the establishment of a sound national economy. I favor, as a practical policy, the putting of first things first."

Roosevelt was correct to say that international trade was not a necessary component of a sound home economy. He concluded by saying that he will spare no effort to restore international economic readjustment "but the emergency at home cannot wait on that accomplishment." Today on the other hand, America regards foreign trade as a top cornerstone of its economy and now is a top cabinet level activity. Balancing the economy is now not on the agenda as infact it suits those who currently benefit from the present structure to claim that US economy is competitive.

Unfortunately, Roosevelt did not, as we have seen, like all the Presidents after him to date have the knowledge needed for restructuring and rebalancing the US economy. It was the best opportunity the US had in its history to set up its economy on a sound balanced basis in which a President was allowed for once to do what he wants to set up a sound economy. Roosevelt's *New Deal* was not an economic plan. The famous British minister and politician Roy Jenkins in his biography of Roosevelt called the *New Deal* a rag-tag.[103]

The *New Deal* was the use of authority of government as an organized form of self-help for all classes, groups, and sections of the country. It was as if the US was an activist committed to providing the individual citizen a measure of security against unpredictable turns of the market as was the norm of the depression. Roosevelt was in effect given $4.8 billion and authorized to spend it as he saw fit, which he used to stop overproduction in agriculture through (AAA), the Agricultural Adjustment Act and applied an early stumbling Keynesian-type attempt to spend his way out of the recession. The NIRA (National Industrial Recovery Act) was intended to raise prices and wages, spread out work to raise employment. Roosevelt in some ways forced alliance of industries and suspended new anti-trust laws, required industries to write codes of fair competition, established production quotas, fixed prices and wages. Employees were given the right to organize and bargain collectively. He attempted to balance the economy through rural development initiatives (Tennessee Valley) and railways.

By the time Roosevelt was through, major corporations unfortunately were already further set up. There were leading corporations in major branches of industry. He ended up fostering the very inequality he was originally complaining about in the industrial structure of the United States because the businessmen who dominated his code drafting wanted guaranteed profits and insisted on the security of their renewed investment and future production. This time, it can be said that while the economic success of the nineteenth century brought in trusts, the depression created a new set of corporations. Roosevelt, however, faced severe criticisms from those who called his government actions a threat to freedom and disliked government compulsory control of production and marketing. The *new deal* did nothing to stop to reduce the poverty and improve the economic climate. Today freedom in the US is equated with freedom to create and maintain monopolies.

Adolf Hitler did more than anyone else to end the US Great Depression because World War II was mobilizing the US economy into a more balanced economy, as I sought to show in my book, *The Science of Economic development and Growth*. Roosevelt's new deal's economic failure was a chance America missed to show that American governments can, given all the resources at their command and with the correct economic science, restructure the economy and create the trust between average American and the government as an economic initiator—a trust that it is presently seriously lacking.

Today's trade enthusiasts will like to tell us the Reciprocity Trade Agreement Act of 1934 that replaced the Smoot-Hawley Tariff was, according to 2006 Economic Report to the President, "a turning point in modern trade legislation" and "a historic shift to greater global engagement."[104] This is as one-sided comment. The other side, the truth, is in what the author of the bill, Secretary Hull, said in 1934 that the bill is "to supplement our almost impregnable domestic market with a substantial and gradually expanding foreign market for our burdensome surpluses." He envisaged a domestic market dominated by local production because the domestic market was almost impregnable to imports. He further told the Senate:

> "It should be kept in mind that American labor at good wages produced billions of commodities we export while our imports in chief measure comprise commodities we either do not produce at all or insufficient quantities with the result that American labor is helped rather than hurt by most of our imports."

Secretary Cordell Hull told the Senate in 1933 (while the Smoot-Hawley was still in operation) that US exported merchandise of $1,647 million and imported goods of $1,449 million of which $878 million was chiefly crude materials, crude foodstuff, and other materials not competitive but actually needed in the United States *to afford work for American labor.* Of this amount, finished imported dutiable manufactures comprised only $189,031,000 while US exported $616,623,000 of finished manufactures. While the United States exported crude materials, US farmers exported crude materials of $590,365,000. It is clear that Hull was describing an America that has today been replaced by China. The Reciprocity Act was in truth a continuation of a US policy of hegemony except that tariffs established with Smoot-Hawley had to be reduced in the face of stronger foreign opposition and revenge from foreign countries. Indeed the then well-known George Peek, one-time head of Roosevelt's Agricultural Adjustment Administration (AAA) preferred barter of US surplus agriculture for non-competitive imports agricultural, and imports and dumping the rest in the international market. Indeed we are told that when the Reciprocity Tariff was passed into law, Hull and Peek each regarded the Act as an endorsement of their strategy.

Much of the economic dilemma the United States faces today were faced by Roosevelt's Secretary Wallace in a publication titled "America Must Choose": He summarized the choice at the time as between the compulsory government control of production and marketing not only in agriculture but in industry in order to reach what he called a balanced nationalistic economy or the suppression of our hereditary initiative and love of freedom and, worst of all, the stifling of individual free thought and speech.

This dilemma is as true then as it is today between the need today for a structurally balanced economy and free enterprise. In a radio address on April 29, 1930, the Republican Henry Stimson summarized what was to be the general attitude of people that matter at the time. He said that Mr. Wallace had pointed out the choice Americans were to make and that he was glad Mr. Wallace announced"his own distaste and opposition to such a process (namely compulsory government control)" and that Wallace "believes that we should try as far as possible to follow the other course, that of trying to restore our international trade." Wallace further said:

> "For myself I have never been able to conjure up any real apprehension that American people would be willing to carry through anything like a complete system of a planned national economy. It would be at variance with their deepest instincts and habits."

Against this were those who labelled Roosevelt as leading a radical, collectivistic, and radical socialist regime. Ogden Mills, Treasury secretary in the immediate past Administration talked of Hoover's *high tariff.* In a speech at the semi-annual dinner of the Academy of Political Science on March 22 1934, he declared, "For my part, I am prepared to cast my lot with the policy of what, for want of a better term, I may call, economic freedom, as contrasted with the rigidity of a controlled and regimented economy." Men like Henry Ford, as will be expected, opposed the *new deal* system, preferring international trade. What played out at the time tells us that over eighty years later, Americans to date don't trust their governments enough to want to hand over the economy to them to direct.

It is against this background of a sudden flood of pro-open economy voices and accusations of anti-democracy against him, as in today's United States, that Roosevelt administration *panicked*. To reconstruct the economy, as he had wanted, was not going easy as it became clear that he had no true economic strategy to offer and he realized that he may have lost time in dealing with international trade, which he had at first postponed. In now seeking to be outward-oriented, Roosevelt realized that he may have lost time in accessing foreign market, which his economic success would have provided him as countries were now imposing trade barriers partly as a result of world depression at the time and partly in retaliation to the United States. Roosevelt needed a fast track approval to deal with the situation by passing the Reciprocity Tariff Act. These pressures were borne by Secretary Hull, the architect of the Reciprocity Tariff Act. In all interchange with members of Congress, Hull always emphasized that there was a grave economic crisis. Can we say that Congress was conned?

With the sense of emergency and urgency, which the Roosevelt administration created, Congress had enormous pressure put on it to pass the bill. The bill was in effect saying that, for the emergency to be dealt with, the president wanted full and special authority.

Some of the amendments/suggestions were:

z. to permit reciprocal trade treaties to become effective if not rejected by Congress within thirty days;
aa. to limit the treaties and the President's tariff powers to three or five years;
ab. to require all trade treaties to be submitted for approval;
ac. to set up an independent body to hear objections of industries affected by lowering of tariff rates and to determine what concessions shall be made to foreign countries.

The President was not prepared to hear any of these.

It is, therefore, incorrect for the Council of Economic Advisers in their historical review of international trade in 2006 to claim that, while the US constitution left members of Congress vulnerable to protectionist demands of special industries and interests, President

Roosevelt and Secretary Hull worked with Congress not only to lower tariffs but also *to make lower tariffs more politically durable* by making Congress not responsible for setting tariffs. The Council further claimed Congress had also intended to permanently delegate tariff setting to the executive. This is also incorrect. Congress gave up the powers because they were told there was an emergency. Secretary Hull made it clear in his statement before the Senate Finance Committee that the executive was asking for a special and temporary authority. The President told Congress, "Trade agreements shall be terminable within a period not exceeding three years."

On the hardened high tariffs, Republicans asked Secretary Hull whether it will be possible to complete reciprocal treaties before the currency was stabilized. Hull replied that it will be best to go ahead (that is you vote for) and that meanwhile currency stabilization would be coming along. Mr. Hull was intentionally not giving his questioner the impression that the tariff reductions for which the president was seeking authority were to be permanent. It is further necessary to probe the minds of the architects of Reciprocity Tariff to see how and whether their thinking differs from those who are at the moment driving the United States free trade agenda. I will again choose Hull, Roosevelt's Secretary of State, a democrat from Tennessee. It was the North that originally wanted protection for manufactures, while the South was interested to export primarily its agriculture. In his memoirs, Hull said that from early in his life, he had fought battles in his home grounds on whether tariff was good or bad for the United States. "Only during World War I did I see the international perspective of trade" he said.

In 1916, he made a speech in Congress calling for a post-war trade conference which never took place. He repeatedly claimed that tariffs were a threat to world peace. His appointment as Secretary of State in 1933 came at a time Roosevelt was fighting the Great Depression and being accused by his opponents of applying undemocratic means, as I have already described. Hull developed the set of ideas that formed the basis of the Reciprocity Tariff of 1934. He was to elaborate on these in his statements I earlier referred to, to the US Senate Finance Committee on the bill.

The Act was, in truth, a continuation of a US policy of hegemony established since the nineteenth century except that tariffs had to be reduced in the face of realities that foreign countries were becoming stronger and beginning to retaliate against the high US tariffs. Unlike the UK hegemony, which in its time was backed by its imperialistic colonial power, the Reciprocity Tariff Act was a realization by the United States that it needed to engage in a new diplomacy in order to promote and continue its desired hegemony of using foreign markets as the destination for its carry-over production surplus, or as Secretary Hull called it on another occasion, taking from outside only what the US could not produce or what it is not producing in sufficient quantity.

In his message to congress requesting the needed authority for the new Tariff Act, Roosevelt emphasized that the adjustment must "rest on the premise of undertaking to benefit and not to injure sound and important (US) interests." As we know at the time, the US had lots of surplus agricultural production, in which, as we saw before, farmers were dumping and destroying agricultural produce. The country badly needed not only to sell agricultural products but also to reduce agricultural production. Indeed the well-known George Peek, one time head of the Agricultural Adjustment Administration (AAA), preferred barter of surplus US agricultural products for noncompetitive imports, agricultural products, and dumping the rest in the international mar ket. The Reciprocity Tariff Act was by no means a liberal stance on trade, based on current trade economic theorizing, as White House economic advisers to the President at the time tried to make out. Indeed we are told that at the time the Reciprocity Tariff Act was passed into law, Hull and Peek each regarded the Act as an endorsement of their strategy.

Following the enactment of the Reciprocity Tariff Act, the United States under Hull set about to negotiate trade with counttries. By November 1938, twenty agreements were concluded with eleven from Latin America. On the whole, the United States did not achieve a lot in a world that was basically full of protection arising from currency devaluations and countries like the United States battling general depression at the time. Condliffe in a prophetic comment stated in 1940 that "If an international system is to be restored, it must be an American-dominated system based on *Pax America*." This, as we will see, happened in 1944/1945 as World War II was finishing. It was all now about politics.

Hull from his early days regarded international trade as a means to avoid international conflict and enthrone peace. I have always felt that that is wrong. One should not mix economics and economic well-being of Americans and international politics, which is the hallmark of many recent US administations. Hull many times called his tariff crusade as "movement for peace" and "economic disarmament." Yet, not long after, World War II started. This *political* reasoning was again to be used by the United States in 1944/1945 which, to some extent, is the start of current US trade policy makers. Sometimes, US officials unfortunately call trade talks *the economic side of peace*. This view of international trade has unfortunately come to dominate current US strategy.

World War II shaped the US economy in distinctly new directions and heralded new trends which gave Roosevelt what he could not get before. The first was rapid growth in production. It was estimated that between 1940 and 1943, output in Germany and Russia doubled. It quadrupled in Japan, but in the United States, it increased by twenty-five times.[105] The gross annual product increased more than 50 percent allowing for price increases. The volume of manufacture tripled. The US was said to have performed a miracle in out producing the Axis powers so soon after the war. The war economy ended the long depression and ushered in a period of sustained economic growth. Neoclassical economists have sought to explain this *miracle* by claiming that it was Keynes at its best. It was not Keynes. It can only be Keynes as claimed by Keynesians if increased consumer spending had triggered new investment in line with Keynes claims, which was not what happened.[106] Indeed during World War II, many consumer items were scarce and often rationed because production was geared to war needs.

Other neoclassical economists have claimed the rapid growth of the US economy at the time was because of vast increases in labor productivity and of Total Producton Factor (TPF). However all these analysts forgot that private investment during the war was far less than in 1929 and 1930.[107] So the vast growth of the war economy cannot be due to rapid investment. The drop in private investment meant that this normal source of capital concentration and intensiveness in the economy was removed. US operative factor proportions improved. War investments were, as to be expected, emergency skeletal low capital make-do structures. They also involved more intensive use of existing facilities and bringing back into production previously discarded installations. Halfway between 1942 and 1945, the net capital increase in the economy was less than the wear and tear on existing capital. The large civilian labor input increases were a combination of full use of all employable hands as well as women and longer working hours. Women worked in shipyards, aircraft industries, machines shops, ammunitions works, and on precision machines. The economy was, therefore, far more labor-intensive, less material-intensive than at any time since the beginning of the century and after the war. For example, between 1939 and 1945, the value of capital assets in the aircraft sector (so important to the war) reduced by twenty-five times while labor increased by over twenty-five times. My book, *The Science of Economic Development and Growth,* presented a very detailed scientific structural factor proportions analysis of the World War II US economy to show that structurally it was similar to the New Economy of the 1900s and late 1890s in that America had structurally balanced economies at this time.

It was with this dominating World War II balanced economic structure that the US invited the forty-four allied countries to the Bretton Conference in 1944. Bretton Woods was an instrument of US hegemony. In an editorial, the *New York Times* observed that the final text of the articles of agreement of Bretton Woods' conference "differs little, except in the elaboration of details from the proposals submitted (by the US) before the conference..." The editorial correctly said that it made the conference "a rubber stamp."[108]

The following is the full reporter's account of American official's plans and hopes from the 'rubber stamp' conference:

> "Confidence was expressed today by members of the American delegation...That the level of American export trade can be raised from the average of $3,000,000,000 annually of the prewar years to around 10,000,000,000 if the proposed International Monetary Fund and World Bank for Reconstruction and development are established."[109]

The two institutions that the conference was expected to approve would vastly facilitate American foreign trade. Surveys showed that for the five years prior to the war the average American exports was $3,000,000,000. They insisted this country must have at least $7,000,000,000 more exports after the war to avert serious unemployment. The experts felt that if the planned monetary fund was approved by the conference, there was a good chance that US exports could reach the $7,000,000,000 level and if the bank was established as well, the US exports should increase to $10,000,000,000. A gain in trade of this size would involve a 60 percent increase in the physical volume of American exports, taking into account the changed purchasing power of the dollar.

It was repeatedly emphasized by the experts at the time that the institutions under consideration to be created in no way can alter the requirement that the United States, as the world's largest creditor nation, shall maintain policies after the war which encourage imports as well as exports. The reasoning at the time was that unless we (the US) buy as many things as possible from abroad, the nations we count on to be customers will lack the dollars they can only obtain [through] sales of goods to us, with which to pay for our exports.

The World War II economic success and prosperity led Americans as a nation to believe that the country's future prosperity lay in the promotion and control of international trade. Most Americans at the time saw the conference as a means to establish US hegemony and dominate world trade. A journalist asked one US delegate at the conference what would happen if the US permanently maintains a favorable balance of payment, exporting more than it imports, and, therefore, little or no need to exchange dollars for foreign currency. The delegate, characteristically, said he thought that after the first few years following the war, during which the rest of the world will need large amounts of US products, there might be a change in the situation.

He continued: "If the United States succeeds in its post-war goals of high production, high employment, and high national income, we will need increasing imports of *raw materials and* some *finished products.*" He also said that within a few years after the war there should be large tourist expenditures by Americans abroad and a return of capital that fled to this country before the war to countries that succeeded in stabilizing their economic structures. "Both would mean an increased American demand for foreign currencies," he said.

Bretton Woods up to about late 1950s was a period of unchallenged US economic and political hegemony. The 1960s up to late 1980s is a period in which the US economy suffered bouts of recessions and increasing balance of payment deficits. The patient became sick and feverishly tried to find cures for his illness but did not succeed. The 1990s to date, the patient has paralysis, namely a permanent and growing trade deficit. The patient has given up looking for a cure and sometimes says that he has no illness.

Post World War II United States was riding on the crest of Bretton Woods and enjoyed rising exports and trade surplus. The surpluses were adding to large growing reserves. The 1947 Economic Report to the President summarized the US economy as follows:

> "As the year 1947 began, the state of our national economy presents great opportunity for all. We have virtually full employment. Our national production of goods and services is 50 percent higher than in any year prior to the war. During five years, production facilities have expanded in almost every field."

The 1950 Report stated:

> "The United States position changed over the last fifty years. Fifty years ago, the country was devoted to internal affairs. Today the population has doubled. National production rose from $50 billion in today's prices to $255 billion a year. We have a more productive economic system and greater industrial production potential than any other nation on the globe."

Authorities decided that they needed to reverse the US increasing reserves in order to create new markets for US bourgeoning manufacturing output. So throughout much of the 1950s, the United States deliberately maintained a deficit. At the same time, the modest credit facilities of the newly created IMF were found to be insufficient to cope with Western Europe's massive balance of payment deficit. The problem was complicated by the IMF board, which stated it could only make loans to countries for current account deficits and not for needed capital and reconstruction purposes in those countries. The IBRD (International Bank for Reconstruction and Development) itself had with it only the US contribution as other countries were not forthcoming. By 1947 the IMF and IBRD were admitting that they could not deal with international monetary system's economic problems, as had been hoped at the conference.

As part of the planned outflow of dollars, the US embarked on the Marshall Plan (the so called European Recovery Program) to provide favored European countries with grants to reconstruct and rebuild their economies. In my book, *The Science of Economic Development and Growth*, I dealt extensively with the Marshall Plan and wondered whether it was more of a political strategy than an economic aid. I concluded that, among other things, the Marshall Plan was intended for America to claim credit for Europe's economic resurgence after World War II. It was also aimed politically to drive Western European countries firmly in the non-Soviet camp. The so-called Truman doctrine entailed providing aid to pro US Greek and Turkish regimes, which were at the time suppressing socialist revolution. Funds were also spent to assist regimes in the third world to keep them within pro free world anti-communist sphere. Aid was also made available to assist Japanese recovery aimed at expanding US markets. The US also financed its military adventures in Korea, Vietnam, and NATO (North Atlantic Treaty Organization) alliances. That was the start of US proliferous spending in international arena which continues today. We became a self-appointed world policeman.

Bretton Woods created what has been called *a system of triangular trade*. The United States will, as the plan goes, use its convertible finance system to trade at high profit with developing countries, and, thus, expand its industries to secure cheap raw materials for them. It will send the profits as dollars to Europeans to rebuild their economies and create markets in Europe for the United States. This will in turn make it possible for European countries to buy from the third world. This triangular arrangement was intended to reinforce the United States role as guarantor of economic stability. In the process, third world countries began to regard export to the United States as a primary goal, a trend that gained momentum as years passed. It has since become a tsunami.

In the end, things did not work as the United States had planned. The hoped for profitable circulation of the US dollar overseas failed to increase the size of the US gold base even as international trade under US charge grew. From 1957–1958 the US faced a recession, the so-called Eisenhower recession, with significant decline in production and employment. The United States faced the crisis of a negative balance of payment. That was the first heart attack the US economy suffered. Eisenhower complained in 1960 that:

> "Our surplus from foreign trade business transactions have in recent years fallen short of the expenditures we make abroad to maintain our military establishments overseas, to finance private investment, and to provide assistance to less developed nations. In 1959, US deficit of payments approached $4 billion. Cutting deficits of anything like this magnitude would, over time, improve our own economic growth and check the forward progress of the Free World. We must meet this situation by promoting a rising volume of exports and world trade."

The Eisenhower administration, in a reversal of US new free trade stand, placed import quotas on oil as well as other restrictions on trade. Unfortunately it did not act on other drastic measures proposed to save the US economy. The decline of the dollar resulted as US share of international reserves slipped to 16 percent by 1970. This further decreased US economic leadership. It was another heart attack because by mid-1960s, the European countries and Japan had fully recovered from the war and had become international economic powers on their own. With their total reserves now exceeding that of the United States, they had narrowed the gap between them and the United States. The shift to a pluralist distribution of economic power meant that the markets created by US profligacy were not always there for the US to dominate. By the late 1960s, the situation worsened for the US. The belief that the deficit could be solved by even greater pace of trade was such that by 1969 and 1970, US balance of payment deficit increased even more to an annual level of $3 billion and in the first half of 1971, the deficit increased to an annual rate of $9 billion. In August 1971, President Nixon pulled the plug and finally killed Bretton Woods. The present belief of the US up to recently, that it can get out of the trade deficit hole by more trade is a continuation of immediate past follies.

The fall of the US international trade should have prompted future administrations to review the country's trade/economic strategy but it did not. President Truman at the peak of US international eco nomic power signed the General Agreement on Tariffs and Trade (GATT) bringing the United States into multilateral trade agreement in pursuance of its hegemony ambitions. But when Kennedy came into power, it was clear that Bretton Woods had all but collapsed. One would have thought that US failure along the path of trade would give it the opportunity to review its liberal trade policy and go back to what the early people who sought to restructure the US economy did. Many pro-trade commentators described Kennedy's Round as the most significant development in the move to advance free trade since World War II. It can be said that Kennedy was the first full blast total acceptance of comparative advantage of trade.

For the first time in its history, the country accepted, as a point of policy, that international trade can or even should lead to loss of jobs in the United States. Congress, as an incentive in support of the new liberal trade bill, provided assistance for such workers through the so-called Trade Adjustment Assistance program. This was a historical reversal of policy. Kennedy's remarks that "Lowering of our tariffs will provide an increased flow of goods for our American consumers," were also the first explicit US statement in history that increased consumer goods import was a cornerstone of trade policy. His statement that "freer competition with industries of other nations for an even greater effort to develop an efficient, economic and productive system," was the first US stated mistaken objective that imports are needed to keep the US economy strong. Kennedy went out of his way to seek the cooperation of the Europeans. He said:

"Together with the Common Market, we account for 90 percent of free world trade in industrial products...and I think this is most important in this vital period—the greatest aggregation of economic power in the history of the world. We now have the means to make certain that we build our strength together and that we can maintain this preeminence."

The United States was repeating this fancy that its market and that of the European Union (EU) combined have so much economic clout that free trade between them will bring prosperity to them and solve their declining economic fates. Of course, the union with Europe at the time with Kennedy never materialized. The Europeans were harboring resentment about the United States backing away from Bretton Wood *guarantees*. Kennedy, like all presidents after him, was driven by geopolitical ambitions in pushing the trade expansion.

He said that the expanded trade bill could "affect the unity of the West, the course of the Cold War, and the growth of our nation for a generation or more to come." He was again, like Bretton Woods, mixing economics with foreign affairs ambitions. The 2006 Economic Report by the Council of Economic Advisers claimed that Congress approved Kennedy's Trade Expansion Act "with substantial support." This is not correct. While the 298/125 vote in the House may indicate substantial support, *Time Magazine* of July 6, 1962 stated that the passage was in fact much harder fought than the votes indicated and that the outcome was in doubt until the final hours of the vote. It stated that many Democrats as well as Republicans in Congress were resentful of the high-pressure lobbying tactics by the Kennedy Administration. All living ex-presidents, Republican Hoover and Eisenhower as well as Democrat Truman, were wheeled out to drum up support for its passage in the House.

By 1962, the US economy had suffered three recessions since the war. Kennedy was also faced with a problem currently facing present US policy makers—technological unemployment. He said he was concerned to stop the waste of able-bodied men and women who want to work but whose only skill has been replaced by a machine or shutdown.

The Manpower, Training and Development Act was put in place to train trade-displaced workers in new skills. Recall Bernanke proposing the same remedy in 2007. As of today, as we will see, the problem is still here in the United States. The basic problems of the US economy reached a new level during Nixon's presidency. The groundswell of the adverse effects on businesses led Congress to propose the Trade Bill of 1970. Professor Canto in his historical account of the period described the bill as "as a sharp departure from more than thirty years of US leadership toward liberalizing trade." He said that it was "the most protective protectionist legislation since the Smoot-Hawley Act of 1930."[110]

Another attempt to pass another *defend-yourself* bill, more popularly called the Burke-Hartke bill, was made in 1972. This bill went further than the 1970 bill to add new forms of defensive strategies including restrictions on direct foreign investments, which have always, in my view, had mixed macroeconomic results in the United States. Nixon himself in a message to Congress on December 1,1971 transmitting the annual report on Kennedy Round (which was being implemented between 1967 and 1972) admitted that direct result of the increased international trade was that the United States "for the first time in this century faced the prospects of a deficit in its balance of merchandise trade." In 1971, the deficit was over $9 billion including $3 billion on trade account. Nixon launched a new Economic Program in August 15. He was confident that:

> "The deterioration in our merchandise trade balance, which was threatening at the end of 1970 and which reached intolerable proportions in the spring of 1971 will be sufficiently improved that the present US surcharge on imports will be removed."

Nixon did not succeed. The 1974 Trade Act was described by *Time* in an article Monday, April 2, 1973, at the time the bill was tabled as a "trust-Nixon" bill. It said that the bill could not be characterized "as either free trade or protectionist."

"The proposals," it said, will give the President "unprecedented authority to move just about as far as he chose in either direction." While the Act authorized the president to begin negotiations to strengthen GATT system of free trade, it also provided that an industry no longer needed to demonstrate that its injury was caused by imports resulting from an earlier tariff concession or that imports are the "major" cause of its injury. The industry only needed to show that imports are a "substantial" cause of its problems and if the recently set-up US International Trade Commission (ITC) finds injury, the industry will be entitled to trade restriction or adjustment assistance, and that Congress can override the president and institute the relief recommended by ITC. The authority of the president to impose quantity restrictions on trade was increased. Use of voluntary restraints agreed with importing countries was expanded. Under this Act, the president entered into the so-called Tokyo Round to cut tariffs further. The president recognized the other reality, which confirmed that the United States was going down the ladder and that the European Community was now "the world's largest trading entity." Nixon always made it clear that US liberal trade policy was driven by the needs of US foreign policy. He said trade was fundamental to US relations with Europe, Japan, and Canada with whom United States "has political and military relations." He said that only Communist countries will benefit from a breakdown of economic cooperation in the non-Communist world.

It is noteworthy that the President appointed a Commission on International Trade and Investment Policy to study the principal problems faced by the United States in this field and produce a set of policy recommendations for the 1970s which would take account of the changes that have taken place on the world economic scene since the end of the War (i.e. World War II). The commission, made of twenty-seven members drawn from business, labor, agriculture, and universities, was high powered. Nixon was seriously looking for a lasting solution to the trade malaise. The report published in July 1971 was good on wishes. It came out with vague recommendations like how to strengthen the capacity of US industry and labor to *compete more effectively* and how to negotiate with US major trade partners. Like many current economic reports one currently reads on the US economy, this report showed a lack of knowledge of the structural issues facing the United States. The Council of Economic Advisers said in 1970 that the surge in US imports was due to US inflation and was sure that as US inflation slows, trade balance will improve. It did not. Instead it got worse. In 1973, Treasury Secretary George Shultz said he will make the trade deficit problem his top priority to no avail. America should have used the opportunity to realize that international trade was harming its economy.

The 1980s was not a good decade for US international trade. It got worse. By 1983, trade deficit was $65 billion, approximately twice the previous record set in 1982. Authorities forecast that it will climb to $110 billion in 1984, three times that of 1982. The Council of Economic Advisers in their 1984 report put on their thinking cap to diagnose the growing trade deficit. The advisers said:

> A common reaction (that is of the growing trade deficit) is one of concern. It is easy to draw the impression that there is a serious adverse long-run trend in the competitive standing of the United States in the world. The greatest danger is that such ideas will come to be believed, and that as a result, the Nation will opt for major departures from its traditional economic system.

The Council was not only deluding itself but more regrettably it was misleading ordinary Americans because the problems were real and technically structural. The advisers claimed in their wisdom that the deficit was due to three factors, each of which in retrospect, we know is wrong:

ad. to the appreciation of the dollar;
ae. loss in net exports to *debt-troubled* countries;
af. The United States is experiencing more rapid growth in income, and, therefore, in imports than Europe and Japan.

They famously concluded, "These three factors concern economic perturbations that though large, are believed to be temporary!" Believe it or not, they advised that US trade deficit was temporary and the problems were mere perturbations!!

The advisers additionally claimed that the deficit may not be as large as it is because export in services had "a gradual upward trend." They claimed that export of services, which they hoped will help the trade gap, was likely to be greater than recorded because of measurement errors. Here is a group who refused to recognize the economic malaise facing their country. They had earlier said that Americans should not accept fears that the United States was losing its competitiveness but indeed the United States was increasingly losing its competitiveness. That is what I classified as ignorance in chapter 3.

The industrial landscape was so disturbed that on October 14, 1984, the Head of the United States Trade Commission Paula Stern charged that the administration and other federal policy makers have allowed American manufacturers to be savaged by foreign competition that the nation risked the loss of much of its industrial base and jobs. "American industries are being savaged by imports in both recession and growth periods due to Federal economic policies that ignore the important role trade has established for itself in the economy," she said. In the US, the solution for unsuccessful trade is more trade. This remains to day as Obama in his last days in office is scavenging for more trade territories in the world.

Reagan was basically pro trade. His administration launched the Uruguay Round in 1986 that powered global tariffs and created the WTO. His administration won the approval of the US-Canada Free Trade Agreement 1988, expanded later to include Mexico in the North American Free Trade Agreement. He vetoed the textile bills in 1986 and 1988. He vetoed bill to impose tariffs on steel. His voluntary import quotas and tariff on motorcycles have been described as "tactical retreats designed to defuse rising protectionists pressures in Congress." He was said to have championed "free trade while selectively deviating from it."

The worrying thing is that Reagan's open-trade leanings were rooted primarily in geo-political philosophizing and not on economics. He moved one step further than Kennedy who was intent to use free trade to unite the free world against communism. As communism became less of a threat, Reagan talked of using free trade as an instrument for spreading democracy and liberty: freedom, free trade, free speech, and all the other freedoms. He said that he recognizes "the inescapable conclusion that all of history has taught: The freer the flow of world trade, the stronger the tides of human progress and peace among nations."

Discussing with the Japanese Prime Minister Nabonu Takeshita on January 13, 1988 Regan told him, "We share an abiding commitment to democratic institutions and to free trade markets to protect freedom and human rights." In his last State of the Union Message, January 25, 1988, he boasted, despite the large trade deficit, that, "Today America is strong and democracy is everywhere on the move. From Central America to East Asia, ideas like free markets and democratic reforms and human rights are taking hold."

The United States has always made trade, not just a central issue of economic growth but an instrument of international relations. While the report he submitted to Congress in 1987 and a national TV broadcast made brief references to US trade deficit, Reagan also submitted an eleven page summary of recommendations for legislative proposals to solve the trade deficit. It contained the same hard-worn ideas that we hear today about investment in human/intellectual capital, literacy, mathematics, science and technology, youth employment, dislocated workers, intellectual property, guarding intellectual property and copy rights from foreigners, all of which had nothing directly to deal with the crisis on trade.

When Clinton came into office, he took a low-keyed but vigorous pro trade stance. He believed that trade was a win-win endeavor (Ricardo's comparative advantage at play). In his State of the Union Message in 1997, he said that trade was more than economics. "By expanding trade, we can advance the cause of freedom and democracy around the world." The same theme was in Clinton's State of the Union Message in 1999: "Our purpose must be bring together the world around freedom and democracy and peace and oppose those who would tear it apart." In his 1998 State of the Union Message he more explicitly said:

> "In the last five years, we have led the way in opening new markets with 240 trade agreements that remove foreign barriers to products bearing the proud stamp 'Made in the USA.' Today record high export accounts for one-third of our economic growth. I want to keep this going, because

that is the way to keep America going and advance a safer, more stable world."

Indeed this was not true. In 1996, exports at $582 billion were 7.7 percent of GDP, and imports at $790 billion were 10.4 percent of GDP. Clinton said that those who oppose trade had unfounded fears (a) that trading partners have lower environmental and labor standards and sometimes use infant labor; (b) workers will lose their job. He opted for legislation to fight intolerable labor practice and above all child labor in other countries. He offered help to communities where factories closed *which has nothing to do with trade*. He did not seem to believe that trade had anything to do with factories closing. Clinton believed in his 1995 message that "in a truly open market, we can outcompete anyone, anywhere on earth."

When Clinton stated in his speech that the world's economies are more and more interconnected and interdependent and that what economic crisis anywhere can affect economies everywhere and that if other people's economy sinks, they will not be able to buy from us, if their currency loses value they will flood us with cheap goods and make it difficult to compete. Clinton had converted to a disciple of *one-worldism*.

Clinton made democrats and unions in the United States believe that if only 'higher' labor standards, establishment of trade unions and end to child labor were put in place in the third world, America will improve its exports to these countries and keep US employment high. With the influence of Al Gore, environment was thrown into the debate about US international trade. I want to make clear that this is not to belittle the importance of environment but to sug gest that on trade it was a political distraction.

So successful was Clinton in his labor and environment twist to the argument that in 2007 that some democrats threatened to make labor standards and human rights part of any deal to get China into the WTO, as if these were the things that account for America's loss of trade advantage with China or other emerging markets for that matter. Labor, food safety, environment, and intellectual property were things thrown in by drowning trade failures. From time to time, Clinton moved to restrict imports when loud complaints about labor standards and environment were made. But the country had no trade strategy other than to charge ahead with new trade agreements in a doctrinal belief on free trade. Clinton told Congress in that 1999 message "the only direction forward for America on trade is to keep going forward." Clinton did not acknowledge that the patient has suffered a heart attack. To him, the patient was doing just fine.

When George W. Bush came into the scene, the US trade profile did not change. In August 2002, he signed legislation (Trade Act of 2002) that re-established fast track trade nego tiation authority, which Clinton was not able to renew due to opposition by democrats. Free trade as a doctrine of America's political mission of democratization of the world was explicitly espoused by Bush in his 2002 "National Security Strategy" in which he said:

> "We will actively work to bring the hope of democracy, development, free markets and free trade to every corner of the world…America must stand firm for non-negotiable demands of human dignity: free speech, freedom of worship, limits of absolute power…equal justice for women and respect for private property."

Free trade, according to this Bush's statement, is essentially part of democratic, political liberation movement and not just an instrument of US economic strategy.

President Obama came into office determined to push trade. He promised to double US exports in five years. He stated that that "It is time to finally slash the tax breaks for companies that ship our jobs overseas and give tax breaks to companies that create jobs in the United States. He set up the National Export Initiative—the first ever government wide export promotion strategy focused at the Presidential and the cabinet level, a sort of Export Cabinet. He also set up a President's Export Council. In the 2010 State of the Union Message, he set up the goal to double US exports over the next five years intended to give employment to two million people. In his remarks at the Export-Imports Bank's Annual Conference on March 2010, he said, "it is absolutely necessary for us to get beyond those old debates" about the differences of opinion on trade. In effect he had implicit belief in comparative advantage of trade.

In seeking fast-track trade authority to achieve Trans-Pacific Partnership of US and 11 other Pacific Rim countries in 2015, Obama and his supporters regretfully succeeded to treat the problems of labor in the US as an aspect of trade which could be treated on its own. In Chapter 5, I endeavored to say that the basic problem is that international trade causes technical structural economic imbalances which make the US macro-economy unbalanced and uncompetitive, and therefore, a source of US economic decline. The Chinese economy as I showed is structurally balanced and its pattern of imports, which is still a relatively small size of its total economy and intended to cover mainly goods not manufactured in China.

Obama came up with many administrative initiatives intended to boost international trade, on top of which were these two new agencies he set up at the presidential and cabinet level. He had broadly a number of things he wants to do to meet the goal he set. First, he was sure that one of the main obstacles to US increased trade was that others have not played fair and he was committed to see that trade agreements were enforced. Second, he was going to show those opposed to any trade that "there are new markets and new sectors out there that we need to break into." Ninety five percent of the world's customers and the world's fastest-growing markets are outside US borders we were told. Third, he will press with signing trade agreements with countries, and he wants the United States to compete with those pursuing trade agreements with growing markets. Fourth, he wants financing for exports to be increased under National Export Initiative. It is planned to install a one-stop shop the US and the US embassies and consulates to help US businesses.

Fifth, he wants the government to improve its advocacy abroad. The President signed a Travel Promotion Act, which in part is to encourage foreign citizens to visit the United States, including trade and reverse trade missions. Sixth, the United States will protect its intellectual property and USTR is to be encouraged in this effort and to enforce controls on the export of US most critical technologies. Seventh, it is intended to streamline and fast-track processes for US companies to get their products out to the market. Eight, the United States will eliminate unnecessary obstacles for exporting products to companies with dual-national and third-country-national employees. He hoped early in his second term to complete talks on the Trans-Pacific Partnership intended to reduce tariffs on a wide range of goods in which eleven countries are participating possibly including Japan. A Transatlantic Trade and Investment with the European Union was planned. There were initiatives to engage in international trade in services with twenty countries nearly two-thirds of global trade in services. These eight initiatives cannot save the US because they are all administrative initiatives and had nothing to do with solving US structural economic problems some of which the US acquired though international trade. It did not occur to the President and the vast conventional economists in the US that America is structurally uncompetive Obama completed negotiations on the Trans-Pacific Trade Agreement and sought a fast track approval of the agreement intended to reduce tariffs on a wide range of goods among eleven Pacific countries including Japan. The Agreement was partly trade, but more a political move against China. Obama had sought to leave the Trans-Pacific Trade Agreement as his legacy. Interest for a North American union of Canada, US, and Mexico is based primarily on security objectives despite a 2014 report, which stated that "Twenty years after its implementation, NAFTA has fallen short of generating jobs and the deeper regional economic integration its advocates promised decades ago." All attempts over the years to solve the NAFTA have not succeeded because these problems are structural.

Forty years or so ago after the US had the fortune when Nixon got Saudi Arabia to agree to sell its enormous supply of oil in US dollars in exchange for giving the country military protection, the Saudis in 1975 finally got OPEC (Organization of Petroleum Exporting Countries) to go along. The era of petrodollars had arrived. America had a petrodollar power/empire. Every country stuffed their central bank with dollars with which to buy oil. So countries had either to borrow dollars or sell to the United States to get dollars and sell they did, with Japan opening up with selling us cars while the Fed printed dollars at little cost. Those selling to America loved the American consumers. They stuffed Americans with their cheap goods. Soon America's supply of dollars ran out as a result of an economic mismanagement. The result that was America went out to borrow from those that accumulated its dollars. They called it petrodollar recycling. Today the Iranians, the Chinese, and BRIC countries are a long way in getting the world into abandoning the dollar as I will elaborate in chapter 10. Dollar will probably end up only as a safe-haven currency. America's trade history is one in which for the past years or so, we still believed that we will still find answers by stepping up trade.

In contrast, China in 2015 bought US $1.682 trillion worth of imported products down by 3.5 percent since 2011 and down 14.1 percent from 2014 to 2015. The fastest growing imports of China from the US are collector's items, cereal, milk preparation, perfumes/cosmetics, aircraft, space components, food preparations, meat, fruit/nuts, knit/crochet, and pharmaceuticals. It is clear that these are things that China doesn't manufacture. Their import does not materially affect China's economic structure On the other hand, exports from China to the US averaged 557.39 USD HML for 1983 until 2016 reaching all time high of 2275.13 USD HML in December 2014 and higher to $419 million in 2018.

After about 100 years on international trade, US has ended up as a country with persisting /increasing trade imbalance. It was originally intended, as Eisenhower stated, that the US produces for exports to capture the world. President Trump who had complained about US trade imbalance before he became President in 2018 initially imposed new tariffs on steel, aluminium, washing machies, solar panels and later new tariffs totaling $200 billion on Chinese US imports because he realized that the US has failed to capture the worl. The President had been of the view that foreigners were taking advantage of the US following as indicated in this chapter of the history of Presidents before him who rushed into trade agreements as the means to spread democracy in the world. He had earlier cancelled the bulk of earlier group trade agreements insisting that US will seek to conclude one-to-one trade agreements as he sees it fit. Instead US trade balance in 2018 grew to $621billion, as deficits with the EU and Mexico grew more than 10%. Some US economists attribute this deterioration to the possible slow down of the Chinese economy and strength of the dollar in international markets that made American goods more costly and cheaper for Ameicans to buy more imports. Additionally, it is argued that Trump's tax reductions put more money in Americans' pocket with which they rushed out and bought more imports. If the US economy is competitive, this will not happen.

Americans now regretfully come to increasingly think that their growing trade deficit and international trade do not deserve priority as shown by a lead article in the NYTimes of March 17,2019, titled "US Trade Deficit Under President Bulges to Record" in which the two authors Tim Tankersley and Anna Swanson told us that most economists (and I presume, mostly American economists) now view trade deficits not as a sign of economic strength or weakness, "but a function of macroeconomic factors like flows, fluctuations in the value of currency and relative growth rates." For good measure, the authors quoted Larry Summers as saying that 'I'd rather live in a country that capital is trying to get into, rather than get out. The reason we have a trade deficit is (because) are investing in America." In a Wall Street Journal article of March 7,2019 by Paul Kierman and Josh Zumbrunand titled "Deficit in Goods hits a Record" the authors drew attention to the raging arguments among conventional economists who, we are told, argue that a large trade deficit reflects a dearth of national savings and that they disagree with the view that a deficit is a measure of a nations'overall financial or economic success. The article concluded that that many economists believe that the shortfall was fuelled in part by Trump's tax cut and resultant capital-spending increases that juiced demand in the US for imports. US consumers would'nt have increased imports so speedily if the US economy was competitive. Yellen once said that she did see unfair practices in China or elsewhere as what is responsible for US deficits. She believes that Americans spend more than they produce. There therefore seems to be a decreased interest in the US in international trade as Americans now realized that they cannot dominate international trade as their forebears intended.

In chapter 5, I reviewed the now moribund theories of trade that were expounded by US economists in the '80s to show the importance the US through history attached to international trade. International trade was pushed by the US following its World War II victory as a means to assert its hegemony. By the time the first trade deficit occurred in about 1958 to the 1980s, we had these trade theories by top conventional economists intended to reinforce support of international trade. In his 1988 book titled "Age of turbulence" Greenspan called those who did support free trade "intellectually uninformed." Are conventional economists now telling us international trade does not matter and that America's growing trade deficit does not matter?America's trade deficit is growing because (in line with theme of this book), American economy is structurally unbalanced and continues to be less competitive as it declines. Capital is coming to the US because it is safe in the US and because America cashed in with petro-dollars at the right time not because the US economy is competitive.

Chapter 7

Globalization (An American Recipe
for Economic Disaster)

Another subject on which American economists are misleading
Americans is globalization. The reason is that most of those who profess
to be experts in globalization lack in-depth technical knowledge of
the subject. Americans are told that they must embrace globalization
because it is inevitable. They are also told that globalization presents
them the best opportunity to prosper. The voices of those who urge
caution with globalization or oppose it are increasingly silenced and
scoffed at.

Most claimed experts who write about globalization, however, are
not clear what precisely globalization is. Professor Bhagwatti wrote a
book titled, *In Defense of Globalization*. He started his definition of
the globalization by saying that globalization can mean many things.
He then said he was focusing on economic globalization. He defined
economic globalization as "the integration of national economies into
the international economy through trade, direct foreign investment, and
short time capital flows, international flows of workers and humanity
generally, and flows of technology..." The list is the consequences of
globalization but does tell us what globalization is. Professor Bhagwati
further said that globalization is a phenomenon without saying what
the phenomenon is. The economist Jeffrey Frankel, Harpel Professor
Kennedy School of Government at Harvard University in 2006,

defined globalization as "the increasing integration of national markets, including goods, services, capital, and labor." Professor Stiglitz in his books, *Globalization and its Discontents* and *Making Globalization Work* similarly described globalization as the closer integration of the countries and peoples of the world which has been brought about by the enormous reduction of costs of transportation and communication, and the breaking down of artificial barriers to the flows of goods, services capital, knowledge and (to a lesser extent) people across borders.

He added that globalization has been accompanied by the creation of new institutions that have joined with existing ones to work across borders. The IMF defined globalization as "the growing economic interdependence of countries worldwide through increased volume and variety of cross-border transactions in goods and services, freer international capital flows, and more rapid and widespread diffusion of technology."

The trouble with all these definitions is that they were telling us the effects of globalization and not telling us what globalization is. Professor Sachs will tell us in his book, *Common Wealth,* that the first great wave of globalization was in the nineteenth century and ended up in "the blood-drenched trenches of Europe in World War I."

Professor Sachs's claim cannot pass as economies up to World I were not integrated nor can Thomas Freedman' claim in his book, *The Lexus and the Olive Tree,* that globalization is a historical era that replaced the Cold War era. Later in his famous *The World Is Flat* book, Friedman wanted us to believe that globalization is creating a flat (economic) earth. If he was singing the praises of globalization in these two books why was he in his later joint book with Michael Mandelbaum titled, *That Used US: How America Fell Behind in the World it Invented',* regretting that globalization has enabled other countries to catch up with the US. Friedman wrote a lot of misleading things about globalization. Greenspan in his book, *The Age of Turbulence,* said that globalization is "the deepening of specialization and extension of the division of labor beyond national boundaries—" He didn't do any better than the others in defining globalization. Later, in the book in another attempt of defining globalization, he said that globalization is "the extension of capitalism to world markets."

Greenspan's second attempt at the definition of globalization is significant because for the first time, we learn that globalization is capitalism in action. From Greenspan we get the first glimpse that globalization has a political motive: the spread of capitalism. In effect he is saying, correctly, that globalization is the spread of an ideology (capitalism). The best attempt so far at the definition of globalization is by Professor John Gray in his book, *The False Dawn,* in which he said that globalization is "the worldwide spread of industrial production and new technologies that is promoted by unrestricted mobility of capital and unfettered freedom of trade."

It is a best attempt at a definition because, combined with Greenspan's statement, we recognize that that there is motive force behind globalization—capitalism in action—pushing for free movement of capital using Western technology originally from the United States and that this involves the spreading of capital and industrial production (foreign investment). One is immediately aware from the definitions offered by John Gray and Alan Greenspan that there is or was a political motive force behind globalization that was American driven. Stiglitz told us that it is American corporations that are the purveyors of global technology (capital).[111]

Globalization: An Original American Idea

Globalization, as an original American idea, was therefore politically intended to spread American capital and technology. Resentment against America for its aggressive and interventionist global economic hegemony, which one would expect to be coming mainly from non-Western nations, was once intense in Europe. In his book titled, *Uncouth Nation: Why Europe Dislikes America,* Andrei Markovits said that America represents the face of globalization.[112]

Europe initially resented US neoliberalism that capital should move unfettered anywhere. Stiglitz talking about the East Asia crisis said that American free trade capitalism was imposed on the international financial system through complete capital market liberalization and unfettered flow in and out of short-term speculative capital. Greenspan stated in his *Age of Turbulence* that capitalism had been a central theme of the West since the eighteenth century. The Americans' belief in their intellectual superiority and worldwide economic domination came to the fore as the US economy triumphed around the end of the nineteenth century. A US senator declared in 1898,"We are a conquering race and… we must obey our blood and occupy new markets, and if necessary, new lands…The trade of the world must and shall be ours."[113]

The blossoming capitalism worldwide is a post-World War II phenomenon, which kicked off with the Marshall Plan and Bretton Woods. The Bretton Woods institutions were to invest in poor countries. The US private sector investment in the world gradually picked up. The 1990s were a period of unprecedented long run prosperity in the United States. Americans made a lot of money during the period called New Economy. That gave spur to globalization as Americans were once again gearing to gamble the capital they accumulated as well as their technology all-round the world supported by their new faith in the new world of IT technology leadership that they acquired during that period. Greenspan nicely summarized this when he talked of, "The newer technologies (that is IT) increasingly drive this unforgiving capitalist process on a global scale." The IMF in effect heralded the arrival of what we now call globalization around the year 2000.

The best way to judge America's globalization position today is to assess the extent to which the United States achieved what it originally set out to achieve. By 1938, the gross value of US assets abroad amounted to $11.5 billion, a large sum even by today's standards. At the end of the World War 2, US was firmly a net exporter of capital. The US was a significant international creditor, reflecting persistent current account surpluses in the period following the end of World War II. Since then, persistent current account deficits have resulted in a significant buildup in its net international liabilities. From 1982 to 2007, US international investment position shifted from a net asset position of $0.2 trillion to a net liability position of $2.5 trillion and of $4.0 trillion in 2011 and $ 9.627 trillion in 2018. The country that started off as the largest investor overseas now turned to be the largest recipient of direct investment in the world.

All told, US international assets rose from just $1.00 trillion in 1982 to $10.00 trillion in 2004 but US investment fell sharply in 2005 to $21 billion or less than one-tenth of the $252 billion invested abroad in 2004. US international liabilities rose from $0.7 trillion to $12.5 trillion over the period. By 2009 ending, the US international investment position was a negative of nearly $2,750 billion. By 2012, the net international investment was $4,663.4 deficit and $9.627 in 2018. This dismal posi tion would have been much worse but for the fact that for some time most other currencies against the US dollar had risen in value and that a significant investment into the United States is because it is regarded as a safe haven. Dollar was also by now a world reserve currency.

By 2007, US capital position was such that its major Wall Street institutions for the first time had to reach outside the United States for capital to boost their portfolios. Morgan Stanley raised $5.5 billion from China's Sovereign Wealth Fund (9.9 percent equity), Blackstone raised $3 billion (10 percent equity), Bear Stearns $1 billion (6.6 percent equity). Wall Street Journal commented that these moves by Sovereign Wealth Funds underlined "the growing importance" of the funds and *their increasingly bold moves to take advantage of the need for capital among Western financial institutions.* Citigroup got $7.5 billion from Abu Dhabi Investment Authority (4.9 percent equity) and $12.5 billion from Singapore Investment Corporation and Kuwait Investment Authority. Merrill Lynch got $6.2billion from Ternasek of Singapore (10 percent equity) and $6.6 billion from Kuwait Investment Authority and Korean Investment Fund. Morgan Stanley got $5.0 billion from China Investment Corporation (9.9 percent stake). Blackstone Group further got $3.3 billion from China Investment Corporation (10 percent stake). Carlyle Group got $1.4 billion from Mubadala Development of Abu Dhabi (7.5 percent stake). AMD got $0.6 billion from Mubadala Development (8.1 percent stake). Och-Ziff Capital Management got $1.3 billion from Dubai International Capital (9.9 percent stake). China Investment Corporation early 2008 also made available another $4 billion to J.C. Charles in the US to invest in smaller US banks that were in financial problem. Eighty-one percent of the delegates to the 2008 World Economic Forum meeting considered sovereign funds as *the new power brokers* of world financial markets. By 2012, the world's top thirty-six SWFs totaled nearly $5 trillion. It is expected that SWFs will be valued at $5.6 trillion by 2013 and $8.1 trillion by 2018. Nobody in the US would have thought of selling equity in prime US commercial institutions to foreign governments or agents some years earlier.

In his New York Times best seller, Jerome Corsi put out his 2009 book: *America for Sale*, and Matt Talabi in his book, *Griftopia*, talked about eager buyers in the unregulated sovereign wealth funds, who were buying up US assets. The idea that the country is for sale was an attempt by Corsi to put into a few words what the ordinary American felt at the time about developments in the United States. America set out to invest in Europe in 1945 and thereafter, in poor countries to develop them for its own benefit. Today, the reverse is the position in which America *needs* foreign investment in order to *maintain* its economy.

New Global EconomicTheories.

As will be expected, the New Economy wealth-induced capital outflow euphoria of the late 1990s set conventional American economists thinking on their feet to manufacture and invent supporting globalization theories—just as earlier they did for free trade—to justify America's quest to conquer a globalized world. Professor Maurice Obstefeld is one of the early theorists of international trade. He had earlier written a book with Paul Krugman in 1997 on international trade. Now later in 2004, Obstefeld and Professor Alan Taylor in a book titled, *Global Markets: Integration and Growth,* sought to lay down needed global financial theories. They claimed that, "International financial market allows residents of different countries to pool various risks, achieving more effective insurance than purely domestic arrangements can allow."[114]

Note the word *risk* and pooling risk which in time turned the financial system on its head with derivatives and so on. It is the frightening risks that banks and institutions *shared* across countries that gave us the global financial crash of 2008. Trillions of dollars' worth of new mortgages of varying qualities were packaged and securitized given Triple A status and distributed all over the world spreading the virus of toxic assets.

Obstefeld and Taylor also claimed that global financial market made it possible that a country suffering a temporary recession or natural disaster can borrow from abroad. They claimed tthat developing countries with little capital can borrow to finance investments, thereby, promoting economic growth without sharp increases in savings rates. They further claimed that international capital market channels world savings to their most productive uses irrespective of location. The other main role of international capital market, according to them, is to discipline policy makers who might be tempted to exploit a captive domestic market.

Unsound policies—excessive government borrowing or inadequate bank regulations –would, according to them, spark speculative capital outflow and higher domestic interest rates under conditions of financial openness. In theory at least, they claim a government's fear of these effects should make rash behavior less attractive. Much of the financial crisis of 2007 and 2009 in the United States and Europe is due to the initial adoption of these and similar theories that had no connection with the real economic structure of counties. The immediate effect of US global investors rushing out again into developing countries with their newly acquired *New Economy* capital gains in late 90s was to trigger economic crisis in those countries in the mistaken conventional economics that capital coming externally was synonymous with economic growth in those countries.

In the early 1990s, Mexico was feted as a country that got its economy right after a previous *Brady bond* support from the US. The 1993 NAFTA was essentially a culmination of Mexico's new profile. Toward the end of 1994, despite the flow of foreign capital it received, US foreign reserves fell to just above $10 billion. When such economic failures occur, the same people in Washington who encouraged third world countries to borrow from the US capital adventure were the ones that turned round to blame the third world for mis management of their economies. The economic failure in Mexico and other countries were due, not to *mismanagement* as alleged but due to technical structural imbalance that invariably occurs when capital-intensive factors proportion activities are introduced to lie side by side with predominantly labor-intensive factor proportion activities of a poor country. Mexico received a US-packaged $49.8 billion assistance and sedative packaged by Robert Rubin. Luckily Mexico was able to repay it off. Mexico's economy today is nothing to write home about despite NAFTA. Next was East Asia in 1997. On January 30, 1995, barely twenty-four hours before President Bill Clinton orchestrated the Mexican bailout, the world's financial system fed by the rapid movement and transfers of money in the global market system was in frenzy. As the news that Mexico was in default spread, capital fled from Brazil and Argentina and even countries as far away as Poland and the Czech Republic. But soon after, East Asia got its share of the fallout, which sent the economies of these countries who had only just been given the title of Asian Tigers into a spin. Here again, those in the United States who provided the foreign capital as well as the US based institutions who were only recently cheering the East Asians now turned round to blame the East Asians for alleged corruption, bad financial infrastructure, and making bad internal loans. American economists are very good at coining these new economic terms. That was the time the terms *hot money, contagion,* and *herd instinct* were coined. Some economists now added to their ever-changing self-serving economic theories by saying that a third world country can get too much capital for its own good, a major reversal of initial globalization claims that were hinged on the economic efficacy of the unimpeded free movement of global capital.

American economists had a field day producing some outlandish explanations for the Asian economic recession of 1997. I analyzed these 'explanations' in full in my book, *The Science of Economic Development and Growth.* The thing to note is that all the "experts" who have published on the Asian crisis in total think that the cause of the crisis was bad financial management and *hot money.* Greenspan said in his book, *The Age of Turbulence,* that, in South Korea, American authorities found out that the government *was playing games* with the country's reserves. By playing games, he meant that governments sold or lent most of the dollars to banks who in turn lent them into bad loans. In his view, the crisis was not the fault of America but due to faulty Korean financial management. A detailed structural study of the Korean macroeconomy, which I carried out in *The Science of Economic Development and Growth* showed that the South Korean economy had been structurally bleeding…I called this structural imbalance economic hemorrhaging in my book…caused by Western-style capital and technology. On the heels of East Asia, Russia also came collapsing in August 1998 on the vast dollar loan it received as overseas speculative capital took flight. Russian collapse was closely followed by Brazil for which the United States also had to organize another rescue working with the IMF.

Here was how US frittered away the capital it accumulated from the New Economy at the time. America in effect repeated its Bretton misadventure. Repeating economic mistakes is what happens when a country has no guiding economic principle because it is a free enterprise.

Structural Economic Damage Caused by Globalization in Poor Countries

The structural economic damage done to developing economies by globalized capital should not be difficult to be demonstrate. This flies in the face of claims of the wonderful things conventional economists claim that Western foreign investment does to third world economies through globalization. The three *financial* crises we just described: in Brazil, in East Asia, and Russia were economic crises resulting from free injection of Western global capital into these countries. In particular, the history of East Asian crises was that of countries that initially sought to grow on a capital-intensive base, causing structural economic in-equilibrium.

I want now to take up the position in most third world countries that does not necessarily result as of today from any financial crisis on the scale of East Asia, Russia, Mexico, or Brazil but from a position in which everyone: World Bank, IMF, Aid agencies, and our American development experts feel that what these countries need is foreign capital investment as part of a globalized world. Third World countries can be very roughly divided into four groups:

    ag. high population and high natural resources;
    ah. low population, high natural resources;
    ai. high population, low natural resources;

aj. low population, low natural resources.

The selection of the appropriate factor proportions (technology) will in case of:

ak. should be high natural resources, high labor, and on the basis of one unit to be low capital levels because it had a lot labor to combine with material for capital.

al. Can be a capital-intensive system because even though there is a lot of natural resources, there is not enough manpower to combine with material to produce capital. There are very few such third world countries. They are mainly mineral explorations.

am. should be natural resources needs a labor intensive system.

an. This will be low capital because both natural resources and labor are low.

It is clear that out of these four factor positions in poor counties only one might justify a moderate capital intensive development. It is therefore incorrect for American economists to make it that all Third World countries need to be linked in globalization through Western capital-intensive technology.

Fig. 7.1 is the structural scientific analysis of the situation in third world country when a capital intensive investment is introduced into its economy. It is a three-dimension presentation of the position. Fig. 7.1 is an attempt to demonstrate economic dualism.

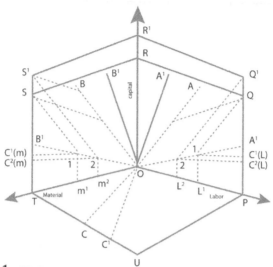

Fig.7.1 *TITLE:*
Two-sector, three-factor construct of third world
country receiving inward capital investment.

It shows structural changes which occur to a third world country's factor endowments before and after the increase in capital stock from foreign investment as depicted by the boundaries of the multi-sector Edgeworth boxes, OPQR, ORST, OTUP. The initial economy is depicted by in three factor construct OA, OB, and OC. Capital introduced into the economy through foreign investment RR1 (=QO1 and SS1) has its material and labor components. The labor component will interact to reduce labor in the original economy from C1(L) to C2(L) while the labor in the foreign investment will interact to reduce labor in the original economy from L1 to L2. The material component of the capital introduced by the foreign investment will interact with the existing economy on the material side by taking away the material on the existing capital from C1(m) to C2(m), while the material in the existing economy is also reduced from m1 to m2. The net result is that the existing initial economy is now adversely disrupted by the capital intensive foreign investment and loses factors of production to the new capital investment which now comprises three changed components: OA1 instead of OA, OB1 instead of OB and OC1 instead of OC. My conclusions here are in the same general spirit with Rybczynski theorem which essentially said that an increase in one factor endowment will increase by a greater portion output of good intensive in that factor. It should be apparent that the effect of foreign investment on a third world economy in Fig. 7.1 is the same as the effect of a growing capital intensive sector in the is in Fig. 1.2 to the rest of the economy as indicated in Fig. 1.2 and Fig. 1.3. The conclusion is that foreign investment acts as a break to indigenous third world economies by diverting factors from preexisting economy, increasing instead of reducing poverty and creating structural imbalance.

The trouble with those who praise and endorse globalization foreign investments as being beneficial for poor countries is that they are not aware of the structural issues I have just discussed. They, like Professor Bhagwati, wrongly, equate capital investment/formation arising from globalization as synonymous with economic development. Bhagwati confirmed this with one sentence in his book when he said, "By supplementing meager domestic savings, foreign funds would increase capital formation and hence jobs (in poor counties)"[115]

Jeffrey Sachs, an expert on poverty and Millennium Development wrongly asserted in his book, *Commonwealth,* that: "The spread of prosperity is fuelled by globalization—and which helps spread the technologies that underpin productivity and economic development." The issue is that from the original four factor proportins I listed at the beginning of this chapter, the technology Sachs was endorsing (capital intensive technology) is the wrong one.

Most commentators on globalization know that it has many problems but set out to point out only the inconsequential ones. Professor Stiglitz's book, *Making Globalization Work,* personified this error, when for example, he complained that developing countries received only 30 percent of the gains from trade, even though they have 85 percent of the population and that developed countries imposed tariffs that were four times higher than against the developed countries. Stiglitz has also written extensively of the need to make globalization more *democratic* but problem has nothing to do with democracy. The problem is that economists like Stiglitz who write on these issues lack the technological insights I have just discussed. Stiglitz knows that there are problems with globalization but wrongly assumes that the technology of globalization is right and praised American corporations for being purveyors of this technology.

In a respected 2018 recently published book titled *The Divide* by the famous anthropologist Professor Jason Hickens, his view, summarized, is that to close the divide between the poor and rich in the world, "real justice like debt forgiveness, democratizing the institutions of global governance and rolling out international minimum wage etc were needed." Here again, Professor Hickens like others expect globalization technology to take command everywhere with compensations for those who suffer from it.

The way it works is that it is the pressure groups and the NGOs who are on the ground in poor countries that see and listen. They see poverty increase in the face of foreign *development programs* and corruption etc. They know that *development* capital-intensive activities often backed by Western governments and private investors over the heads of ordinary people only succeed in creating economic inequilibrium and resentment, which has wrongly and increasingly fueled terrorism all over the world. The pressure groups speak out, often on moral grounds, as if those who promote globalization are immoral. This is not necessarily true because many people involved in globalization work have been made to think that capital intensive projects provide economic benefits to poor economies.

Similar ignorance of the structural issues was reflected in what Robert Rubin stated in his book, *In an Uncertain World,* talking of his time in government. He stated:

> "Most vocal critics rejected outright the premise that underlay our thinking that globalization and open markets were on balance greatly beneficial, both to the United States and to the rest of the world and that what was needed was to make it work better. The vast majority of those who took issue with us on some aspects of policy or another shared our broad view in favor of globalization and saw market-based economics and economic integration as the most promising approach to raising living standards around the world."[116]

Increasingly doubts are beginning to be expressed in America about the benefits to the United States of globalization. Not too long ago, a former Treasury secretary Lawrence Summers cast doubt about the benefits of globalization to the United States. He said, "Since the end of the Second World War, American economic policy has supported an integrated global economy... Yet America's commitment is ever in doubt...the indicators are disturbing." He stated:

> "Policy debate in the US, and probably in some other countries as well, will need to confront a deeper and broader issue: the gnawing suspicion of many that the very object of international economic policy—the growing prosperity of global economy may not be in their inter est...In a world where Americans can legitimately doubt whether the success of the global economy is good for them, it will be difficult to mobilize support for economic internationalism."[117]

The basic reality is that as US capital causes economic disruption in poor countries, at the same time as America is losing its capital base in uncompetitive economies so created in these countries. Forecasts of the future of America in a globalized economy are becoming common, all clearly pessimistic. Jim O'Neill, for merly of Goldman Sachs, forecast that between 2010 and 2015, world economy will grow by 25 percent due to the high growth in Asia, Africa, and Latin America, but there will be little growth contribution from America and Europe. He forecast that investment in America and Europe will be below 2007 level over this period, representing a cumulative deficit of $5 trillion by 2015. The World Bank forecast global growth at 2.9 percent over 2016. America's growth trends, once above about 4 percent, according to the forecast, are set to go down below 2.8 percent.[118]

The global trade outlook for 2019 was not bright.

A kind of fatalism mixed up with a refusal to accept failure of its globalization adventure also afflicts the United States. Under the make-believe that it is gaining from globalization and that it has to give up things in exchange, the use of an increasing basket of safety nets to *compensate* the losers in the United States has become a cornerstone of its economic policy.

How East Asian Countries Came on Top

I find Professor Stiglitz's account of how the East Asian countries achieved the economic success which today has enabled them take over the present global control in his book, *Making Globalization Work*. He told us that the emerging countries of China and Asia succeeded by managing globalization without being taken advantage of by globalization.[119] They applied economic science in their economic strategy.

I will summarize the actions Stiglitz—a pro-globalist—enumerated actions these countries took that enabled them to 'manage' globalization or to bypass and/or exploit globalization.

a. China ignored the IMF and followed what Stiglitz called "standard expansionary macropolicies." The result was growths of 7 percent to 9 percent. If China ignored IMF, then it means that China rejected much of Washington's consensus, which required an open economy including free capital inflow and foreign investment. High growth rates can only be the result of a structurally balanced economy, which could not have been achieved with high levels of foreign investments that would have structurally unbalanced the Chinese economy.

b. The governments made sure that the benefits of growth did not go to a few but were widely shared. China witnessed a rapid fall of poverty. In my view this required a balanced economy (based on Chinese factor proportions) without capital intensive American-type of foreign investments.

c. The economies/markets were far from unfettered.

d. Globalization required an open internal market.

e. Governments played a strong role in development by ensuring that new jobs were created in place with new entrants to the labor force. That is to say that they pursued a balanced structural economy.

f. South Korea and later China led in high-tech industries.

g. Governments intervened carefully and played major role in planning and advancing technology. They made great efforts to develop local industries not foreign investment. Local industries were more likely to conform with local factor proportions.

h. Governments played a major role in planning and advancingtechnology, namely "indigenous" technology and to make up for what traditional free market can miss out by coordinating economic activities and sectors. The economy was not a free for all free economy and there was a degree of economic planning. These are all against the basic tenets of globalization.

i. The countries did not look for foreign investment as a source of capital. The countries ensured that money for investments came from their own people's savings so that they "did not have to depend on volatile capital flows." Those that invited foreign investment did it for a purpose: to 'transfer' technology and train local people.

j. They limited imports that would undercut local manufacturing and agriculture.

The East Asian countries learned from their financial crisis that their outward posture of capital-intensive capital imports in the 1980s and 1990s caused their economic imbalance and collapse. They realized that what they needed was to pursue an inward-looking development strategy. The financial crisis convinced many South Koreans that it isn't enough to be a *developed* follower of the advanced economies. South Koreans were determined to create an advanced economy *powered by their own non- capital-intensive inventions and talents and inventions.*

The crisis also revealed the flaws in the South Korean economy: the family-dominated over-capitalized chaebols (business conglomerates), which dominated the economy before 1977. The chaebols exported huge amounts based on technologies from the United States and even from

South Korea's former colonial overlord Japan. Chaebols were one of the major casualties of the Korean crisis.

The irony of Stiglitz's account of why the East Asian countries triumphed is an account how only not to comply with globalization but also how to take advantage of it.

Latin American Failures

Latin America is a region marked out by Stiglitz as presenting a different picture from East Asia. I will review the Latin American position since the 1990s global financial crises as Stiglitz did. He described Latin America as the region that embraced the Washington Consensus policies more wholeheartedly than any other region. Latin America today, as a result, faces many problems. According to the IMF, one of the most pressing problems of the region is how to step up its slow pace of economic growth. Under pressure from the IMF, the World Bank and the United States, the region was in the 80s and 90s characterized by a wave of economic liberalization. The people in the region call it neo-liberalism entailing free flow of capital. All the countries in the region were encouraged to embrace *democracy* and free and fair elections, as a gateway to economic prosperity.

Democratization meant IMF type economic liberalization and reform. Yet today the region remains poor. Poverty is still rampant, averaging at over 35 percent of the population: 10% in Uruaguay, Argentina and Chile and 37% in Nicaraguay and 50% in Guatemala. Unemployment in the region averaged 7.8 percent in 2018. The region continues to run external-oriented economic policies, with high external debts—Brazil with around $191.2 billion, Argentina with $109.7 billion, and Chile with $47.71 billion. Brazil, the top economy of the region, is afflicted with many economic problems. GDP increased from 1.7% in 2018 to 2.8% in 2019. The Economist of January 17, 2008 summarized the Brazilian current position as follows: "Brazil knows about economic and financial crises. The original squabbles afflicting America and threatening Europe look like a gentle breeze when compared with the frequent and violent blow-ups that litter Brazilian economic history."

Integrated into the world market, most of what Brazil today produces for export is in the form of primary goods and commodities, so that its financial export growth correlates strongly with commodities' prices. Brazilian economy still suffers from problems that make growth above 5 percent look like a stretch and dependent on the ebbs of a foreign-investment dependent economy. (In 2012 GDP growth was 1 percent.) By 2015 and 2016, Brazil's GDP contracted value by nearly 5 percent and may have a growth of less than 1 percent in 2016 and 2017 hoping to achieve 2.6% in 2018. Forecast for 2019 is a deceleration from 2018. Its growing output is unfortunately based on the export of its large number of commodities to China. The country has largely turned itself against the US in favor of China. The globalization frustrations caused in the Latin American countries by IMF and World Bank and the over the past decades have in the recent years taken their toll as a wave of socialism and anti-Americanism in the region has surged.

Globalization and Finance

Just as I will show in chapter 9 that Wall Street has overshadowed Main Street in the United States, I intend to show here that global finance has overshadowed the real economies of all countries. The global finance world is intent on increasingly taking control of the economies of the world.

Take Europe as an example. European Union was set up as an ideal free trade and mini-globalized unit intended to be the economic leader of the twenty first century. That mini-globalization of European countries has turned out as a disaster. Growth is notmore than 2% going forward. It was 2.3% in 2017, 2.1% in 2018, forecast 2.0% in 2019. The Chief Economist of Lombard Odler in Geneva once stated that "All open economies (i.e. in the Euro)have hit a brick wall." Unemployment is at over 8 percent. European youths have borne the brunt of this. In January 2018, 3375 million youth below 25 were unemplyed Average unemployment in Zone had drpped to 8.95% in 2018. We are dealing with a region where the economic growth is varied depending on where you are because EU has structural inbalance. It is essentially a political union.

Such abysmal economic results will obviously show up as public debts. Debt is the *result* of a bad structural economy and not the cause. Many European countries are owing up to their neck. Global finance and European banks have from early told EU that the way to get EU economies out of the mess they are in is to borrow money. When the Greeks realized the size of their debt, could you believe that what they first did was to hire some well-known banks at very substantial fees to advise them on how to hide the extent of their debt?

Eventually, the Greeks went to borrow from both the European Bank and issue bonds all at huge profits of the global finance operators. Another country Spain, which, not a long time ago was expecting its economy to overtake that of Germany, found its debts out of control. Joachin Fells of Morgan Stanley was once involved in advising Spain as his firm was collecting good fees for advising on Spain's austerity.

Rising and the debt level rising. So it was back to further borrowing and profits for global financial investors. As Spain deepened in further austerity, it ended up after five years of financial expedition with unemployment of 27 percent by early 2013 and current GDP: debt around 98.3%. 2018, debt for Italy was 2331 billion Euro, France 2322, Germany 2052 billion Euro and Spain 1175 billion Euro. When EU noticed the collapsing wall of debts in almost all member states, all it did under the influence of the ECB, was to request that member states cut government spending and raise taxes to bring their budget in line with European rules. To date nobody has thought of how to deal with the serious structural economic problems of most European countries. The long-term-prospects for the EU is a deteriorating economic region in line with their cousin in the US because each of them thinks that economic growth is all about finance and banks. Today the European debt crisis brings many of EU countries near recession but for Germany that runs a slight surplus. A major reason for Brexit vote is the poor and deterioration of ground-level economic conditions in the Euro in Britain.

'Omnipresence' of Globalization

There are many who believe that globalization deserves to cover all countries in the world. Greenspan told us that while communism and capitalism at one time competed for the control of the world economy, capitalism won. He believes that globalization and capitalism are one. He, therefore, believes that the fall of Communism gave capitalism a clean bill of health to take control of the world economy. Greenspan said that no one nation can rein in the forces of globalization. According to him, the global market is so huge in size with millions of financial transactions moving with too great speed for any meaningful intervention by regulators.

He praised the international global market for being competitive. According to him, crisis in one country is an opportunity for another country. To him, the global financial market is one which no country can refuse to be part of and which every country must compete in. Greenspan is avowedly in favor of a globalization that is uncontrolled, unregulated, and free. He thought that the global finance cannot be regulated. He feels that consumers and politicians in all countries should not be worried about the speed of change arising from globalization and the potential for crisis spreading through linkages in a free global financial market.

He gave this comfort to consumers and politicians because he sees balancing forces through the invisible hand that will avoid global crisis. According to him, "Even in crisis, in the global economy, economies seem inevitably to right themselves" (through Adam Smith's invisible hand). Years later the United States and European crises now show how wrong Greenspan was because the deteriorating global market is getting worse and not righting itself. Long-term growth prospects in the US and EU are poor. In chapter 9, I showed that Adam Smith's invisible hand does not apply in financial markets but Greenspan and other financial market operators evoke Adam Smith for their egoist theorizations.

Despite the hope he raised about globalization, Greenspan turned around at the same time to say that he did not know where globalization was heading. He considers that the world economy has become too complex and interlinked. "Too often we have to deal with incomplete and faulty data, unreasonable human fear, and inadequate legal clarity." His book was punctuated with words like *puzzling, surprising, mystery, conundrum*, and *irrational* to describe globalization. In effect, by going forward with globalization, he is saying that we are wandering into a dark room. With the uncertainties about globalization on his mind, Greenspan concluded correctly that something fundamental that he did not know seemed to be going on that had altered how one knows when the US economy is out of balance. He is saying that he has no means of saying how and when the US economy can go out of balance being part of the global economy. That was not a great comfort to Americans. These statements coming from a man of Greenspan's stature and of such close knowledge of the global finance are worrying. I believe, therefore, that most people who currently talk about globalization don't know its full ramification. Professor Stieglitz said that capital market liberalization has been pushed despite the fact that there is no evidence showing it spurs economic growth. But capital market freedom is the core of globalization. I concur with someone who said that "the cowboy culture that created Bear Sterns has been exported to the far-off corners of the world. The only difference is that the far-off corners aren't far off at all."

How the US Lost Out On Globalization

I need to summarize on a broad level how the United States has lost out on globalization. The Fed over years told Americans that in cooperation with other Central Banks in the world, it has reduced inflation worldwide and that America with other countries will reap the benefit of a world economic growth based on the wrong assumption that low inflation is the gateway to economic prosperity.

Greenspan in his book told us the puzzle that inflation posed to him as Fed chairman. He observed that inflation had been subdued virtually across the globe by central banks. He concluded that the *movement of workers into marketplace reduced world wages, inflation, inflation expectations, and interest rates and accordingly contributed to rising world economic growth*. He, therefore, equated low inflation and low wages with global economic growth. He said that even though the aggregate payroll of the newly repositioned work force was only a fraction of that of developed nations, the impact was pronounced.

According to Greenspan, the international movement of workers not only reduced world wages but also led to low-priced imports displacing production and hence workers in developed countries. He heralded that the competitive effect of the formerdisplaced workers seeking new jobs also suppressed the wages of workers not directly in the line of fire of low priced imports. Here was the ignorance we described in the last chapter on the claimed benefits of international trade. In addition, according to Greenspan, migration to Western Europe of low-priced workers exposed part of the homegrown workforce of Western Europe to enhanced wage competition. Finally exports from previously centrally planned economies competitively suppressed export prices of all economies.[120]

He added that it is the pace, the rate of change, of movement from centrally planned employment to competitive markets that determines the degree of disinflationary pressure on developed nation's wage costs and hence prices. Because of indirect effects of competitive imports and immigration, the addition of new low-priced workers affects the whole structure of labor costs in developed countries. Greenspan's claims were intended to get Americans to support globalization because, according to his one-worldist belief, increased global growth automatically benefits the United States. Greenspan's theorizing is empty conventional economic intellectualism with no structural economic science content.

The topic of low world inflation was also the topic of an important lecture by a former Fed governor, Randall Kroszner, at the Catino Institute Monetary Policy Conference, Washington DC on November 16, 2006. He called his lecture, a lecture about the conquest of worldwide inflation. He said that the globalization, deregulation, and financial innovation, in part spurred by experiences of high inflation in the 1980s, have fostered currency competition among countries that has led to improved central bank performance and hence recent conquest of worldwide inflation. He argued that increased competition among currencies has changed the ability and the incentive of governments and central banks to pursue high-inflation policies.

He argued that such changes have allowed improvement in central bank independence, governance, and credibility, thereby leading to better inflation outcomes. Greater bank credibility, he maintained, allowed the development of long-term bonds in many countries where such markets did not previously exist and flattened of yield curves around the globe as concerns about future inflation risks declined. In his own case, the so-called *defeat* of global inflation was used to claim that globalization has helped stable international currency system—another reason Americans were expected to be happy that there is globalization.

In contrast to the apparent arms-length treatment of inflation by the Fed, which Greenspan conveyed, Kroszner seems to say that concerted actions by central banks were crucial in reducing world inflation and so beneficial to the US. His stand that deregulation and globalization contributed to the conquest of world inflation was also going in the same direction as Greenspan's contention that low international wage (low inflation) was due to globalization. Predictably, the claim that globalization has altered the parameters of individual countries' inflation process was not endorsed by everybody.[121] Americans were made to believe that they have economic growth coming from global growth. This is what Trump did not want to hear.

Another great disappointment Americans had was being sold is the idea of global one-worldism as I had earlier mentioned in chapter 3. They were told on that basis that they cannot prosper on their own. Greenspan stated that globalization has created "the deepening of specialization and the extension of the division of labor beyond national borders…"

He encouraged Americans to develop a growing capacity to conduct transactions and take risks throughout the world, thus, creating a truly global economy. It is better to quote the requisite paragraph in his book. He reasoned that in the global world:

> "Production has become more and more international. Much of what is assembled in final saleable form in one country increasingly consists of components from many continents. Being able to seek out the most competitive sources of labor and material input worldwide rather than just nationwide not only reduces costs and price inflation but also raises the ratio of the value of inputs to inputs…

the broadest measure of productivity and a useful proxy for standards of living." He in effect sopports large-scale US outsourcing. Coming after US disappointment from international trade and rising trade deficits, this was hard to take.

He claimed falsely that hundreds of millions of people in developing countries have been elevated from subsistence poverty through globalization. He claimed that hundreds of millions are now experiencing a level of affluence that people born in developed countries have experienced all their lives.[122] America's one worldist economic policy has been particularly evident, by the way, since 1999 when America had gone out its way to cultivate China as source of cheap imported goods and hogging for China's market for American capital goods.

We Have Created a Monster

From everything I have said, it is clear we have created a monster called globalization. One group says that the monster is so strong that it is better to let it roam. The other wants the monster to be controlled but does not know how. There is a fight for the soul of globalization however bad its health is.

It is the blind leading the blind. In articles and speeches, Greenspan has always said that the problem of globalization is not the lack of regulation but unrealistic expectations about what regulators are able to prevent. He said, "Regulators, to be effective, have to be forward-looking to anticipate the next financial malfunction. This has not proved feasible. Regulators, confronting real-time uncertainties have rarely, if ever, been able to achieve the level of future clarity required to act preemptively."

In a CNBC television interview on April 2008 Greenspan also said the ordinary regulator is dealing with very clever people and crooks. I respect Greenspan's candidness, which is fresh air because with most others in the global world you are dealing are people whose views change like the weather and who will want us to believe they know all that needs to be known about the globalization. Greenspan's predecessor Volcker expressed a similar view when in the same month following the 2008 collapse of the US financial market he said that, "Any return to heavily regulated bank (i.e. Fed) dominated, nationally insulated markets is pure nostalgia, not possible in this world of sophisticated financial techniques made possible by the wonders of electronic technology." He wanted to separate trading activities of banks from their investment activities which did not mean he was advocating regulation.

Globalization Under Its Own Threat

Many countries treated the 2001 US recession with a shrug of the shoulder. To them, the biggest engine of world growth simply developed a fault. They were sure that it will not take too long for the machine to be put back into operation. 9/11 additionally attracted sympathy and support for the United States. The tearing up of globalization started when the US 2008 financial crisis started. People out there particularly in Asia realized that they are dealing with they regarded as an old sick patient. Central banks around the world began asserting their independence from the United States. Some were thinking of forming global regional groups that is to leave the United States out. For the first time, Europeans were telling everyone that their own European economies were doing well and that any slowdown in their economy is from external sources, namely the United States. In a communiqué of four EU leaders from Britain, France, Germany, and Italy and EU President Jose Barroso in January 29, 2008, they insisted that, "The fundamentals of the European economies remain strong with employment still rising."

They said they were meeting to look at a series of measures to make global economy more resistant to future cross-border crises with US in mind. Italy suggested creating a pan-European regulation body to regulate the global system. This was a protectionist stance against the United States. Mr. Barroso asked for calm and warned European leaders at the meeting, "We must not be tempted into protectionism (against the US) or futile attempts to stem financial globalization or artificial stimulus of the economy." He advised against *knee-jerk reactions* but advised actions that were *both targeted and proportionate*. When the US

Fed was lowering interest, EDB was instead raising it saying Europe's problem was inflation not US economic stimulus.

As countries started throwing off central US global influence, differences in and lack of communication among major central banks in dealing with the global market increased. In the midst of the liquidity problems coming out of the United States, the IMF on January 29, 2008 has called on the world's top central banks to narrow their differences in the way to combat market strains that were global in nature. It argued that "In a globalized world, it makes sense to have as similar as possible systems and procedures. It would be good to have more convergence." It said the IMF is looking for natural *convergence* not *full harmonization* given the differences in the structure of financial systems in different economies.

The same problem of global fragmentation was mentioned by the Bank of International Settlement at the 2008 World Economic Forum by its Chief Executive, Malcolm Knight. He worried that the major challenge facing financial regulators was "the balkanization of regulation—fragmentation across market segments, across national jurisdiction, and yet they want to have a global financial system."

He said that what was required was for regulation to be consistent, so that the same risk gets the same treatment irrespective of who is holding them. This crisis was taking place at a time when financial flows, and therefore, financial risks were crossing borders of countries at a frightening speed and residing in ever shifting global companies, whereas those supposed to be supervised were located within the confines of a country.

So the world had no effective monitoring system. There was also no cross-border crisis management, a position likely that was worsened as national jealousies and rivalry intensify as US world economic influence diminishes. The Chief Economist of the World Bank's IFC Michael Klein, at the same time, summarized the position that: "Disparate national interests may pull [countries] in different directions and render global actions more difficult."

Europeans, more open than the United States where financial and market regulations were up to, now regarded any regulation as an attack on the free market. The UK Financial Services Authority in the midst of the US sub-prime mortgage crisis, expressed worry that UK consumers could lose faith in the financial system and its regulators. The four EU leaders, I earlier referred to their meeting in January 2008, worried about what Angela Merkel of Germany called a growing "lack of trust" that she said was undermining faith in the capitalistic system. The communiqué by the four leaders called for "improvement in the information content of credit ratings to increase investor's understanding of the risks associated with structured products." It also called for the sector to address conflicts of interest between the agencies and the institutions they assess. Unlike the United States, the leaders said that while they preferred market-led solutions, they stood *ready to consider regulatory alternatives* when Greenspan had earliersaid regulation of the global finance was not possible. Mr. Sarkozy the French President at the time added, "We have the sort of capitalism that encourages entrepreneurship, not speculation." That was a subtle throwback to the United States. Despite the relatively checkered short life of globalization, Gordon Brown of Britain was in January 2008 calling those he called "progressive business and government voices should come together to agree to a manifesto for successful globalization." He said that the global economy was facing "the biggest test in more than a decade." He said that the global economy system—its organizations, auditors, credit agencies, firms, and regulators was enveloped in a *deficit of transparency*.[123] All this was a serious indictment of the global financial system coming at a time when the ordinary American was being asked to trust glo balization. All this was a serious indictment of the global financial system coming at a time when the ordinary American was being asked to trust globalization.

Brown wanted the IMF to act with the same independence as a central bank responsible for surveillance of the world economy and for information and educating the market. He argued that to enforce transparency throughout the system, IMF should work with other global supervisors to create an early warning system. "We should consider how the IMF's responsibilities for financial stability could be clearer.[124] The G7 finance ministers in turn instructed that the IMF and the Financial Stability Committee (the Committee of Central Bankers) to report on "identifying early warning systems." The IMF, who was to lead this early warning system, no doubt knew as to how difficult the whole venture is. Its Managing Director at the time said that today's financial crises were more difficult to read than when trade was vulnerability quickly showed up in current account deficits. "Now," he said, "imbalances can spread through diverse channels."

He was in effect saying that there cannot be a valid warning system and that they were creating a monster that no one can follow or control.[125] In February 2008 after the IMF Managing Director thought about the IMF's mandate of early warning, he said that while it was a "laudable goal," "we must be realistic about our ability to predict crises."[126] Mr. Greenspan was telling us the truth when he said, "Regulators can still pretend to provide oversight, but their capabilities are much reduced and declining."

Robert Rubin, as I had earlier mentioned, suggested an IMF warning system years before in his book following the East Asian crisis. The warning system idea is, therefore, not new. Conventional economics has no scientific basis to forecast economic disruption. In any case, the IMF cannot originate data for countries for its early warning system job unless the countries are willing to provide it. Data are only as good as the country supplying it nor can it be assumed that countries that have problems will necessarily want to share them with others including the IMF. An early warning can in the peculiar psychology of the financial world instead precipitate unexpected financial crisis.

Our world is increasingly polarized and contentious. Foreign policies of countries are becoming more dysfunctional. The harmonious world that World War II was to usher in on the back of free trade and subsequently by globalization has not occurred. The close national and international coordination which globalists needed if their global financial system is to be sustainable is increasingly missing in the face of growing balkanization and fragmentation of the system. A new type of protection by countries against unknown risks that will result from this fragmentation and balkanization of the system was looming. America should protect itself from this eventuality. The G20 will not solve the problem. America needs to go back and solve its structural economic problems.

Last Ditch Effort to Save Globalization

The former British Prime Minister and long-term British Chancellor of Exchequer Mr. Brown stated that in the early 2000 decade, a "new but unsustainable" balance in the world economic activity emerged. The populations of America and Europe, he said, were being outproduced and outmanufactured, outexported and even outinvested by Asia and the rest of the world. The IMF figures suggest that from 2010, America and Europe will have less than half of the world's economic activity. Goldman Sachs suggested at the time that America and Europe will account for less than 40 percent of the total investment the economies of the world would make. This is what globalization brought to America and Europe. The answer should have been for Europe and America to abandon globalization and find out what has gone wrong with their economies. East Asian countries acted outside globalization and got the economic reward, now being envied.

People like Gordon Brown instead wanted to come up with a new plan to resuscitate and save globalization in a book, *Beyond the Crash.* He asserted that everyone in the world, including the losing America and Europe, will gain in economic growth if total global economic output grows. Americans, whose long-run economic prospects have continued to dim and whose global losses have continued to grow, were being told by Brown that if global growth increases, US unemployment and its declining economic profile will auto matically disappear because the United States will suddenly find new markets. It is this fixation with finding new markets through globalization that has deterred Americans from sorting out their internal economic problems.

Americans and Europeans were told by Brown that to achieve this change, they should recommit to an even greater globalization. This time, it is going to be a globalization controlled not by the United States as before, but the G20. Brown pulled out an IMF study produced for the G20 in June 2010 that claimed that cooperative global action by countries could bring in about $1.5 trillion more economic activity in the world by 2014, 2.5 percent higher than the global GDP which should translate into more than thirty million more people jobs worldwide and tens of million people taken out of poverty. All these were pipe dreams.

At the Toronto G20, the IMF stated that the difference between what it called "good" and "bad" global coordination is of the order of $4 trillion by 2014 or a 5.75 percent higher global GDP, which it claimed will make a difference of fifty million jobs worldwide and ninety million out of poverty. The IMF claimed that good global coordination will eliminate the present imbalance in the global economy because it will, for example, create new sources of consumer demands, which was lost during the recent recessions in Europe and the United States. All this, according to Brown, will make poverty in the world a thing of the past and will resuscitate American and European collapsing economies.

Brown, therefore, wanted the world to *devise a [new] properly coordinated plan for global growth.* He also stated that the 2007 crisis was not only global but that it was *the first crisis to have its roots in the very process of globalization.* He was of the view that today's problems of global capital, markets and global sourcing of goods that have resulted cannot be solved in the same old way of *national–only* solutions. He called for *more academic work on a new global growth economics.* Here, he was almost reechoing Greenspan's statement that people don't fully understand globalization. We are still waiting for the academic research he called for. Nothing has happened. Brown had the perception that globalization and finance are science that can be researched, forgetting the tragedy of the 2008 financial crisis, and its operators' attempt to make finance a science through financial research and sophistication.

A major component of Brown's global growth plan is the establishment of some global monetary, financial, and fiscal policy. He stated that while the founders of Bretton Woods *devised rules for a world of global limited capital flows, we must devise new rules for a world of global capital flows.* Brown stated that it was essential to lay down *a route map for sequencing capital account liberalization.* Central to the global economy he had in mind is a global financial regulation, a global financial crisis prevention and resolution, and a global social code.

Brown's global economy ideas are flawed. He is wrong because, as I have already shown, unimpeded global capital flow brings with it technology consequences that cause structural economic problems of poverty particularly in the third world and with them increased global inequality and political tensions. Greenspan made it clear that even the greatest enthusiast of globalization does not understand globalization. America's future, therefore, cannot lie in a hoped new global economy with its unknowns. What Brown proposed is old wine (globalization) in a new bottle. As one can see, if the medicine prescribed does not solve the illness, the answer, according to Brown, is to increase the dose. Brown has since vanished from the globalization scene ever since the UN gave him a job on education. Brown's idealism cannot fly in a situation that there is increasingly lack of trust in globalization as countries are too ready to commit to economic sanctions targeted against the very assets committed by others to globalization.

Ineffectiveness of the G20

I needed finally in this chapter to underpin the ineffectiveness of the G20. G20 was set up in 2008. It was composed of countries with a total of 82.2 percent of the world's GDP and 80 percent of its trade. The BRICS was later added. The alleged instability and contradictions of the G20 were such that BRICS tended increasingly to stand alone. The accusation against the G20 is that G20 has increasingly focused on developed economies' problems, especially those of the EU countries. In 2012, the then President of China described the BRICS countries as the defenders and promoters of developed countries and world peace.

As the 2008 financial crisis in the United States spread to other countries' financial systems, the G20 decided to step in. In 2009, under the singular initiative of George Brown, the then British Prime Minister about the time the rotating chairmanship of G20 passed to Britain. Brown felt, by his account, that there was need for the G20 to take a *make or break* action to move the world out of recession, which he correctly stated was the worst since 1933.

In a major world conference before the G20 meeting, he told the world that this day the world came together to fight global recession. Brown concluded that what was needed in line with his ideas as to how to stop recession was:

k. To restore confidence in the world's financial system;
l. To inject $1 trillion into the system.

He was confident that by this action, the world will quickly achieve a pre-crisis rate of growth by end of 2011. At the G20 summit in London in April 2009, which Brown organized and chaired, the G20 leaders agreed to what was the largest financial rescue package in history. In addition to the $1 trillion rescue program underpinning the economies, the G20 agreed on actions to ensure that world monetary and fiscal actions were to be coordinated *on a level never seen before*. Independent central banks were for the first time now working in unison in their plans to inject new resources into economies; increased supply of money through quantitative easing was happening all over the world and very critical extension in bank-to-bank currency swaps was providing the funds necessary to address recession. The central banks developed swap credit lines with other countries up to half trillion dollars. In total, a sum of $3 trillion was injected into the budgets of national economies to take them out of recession.

The then President of the World Bank Robert Zoellick was so overwhelmed with this united global effort that he described it as the thing that *broke the fall* of the global economy. Brown said that there was trepidation among some of the G20 delegates at the meeting about the scale of the size of the rescue that was being planned to be injected into the world system.

Brown claimed that three months after the G20 action, the collapse in global domestic product of 2008 and 2009, which had gone on for five successive quarters was halted in contrast to the 1929 to 1930 fall when the global domestic product continued to drop for another two years after the initial five successive quarters. Brown was, however, comparing oranges and apples. The 1929 episode was a depression. We have not had a depression since 1929–1933. It was not inevitable that the 2007 recession will turn into a depression. It was, therefore, incorrect for Brown to claim that the 2009 G20 action prevented a depression within three months. What the G20 told the world in their communiqué was that they wanted to bring the world back to pre-crisis global growth rate by the end of 2011.

Despite all the colossal unprecedented sums the G20 poured into the system, they failed by 2011 to achieve anything near the pre-crisis growth rate. Instead, Europe joined the United States as problem economies. More than after three to four years after the much heralded G20 make-or-break global action almost all countries in Europe were in recession, while the United States was limping. In a June 7, 2011 Global Economic Prospects Report, the World Bank declared: "Two and half years after the crash of September 2008 and two years after the end of the US recession, it is clear that none of the underlying problems that plagued the world into the deepest slump since 1930s have been resolved."

The report stated that: "On the contrary, the anemic recovery is faltering—growth rates are slowing in most of the world, and the financial system is again teetering on the edge of the abyss." The report said the world economy will expand by mere 3.2 percent in 2011, dramatically lower than the modest 3.8 percent for 2010. The G20 of April 2009 was an example of what IMF called *good* global. The so called world economy has today not recovered from its very low growth since 2008.

Nothing more than the World Bank report could be more indicative of the G20 general ignorance of the global economics and the impotence of globalization. The G20 with the fractionalized and collapsing state of the 'global' economy as US and Europe's economies falter is today an almost irrelevant decoration. The world finance has long been taken over by the financial industry that is reaping it off based on the belief by governments especially in the West that it is international finance that governs the economic development and growth of all l countries.

Mr. Brown himself admitted that "At no point in history (during the 2009 G20) have governments ever injected so much money into buying up assets in the banking system, with capital and guarantees running into trillions." But it did not increase global GDP. Finance they needed to know does not create economic growth. According to Brown, between 1990 and 2008, "Finance went global, far outstripping growth in the rest of the economy, and became the biggest industrial-scale money making machine the world has ever known." It was the monster I had earlier referred to. Between1990 and 2008, global money flows went up by 6,000 percent that translated into flows of $130 billions a day. Such intensified international trade and globalization flows are pushed by the powerful worldwide financial industry not because of the sustainable economic benefits to countries of international trade and globalization but because it gives the financial industry the justification it needs for its existence: profits.

The position today is that each of these Western countries is pushing on the global front end with an economy that is structurally unbalanced. The global finance industry profits is leaving each economy in a worse structural economic position because they only know how to push on conventional economics based on capital investment.

Take Japan as an example I had earlier referred to. Here is a country that was seeking ways to build its economy after the serious economic disaster it suffered in World War II. In 1949, it set up a super ministry: the Ministry of International Trade and Investment (MITI). The ministry was in charge of industrial policy. It was in charge of investment in plant and equipment, expected to establish and grow productivity and employment. Japan is an island with very few natural resources, little energy resources. Its population density of 327 per square km, compared to 119 for China and 7 for the United States clearly called for factor proportions that are low in material and capital and high in labor. But MITI set out to make Japan a major capital-intensive economy. Japan imports much of its raw materials and energy. It does not have what is needed to support a capital-intensive economy. By the 1980s, Japan was about to overtake the US economy as its industrial output and export soared.

Gradually, as was inevitable, Japan's economy buckled with a structurally unbalanced economy, worse in some respects than the United States, which has a higher material endowment. Japan has had to go into a long sleep, an *unexplainable* deflation as a result of a serious structurally unbalanced economy. Japan today has currently the highest ratio debt/GDP of 233 % worst of all advanced economies with unemployment of about 2.4 percent. Japan's immediate problem is not exports but the wrong exports. The huge gainers are the global financial markets. Japan will never succeed without structural factor proportion changes just like the United States that needs structural changes to be competitive.

The possible slow death of globalization arrived following the US Great Recession and was demonstrated when in March 2013, the IMF hosted a conference of some of what it called the *world's top macro-economists* to assess how the most intense global financial crisis since the Depression has changed the profession's collective understanding of how globalization works. The first to speak was George Akerlof, a Nobel Prize-winning economist from Berkley, who compared the global economy with a cat stuck in the tree, afraid to move.

Realizing after the conference, that after five years of trying to solve the global crisis since 1998, there is great uncertainty among these best international globalization brains on what to do to prevent more global crisis. The IMF Chief Economist Oliver Blanchard, the host, concluded, at the end of the conference, that "we don't have a sense of final destination. Where we end up, I really don't have much clue." The clue, in my view, is to throw globalization into the dustbin.

It was at the height of the US financial crisis in 1998 that President George Bush issued invitation to countries which eventually were called the G20. The G20 has initially claimed through Mr. Brown that it stopped a world financial crisis and stopped a world depression from taking place! The G20 has met since then every two years with a rotating chair but has nothing to show for it. The fact that the G20 pumped $3 trillion into economies spearheaded by Brown in 2009 with no result did not prevent the G20 meeting in Australia February 2014 from making another joke of itself in deciding to add more than $2 trillion over the next five years to the world economy to increase investment, boost employment and private investment with no result. In an article by Lowy Institute for International Policy in Australia, the host country for G20, the institute talked of "The Challenge of Repairing G20". The article stated that the objective is to invigorate the G20 in its claim as the "foremost global coordinator." This the article said, comes as "some emerging economy members are buffeted by the spillover of uncoordinated macro-policies in advanced countries" for example, United States Fed expanded its QE, and sent much of the money the Fed was pouring into the financial market in the US into emerging markets by institutions that leveraged their portfolios, which drove up their exchange rates, eroded their trade competition. When in late 2013, the Fed announced that it will start slowing down and will finally wind up QE, a sudden rush of the money out these countries started, pushing down exchange rates, deflating equity prices and driving up interest rates. This is exactly what Asian crisis in the late 90s was about except that the rush out of money then was due to the structural collapse of the Asian economy. What we had with QE is a situation which the United States Fed felt it was entitled to take unilateral action without clearance with anyone in undertaking an action which was the cause major ripple in international finance. G20 is ineffective even as its membership lacks cohesion of objectives and as globalization itself becomes a mere means for private operators of globalization to continuously exploit the rest of us. All the dreams about a global financial system monitored by G20 with all the controls/regulations and early warning systems in a rising global economic growth and prosperity have come to nothing.

Two new key features in reviewing the future of globalization need to be commented on. First is the increased effort to avoid future world financial crisis the type that followed the US recession of 2017. It is an international effort to stop the divideness that followed that crisis as I have earlier described. A Financial Stability Board was formed under the aegis of the G20, based in International Bank for Development intended to monitor/assess vulnerabilities afflicting the global financial system and to proposes actions neededwhich are not legally binding on the members. The Board monitors and advises on market and systemic development and their implication for regulatory policy. It is a major change from the recriminations and divisiveness that followed the US last recession as I earlier described.

A second key change in globalization is the Chinese recent emergence in globalization. It is the result of years of learning and preparation. In chapter 4, I stated that in a countrywide scientific conference in 2003 in China, the topic was to study globalization, how to avoid its pitalls and how to take command and advantage of it soon after China got its WTO membership in 2001. US wrongly thought that Chinese membership of the WTO signaled China's intention to abide by the international WTO-based rules of international trade. When therefore President Xi in key speech at the World Economic Forum in Davos in 2017 defended international trade and economic integration, he was taking up from the study/movement which China started in 2003 of how China can make globalization a servant of China. Mr Xi in Davos, in this context, for the first time asked the the world to say no protectionism and push free trade. That was at a time the US was beginning to doubt globalization and losing leadership just as the Chinese wanted to take over globalization. At the first China International Import Expo in November 2018 in China, the Chinese president declared that "China will not stop its effort to pursue high-quality opening up. China will not stop its effort to pursue an open world economy." China in effect was in effect wanting to spread its wealth and economic success throughout the world. China in 2013 devised its Silk-Road infrastructure project, the same year as its countrywide conference on globalization. The Silk Road was a (Chinese) ancient road that promoted trade between the East and West. In modern times, its name revival should tell the world about the ambitions of China to take over globalization. The basic difference between the US and China in their globalization strategy is that the first was private sector seeking profit while the Chinese was led by the Chinese government. Silk Road is a Chinese development $ 1tn strategy involving infrastructure in 152 countries and institutions in Europe, Asia and the Middle East. While we are watching the Chinese were next in the former Eastern Europe expanding port facilities in Bulgaria, high-speed railway connecting Hungary and Serbia. 16 central and eastern European countries, including 11 members of the EU have formal business relations with China. EU leaders have recently become increasingly alarmed by what they consider Chinese aggressive incursions into the continent's economy as confirmed by a Chinese Silk Road port development in Italy in 2019 as it became the first G7 country to sign an

MOU endorsing China's Belt and Road initiative. Italy is a country seeking aid andwhose economy shrank in the 2018 derving little benefit from its membership of the EU. The Italian prime minister admitted that "as China exerts a stronger influence on the world economy, it is going to exert increasing influence also at the political level." He spoke admiringly, as reported in the Wall Street Journal March 31 2019 of Chinese efforts to become "a world leader intechnology and innovation." Italy was followed by France that signed a good number of trade and investment agreements with China trying to live up to Germany that already has strong trade and investment relationships with China and whose rail industry has been reinvigorated partly by Chinese investment, as the German city of Duisburg has become an important stop in the Chinese Silk Road project. Many French wineries are today Chinese-owned tied to powerful growing wine industry in China. The EU in a 2019 report on China was aware of the looming Chinese power. The EU described its dilemma with China by saying that Europe should appreceate that Chinese foreign investment "may result in high level indebtedness and transfer of control over strategic assets and resources." The report feared that if China is allowed to get away with its plans "China will behave like a mercantilist power that favors national champions over foreign firms to dominate world markets." China has its national industrial Champions waiting. Brussels is passing laws in attempt to counter China's influence in the EU. European lawmakers and political leaders agreed on a system to scrutinize investments in the EU as a way to protect key industries from China. Mr. Geraci, the Italian Under-Secretary who put all the Italian package together stated that he did not see what is the difference between what Italy is doing with China and what others have done with China. "Once the first domino topples, speaking of Italy's decision, "the others will follow" he said. When Richard Grenell, the US ambassador to Germany threatened in 2019 that the US would scale back its intelligence sharing with Germany if Huawei (of China) played a role in its 5G infrastructure, Ms. Merkel shot him down, "We are determining our standards for ourselves.". Ms. Markel had earlier herself has said that "We, as Eurpeans, want to play an active part in the new Silk Road project." Mr. Xi said that "a united and prosperous Europe corresponds to our vision of a multipolar world" a seeming turn away from the US which had recently as 2017 witdrawn from many bilateral trade and regional agreements. United States has seen the Silk Road project as a challenge. A former US Secretary of Defence has described it as "long-term designs to rewrite existing global order." He suggested there were three ways which were all military. He failed to realize that the issue was fundamentally economic as China's economy seems to dominatet US economy, the subject of this book. In April 2019 in an effort to see the Silk Road Project in a forum hosting dozens of nations in which China sought to seek international and private finncing into Silk Road projects of whichM/S Lagarde of IMF said was welcome. She said that financial centers in Europe and Asia lining up to share [in Silk Road]. Could this be a new globalization?

THE US REAL ECONOMY

Chapter 8

The Problem Called the Fed

Complaints against the Fed have recently increased from within Wall Street financial operators and outside. The general tone devolves on complaints about the Fed's incompetence and its inability to explain its economics, not when, for example, Bernanke and Yellen could not even explain what causes unemployment during their nomination hearings which I will get to later. In a June 6, 2016 *Market Slant* article, "End the Fed…and Move the Country Forward," Shah Gilani declared that the name "Federal Reserve System" is supposed to conjure up nice, comforting images of a safety net, of a system to safeguard the economy of the United States. In fact, he said, the creators were adamant about now calling it a bank—because banks were feared and loathed then—as they are mostly now. He declared that the truth is that the Federal Reserve System (remember, it is not a bank it is a "system") is killing this country. They are false prophets with a god complex— the most dangerous kind. In his 2018 publication, "All Hail the Fed," Kesley Williams stated that the Fed represents "the culmination of decades of irresponsible financial policies and a complete abdication of fundamental economics."

What the world refers to as the Federal Reserve Bank or America's central bank, while believing it's a U.S. government body—in fact is a private enterprise system, secretly despised by bankers and their pet politicians on Jekyll Island Georgia in 1910. After a great deal of manipulation, the outline of the plan drawn up at J.P. Morgan's private hunt club of an island became legislation: The Federal Reserve Act. The legislation was quietly signed into law before Christmas Eve 1913 by President Woodrow Wilson—a former Princeton professor plucked from obscurity by bankers and politicians who engineered his election, in part to bring the Fed to life.

With the Federal Reserve Act, Congress ceded the creation of money to the Federal Reserve Bank system. The dollars in our pockets he reminded are printed by the US Treasury and signed by the Secretary of the Treasury, but they are neither issued nor owned by the US Treasury. The dollars in our pockets are Federal Reserve notes. The Fed owns the money and, by extension, it owns the country.

It is the place we call Main Street that harbors the poverty, the unemployment, the inequality and all the things we regard as evidence of the poor economy of the United States. Wall Street/Financial Market under the Fed is an outer coating which, according to the economic thinking in America, only has a financial connection with Main Street but thinks that it is in charge of it.

The US macroeconomy is supposed to be under the charge of the Fed. The economic idea is that the Fed is charged with maintaining the health of the economy by controlling the money supply in the economy. Here is the difference between China and the United States and many other countries. Whereas China sees its central bank as a lubricant for the economic engine, America sees its central bank as the designer and the driver of the economic engine. The collapse of development economics in the 1950s in the US, as I discussed in Chapter 1, prevented economics in the US from embracing economic science. Conventional economics that took over after the collapse finally ended in a financial dead end unable to provide a scientific analysis of the economy. China, on the other hand, as I discussed in chapter 4, has matured its economic experiments and studies into an economic science.

Economic science, as I have indicated, is hinged on structural economics based on the three factors of production of labor, material and production aid (capital)—in 3D. The essence of economic science is to achieve the expanding and efficient use of natural resources of labor, raw materials and production aid through the adoption of appropriate factor proportions.

The essence of "appropriate factor proportions" is the essence of technology. Technology is the science of factor proportions. It is therefore important, as I start this last section of the book, to state that finance is not economics. All finance is in our imagination. Finance has no physical existence but an agreed basis of value from the days of barter. In one of its "FAQ's and Answers", the Fed admitted that "—it is difficult to gauge precisely the effect of monetary policy on the economy." As economic development is to top-most agenda for China and as China's economy is about to overtake that of the US, can the US continue the luxury of handing its economy to the Fed which cannot scientifically establish the connection between its work and the US economy.

Fed Twin-Objectives

It was the appalling history of unemployment in the post-World War II United States economy in the mid-1970s that brought the issue of unemployment to national attention. The Federal Reserve Act section 2A 1977 was an attempt to fix the problem. The dual mandate of the Fed, was a 1975 resolution of the Congress which was later made an amendment to the Federal Reserve Act 1977 that specified that the Fed:

> Shall maintain long-run growth of the monetary and credit aggregates commensurate with the economy's long run potential to increase production, so as to promote effectively the goals of maximum employment, stable prices, and moderate long-term interest.

The Act is technically deficient because it arose from the mistake of regarding the quantum of monetary and credit aggregates as commensurate with economic production. It is the faulty stance that it is only finance that is the means to economic growth that has dragged down US economic growth since. The fact that the Fed had never promoted the economic growth and high employment of the US economy is evident in statements from the Fed itself. For example, in one statement in January 25, 2012, the Fed said that "The maximum level of employment is largely determined by non-monetary factors that affect the structure and dynamics of the labor market." It said that "These factors may change over time and may not be directly measurable. Consequently, it will not be appropriate to specify a fixed goal of employment...." In other words, the Fed is saying it does know the factors that determine maximum employment and that they cannot be measured as part of monetary and credit aggregates and that whatever they are that they also may change with time. The target unemployment rate which the Fed uses as a basis is not from any structural knowledge of the economy but by a paper vote of the FOMC members every three months based on models.

I decided to see what Greenspan would say in his two books to date (The *Age of Turbulence*—531 pages, *The Map and The Territory*—388 pages) about the Double Mandate especially *The Age of Turbulence* which was Greenspan's broad sweep of his career and accomplishments. Nowhere in the two books did he mention the Double Mandate. He talked a lot about employment in the books but never made a claim that the Fed pushed employment as part of the Double Mandate. It is because he probably was not willing or able to make such a claim.

The truth is that when the law setting up the double mandate was established in 1977, people in the Fed found the double mandate a bit of embarrassment up to Greenspan's time. Daniel Thornton in his Federal Reserve Bank of St. Louis Review March/ April 2012 article "The Dual Mandate: Has the Fed Changed its Objective?" pointed out it is not until thirty years after the law was set up that the governing body of the Fed (FOMC) ever made any public reference to employment as its objective. It was only at the first Federal Open Market Committee meeting of the Fed in 1995 that the first major discussion of the dual mandate was held between the then President Yellen of San Francisco Fed and President Broaddus Jr. of Richmond. Thornton gave reasons for this. The principal one was that while people in the Fed agreed that their policy actions can have a direct effect on economic growth via interest and/or the growth of monetary and credit aggregates—which was wrong in itself—there was little agreement among them on how their policy actions on the economy by the Fed can have any direct effect on employment growth. There was therefore a deliberate policy to avoid mentioning double mandate in Fed policy papers over many years.

In fact, according to Thornton, FOMC members found some of the double mandate requirements of the law troubling. The law with its errors had remained the same till today. What has happened is that in the recent years, the people in the Fed have decided to acclaim the double mandate despite its basic economic fallacies helped by the fact that many of their group have come to believe—falsely though—that low inflation can increase economic growth and employment and as they came to believe they can succeed with employmentby keeping inflation low. What we now have today in the United States is that there is public deception by the Fed that makes it out that it is working to turn the United States into a high employment economy and has the expertise to do so. The truth is that no one in the Fed has the structural knowledge about how to grow the economy and employment of the United States.

Despite these untruths and ignorance about the double mandate, the Fed and its officials under Bernanke and Yellen have always tried to live with it and to acclaim it. I have the impression that they are telling us "If you believe that the Fed can solve unemployment, then we will also believe it and will help to convince you further that it is true."

Bernanke's speech on February 24, 2006 titled "Benefits of Price Stability" at the Center for Economic Policy Studies at Princeton University was such an initial attempt to claim overall control of economic growth. Bernanke told his audience that the Fed's mandated objective of price stability is an end in itself. According to him, price stability promotes efficiency and long-term economic growth by providing a monetary and financial environment in which economic decisions can be made and markets can operate without concern about unpredictable fluctuations in the purchasing power of money.[127]

Sometimes the Fed says that employment requires price stability. At other times they say it is low price/low interest that cause employment. From 2008 to 2013—5 years—despite low and negative interest, unemployment in the United States dropped from 10 percent to 7.3 percent. The drop was an inevitable drop as the economic cycle returns to "normal" from recession. At her nomination hearing in November

2013, Yellen tried to claim credit that "since Quantitative Easing started, unemployment had decreased from 8.1 percent to 7.3 percent" even though she readily accepted under questioning that true unemployment might be more than 10 percent. These Fed claims are false. It is not true, as I had earlier said, that price stability guarantees long-term economic growth. Economic growth is a structural economic activity determined by creating the structural determinants of the correct application of production factors as I have already summarized. Growth has nothing to do with price stability. A structural economic activity is not a financial activity. Price stability, to put it the other way around, is the result of strong, balanced (structural) growth but cannot be the cause of strong balanced growth. The only recent time the US economy grew very fast was the period that was called the New Economy of the 1990s. It was the period that the Fed erroneously expected inflation to jump up on the wrong thought that the resultant high employment will overheat the economy (NAIRU) and cause inflation to rise. Instead the rise in employment during the New Economy resulted in stable low prices despite the Fed's attempted rate increases. The point was made by Bob Pollin, founder and coordinator of PERI Institute, author of the book *Back to Full Employment* when he said that "Where we have gotten essentially in [conventional] macroeconomics analysis and policy is really to say, 'Well we can't really do anything about employment through government policy. We can control inflation, so let's just stick with inflation and let job creation land wherever it lands.'" That is precisely what the Fed is doing.

Employment and economic growth specifically came up for discussion during Bernanke's confirmation hearing in November 2005. Senator Robert Bennett asked Bernanke the relationship between inflation and growth. Bernanke responded as follows:

> "Senator, growth itself and growth capacity is ultimately determined by productivity, which again, depends on issues like regulation, taxation, innovation, technology, and the like, and also by employment growth, the number of workers available and the increase in their labor supply. So those are the fundamental factors that determine growth. The amount of available growth varies over time

according to economic conditions. It can be high. The United States has had good economic policies that have promoted growth in recent years—good technologies. And so, in that sense strong growth does not create inflation. If financial conditions are such, though, that aggregate spending is greater than even the growth that underlying conditions can permit, then there can be increased price power, excess demand, and pricing pressures could increase. In that case, you get some inflation. I agree with your original statement, though, that in the long run sense the most important relationship is between low inflation and high growth. That is, when inflation is kept low and stable and expectations are kept llow and stable, then the economy will be more stable and more growth will be possible."

In this very long winding statement, Bernanke was unable to tell Senator Bennett how the Fed grows employment and even though he claimed that growth in employment grows the economy. He never mentioned the double mandate.

Instead Bernanke claimed categorically (and wrongly) that economic growth and growth capacity is ultimately determined by productivity, which itself, according to him, is determined by another set of factors: technology, regulations, innovations, and *"the like."* All these technical issues (innovations, technology, regulations etc) are clearly not within the knowledge of the Fed and have nothing to do with Fed's claimed inflation control. Bernanke told the senator that the only time inflation will be relevant in regard to growth is if aggregate demand/spending is greater than growth.

I am glad some monetary people recognize the facts I have made. For example, the Federal Reserve Board of Richmond in its Federal Open Market Committee (FOMC) statement of February 25, 2012 stated that "The maximum level of employment is largely determined by non-monetary factors."

Most people in the United States are not aware or have forgotten Bernanke's admission in the 2006 speech that "Research is not definitive about the extent to which price stability enhances economic growth."

He said at the time that "We do not have controlled experiments in macroeconomics, and inflation and growth are both endogenous variables that respond to many factors." Here again, Bernanke was confirming that he was not sure whether there are any financial links between growth /employment and inflation.

Despite this, on another occasion, Bernanke went on another occasion to tell his listeners that nevertheless he was "*confident* that the effect of price stability on growth/employment is positive." He instead argued this time that "it is the *consensus* view among economists that mandated goals of price stability and maximum employ ment are *almost entirely* complementary." Hanging on his point further on claims of consensus—this time it was the consensus of central bankers, economists, and people he called "*other knowledgeable observers*", who *believed* that price stability contributes to economic growth and employment prospects *in the longer term and moderates the variability of output in the short to medium run.* Elsewhere he said that in the pre-1970s that high inflation was thought to be best way to achieve low unemployment but that that view surprisingly has now been reversed.

The Fed in recent years makes a desperate attempt to cling to its claim that it boosts employment because it is a big image and political booster. In an earlier speech in 2003 as a Governor of the Fed, Bernanke tried to use economic history to back up this claim. He told us that periods of unstable prices *tended* to be marked by instability in output and unemployment.[128] He reminded his listeners that the US suffered precipitous deflation from 1929 to 1933. He claimed the 1929 to 1933 deflation ushered in, and to a significant extent, was the cause of the broad economic collapse we now know as the Great Depression. I have shown in chapter 1 that these claims on the Great Depression are incorrect.

Clearly the Fed has succeeded in *convincing* a large of section of US population that it controls employment (and so economic growth) of the United States. In announcing the nomination of Yellen as the Chairman of the Fed, the New York Times of October 10, 2013 headlined: "Yellen's Path From Academic Theorist to the Fed's Voice for Jobs." So, New York Times believes that the Fed is the voice for jobs in the US.

Yellen was herself intent on boosting the claim about the Fed's employment promotion expertise claimed at her nomination hearing that "Too many Americans still can't find a job and worry how they'll pay their bills. The Federal Reserve can help." Yet a few months earlier in a speech February 11, 2013, the same Yellen was saying that "It will be years before many workers feel like they have gained the ground lost since 2007."

The Chinese central bank does not make these wild claims. It knows what its job is—to lubricate the economy, to simply assist to make money available to people who need it to pursue the planned development programs. The current Chinese central bank governor follows developments in the US and differences with Fed and the financial market in the United States very closely.

The Bank of China does not make the wild claims the Fed makes about its twin role and control of the economy. Zhou Xiaochoun the Governor of Bank of China, without specifically referring to US economists' constant reference to the Great Depression warned against what he called *misreading history*. He stated that every person was likely to have his or her own bias in interpreting history.

He added: "This is especially true for a researcher whose established approach and school might affect the methodology and perspective of analysis and interpretation and disturb the pursuit of a correct prescription." He specifically pointed out in his speech that Bernanke is a follower of Friedman. Bernanke is famed for his research on the 1933 depression which he later told us he found very handy in dealing with the 2008 and 2009 financial crisis. Xiaochoun cautioned that "the viewpoints of Nobel Prize winners [of whom US abounds] might not be completely correct as many of them in any case have conflicting ideas."

He warned against ready adoption of *superficial reasons* as against *deep rooted causes* in interpreting history. The Chinese *Central Governor* clearly did not believe or agree with what Bernanke and Fed were claiming.[129]

In a major speech, as a governor of the Fed in 2006, Randall Kroszner clarified Fed's price stability claim as follows: "Stable prices encourage the growth of financial intermediaries and financial markets." He further said, "According to numerous studies, there is a strong *link* between financial market development and economic growth."[130] Again notice he was loosely talking of *links*. The first link is between stable prices and financial intermediaries/ markets. The second claimed link between financial market and economic development is patently false. It is acceptable that stable prices are good for the financial market, the next jump over in analysis, namely the link from stable prices to economic growth is false for structural reasons I have given.

Bernanke demonstrated this error of thinking when he argued in his 2006 speech that economists argue that money belongs in the same class as the wheel and the inclined plane among ancient inventions of great social utility. Price stability, he claimed, allows inventions to work with minimum friction. He was incorrect. It is the designed structural balance in the wheel and inclined plane that ensures there is no friction. It is not the lack of friction that creates the balanced wheel or inclined plane.

Inside the Fed, there were people who don't accept the Fed's age-old claim about its role in creating economic growth and maximizing employment and have had the courage to say so openly. On April 2, 2013, in a public debate in Richmond Virginia, two of Bernanke's colleagues in the Fed disagreed on the Fed's effort to stimulate the US economy. Jeffrey Lacker, the President of the Federal Reserve Bank in Richmond, said he did not expect the Fed to recover the losses the economy sustained during the 2007 through 2009 recession. He doubted whether monetary policy has the power to increase economic growth. He said he saw little evidence of the Fed's efforts of increasing economic growth including the new experimental strategies. He accused the Fed of repeatedly exaggerating the strength of the recovery.

Charles Evans, a member of Fed who did not describe himself as a critic of Fed policy, will only say that recovery has been postponed rather than cancelled. He admitted that "Our (the Fed) credibility will ultimately be judged by how we do on both of these mandates, not just the price mandate." He concluded that: "I think we will be judged very badly" if we do not reduce unemployment." The Fed is a club to which members almost swear an allegiance of secrecy.

The *New York Times* commentator stated, at the time, that the Fed's course continues to be set by its Chairman, Ben Bernanke, with a centralist majority he has carefully assembled. Not everybody in the Fed obviously agrees with what the Fed claims.[131]

The relevant part of the Federal Act that set up the Dual Mandate is therefore technically mistaken and not economically sound. The Mandate is therefore technically deficient and is unimplementable. Growth is not a financial process.

Fed's "Management" of Inflation

Inflation is like a virus that spreads through the body in an unpredictable manner. Like friction that occurs in an irregularly unbalanced machine, inflation cannot be predicted. The Fed has no medicine with which to treat this virus despite all its pretensions. The virus goes away and reappears when the doctor thinks that it has been subdued. The doctor has no idea about the character of the virus he is treating.

The following are the comments of Fed Vice Chairman Donald Kohn at a conference of experts on the subject of "Understanding the Evolving Inflation Process" in March 2007.

ba. Even today, we face a number of uncertainties about the nature of the inflation process;

bb. We do not yet have a consensus structural model of inflation dynamics...

bc. Monetary policy operates in an environment of pervasive uncertainty...

bd. We should always keep in mind how little we know about the economy.[132]

Governor Mishkin said, "Substantial gaps in our knowledge (of inflation) remain and forecasting is still a famously imprecise task."[133] Ivan O'Kitov wrote that there are numerous definitions of inflation resulting in different values. He said, "Inflation is an obscure variable."[134]

Kelsey Williams in his 2018 publication titled'Inflation titled "Inflation—What it is, What it's not—"stated that inflation "is "legalized version of Ponzi sheme." Why then do the Feds put up a face of mastery of inflation?

There have been historical changes on how conventional economists explain the cause of inflation. In my days as an economics major in the early 1960s, my teachers used to say that inflation was caused when too much money were chasing a few goods. Then the next economists linked inflation with the *velocity* of money. This was what I may call the quantum approach to inflation. In the late 1960s, Friedman and Edmund Phelps, a Nobel laureate, independently overturned the quantum view of inflation. Their reason was that wages and other prices might not change immediately due to changes in the quantity or velocity of money. Economists, following the lead of Friedman and Phelps, changed course and resorted to behavioral *sciences.* They decided that it is the psychological outlook of the price setters in an economy that determines the price changes in the economy. Firms and households are supposed to take account of demand and supply conditions that will prevail until they reset their prices. Behind all these expectations are, we are told, their price increase (inflation) expectations. These experts have failed scientifically to answer a more fundamental question: what is it that determines price changes that are presented to the minds of the price setters? Bernanke told senators in his confirmation hearing in 2005 that:

> If financial conditions are such that aggregate demand, aggregate spending is greater than even the growth that underlying conditions can permit, then there can be increased pricing power, excess demand, and pricing pres- sures could increase. In that case, you can get inflation.

The Fed cannot solve inflation if in fact it lacks full scientific knowledge of its nature and its causes. Bernanke's description of inflation is deficient because it did not tell us why and in what way demand can just increase above the capacity of the economy. He has not told us how he can define or measure the capacity of the economy. In so far as the Fed cannot answer these basic questions, it has been gambling with the US economy.

Bernanke's inability on various occasions to give us a precise scientific definition of what causes economic growth makes the Fed unqualified to pursue strategies that will grow the economy and employment. We are witnessing economic gambling on a large scale that will eventually stall US economy's growth. As Kesley Williams put it in respect to the Fed: "Where we are today is the culmination of decades of irresponsible financial policies and a complete abdication of fundamental economics."

We all experience the effects of inflation because we experience price increases in our everyday life. That is not enough as a basis to understand what inflation is. Friedman, the legend of conventional monetary economics, had incorrectly told his followers that "Inflation is always and everywhere a monetary phenomenon." In seeking to manage the illusive phenomenon called inflation, the Fed and US economists have experienced serious reverses in their beliefs. They have been using the US economy as an experimental laboratory and still have not found an answer. At first, they believed as an article of faith that there is an inverse relationship between the rate of inflation and the rate of unemployment. The so-called Phillips curve put this graphically as the relationship between unemployment and wage inflation. This was a piece of empirical evaluation. The Nobel laureates Paul Samuelson and Robert Solow led their followers to take the Phillips curve as the mainstay of inflation management. In Friedman's and Phelp's view, the Fed could make a permanent trade-off between unemployment and inflation rates on the basis of Phillips curve, choosing unemployment required against inflation to be expected and vice versa. So for a time, the US economy was run on this fantasy. Then at the height of the Phillips curve popularity, Phelps and Friedman challenged its theoretical underpinnings...which there were none. There were none because all conventional economic theories are empirical with no scientific/ structural base. Behaving as if they knew better, Friedman and Phelps led economists to a new empirical conclusion that the government cannot juggle unemployment and inflation rates at will. They argued that at each level of employment, wages will adjust to make supply and demand for labor equal and that there will be an unemployment level equivalent to that wage level. This level of unemployment they called the *natural rate of* unemployment. Therefore, for a given rate of inflation, there is a natural rate of unemployment, fondly called NAIRU (Non Accelerating

Inflation Rate of Unemployment). From 1979 to 2003 Federal Chairman Paul Volcker and his successor Alan Greenspan exploited the idea of NAIRU that as unemployment falls too low, inflation goes up, and vice versa and by using interest rate to push up unemployment in the hope of achieving lasting reductions in inflation. But as usual with conventional economics, NAIRU came to a dead-end during the New Economy when unemployment was reducing as inflation did not increase. Greenspan at a November 13, 1996 meeting told his audience that the evidence that there is a significant shortfall in measured wages from the predictions of our wage-NAIRU econometrics is pretty clear.

In a February 4 to 5, 1997 meeting the Vice Chairman of New York Fed admitted that "one of the things we have become rather convinced of is that the NAIRU is a very interesting analytical tool, but it is a very poor forecasting tool…" Greenspan, as I already mentioned, during a Congressional testimony, which the *New York Times* called an "epitaph" to NAIRU in July 2000 told congress that:

> My forecast is that NAIRU, which served as a very useful statistical procedure to evaluate how the economy was behaving over a number of years ahead as a useful, like so many types of temporary models which worked, is probably going to fail in the years ahead as a useful indicator.[135]

The whole Fed is all about experiments and illusive conclusions. The collapse of NAIRU during the New Economy after a time when it was the key the Fed has all but silenced further noises of economists about NAIRU. But not gone are the losses and damage done to the US economy over the years by NAIRU theories that had no scientific foundation. The original Phillips curve metamorphosed as expectations-augmented Phillips curve developed. It became a fundamental element of almost every macroeconomic forecasting model used by the Fed and businesses. It became also the fashion in Europe. The present Fed once based the bulk of its inflation reputation on inflation expectation, almost a complete departure from Greenspan's NAIRU. Greenspan did not mention the Phillips curve even once in his 531 page book on the US economy. As this stage of the dance goes on, Americans are being short-changed, fooled and misled. As Kesley Williams stated that since the Fed's inception in 1913 the US dollar has lost more than 98% of its purchasing power. He added that that:This is the price we have paid for hoping and believing that a small group of individuals can manage the economic cycle—."

Some people were given a Nobel Prize in economics because they *discovered* this obvious truth that the Fed does not control inflation/ price. What people think was then termed "people's expectations". The Fed now decided to move strategy so as to be relevant and remain in the driving seat on expectations. It now argued that because of the importance of this expectation, the central bank needed to upgrade its communication strategy with the private sector so as to influence and monitor this expectation. Bernanke's Fed sought to broaden the scope of this communication by seeking to help households and businesses to make more "informed" decisions and help *anchor* the private sector's inflation expectations in the hope of achieving long-run low and stable inflation by *anchoring* it. But how can the Fed do this when its quantitative knowledge of inflation is itself deficient that brought it to the point that Nobel Prize winners in effect told it that the Fed did not have what it takes to control inflation. Indeed the Nobel Prize winners were themselves limited in their study. Their study was concentrated on how much ordinary people made an input into the determination of inflation/prices. It did not occur to them that prices/inflation can be subject to structural factors and that what they thought was people's expectations were set by the structural factors.

The Fed's speculations which I have described fail to address the issue of why prices change and what determines the quantum of inflation expectations. If the quantum of inflation changes, no amount of Fed communication can produce stable prices or anchor inflation expectations. The Fed cannot anchor inflation expectations, despite its claims, if, as can be expected, the private operators cannot them- selves predict inflation because the changing quantum of inflation is dependent on the changing state of the structural imbalance in the economy. In January 2008, the US producer price index for finished goods increased by 1 percent causing a wholesale price jump of 7.4 percent for the year, the highest increase in twenty-six years. This happened at a time of so-called stagflation. Where were the Fed and its inflation expectation anchoring and its key task of ensuring price stability? The Fed should have better spent its time studying the dynamics of the basic US macroeconomic structure and how that determines the character of inflation instead of playing the economic psychologist.

Expectation theory is already under attack. There are people in the Fed itself who have no faith in inflation expectation as a policy threshold. In his comment on a paper on "Understanding the Evolving Inflation Process" by four authors, Fed Vice Chairman Donald Kohn on March 9, 2007 commented:

> The issue of expectations illustrates our ignorance. As I have already indicated, inflation expectations are among the most important variables policymakers monitor, but we do not always have the answer to our most basic questions about them: Are available measures suitable indicators of true inflation expectations by household and businesses?

My answer is no. He continued:

> How are expectations formed and in particular what are the respective roles of central bank talk, central bank actions, and the actual inflation outcomes? And how do expectations influence price and wage setting? In short, although I believe inflation expectations are critical to assessing inflation outlook, I cannot be sure (particularly in real time) that our expectation measures are accurate and so cannot know what precise role expectations play in wage and price dynamics.[136]

The Vice Chairman was in effect saying that he does not believe that inflation expectation enables the Fed to understand the wage and price dynamics of the United States, a point I have already made. Ben Bernanke's full outing with inflation expectation and Phillips curve started at the National Bureau of Economic Research (NBER) on July 10, 2007.[137] Bernanke made about a dozen references to the Phillips curve in this lecture, a concept that you would not hear his predecessor talk about. He told his audience that "the state of inflation expectations greatly influences actual inflation and thus the central bank's ability to achieve price stability."

On the other hand, he, like his Vice Chairman at the time acknowledged that the Fed had no satisfactory means of measuring inflation expectations. He admitted that the Fed's ability to forecast inflation and predict how inflation will respond to [financial] policy actions depends very much on the Fed's capacity to measure and understand what determines the public's expectations of inflation. I think the position with the Fed is like being in a jungle of vicious circles. Bernanke correctly admitted that the US economy is constantly evolving in ways that are imperfectly understood by the public and policy makers. This is because of their lack of knowledge in structural economics. The Fed has been fooling Americans that it can master the economy with financial modeling and econometrics of concepts which have no scientific base. In a *Financial Times* article on March 19, 2010, Samuel Brittan bade inflation targeting good-bye when he said that "from the onset of the financial crisis in 2007 and the subsequent recession, inflation targeting broke down in spectacular fashion." He stated that what really broke down was *the doctrine, spelt out in dozens of central banker speeches, that their pursuit (of targeted inflation) would bring reasonable stable economy.* The basic idea is that monetary and fiscal policy cannot *manage demand and output in real terms, as so many post-war experiences demonstrated.*[138]

The Phillips curve, which the current Fed desperately hung on has its critics even within its fold and outside. The debate about rational or irrational behavior of people always surfaces in conventional financial economics. Classical economists argue that inflation expectation based on Phillips curve ignores the fact that people make up their expectations rationally and that when that is taken into account much of the basis of expectations based on the Phillips curve is destroyed. There was talk in the Fed that the Phillips curve seems to have shifted and become flatter, a case of arguing one's way as one goes along by cleverly moving the argument. One excuse for arguing for a changed Phillips curve is that the sensitivity of inflation to activity indicators is lower today than in the past. In a Federal Reserve Bank of San Francisco Economic Letter in 2002, a senior economist stated, "The evidence suggests that the short-run Phillips curve is more likely to be useful for forecasting the direction of change of future inflation rather than forecasting the actual magnitude of future inflation."[139]

In another paper, it is being suggested that there is no relationship between inflation and unemployment and, therefore, there is nothing like a scientific Phillips curve.[140] The truth is, as I earlier stated, that as Bernanke admitted, the structure of the US economy is changing in a way that is not understood by financial policy makers. There is, therefore, no way the Fed can argue that there is a standing relationship between inflation and employment. The two are fairly independent outcomes of an unbalanced economy, and it is not feasible that you can alter one by altering the other.

After Bernanke's wide-ranging NERB academic lecture on July 10, 2007, which I had earlier referred to, on inflation expectations and Phillips curve, Greg Mankiw, a professor of economics in Harvard invited students to forward their comments on Bernanke's lecture. A sample of these comments show that students of economics are not fooled. One said, "To the fact that Bernanke's talk included about a dozen references to the Phillips curve," an economic concept you would not hear Greenspan talk about, Bernanke's predecessor "was a wise man." A second said:

> The reasons his (Bernanke's) predecessor is being wise are the following.
>
> Case 1: "The Phillips curve is bogus; a bad reading of data. Then the Fed chairman Ben Bernanke shouldn't be talking about it because it is bad science."
>
> Case 2: "The Phillips curve is a real thing describing the short-term tradeoffs by the Fed. Then the Fed chairman also shouldn't be talking about it, because if it is real, the last thing we want is a Fed chairman who believes it is real."

A third student said:

"Apparently, Elvis Presley is also alive and well, but who believes it? The Phillips curve is a UFO—an Unidentified Flying Object. To say the economy lies at a point on the curve, while the curve randomly shifts and changes slope is tantamount to saying nothing. And of course, a relationship valid ten years ago without widespread Internet access, etc., might well be invalid today. Now is it a surprise Bernanke advocates this? The Phillips curve gives monetary policy an aura of scientificism and determinism—precisely what Bernanke seeks to promote."

A fourth said:

"Trying estimating (inflation) to two decimal places! Taking these issues into account, another paper at this conference shows how policy makers couldn't even tell if inflation was rising or falling over the past decade. So Phillips curve nutters should take *that* in their pipe and smoke it."

We are being fooled by the Fed. This foolery is passed around in conspired silence. I find it ironic that some past Fed Chairmen take credit that they have significantly lowered inflation from what they call the Great Inflation of the '60s and '70s. Greenspan in his book thought this lowering of inflation was because his Fed had acted in cooperation with other central bankers worldwide. He saw globalization and cheap labor and cheap imports resulting from globalization as contributing to lower inflation. Bernanke and his colleagues, on the other hand, thought they lowered inflation because they have been able to *anchor* people's inflation expectations. All these claims are clearly superfluous as they were based on untruthful claims about globalization.

Since the Treasury-Fed Accord of 1951 that freed the Fed from constraints of fiscal policy and was supposed to have set the stage for the Fed's independent and improved monetary policy, the claim is that the Fed had been able to usher in improved macro-economic policies. The age of Great Moderation was claimed to be the prize to the country for this. The Fed was supposed over the 1980s to have achieved substantial moderation in the variability of both output and inflation which are claimed to lead to more stable employment. Greenspan made the claim that through Fed cooperating with other central banks inflation in many counties was checked. In a speech in February 20, 2004 Governor Bernanke claimed that the achieved moderation was associated with the fact recessions were less frequent and less severe. Most shocking was the claim in the speech that part of the reason moderation occurred was America's "shift away from manufacturing towards services and increased openness to trade and international capital flows." From their claims about the Great Moderation, our monetary wizards were sure recessions may either not occur again, but if they did, they will not occur as often and will certainly be much milder. The 2007-2009 Great Recession was a great shock to them not only because it occurred very shortly after Bernanke made his claim but that it was the most severe since the Great Depression.

The 1960s/1970s surprised conventional economists that high inflation can occur even when the economy is nearing recession and that during the New Economy of the '90s, low inflation can occur even when the economy is growing rapidly. These two surprising incidents should have told the Fed economists that inflation does not drive economic growth. As one of the students who commented on Greg Mankiw's blog said, "The Fed should take the NAIRU and Phillips curve in their pipe and smoke it."

Inflation is not something the Fed can predict or control given the structural imbalance of the US economy. It is not something the Fed can fix in our expectation. Inflation has no pattern because an unbalanced economy has no fixed behavior. The dynamic behavior of an unbalanced economy, from its inflation and recession behavior has an irregular regularity just like an unbalanced motor vehicle in motion. It is, therefore, difficult to see how the Fed can achieve stable prices. The Fed has all the time only been guess-estimating inflation in a situation in which forecasting is a nightmare. We know where the price increases of imported goods come from because Americans took a deliberate decision to import them into the United States. Such price increases should not be confused with structural inflation. Structural inflation should also not be confused by increases in prices that can occur because of shortage in supply due to unforeseen events like draught or adverse weather or accidents.

If inflation is like the friction caused when the moving parts of an old machine rub together, it can give us a rough clue as to how far this machine is performing below its potential capacity. An engineer will call it loss in output. The output of the macro-economy less the loss it suffers is its achievable (effective) output. To improve the effective output will require structural repairs to the machine. You cannot increase the output of the machine by slowing it down so as to reduce the friction between its moving parts. That is precisely what, in principle, the Fed is doing with the US economy by claiming that it needs to put interest up to avoid the overheating of the economy. At the end, the Fed wants people just to trust it that it can handle inflation. Yellen said in a lecture June 30, 2009 to the Commonwealth Club of California: "I will be the first to say that it is always difficult to get monetary policy just right. But the Fed's analytical prowess is top-notch and our forecasting is second to none." We know however that forecasting in the Fed and other forecasting agencies it associates with is a game of darts. That is why the Fed was unable to forecast the Great Recession of 2007-2009.

Today the Fed from nowhere has adopted 2% as its target for inflation. It had no structural basis for this only based on impromptu suggestion by Mrs Yellen in a Fed meeting in 2012. Some people in the Fed now claim that 2% is a Mandate. A balanced economy, as the New Economy experience showed, will eliminate inflation and lose the Fed its biggest claim for its existence. A balanced economy is beyond the competence of the Fed but if suceesful will eliminate the central core of the Fed's double mandate. As I have stated all through this book, America's main economic setback is structural.

The Fed's Independence

The Fed's independence came on the hot burner during the 1970s high inflation in the United States. There was the belief that over the period politicians were often tempted to push for high inflation by the

Fed in order to secure rise in employment for their political ends. It was therefore important, it was reasoned, that the Fed is independent so as to be protected from political directions in this context. The belief was that employment can be controlled through inflation management through interest management. If the claim that the Fed can control employment through inflation management is false, then the need for a Fed independence ceases.

It is noteworthy that in recent times, people at the Fed do not now justify the Fed's independence as intended to prevent politicians in power from pressing the Fed to manipulate interest rates to boost their election fortunes. People in Fed over time realized that the Fed has no such control of the economy. They have shifted to the claim that they need the Fed's independence in order to protect the financial market. This is because the people in the Fed know they need the powerful continuing lobby support of Wall Street.

When Ron Paul successfully raised concern about the Fed's independence in 2009, the Fed Vice Chair Donald Kohn vehemently argued at the House Financial Services Sub-Committee that "Any substantial erosion of the Federal Reserve's monetary independence would lead to higher long-term interest rates as investors begin to fear future inflation."

Asked in his first town hall meeting on July 27, 2009 why he thought it was important to retain the independence of the Fed, Bernanke said it was because financial markets will be unhappy if they felt that interests were being decided through political interference. The Fed has also fallen into the habit of justifying its independence by telling us that other central banks especially in the West are independent. They would not say that these countries copied the United States when the US economy was the shinning star. If early US economic history had taken a different path, they would not have copied the US central banking system.

The mystic awe people have about the claimed deep economic knowledge possessed by the Fed and its famed control of the economy have contributed to a situation in which people don't want the Fed's claimed vast store of knowledge and resulting control of the economy to be questioned. The truth was summarized by Roger Loweinstein in an article titled "The Decider" in *The New York Times* of January 20,

2008. He said,"There is a general notion that the Fed has vast powers over the US economy.""Actually," he said, "it has little influence over the (US) economy itself."

John Hussman has put the shaky knowledge of the Fed very well by stating August 25, 2014 (Hussman Funds) that "before the 15th century, people gazed at the sky and believed that other planets would move around the Earth, stop, move forward for a bit, and then move forward again. Their model of the world—that the Earth was the center of the universe—was the source of this confusion. Similarly, one of the reasons that the (US) economy seems confusing is that our policy makers are following models that have mixed evidence in reality. Worse, when extraordinary measures don't produce desired result (their) response is to double the effort without carefully asking whether there is a reliable, measurable cause and effect in the first place." If I put what Mr. Hussman is saying straight, I will say he is telling us that the Fed's monetary macroeconomics is faulty. The Fed, as Hussman's statement implies, thinks on its feet and has passed this habit to other central banks in the West/EU and Japan with the result that these countries (the developed economies) are in various state of economic instability. Being guided by varying empiricism, the Fed will always wait to recieve data and information on its actions so as to decide its next action and timing. The Fed is all the time experimenting with untested ideas and therefore unable to predict the result of its actions. For example, its announced plan to increase interests in 2016 has come undone because the economic recovery it betted on did not materialize to justify the promised interest hikes. Its plan to increase interest rates in 2018 were curtailed after interest increases in September and December 2018. The Fed increase its rate late 2018 was in the false belief that the US growth was rising.

China is an example of a country where the central bank is not independent but actively contributes to economic development. Monetary policy in China and the Chinese central bank are intended to support the Chinese Communist Central Working Committee and State Council work of maintaining a balanced scientific economy strategy in China. For example, as early as June 5, 2003, the Governor of China's central bank stated that the bank's role in the following words:

"Given the unique features of Chinese economic transition, the People's Bank of China also rendered its support to the economic structural adjustment (by the Central Working Committee/State Council) through its monetary and credit policy."

On November 23,2006, the Deputy Governor of the bank stated:

"The balanced development of the national economy is the prerequisite for rapid development of the national economy and the main content of sustainable and healthy economic growth...the PCB will continue to implement a sound monetary policy, focusing on both short term liquidity management and medium and long-term objectives to further intensify economic structural adjustment and promote a balanced growth of the economy."

The Governor on July 3, 2009 said:

"The scientific view on development conceived and established by the party and the Chinese government covers many aspects of the needed reforms and structuring, including putting people first, expanding consumption and domestic demand, environmental-friendly growth, promoting urbanization, developing the service sector, trade and investment facilitation...Though the quest for specific rules and routes toward sustainability involves trial and error, experimentation and knowledge renewal (by the Central Working Committee of the party), I am confident that...we will find a path to sustainable and scientific development."

What we have in China stands in stark contrast with the United States. In China, the Central Bank is a means to an end, a lubricant to the engine of growth as an agent of Chinese economic science. Chinese Central Bank involves itself intimately with all parts of the real economy whereas the US Fed regards itself, incorrectly, as the driver of the US economy and yet has little direct contact with the real economy.

The Fed in the United States is an ivory tower that does not meddle itself with the unexciting realities of Main Street. The Fed is often fondly called the Keeper of the Temple. The keeper of the temple lives in its ivory tower almost despising the busy Main Street below it. As the Janet Yellen said at her nomination hearing in November 2013, that the tools of the Fed allow it to reach the Main Street in part through Wall Street. The indirect link to Main Street which Yellen was talking about is a loose financial link which the Fed has had over time with community banks who serve Main Street. Community banks have however begun to disappear as they get swallowed up by big banks and very few new ones are coming up. An independent Fed therefore is isolated from real activities and day-to day activities in the real US economy.

Fed: An Agent of Wall Street

The Fed and the US Treasury are agents of Wall Street. I have tried to show that the Fed has no economic growth competence. It has no scientific knowledge of the economy. The Fed—it has also to be emphasized—is not a public institution. It is a *private* entity. Its shareholders are the major banks. All Fed's actions are based on satisfying the financial market. It goes a long way to deny this but when matters get to a crunch, the Fed knows which side of the bread is the butter. The financial crisis of 2008 made it necessary for the Fed to make sure Wall Street and its banks were preserved in the untruth that the economy needs Wall Street to survive.

In August 2007, as the economy was slipping into recession, there were strong speculations in the market that the Fed will cut the discount rate. The Fed saw the recession as a financial problem based on conventional economists' understanding of recession as we exhaustively discussed in chapter 1. The Fed had no structural understanding of the causes of recession and did not know that there are no financial solutions for structural macro-economic problems that drive recessions. Seeing the recession only as a financial crisis, it believed that Wall Street and Wall Street banks must be saved at all costs. Following heavy financial market panic selling of financial stocks in the week ending August 17, the market closed on August 16 with strong rumor in Wall Street that the Fed will cut rates. Indeed it did cut discount rates by fifty basis points the morning of August 17. Still this did not satisfy the market that was now seeking to be treated like a helpless baby.

Roger Lowenstein's account of what followed the August action contains some insights that collaborate what I am saying. According to him, in what to me was a futile attempt by the Fed to forestall criticism of bowing to Wall Street, a Fed statement after its decision to lower interest again in October 2007 said that "the upside risks to inflation roughly balance the downward risks to growth" was an attempt by the Fed to say that it will not lower interests anymore any time soon. But still Jim Cramer, the loud CNBC broadcaster gloated on the October rate cut, "The Fed has got your back," implying gleefully that the Fed would protect Wall Street investors at all costs. The Economist charged that Bernanke was a *pushover* for Wall Street.

The Wall Street Journal once said that the Fed had become a *Pavlovian* slave to the market. Lowenstein correctly pointed out the Fed's dance with the futures market is *a pressure-packed* aspect for Bernanke who knows that investors stake millions every day on what the chairman will do and also to react to it with the short-term horizon. Investors have to watch the Fed, but the Fed has also to take pulse of investors. Fed Chairmen and our Secretaries of Treasury have a habit of double talking even glossing over serious economic problems that concern ordinary Americans because of the impact of what they can have on Wall Street. Writing in September 2007 as the sub-prime problem was beginning to come into public attention, Steven Schwarcz, a Duke University law and business professor, said that the Fed's cutting of discount rates only impacted banks but did not directly impact financial markets because in his view it is the markets not the banks that were at risk. He feared that the sub-prime crisis could trigger systemic risk, that an economic shock such as market panic or institutional failure may trigger a domino effect, causing the failure of chains of markets and institutions. He did not know at the time that the real problem was a looming recession.

He felt that such systemic financial risk needed government action, because individual market participants "do not have sufficient incentives to limit risk-taking." He suggested that apart from interest cuts, government should create a "lender of last resort" that in situations like this that would stabilize collapsing markets by purchasing securities in those markets. He thought the Fed was best placed to act in this function. It was clear that to people like the professor that the Fed, the *market* is the US economy and needs to be protected. Ironically, what he suggested was the blueprint of the Fed actions in 2008 as Wall Street started to collapse.

On the other side about the same time as the professor was writing, Tyler Cowen in *The New York Times* was making another case for Fed's salvage intervention in the market. He felt that ordinary Americans feel that the Fed's actions of *keeping short-term interests from rising and injecting additional liquidity into the economy* can be seen as *bailing out the speculators* that bought securitized loans heedlessly and spread financial risk. He thought that wealthy financiers and hedge funds can be easy targets for the jealousy by the rest of us. He observed that:

> "Liquid markets are good for many investors, and if the Fed succeeds in keeping markets running, that helps hedge funds too... (and) keeping loan markets open is not a bailout: it is simply getting part of the economic infra-structure back on line, much as the police clearing a road after a traffic accident."

Note again that all these people talked only of investors/speculators/ markets as if the problem facing the Fed was just a financial market problem. The truth unfortunately, as I earlier indicated is that the Fed also saw the coming recession when it came to them as only as a financial market problem In November just after the October interest cut, Wall Street began to agitate for another third rate cut. Bernanke and his vice chairman began to indicate they were willing to further cut interest because bank credit was tightening. In December, Wall Street indeed got another rate cut, but only got a quarter point. Loweinstein described the reaction that the markets went ballistic: Dow Jones plummeted 300 points or 2.1 percent. S&P and NASDAQ fell 2.5 percent. Wall Street felt that their dad (the Fed) had not done enough. Some traders even interpreted the Fed's action as a betrayal. Paul McCulate, a managing director at Pimco a major bond-trading firm accused the Fed of *breaking a covenant* [with Wall Street]. John Derrick of US Global Investors said, "The Fed needed to cut more now in order to fend off the credit crisis that has intensified in the past month."

On the other hand, one market expert stood up and said investors were wrong to think that the Fed would keep cutting interest drastically just to save banks and troubled borrowers. "People (in the market) don't' want to hear that but it is the real world," he said. On January 30, 2008, Wall Street got what it wanted like a spoiled baby, which was another rate cut of ½ point to 3 percent, all this with growing threat to the US dollar. They were like the drug addicts just seeking to get the next fix.

August 2007 to January 2008 and we saw the continued slashing of zero. In its ignorance and panic after there was no more interest to cut, the Fed decided to pour money into the economy into the economy in the hope that that will do the trick by flooding the financial system with funds demand in the new belief that it was loss of demand that caused the recession. We see the false idea that to get this demand back, you need to get money to people. Stimulus they sometimes called it. After all, Krugman in his book, *The Return of Depression Economics and the Crisis of 2008* defined recession as "insufficient private spending to make use use of available production capacity." He further claimed that recessions can be cured with *surprising ease* by the Fed prtinting more money. When the Fed has no more interest to cut, it started to pump $20 billion every week into mortgage security, all business loans, car loans, and consumer credit and purchasing $350 billion of commercial paper. It stocked up on treasury bonds. Still, instead, the economy continued to slide further and further into recession. From February 2008 for six months, GDP fell at an annualized rate of 6 percent. The 2007 recession ran its full course and the Fed had no answer.

The Fed's Quantitative Easing

Quantitative easing is a good example of the disadvantages of conferring independence to an organization in an area in which its knowledge and expertise are limited. QE was a case in which the Fed was going into what it had never done before. While it knew what it was seeking, it was not sure whether it will work, but because it was not accountable to anyone or subject to any scrutiny, it was no problem for it to deploy historically unprecedented quantity of money in the gamble.

QE was a desperate effort in uncharted territory intended to make believe that the Fed knows what to do to stop the deepest recession that faced the United States. Bernanke at the time admitted that QE was an action in place of no action. Recession is a structural illness and QE was based on the continuing *belief* by the Fed that it is a financial illness. Quantitative easing is a term which was first widely used in Japan in the 1990s with no agreed definition. QE was pursued in the 1990s by Tokyo with little success. The desperation of the Fed after it exhausted interest rate tools was apparent as it needed to appear to be doing something and appear to be in charge, even though the Fed knew that Japan did not succeed with QE. It is absolute madness to continue to think that by throwing money into the economy you will reduce interest, create demand, create investments, and resurrect economic growth.

It is the Fed's continuing stimulus. Bernanke liked to say that his research into the 1933 depression taught him that recession must be tackled aggressively. With the Fed throwing artificial money around, the banks, insurance companies, and pension companies now have new money in their accounts. This is supposed to boost the money supply in the economy in the aggressive hope that the new money will be lent out at lower interest for new business activities, increasing consumer spend-ing, and invigorate investment all of which are supposed to revive the economic growth and employment.

Economic growth does not depend on control of inflation as I have phasized many times. What is worrying is that there is a conspiracy of silence and ignorance in the economic profession except for a few strong voices like those of Larry Summers, who expressed tepid opposition to QE. The profession was regrettably quiet because it knows that there is no immediate alternative macroeconomics to adopt.

In a first-hand account of the arrogance and ignorance with which operators in the Fed handled QE, a former Fed staff Andrew Huszar who was involved in the initial implementation of QE told Americans in November 2013 that the QE was the greatest Wall Street bailout of all time. This was coming in the heels of the mighty Wall Street bank bailout of 2008. In what is supposed to be a free-market economy, the QE turned out as the largest financial markets intervention by any non-government institution in the history of the world to date with no discernible change in economic fortunes. The Fed got away with all this because it is independent. The US banks hadn't just enjoyed lower cost of making loans from QE but had their collective stock price tripled since March 2009. The biggest banks have become more of a cartel: 2 percent of them control more than 70 percent of the US bank assets. The German Minister of Finance Wolfgang Schauble (the equivalent of the US Treasury secretary) at the time described the Fed's action as clueless. The Fed's purchases were an absolute coup for Wall Street, as Andrew Huszar said.

Huszar, fully aware that America's economic problem is structural, not financial, regretted that QE "has killed the urgency for Washington to confront a real crisis, that of a structurally unsound US economy." He complained that with QE "*the country remains overly dependent on Wall Street to drive economic growth.*" Wall Street does not drive real economic growth as I have gone to great pains in this book to show. The correct way to frame Huszar's statement is that QE helped to push the Main Street (the real US economy) further into ruin. Billionaire Stanley Druof wealth from the middle class and poor to the rich.*

Janet Yellen's defense at her nomination hearing claimed that the wealthy Wall Street and banks needed to receive the QE windfall before the economy could revive. The Fed's QE largesse created the situation in Wall Street in which Dow Jones index in March 2013 reached its highest level in seventeen years reduction in unemploy ment to 7.8 percent the month of March at a time when the economy was barely growing at a pace below the long-run average of the US over the past century. Hardly a week later after the record Dow Jones there was a hint that the Fed may not keep to its promise to keep pumping QE 3 funds until unemployment drops to 6.5%, there was wide sell-off in Wall Street! It is a drug fix for financial operators. The amazing thing is that the American public accepted and shrugged off these economic abuses because the Fed has managed to convince Americans that it has the secret to running the US economy. The Fed might better have better "succeeded" if it handed this money to people in the streets.

By 2013, the Fed has created more than $3.2 trillion to buy $1.77 trillion Treasury bills, $1.08 trillion for mortgage-backed securities (MBS) and a handful of other debt instruments. In addition, it was buying $85 billion a month in Treasury and MBS, which could have brought its balance sheet to above $4 trillion by 2013 without any sign of economic revival of the US economy. All this money was handed to Wall Street and the banks making the rich much richer.

According to the Congressional Research Service (CRS) report of February 19, 2013, it is not clear how much the QE has affected private borrowing rates and interest-sensitive spending. The Fed, according to CRS, has fed the financial market with liquidity while the real economy is in poor state. It wants irrational exuberance. The CRS report was suggesting that legislation may be necessary to bar QE if it becomes clear that it is causing some unintended consequences. The CRS was obviously not in support of QE. As the Fed was entering the second quarter of 2013, there were growing concerns about the cost of QE. The CRS report stated correctly that monetary policy alone is not powerful enough to return the US economy to full employment consistent with its position that monetary policy has nothing to do with employment creation.

The 2012 Annual report of the global "central bank for central banks," the Bank for International Settlements (BIS) stated correctly— with regard to the US—that the near zero policy (interest) rates of the Fed, combined with its abundant and nearly unconditional liquidity support to Wall Street weakens the incentives for US fiscal authorities to limit their borrowing requirement and reduce the country's deficit. In simple terms, the BIS was saying that the US Fed was disrupting the US fiscal management. The Fed could get away with this because it is independent. The Fed had over the period of the 2007–2009 recession and the slow recovery quarreled with US fiscal management. Its Chairman Bernanke used opportunities provided by his statutory testimonies to Congress always to blame US fiscal management and had the audacity to claim that it is the errors in fiscal management that were contributing to the Fed's monetary failure to achieve economic recovery.

Janet Yellen at her nomination hearing in November 2013 suggested that fiscal management should aim at deficit sustainability in the medium term but claimed that near-term deductions being made in current expenditure were detracting on the momentum of recovery because it will adversely affect demand and make for a fragile recovery and detract from the Fed's effort on the recovery. This was a self-serving comment intended to cover up for Fed's pretenses and ignorance on economic recovery. Bernanke, as I observed in chapter 3, also blamed fiscal policy for helping to hold back economic recovery this time instead he said it was because current expenditure was too high and reduced investments that could have engendered growth!

It is not to be forgotten that QE and related activities also tended to reduce the value of the dollar, resulting in consequences that were outside the realm of monetary policy. The Fed could act like this with impunity because it is independent. QE was a desperate financial intervention, the result of erroneous assertion that low interest rates increase economic growth. QE does not advance economic growth. The Fed's QE never advanced the US growth out of the recent recessions.

QE was in truth a financial tool that was used in a panic because the magician ran out of tricks. It was Larry Summers who pointed out that the route of QE might next time call for sums the country may not afford only to be passed out to wealthy people in a wealth transfer that has no justification.

Terminal End to Monetarism

In order to conclude this chapter, the potential danger which the Fed poses in pushing the decline of the US economy needs to be specified. The Fed acts as the chief economist of the country. In doing all this, the Fed was taken over monetarism as its sole tool for US economic management.

The Fed had over time continued to expand its power and influence by expanding the scope of monetarism and interpreting all economic issues and problems in monetary terms. For example, QE was unnecessary and was not the correct economic solution to the Great Recession. It made no sense that an economy marked by serious inequality will instead artificially introduce a higher level of inequality by passing billions to the financial market by artificially dreaming up QE.

The idea of QE is not economics. It is what you and I as ordinary people will imagine will happen if everybody suddenly had a bit of cash in their hands. We will imagine that that will make everybody rush to buy things and create demand. But in fact, it does not happen that way. People can in period of recession instead save the bulk of the money. In the case of QE, the money was instead handed to Wall Street.

The Fed since 2004 has claimed to have achieved what it called Great Moderation, namely that central banks achieved the decline of macro-economic volatility, which it believed resulted in reduced recessions. The Fed claimed that the Great Moderation was achieved in three ways. The first was what it described as structural: by replacing manufacturing with services, by widespread use of computers, increased openness of the US to trade, and just-in-time deregulation. The second was improved financial monetary management. The third was what Bernanke called good luck. The Fed badly needed luck. The Moderation claim follows the claims made by Greenspan about the New Economy of the 1990s. I have shown in my book *The Science of Economic Development and Growth* that Greenspan and the Fed and the Economic Advisors to the President at the time did not understand the structural factor proportions changes that heralded the New Economy due to the development and growth of IT in the US economy, which substantially reduced the capital/labor/and material/labor ratio of the US economy, and which for the first time since World War II yielded a more structurally balanced US economy. Conventional economists were confused what had happened and instead called the New Economy a "knowledge economy" because they saw a lot of IT (computers) around and did not know what to make of it. Bernanke in a speech in 2004 thought the widespread use of computers enabled more accurate decision making, enabled advances in financial system, deregulation and the economy, shift away from manufacturing services." All the IT according to him, helped moderate the large boom and bust cycles *of the past*. From this, monetary economists next claimed a gradual stabilizing of the US economy, as Bernanke did, correlated with what they claim were "increasingly sophisticated theories of monetary and fiscal policy." Bernanke failed to realize that production of IT goods is itself manufacturing without which the services growth he claimed would not have happened.

Kelsey Williams made the very important observation that the "sole and overriding purpose behind the existence of the Federal Reserve" is to keep the US government solvent by maintaining US government's "ability to borrow money by issuing more and more debt" and thereby maintaining and reinforcing confidence in the financial viability of the system. In other words, the Fed gives cover to a failing US economy in which government revenues continue to decline. The New Economy of the 1990s was, as I earlier observed in my book: The Science of Economic Development and Growth," the period in which the US economy expanded fast because the economy was balanced. That is why the period was called "New Economy" because it exhibited new features in the US economy in which the economy was balanced as detailed in my 2005 book "The Science of Economic Development and Growth." Concidentally, the Treasury was flooded with vast incomes that Treasury Secretary at the time Rubens was regarded as genius. It is therefore clear that with a US balanced economy (which generates maximum sustainable) will generate large government incomes so that the need for government borrowing will be reduced (eliminated) and the need for the Fed can be eliminated. Rather than dual mandate with its lack of link to USeconomic growth, the US should move to a balanced economy as I have shown in fig 1.1 at the beginning of this book that the US economy has been increasingly unbalanced from the beginning of this century.

The dot.com bubble of 1999-2001 was the immediate result of Wall Street taking over the newly-born IT system and capitalized on it. When the US finally slipped into the largest recession since the Depression in 2007, the Moderation claim by our financial exprts became an embarrassment. The Moderation claim and Quantitative Easing constitute the Fed central monetary "controls" that have featured in the US economy for the immediate last 20 years, so that as this book goes to print in 2019, the US economy has only limped out of the Great Recession and there are fears that US economy expects more recessions/

depressions and US government debt climbs. It is noteworthy that one of the reasons Bernanke gave for Moderation's "success" is luck. What we have today is the terminal end to Monetarism as the Fed frankly does not know what else to do to change the long-term future of the US economy.

In an article by J. Hill and I. Morris of Blackstone Alternative Asset Management in *Foreign Affairs*, Macrch/April 2016"Can Central Banks Goose Growth?" they stated that "Central banks have already applied almost every traditional policy tool as well as radical ones and yet economy everywhere remains uncertain...." They further stated that "Another downturn—even a relatively ordinary one—requires central banks would, once again, turn to experimentation again and seemingly risk monetary policies." Two words now define monetarism—experimentation and risk. The present sorry state of monetarism can be summarized by Janet Yellen's Semi-annual Monetary Monetary Policy Report to Congress June 2016 that "If there were to be a negative shock to the (US) economy, we don't have a lot of room using one traditional tried and true methods to rely on." She was in effect saying that she does not know if another recession will occur and if it did, there is not much the Fed can do about it.

What is very worrying is Yellen's use of the word "shock". Yellen and others think of a recession as being caused by shock, which she called "negative shock". A shock is an unexpected external factor that disturbs a normal state of equilibrium. I am aware that some prominent conventional economists apart from Yellen and the Fed and some politicians incorrectly think of a recession as caused by (external) shocks. At one time for example, G.W. Bush in 2005 boasted that US economy suffered serious external shocks caused by Hurricane Katrina with its vast physical and economic ravages and economic damages (external shock) and but did not have a recession. In the days of sharp increases in oil price externally caused, people thought a recession was imminent. Key policy figures in the US who harbor these ideas are not aware that recessions are not caused by external "shocks' but are caused by in-built structural imbalances in the economy.

A major problem with the Fed is summarized in a short article in the Wall Street Journal of March 14,2019 titled "The Fed is a threat to

Growth." It will be noted that earlier Yellen had in 2017 prescribed that the Fed had shifted its focus of stimulating the post recession economy to keeping growth at even keel of 2%, stating as Yellen did, that US economy at the time estimated at 2% allowing for a pretty healthy "even keel development'. She will later attack a Trump's planned 3% or more growth as difficult. According to the article, "The last major obstacle to higher growth is the deflatory monetary policy of the Federal Reserve" which believes that any growth of the economy must be accompanied by inflation (which the balanced economy of the 1990s dispproved) hence the Fed's two rate increases in Sepember and December 2018 when the economy reached a 4% growth in the summer of 2018. The Fed has not got over its NAIRU mentality by which it sees inflation in any growth. The two rate hikes in 2018, according to the article, resulted in a fall in growth. When the Fed admitted its mistakes, it decided to forgo its immediate three planned rate increases for 2019. Since the Fed announced the pause, the US economy has shown signs of decline instead. Manufacturing indexes have pointed to a weaker growth. Hiring virtually reduced, retail sales fell in December. I believe that the Fed lacks what it takes to move the US's growth forward and that a strategy for a balanced economy will eliminate the need for the Fed.

Economic growth, as we have seen in China is long-term strategy with its five-year plans. Economic growth in the US presently short-term under the Fed. I was excited therefore when in 2018, I across an article, being a speech by William Dudley, President and CEO of the Federal Reserve Bank of New York because of its title: "The Outlook for the US Economy in 2018 and Beyond" I was expecting for a change to hear from someone at the top of the Fed about Fed's longer term US economic growth strategies. I was disappointed that Mr. Dudley's speech hardly touched issued, almost already well known not beyond 2019. This indicates the problem that the Fed has no long-term growth strategies for the US which is no one's responsibility. The Fed is too short-termist to take on the long-term growth strategies facing the US.

It is in this context that I will end this chapter by reference to the speech of Fred Powell the Fed Chairman to the Citizen's Budget Commission 87th Annual Awards Dinner Feb. 28,2019 titled: "Recent Economic Developments and Longer-Term Challenges." He stated that "By promoting macroeconomic stability, the Fed *helps* to create a healthy environment for growth. But these long-term issues require policies that are in the province of elected representatives. The nation would benefit greatly from a search for policies with broad appeal that would provide labor participation and higher productivity with benefits shared broadly across the nation.' He acknowledged that economic growth in the US has slowed based from 3% growth from 1991 to 2007 and that since 2007 growth had averaged 1.6%. He asked why growth has slowed and "what can we do about it?" He stated that there were two factors at play: low labor partcipation and and low productivity. He concluded by saying that "—these longer term issues require policies that are more in the province of elected representative." First is the question why, as it appeared from the Chairman's speech that the issue of productivity and labor participation in the US as a national study, has been neglected up to now even though the two topics are supposed within the Fed's twin mandate of maximum employment and financial price stability? Past Feds helped lower the growth of the US economy by claiming falsely, as I have shown in this chapter—and confirmed by the Chairman in his speech—that the Fed is not firmly in control of employment and output. Second why did the Chairman say that the two issues were for elected representatives (not the Fed)? The Chairman was implying that these issues have not been addressed before by the Fed— contrary to Fed's claims as I discussed in this chapter that it is in charge of employment and growth of the economy. The Fed has just blundered by its rate hikes in 2008 folloewd by an initial lackluster economy in early 2019 as it was getting its signals mixed. Mr. Powell was saying that it was for elected representatives to deal with them, meaning that action was required to deal with these issues by Congress. The Fed has come to realize, with change its change in leadership that all these years it had taken more than it can digest. These two issues outstanding issues Mr. Powells talked about' in line with the theme of this book' have a lot of science that involve structural economics, the theme of this book, which I have said is presently lacking in the US and leading to a long-term decline of the US economy. Mr. Powell's speech was also muddied because he talked of the US economy as if it is one unified economy and commented on problems of investments in it (contrary to fig 1.2 in this book), which wrong assumption, held by most US policy makers, has made it more difficult for Americans like him uncompetitive economy. The Fed, through Mr. Powell's speech, also confirmed what this book has been saying : that US economy was facing a long-time decline. The Fed did not know, in its announcement in March 2019, when next it will raise interest rates because it did know where the economy was going except it has signs before it that the economy was slowing. It was adopting a wait-and-see stance as the Wall Street Journal report of March 31,2019 called it, oblivious of the long-term urgent economic growth needs of the US economy competing with China's economy currently at 6-7% for world economic supremacy.

Chapter 9

Wall Street: A Main Cause of US Economic Structural Imbalance

The Fed and Wall Street work together in enabling the worsening technical imbalance of the US economy (fig 1.1). In the five years between 2002 and 2007, just before the 2007 recession set in, private fixed capital investment attributed to corporate and non-corporate businesses in the United States rose by 35 percent while US GDP only rose by 17 percent. Announced projects in the Ernst US in 2011 accounted for $135 billion and about 336,000 jobs.[141] That is a capital/labor ratio of $401,785. This additional 2011 capital/ratio addition was almost twice the US capital/labor average in 2006 (the year I used for the chart in figure 1 in chapter 1 for the American economy) less than five years before. I had in an earlier chapter referred to what is the general consensus among US policy makers as summarized by Andrew Smithers when he said that any significant and sustained improvement in the US growth will require marked *acceleration* in the growth of net capital stock of the US. Americans have come to equate economic growth with the growth in capital stock. This results in worsening America's already bad structural imbalance reducing US economic growth potential which we are currently withnessing. As the capital-intensive sector of the US economy (namely the right-hand sector in figure 1 of chapter 1) intensifies, the labor intensive sector (on the left side) continues to be more and more labor intensive as it also struggles to absorb the increasing population of the United States. The result is the ever increasing pace of the structural imbalance of the US economy.

The basic error of Americans as to how to grow their economy was summarized by President Ford in his famous WIN Speech October 8, 1974: "We need more capital. We cannot eat up our seed corn. Our free enterprise system depends on orderly capital markets through which the savings of our people become productively used." The Fed and Wall Street have taken the task of monitoring and growing this capital. But there are a number of major contradictions/errors in this American article of faith on capital as I have tried to stress in this book.

Regretfully, therefore, the Fed and Wall Street's primary task, as seen in the last chapter, is to help build the capital-intensive part of the economy—the right side of figure 1. The twenty top Ernst 2011 investments just referred to by size totaling $42.475 billion only produced 29,000 new jobs in 2011, a capital/labor ratio of $1,464,655, which was structurally unsuited for the US economy. Wall Street is the sponsor of these large capital-intensive projects through huge packages from Wall Street main banks and private equity/funds operations all under the umbrella of the Fed. That is capitalism.

The capital goods production sector of the US economy is the sector that produces the capital goods used in producing the goods and services used in the economy. There are approximately 30,000 companies in the United States in the capital goods production with approximately $760 billion annual current revenue, exporting approximately $160 billion of capital goods. As a sector, the capital goods sector in the United States has managed to mesmerize the rest us by calling what they do as technology. The US International Trade Commission (ITC) affirmed this by claiming that "Machinery industries (in the US) provide essential and highly sophisticated technology for many other manufacturing and services industries."

The ITC further claims that "Process control and other automation technologies enable end-users to maximize productivity of their equipment."[142] The use of the word sophisticated is amateurish and should not be used in serious analysis of technology. The mention of productivity is amateurish. A technology should never be used because it is sophisticated but only because it is essential and in line with US factor proportions. Productivity as I have shown in chapter 1 is another poisoned chalice in American technology. It is the drive to sound sophisticated, as the ITC statement did, that makes American industries adopt unnecessary (sophisticated) process controls and automation intended to eliminate labor and increase 'productivity'. Global Industry Analysis Inc., a leading market research analyst firm, in its report and analysis of the Capital Goods Industry in the United States stated that "...capital goods (in the US) are productivity enhancing tangible assets..." It pointed out that the capital goods industry's focus is on "infrastructure development, increasing use of technology for producing final goods, for instance automation of manufacturing and processing steps and mechanization of agricultural activity."[143]

The Information Technology Industry Council (ITI) headquartered in Washington is a "premier advocacy and policy organization" for the world's leading IT innovative companies. ITI was described by Ars Technica, the well-known technology news and information web site as "a lobbying group with a membership list that includes almost all the heavy hitters of the tech world."[144] ITI is constantly navigating relationships between policy makers, companies, and non-governmental organizations on behalf of the IT industry. Ten of the IT companies in this council are among the world's fifty largest corporations. ITI works to encourage 'innovation' and promote global competitiveness in its members in a quest to increase their international sales and profits by enlarging our economic structural imbalance.

ITI's links with Wall Street are diverse. Its members trade in NASDAQ exchange, which has increasingly gotten more popular as 'tech' companies had prospered. It can be seen that the capital goods production sector's emphasis on technology and innovation is all consistent with the drive of ITI member companies to promote IT as a national policy destination in Washington. This means that US goods and services producing industries are increasingly under pressure to automate and reach for increased productivity by higher capital investment a trend that has gathered great speed in the last ten to twenty years in the United States. The IT industry has largely succeeded in capturing official Washington support with the the White House's keenness to be in the good books of innovation and with Wall

Street's planned $1 billion in the 2013 budget on the basis of which a National Network for Manufacturing Innovation was set up by President Obama. Today, IT companies control over 14 of the total S&P 500's market capitalization. They have a lot of power that has met the ire of the EU and the UK where they are accused of reducing consumer choice. Professor Jason Furman has in a 2019 report in the UK digital market said that "There isn't sufficient competition today." He said correctly that this—(competition)—is one of the most important economic policy issues" in the world today. His three recommendations to increase competition however failed to strike at the most common structural reason for the lack of competition which is the high capital-intensive nature of the industry which makes the entry of new starters difficult.

Because 'technology' changes rapidly, manufacturing producing plants in the United States are under constant pressure to move into more and more capital intensive operations with increasingly short lives as they try to keep up with this "ever-changing technology". The capital producing sector in the United States is also fragmented. Companies in the sector are constantly, in cooperation with Wall Street, acquiring smaller ones in order to increase sales growth and automate, increase product offering, barriers to entry, and broaden their presence in existing markets. The ability for companies in this sector to integrate their acquired firms is important through the creation of necessary synergies assisted by Wall Street Merger and Acquisitions (M&A) consultants. The sector consumes vast quantities of materials and is so very sensitive to commodity prices and foreign dependence on material supplies. The larger the country's industries get more capital intensive, the more this dependence on outside supply of commodities much of which goes into the US capital equipment industry.

The National Association of Manufacturers (NAM), which prides itself as the major association for manufactures in the United States, has demonstrated considerable ignorance of the structural problems of the US economy. In an advert, its president claimed that NAM members' factories are high-tech and that factory renaissance (which means more high-tech) is required in order to turn the US economy around. In March 2013, the Association announced what it regarded as the challenges the US manufacturers face in what the association called skills gap. The association stated that despite unemployment hovering then around 8 percent at that time in the United States, approximately 600,000 manufacturing jobs remain open because employers can't find workers with the skills necessary to fill these positions. The report from the association claimed, like its president, that today's shop floors in the United States are technologically advanced and stated that the majority of manufacturers report moderate to serious shortages of skilled talent. The association claimed that the skills gap threatens the manufacturers' ability to innovate, grow their businesses, and compete in the global market place. The senior Vice President for the association was quoted as saying that, "Manufacturers (in the US) need a skilled workforce to compete in the twenty first century economy." He was thinking of the need for more capital-intesive operations.

There is something worrying in a country where manufacturers establish industries without first ensuring that they have requisite staff to operate them. Something must be pushing them, including the ready availability of Wall Street finance to engage in new technology without necessary staff to operate them. There is nothing like "a twenty first century" economy as the Vice President of the association claimed. It might consist of the factories where Paulson enthused that he did not see any man because everything is automated. What America needs is not a twenty-first century economy (whatever that means) but a growing economy based on factor proportions appropriate to the American economy. The six hundred thousand skilled staff shortage in the United States is evidence of the US economy's structural imbalance on the basis of core of American capital-investment manufacturing facilitated by easy Wall Street finance.

The financial institutions and banks in Wall Street are very interested to transact and profit from M&A dealings in industry but have no interest whatsoever in organizing and running those industries. The M&A people present themselves to the world as outsiders tackling inefficiencies in industry seeking to grow value. In the early days, M&A was about small fellows challenging the big industries as standard bearers of "a democratization of capital" that unlocked shareholder value.[145]

But we have been deceived because the truth is that the most important effect of merger and acquisitions and reorganizations is to increase stock indexes and increase fees and profits. Wall Street banks and accounting and law firms drew about $14 billion in fees on M&A alone in the first quarter of 2013. Just as Wall Street and its clients gamble with shares, M&A is gambling with corporate bodies. The M&A industry has since increasingly kept its industry's annual fees confidential.

Private equity in the United States survived the 2007 through 2009 recession and between 2010 and 2012 business has gone up by 49 percent. The US private equity Q3 2012 was $66 billion (in 433 deals) and in Q4 2012 was $102 billion (451 deals).[146] 2018 is 760 billion of private equity. Acquisitions of $1 billion to $2 billion were regarded as small acquisitions in Wall Street before the 2008 financial crisis. As of 2012, the total M&A was about $285 billion. Berkshire Heinz acquisition for $28 billion by Buffet and the fight for Dell going private for $24.4 billion. By 2013 there were indications that the M&A in the US is strong with Q1 2013 registering total deals of $165 billion. By the first three months of 2016, announced mergers and acquisitions have jumped to more than $800 billion." *Invest Place* correctly remarked that "mergers and acquistions usually line the pockets of Wall Street investment bankers than shareholders." On June 2016 Microsoft added $26 billion to the US M&A bill. In 2013, the US on the whole accounted for 43 percent of all M&A deals worldwide giving one an idea of the rapidly detereotating structural imbalance of the US economy. Special Purpose Acquisition Companies (SPACs) represented 1 in 5 dollars raised in the US IPO in 2017 compared to 1 in 7 in 2013.

Each M&A venture is justified by Wall Street on the basis of financial profits made through the synergies created by its spon sors either in the acquired target or between it and the other units in the acquirer's portfolio. Through synergy, sponsors seek to make 1+1 = 3 or 4 or more. It is in most instances a case of economy of scale at play. The synergy may be organizational or technical or a combination. In almost all cases, the result is staff layoffs and increased capital/labor portfolio. Venture capitalists in the rear guard of the system are to ensure that new business start-ups are shepherded in the direction of high capital intensive development. Wall Street is the coordinator of industrial monopoly of the United States, a thing early US Presidents tried to fight but gave up over the years in the name of free enterprise as we discussed in chapter 6.

Wall Street and US major corporations work together in keeping, maintaining and increasing a highly capital-intensive monopolistic culture of the economy. Short-termism reigns as each corporation's key priority is how to advance their share value and profits. These types of corporations are the ones that transfer labor intensive industrial activities out of the United States to low labor cost countries as they seek higher and higher profits and as they also want to circumvent the increasing uncompetitiveness of the US economy which they helped create.

Bill Moyer, quoted by Thom Hartman in his book, *The Crash of 2016,* has said Americans no longer have a government of, by, and for the people—representative democracy. We have a government by plutocracy—the rule of the rich for the rich by the rich. He added that plutocracy has one purpose, which is to protect financial wealth. Hartman stated that what we have are fewer and fewer companies owning more and more wealth. Competition is destroyed by unrestrained growth of corporate interest. Big companies buy small companies over and over again, until there are no more small and medium-sized businesses for a profit. In 2012, Krugman warned in a *NY Times* article that "There are lots of ugly forces being unleashed in our societies. We may look back at this, thirty years from now, and say, 'That is when it all fell apart.' The point is that the felling apart has already occurred."

These statements by Bill Moyer and Krugman are not the issue. What we are talking about is not democracy or justice. We are talking of the increasing structural economic problems of the US, which people like Krugman can help solve by helping develop a new orientation to structural economic science of the US. In his book, *Capital Offense: How Washington's Wise Men Turned America's Future Over To Wall Street,* Michael Hirsh described the era in which we think that what was good for big finance was good for America, and we came to accept that finance, however, unleashed had come to dominate the economy and Wall Street and became the master of Main Street rather than its handmaiden.[147] Wall Street and the long line of ex-Wall Street US Treasury Secretaries in cooperation with the Fed have led Americans to think that Wall Street is a gateway to the Main Street. The recession in 2007 like all other recessions announced its arrival by the drop in demand in the economy that occurred. Before this recession started, it had already been forecast that there will likely be a housing slump.[148]

Drop in demand is the result not the cause of a recession. By mid-2007, there were $1.8 trillion mortgages securitized by Wall Street outstanding. More than 7.5 million households held sub-prime loans with very poor lending standards, which Wall Street supervised. It should not be a surprise that when the 2007 recession started, housing was one of the first activi ties to collapse. It is clear that it was the recession that finally led to 2008 financial crisis. The recession, enabled us to know, as the famous expression goes, those who were swimming naked.

The failure of Lehman Brothers and the subsequent turmoil in the market were the single event that convinced the three most powerful people in charge of the US financial system at the time (Paulson, Bernanke, and Geithner) that there was a financial crisis and that they needed to save Wall Street, no matter the cost. They reasoned that legislators are more likely to act if they are told that it is the economy itself rather than Wall Street that was in trouble.

At an emergency meeting initiated by Paulson and Bernanke, they told congressional leaders of what they called a national emergency, which required the unprecedented Toxic Assets Relief Program (TARP) authorization. Bernanke told them that the financial crisis in Wall Street will spill into the real economy. Paulson told them that if stocks dropped a further 20 percent that General Motors would go bankrupt and unemployment would rise—to 8 percent or 9 percent from the prevailing 6.1 percent—"if we did nothing". Why did Bernanke bring GM into the discussion? He did this to create alarm about the real economy because at the time GM's possible collapse was in the news, and it was being rumored and the press was harping on the possible serious effect of GM's collapse on unemployment, which was already high.

"It was a matter of days," Bernanke told the members of Congress, "before there is a meltdown in the global financial system." This presentation was enough to get the members of Congress "ashen-faced." When asked by the lawmakers what will happen if he and Bernanke did not get the money they wanted, Paulson exclaimed, "May God help us all."

Paulson told us in his book that he continued to play this scare-the-shit-out-of-them card all throughout with Congress. He said that he and Bernanke "needed to make dire predictions about what would happen to the economy if they didn't give them the authority for what they wanted." Bernanke kept to this strategy when he told lawmakers on March 2, 2009 that "We know that failure of a major firm in a financial crisis can be disastrous for the economy." They succeeded in their scare tactics.

Nancy Pelosi stated that the only reason Congress was approving the TARP was because, "We want to insulate the American taxpayer, Main Street, and everyday Americans from the crisis on Wall Street." "It is a 'buy in,' so that we can turn our economy round," she said. It was not a "bail out" of Wall Street. Representative Boehner said, "If I didn't think we were on the brink of an economic disaster, it would be the easiest thing to say no to this." Many members of Congress emphasized that they had voted for TARP only because they had thought it would help struggling homeowners and that indeed that whole sections of the TARP statute regulated how the Treasury would modify the mortgages once it conducted its originally planned massive purchase of troubled assets.[149] Paulson, in his book, called TARP the "Treasury's most crucial legislative undertaking since the Great Depression", and that it was appropriately or inappropriately called the "Emergency Economic Stabilization Act." In his book titled *"Bailout"*, Neil Barofsky,(a former Special Inspector General in Charge of Oversight of TARP, being as Mr. Barofsky explained "An Inside Account of How Washington abandoned Main Street while rescuing Wall Street") stated that Treasury's attempt to save Wall Street set up the country "for potentially catastrophic losses."

After the Fed and the Treasury rescued Wall Street with taxpayers' money, Wall Street came back to life. The banks that survived became stronger than before the crisis, courtesy of the Fed and the Treasury, with massive profits and bonuses in 2009. Citigroup earned $4.4 billion in the first quarter of 2010, the Bank of America $3.3 billion, J.P. Morgan $3.3 billion, and Goldman $3.3 billion, as the economy was still reeling with unemployment and not out of recession.

While the TARP at $700 billion was considered audacious, the Fed doled out no less than $3,300 billion in loans to banks and companies on its own. Most of Wall Street made gigantic profits by taking advantage of the rock-bottom cost of capital, provided courtesy of the Fed—now that the big Wall Street firms are all bank holding companies—and then turning around and lending it at much higher rates. The easiest and most profitable risk-adjusted trade available for the banks is to borrow billions from the Fed at a cost of around half a percentage point and then lend the money straight back to the US Treasury at yields around 3 percent or more a moment later. The imbedded profit of some 2.5 percent points was an outright and ongoing gift from the Fed to Wall Street. Fed's borrowers included institutions such as Lehman and Citigroup, which were clearly insolvent not illiquid. The Fed accepted collateral that included toxic-backed securities. One tenth of the emergency lending went to foreign banks. Fed's Maiden Lane facility, which accepted some of Bear Stern's most toxic assets were used as collateral for the $28 billion acquisition by J.P. Morgan. By being allowed to keep its risky assets and turning it into a bank holding company on September 21, 2008, and giving it unfettered access to cheap credit, Goldman overnight turned into the world's largest government-backed hedge fund. It was as if, as a commentator put it, Tiger woods broke his golf club and the Fed bought him a new one. At $140 billion in compensations, the 2009 paychecks on Wall Street were the best ever before the crisis. Hedge funds did better. The top twenty-five earned a total of $25.3 billion in 2009— an average of $1 billion each—with the lowest paid hedge-fund manager receiving $350 million.

The overall mood in those days was summarized by Neil Barofsky in his book earlier referred to when he said: "With a government guarantee made all but explicit by the bailouts, the executives (of Wall Street banks) still enjoyed all the short-term profits and benefits of taking outsized risks backstopped by the government. Worse still, the presumption of bailout made the banks more attractive to creditors, who continued to extend credit at prices that did notfully account for risks that the banks were taking and, as a result, failed to provide the necessary market discipline to reign in excessive risk-taking. This "heads I win;tails the Govrnment will bail out "incentive system was firmly in place."

At the end, what Pelosi got was not a turnround of the US economy, but a bailout of Wall Street, the opposite of what she was made to believe that she and the other legislators were getting. It was not the buy-in she wanted but a bailout of Wall Street. While Boehner thought that TARP would bring the US economy back from the brink, it ended up drawing the economy into a real economic disaster. Joseph Stiglitz called the Great Recession evidence of a colossal failure, which has imposed an enormous burden on ordinary Americans.[150]

After Lehman Brothers went under, Paulson fully believed that the loss of Morgan Stanley and Goldman Sachs would follow and that "the financial system might evaporate and with it the economy."[151] This set up the birth of too big to fail: the idea that certain financial institutions' failure will lead to the collapse of the total economy and that in order to save a failing economy these institutions must be saved at all costs: another scare tactics on the economy at the time.

Paulson was sure that the Wall Street banks' illiquid assets that he was trying to buy through TARP were clogging the financial system and threatening Americans' personal savings and the entire economy. This running error of concept among financial policy holders in the United States which continues today in the subtle assumption that a country's economy is its financial system and its financial system is the economic engine without which the economy will collapse.

Here are some thoughts about this whole episode by Sheila Blair, the FDIC Chairman at the time in her book characteristically titled, *"Bull by the Horns: Fighting to Save Main Street from Wall Street and Wall Street from Itself"*. She played a significant role in moderating the three men's desire to change from buying the troubled mortgages and mortgage-related investments of the Wall Street banks to guaranteeing their debts and also giving them large capital injections.

Sheila mused that the mere fact that a bunch of large (Wall Street) financial institutions was going to lose money does not make it a systemic event. "Yes, the steps taken prevented a more severe credit contraction, but the big banks still pulled back. Indeed, between 2008 and 2009, they pulled trillions of dollars in credit lines and their loan balances fell significantly."[152]

Paulson convinced himself, as he said in his book, that Wall Street problems will "see credit tightening, strapped companies slashing jobs, foreclosures rising ever faster: millions of Americans would lose their livelihoods and their homes." He was wrong that Wall Street's failure will result in foreclosures and unemployment in Main Street. The two were not related because when one healed, the other's sickness started and continued.

Paulson, Bernanke, and Geithner in effect all got it wrong because of their lack of structural economics knowledge. The money and credit they wanted to flow from the banks to the Main Street could not slow or stop the recession. The recession is a structural phenomenon and could not have been stopped or reduced by the flow of money. The loss of demand in a recession is structural problem. That is why years after the Wall Street banks recovered from the 2008 financial crisis, the economy of the US was still ill, even after more fund injections were made into the US economy through stimulus, and QEs, etc. By 2016, interest was still at near zero waiting for revived economic growth happened even by 2019.

The truth is that Wall Street has no umbilical economic cord connection to Main Street. The US Main Street does not depend on Wall Street just as I have shown in Chapter 8 that Main Street does doesnot depend on the Fed. That Wall Street and Main Street were not one integrated economy is confirmed by Janet Yellen's well-intentioned statement to a willing audience in 2014 that: "Our goal is to help Main Street not Wall Street," in her attempt to prove that she is helping the poor section of the population. The former Chinese Prime Minister Wen Jiabao said that the problem with us in the United States is "excessive expansion of financial institutions in the blind pursuit of profit." One can safely say that Main Street can thrive without Wall Street but that Wall Street cannot exist without Main Street because a substantial amount of Wall Street's games and gambling depend on the existence and activities of the Main Street.

In chapter 8, I stated that financial policy should be a servant of economic growth employed to mainly ensure that money/ finance is available where, when and in the quantity it is needed as a lubricant of economic activities. The Fed should not use its control of money to attempt to do things it hasn't the macro-economics expertise to do: like unemployment, economic growth, inflation, all of which it pretends to control. At the height of a recession, the US economic structural cycle is in its worst structural imbalance because at that point supply and demand are completely out of phase. The position cannot be corrected simply by injecting finance into the system through (stimulus or QE or by capital investment) nor by injecting staggering sums into banks in the wish that the banks will give them to businesses in the hope the money will initiate demand and make the businesses start production.

It is only when a structural cycle moves out of its worst imbalance position, thereby establishing and increasing to some degree of in-phase operation with demand that demand will gradually move in phase with production. It will not, however, be a sustainable maximum economic growth because the economy is structurally unbalanced. The only way to rectify the economic faults is to balance the basic economic structure of the economy so as not only to avoid recessions but also to introduce sustainable economic growth.

The ready availability of the simple finance required by the Main Street is best achieved when finance is located close to the points of demand. Local and regional banks in the United have always fulfilled this need. Throughout the time Paulson and Bernanke were spoon-feeding the big Wall Street banks during the financial crisis in 2008, it was the small local and regional banks, not Wall Street banks, that kept their credit lines open to businesses even though they did not benefit from all the Federal government largesse. Wall Street therefore was not a component of Main Street's recession survival.

Claimed Supremacy of Financial
Markets Over the US Economy

The above discussions where I showed that Wall Street has vitally no important connection with Main Street nor does Main Street need Wall Street to perform its basic functions was intended to attack the prevailing blind belief in Wall Street's omnipresence.

In forwarding the 2008 Economic Report to the President to Congress, President Bush claimed that over the past six years, "the American economy has proven its strength and resilience." He said that the economy, according to him, "is built on a strong foundation" because the country has a "deep and sophisticated capital market." The President regarded a deep and sophisticated financial market as the strong foundation on which the US economy was built. Hardly had the President made this boast in 2008 than the full effect of the recession started. Alan Greenspan was, as early as 2005, so fascinated by the increasingly complex financial instruments of the market that he boasted that these instruments contributed to the development of a far more flexible, efficient and hence resilient financial system. Listen to Henry Paulson, in another of his speeches to the Chinese in 2007, told the Chinese that America has mastered the management of its economy through the excellence of its financial market. He said:

> I am a strong believer in the power of financial markets to support growth and development and help a society fulfill its aspirations and needs. Efficient financial sectors help allocate scarce resources to their most productive uses and generate significant multiplier effect for economic growth...Efficient financial sectors are, in a sense, the central nervous system of modern economies, making countless decisions all the time to keep the body in good working order.[153]

On another occasion, Paulson said that the US capital market is the lifeblood of the US economy. President Obama told us in his April 22, 2010 remarks on Wall Street Reform that a reformed Wall Street was "an essential part of a new foundation for economic growth in the 21st century." He said that without Wall Street our house will continue to sit on shifting sands… He was sure that by spanking Wall Street by enacting the Wall Street reforms that led to the Dodd-Frank Act that our financial system and therefore our economy will continue being the envy of the world. He called his nomination of Yellen as Fed Chairman October 9, 2013 perhaps his "most important economic decision." He called Yellen "one of the nation's leading economists and policy makers." He further said that given the urgent economic challenges facing our nation, "I urge the senate to confirm Janet without delay". The President, it looks, incorrectly regarded US economic problems as the central responsibility of the Fed. It is clear that Obama throughout his presidency never appreciated the depth and seriousness of the country's structural economic malaise. He, like many Presidents before him in this age of globalization, has not appreciated that the Fed is a major part of the US economic problem as I showed in chapter 8. Simon Johnson and James Kwaki put the problem this way:

> "The conventional wisdom, shaped during the three decades of deregulation, innovation and risk taking that brought us our recent financial crisis is that large sophisticated banks are a critical pillar of economic prosperity. That conventional wisdom has entrenched itself in Washington, where administrative officials, regulators and legislative agree with Wall Street line on intellectual grounds or see their personal interest (financial or political) aligned with the interest of Wall Street, or simply not feel qualified to question the experts in their thousand dollar suits."[154]

In his book, *The Cost of Capitalism,* Robert Barbera, Wall Street investment economist, said that "sensibly regulated free market capitalism does the best job of delivering growth to the citizenry of the world."[155] That is capitalist religion. Politicians have also weighed in on this theme. Newt Gingrich told us in his book, *Real Change,* that "America's ability to win, and not just to complete in the global economy depends in part on our having the most efficient capital market." According to him, "We need substantial reform in this area of America to be the most successful in the world and the best source of high paying jobs…"[156]. US economists and policy makers have also over time come to believe that efficient financial market is the best means of achieving the most efficient allocation of resources. The Fed in order to ensure its relevance has continued to sell this version of the story of what it says it needs in order to maintain an efficient and strong economy as the controller of the financial market. As the study of financial mathematical models and faith in market efficiency found their way into conventional macroeconomics, some leading economists by the 1980s even told us that one of the best ways to achieve maximum development of the economy is simply to maximize stock prices.

Rubin, the Treasury secretary following Clinton's re-election in 1996, made his name as the stock market was soaring with the exploding New Economy economic growth. Bob Hormats, an economic official under Bush I and later Obama said that "For a long time there was a view that New York and Washington were two different worlds." He thought Rubin embodied the reunification of the two.[157] The New Economy was believed to be due to the roaring Wall Street under the spell of Rubin. Overnight, Wall Street was also taking credit for the New Economy.

The dominating influence and prestige of Rubin over this period with his reputation arising from the New Economy were so high that his ideas and philosophy took over the system. He basked in the prestige he won as the commanding and graceful Treasury Secretary who had presided over the highest growth, low inflation of the US New Economy to give the Wall Street the commanding position it achieved. Leon Panetta, the then White House Chief of staff, affirmed that Rubin always represented Wall Street. Rubin defended the interest of high finance.[158]

The Treasury was piling up with such high revenues from the New Economy that everybody thought Rubin was a genius. Rubinomics was the new branch of economics that claimed erroneously that it was Rubin's deficit cutting that led to the New Economy. Rubin himself sought to take this glory when he said in his book, *In an Uncertain World*, "The view that fiscal discipline was being restored contributed to lower interest rates and in turn led to job creation, lower unemployment rates and increased productivity [during the 1990s]."[159] He was of the view that the resulting increases in the financial market confidence, achieved by his and Clinton's administration's actions boosted the New Economy. As a team with Greenspan, Rubin sought that finance and Wall Street should be given unfettered freedom and no controls. The new confidence in Wall Street and its claimed magic effect on the American real economy was sold to Europe to adopt American practices. At Deutsche Bank, there was a shift to US style of investment banking. The theme was that Germany should be more like the United States. The UK financial market changed in the fashion towards Wall Street.

G. W. Bush's advocacy of a free financial market in the belief that Wall Street was the key to American economic growth permeated his administration. His first chairman of the SEC, William Donaldson, promised a kinder, gentler agency toward Wall Street. The second, Christopher Cox was pushed out amid Wall Street complaints that he was too aggressive. According to the Inspector General's report, Cox failed to police the catastrophic decisions that toppled Bear Stearns and contributed to the 2008 Wall Street collapse. With regard to banking regulators, *New York Times* once said that regulators brandished a chain saw over a 9,000 page pile of regulations because they instead wanted "to ease burden on the industry." When the states tried to use State consumer protection laws to crack down on banks' predatory lending, the US controller of currency blocked the effort, asserting that states had no authority over national banks. The administration won that fight at the Supreme Court. Roy Cooper, North Carolina attorney general said, "They took fifty sheriffs off the beat at a time when lending was becoming the Wild West." When the Center for Community Self-Help turned to Congress about predatory practices by mortgage lenders, according to its President, Congress told it that nothing should be done to disrupt the free flow of credit. Simon Johnson and James Kwaki summed the position up by saying that:

> "The conventional7 wisdom, shaped during three decades of deregulation, innovation and risk taking—is that large banks are a critical pillar of economic prosperity. That conventional economic wisdom has entrenched itself in Washington where administrative officials, regulators

and the legislative agree with Wall Street on intellectual grounds or see their personal interests (financial or political) aligned with the interest of Wall Street or simply not feel qualified to question the experts in their thousand dollar suits."[160]

As of today, as we can see, there are still many who, at the highest levels of American administrations, feel that Wall Street and the financial market (especially after Dodd-Frank) are the key to the growth of the US economy. America has no strategy for long-run economic growth of the United States because its leaders believe that the Fed and Wall Street are and should be in charge of economic management and know best.

Wall Street: A Spoiled Baby

Wall Street is a spoiled baby who all the time seeks to get what it wants from the parents. It resists government oversight and uses its enormous lobby powers to stop from Congress making any real inroads into its power. It has become very clever at combining financial games and creative accounting to inflate its own financial assets without the burden of producing anything of real value. It is only since 2012 that some of the corruption in Wall Street started receiving more serious but still relaxed criminal attention.

Wall Street's purpose, we are told, is responsible to raise money for industry: to finance steel mill and technology companies and yes, even mortgages. But collateral debt obligations involved in Goldman trades, like billions of dollars of similar trades sponsored by almost every major Wall Street firm raised nothing for anybody. In effect they were bets—like those in a casino—that allowed speculators to increase society's mortgage waver without financing a single house. The mortgage investment that was the focus of the SEC civil suit didn't contain actual mortgage bonds. Rather it was made up of credit swaps that referenced such bonds. Thus, investors weren't truly investing—they were gambling on the success or failure of the bonds they actually did mortgage. No actual bonds—and no actual mortgages—were created or owned by the parties involved. SEC charges that the bonds were picked by Paulson that failed. Goldman says that Abacus merely allowed it o bet one way or the other. Goldman was not alone in these practices. But either way, such transactions had nothing to do with the real US economy. Proprietary trading fetches the bulk of the bank'sprofits. People gambled on derivatives and made obscene sums of money without spending a dime.

Wall Street activities have over time done those things that contribute increasingly to unbalanced growth of the United States. It has used the Fed and the Treasury, in their incorrect belief that the US financial market and Wall Street constitute the gate to Main Street, to increasingly consolidate its position in the United States. The worst enemy is the one who has succeded to make you believe he is your friend. Twenty years ago, the six largest banks in Wall Street had combined assets of 16 percent of the GDP. Today it is 64 percent to 65 percent. They are today more than 30 percent bigger since Dodd-Frank. Five of the largest Wall Street banks currently have over 50 percent of all US banks' deposits up from 37 percent in 2007. Wall Street institutions have acquired an ever growing proportion of the money in circulation for their private accounts, thereby, accumulating ever growing claims on the society. Wall Street has managed to make us believe that anything that makes profit for Wall Street benefits the society and is, therefore, legal. Currently derivatives, which Warren Buffet once called "weapons of mass destruction" are now worth more than $1.2 quadrillion, 10 times bigger than the entire world GDP. Any crisis this time will be too big even for the US government to solve.

While the consolidation process continues, Wall Street institutions push ahead with new products/inventions to confuse and entice the public more and more. At the same as the US government pushes ahead with international trade and globalization, Wall Street institutions continue to expand, forming overseas and increasing international connections and inversions and expanding risks that stretched the base of their assets. Much of the international trade and globalization push up the US profits of Wall Street while the trade and globalization are adversely affecting the structural base of the economy.

In chapters 5, 6, and 7, I showed that the US economy is degrading itself because of its persistence on free trade and globalization. These topics are still subjects of hot debate in the United States. Wall Street, as should be expected, is a serious outspo ken defender of international trade and globalization. In a 2010 publication by the US Securities Industry and Financial Markets Association (SOFMA) titled "Contributing to a More Competitive US Economy," the association claimed that their Wall Street financial services and products help facilitate and finance the export of manufactured goods and agricultural products, while helping the US become the world's number one exporter of services. It acknowledged that the financial services industry is the largest corporate player in US national politics.

Here is a claim by Wall Street how the financial services constitute a direct involvement in the economic development of Main Street. The $180 billion or so is the business Wall Street gets a month from US export trade. The many learned Institutions and Foundations that abound in Washington are a Wall Street political constituency that wants to preserve and enhance US trade and the global system. The 2010 publication of SOFMA argued with regard to globalization that because a growing share of non-US markets have more than three quarters of the world's GDP, about two-thirds of the world's debt market and 95 percent of the world' financial service requires having access to clients outside the United States. According to the publication, multinational companies and investors seek global expertise of financial services firms for a wide array of activities—research, fund management, corporate finance, and risk management. To compete effectively and serve their customers, many of whom operate and raise capital in global markets, the publication arguedthat Wall Street's financial service firms must have the capabilities to establish local presence in many markets round the world, while providing other services on a cross-border basis. Access to non-US markets, according to the publication, enhances the competitiveness of the US financial services, benefiting its more than 5.77 million employees. It is for these reasons that the publication concluded that the financial services strengthen the entire US economy.

In chapters 5 and 6, I showed however that not only is the US economy largely uncompetitive in international markets and that our further incursion into international trade is simply lead up to increase our trade indebtedness in the long run as US continuing/increasing trade deficits show by exposing it to more unfettered free trade with ever increasing trade deficits. Wall Street is unknowingly helping US economic decline. Wall Street is the base and origin of the exploding capital-intensive sector shown on the right side of fig.1.1 in this book that promotes US economy's structural imbalance. So long as Wall Street is in its form, there is no hope for US short or long range economic growth. US corporations have no loyalty to the United States but only to their profits. US monetary system is designed to serve banks and corporations. What is more important, as I was able to show in chapter 5, is that international trade directly harms and worsens the structural balance of the US economy. In chapter 7, I showed that globalization, very much a Wall Street baby on which the US has depended, is collapsing as US and Europe are losing control of the world economy because of the structural weaknesses of their economies. My recommendation in chapter 8 is that the US should pull back from globalization. Wall Street is on the other hand, for reasons of its financial profits as I have just shown, been pushing the US to continue to move even more vigorously on globalization and international trade. I am impressed how Wall Street, as I have shown, has ingratiated itself with changing US governments and political parties.

In a 2012 article captioned "The Retreat of Globalization" by Kevin Warsh and Scott Davis, the two gentlemen confirmed the adverse globalization trends that are coming. Many people in Washington and Wall Street don't want to hear that globalization "is now showing signs of retreat." The two men stated that the structural fillip that amplifies economic growth and individual opportunity for all Americans was also showing signs of retreat. They pointed out that cross-border and private-capital global flows continue to be disappointing. They stated that capital flows to emerging markets (from the United States) have fallen. Investors appear cautious, notwithstanding the Western Central Bankers' ceaseless efforts to tempt them to buy riskier assets by suppressing yields of government-backed securities.[161]

National Debt of the USA and Other Countries

Wall Street is happy about the US national debt. The higher the US national debt, the more Wall Street's sales and profits from bonds and instruments and interest payments are. Wall Street institutions and companies participate in the debt transactions of other countries, especially European countries that have copied the US systems. The United States had no post World War II national debt. It also did not have a national debt and the New Economy of the 1990s gave us an economy that was debt-free. One would have thought that US economists would have researched into the structure of the US economy during these two critical historical periods to find out what was happening to the economy on those occasions. They did not. Wall Street will lose its structural standing if the US undertakes a structural reconstruction of its economy because the Much of the US national debt will disappear and the economy will launch into the path of sustainable growth. Policy makers in the US, despite the economic problems facing the US, have always weighed in on the need to have powerful Wall Street banks. Paulson in his view reasoned that:

> With a $60 trillion global economy and a $14 trillion US economy, it is inevitable that we will have a number of very large financial institutions whose increasing size and complexity are driven by customer demand in a global market place. Inside the United States which still has 8,000 relatively small banks along with its many big institutions, competitive pressure will also force the industry to continue to consolidate.[162]

He wanted further consolidation to take out the small banks. Other people who seem to have managed their financial sector more efficiently than the United States have spoken out. For example, as earlier reported the former Chinese premier had said, as I had earlier mentioned, that what the problem is, alluding to the United States, is excessive expansion of financial institutions in the blind pursuit of profit.

The need for the fragmentation of the Wall Street banks industry has been very much on the minds of many people since the 2008 Wall

Street rescue, and people have written and spoken widely about it. Their reason for wanting the fragmentation of Wall Street is however basically political. They think that smaller banks will reduce Wall Street's political influence. Reducing political influence is only useful if people know what use to make of the reduced political influence, so as to get the US out of the economic straight jacket it is in. In the early stages, there were over seventy investment banks in Wall Street. Simon Johnson and James Kwaki argued that fragmentation in Wall Street should help dethrone Wall Street from its privileged place in the US economy. They argued that "The end of too big to fail will reduce large bank's funding advantage, forcing them to compete on the basis of products, price, and service."[163] Competing with smaller banks on products, price, and service is structurally not important. Ideas on how to limit sizes of banks vary from preventing them going into certain business activities (Volcker doctrine), and limiting the percentage of total deposit they can take on or limiting control/ownership to a fixed percentage of the GDP. These suggestions are not structurally to the point.

Professor Simon Johnson, a former IMF Chief Economist, having worked on financial crises round the world, told Bill Moyers in an interview in 2009 that the financial system of the United States reminded him more of the embattled emerging markets he encountered in his time with the IMF. He was of the view that the US financial system needed a reboot, through breaking up big banks. He was of the view that:

> "Weakening big banks—should not be seen as an unfortunate side effect of beneficial medicine. It is exactly what we need to do under the circumstances. Unless and until these banks' economic and political influence decline, we are stuck with too many people who know exactly what they can get away with because their organizations are too big to fail."[164]

Krugman put the point this way in his *New York Times* column of April 23, 2010 that "A growing body of analysts suggests that an oversized financial industry is hurting the broader economy. Shrinking that oversized industry won't make Wall Street happy, but what's bad for Wall Street would be good for America." Unfortunately, the US financial industry is getting even larger. As Brian O'Brien stated in his book *The Tyranny of the Federal Reserve,* "we are a nation run by corporations with a government of corporations by the corprations and for the corporations …. These corporations have no loyalty to the United States but are loyal to profit and to the globalistic vision of free trade—." I have earlier shown that loyalty to the financial market is a cross-party fact in the US.

What I have done is to pinpoint how Wall Street harms the US economy particularly how it is a major agent in promoting the structural economic imbalance of the economy. I also wanted to point out that US corporations and monopolies are guilty of causing the structural imbalance of the US economy. Fragmenting Wall Street banks alone is not enough if Americans don't know what they want so that even in the fragmented state of banks Wall Street will continue to constitute a major structural danger to the US economy.

My Pessimism about the United States

One of my biggest sources of pessimism about the future of the American economy, as I had earlier stated, is that, despite the economic mess the United States is in, a substantial portion of Americans do not know the extent and depth of US economic decline, and many don't trust or want their government to step into economic reconstruction of the US economy. Others are sure that even if the government wanted to step in, it cannot succeed because it lacks the knowledge and because it is too tied up to Wall Street and politics, and that the depth of the economic chasm has created an almost impossible political condition for a cross-party agreement as to what to do. My review of the White House and Treasury's agencies concerned with framing economic policy and strategy in chapter 3 showed that policy makers lack the competence and knowledge needed to understand the scale and nature of America's growing economic decline. My regret, as I observed in chapter 6, is that FDR's failure to make an economic success of the New Deal was an opportunity lost in the US history to lay the foundation for enduring government involvement in US economic management. US presidents through history are politicians first and foremost. Americans therefore do not trust their Presidents as the people to hand the economy to change. Wall Street's dominance of Washington is likely to continue that will complete the vicious circle. All talk of subduing Wall Street is not likely to succeed so long as there is a revolving door between Wall Street and Washington, and in so far as those in Washington think that it is finance from Wall Street that that makes US economy, and in so far as all the politicians look to Wall Street for their election campaigns. Even as Congress was debating the financial regulation that led to Dodd-Frank in 2010, the financial industry was conducting a bidding war between parties with an eye on campaign contribution for the elections. Today, much of the relatively watered down regulations of Dodd-Frank have been further eroded following the changes that subsequently flowed from it because of the clout of Wall Street. Wright of FDL News Desk correctly stated that "it is an open question if what remains of Dodd-Frank is even worth trying to save." Dodd-Frank was not about the US economy. It was only about the financial sector to prevent another financial crisis. It was not the financial crisis that started the recession. So Dodd-Frank cannot stop future recessions. Dodd-Frank wanted to achieve only two things (a) to stop too-big-to-fail by requesting higher capital base of banks and (b) to step up consumer protections.

Robert Rech, a former US Secretary for Labor and Professor of Public Policy at the University of California Berkley, in the *Financial Times* of April 26, 2010 said that:

> "Washington's relationship with Wall Street is growing more schizophrenic by the day. On one hand, (as the mid-term election loomed in 2010) Congress went out of its way to show how tough it can be on the financial sector by enacting a law ostensibly designed to prevent another melt down and taxpayer supported bailout. At the same time, both parties were going to Wall Street seeking cam paigns donations...In the recent years the financial industry has become the second largest source of campaign con tribution—just behind health care."

The goal to distance Washington from Wall Street has been made more difficult since the Supreme Court's decision in 2009 that holding corporations including financial firms have a right to spend unlimited amounts on political campaign. The sad position in which the United States finds itself can be summarized in the following words by a Wall Street insider: "There has been an increasing disconnection between the real and financial economies in the past few years." He continued: "The real economy has grown at brisk rate (that is at the time), but nothing like that of the financial economy, which grew even more rapidly…" According to him, "there has been the rise in securitization and development of structured investment vehicles, conduits, hedge funds, private equity, leveraged loans and the like." He said that these were probably the biggest stimulus to credit multiplier. "The process has been driven by agents that have grown up (and made big profits) in unregulated areas without taking account of the basic share values," he stated. These have done nothing toward possible balancing of economic structure needed for US Main Street growth.

Mary Shapiro, chairman of the Securities and Exchange Commission, in defending derivatives told Congress in June 2009 that those derivatives "allow parties to hedge and manage risk, which itself can promote capital formation." She wrongly thought that capital formation meant economic growth. It is this kind of thought locked in economic and political leaders' thoughts that make them think the country cannot progress without Wall Street at the front.

Wall Street Plans to Come Back

Wall Street became the American public's villain less than a year after President Obama took office following the large rescue of Wall Street. Similarly, Wall Street was the villain as FDR was being inaugurated in 1933. FDR inherited a population that was enraged by what it considered the greed of the market crash of 1929. The Pecora Commission, which was set up a year before FDR was inaugurated to probe the sins of Wall Street some seventy years ago unearthed the reasons for the crash and accused the banks for what Robert Sloan called a rigged game. Robert Sloan called the action of the commission a political defenestration of several well-known Wall Streeters of the time.

FDR populist rhetoric set off waves of anti-Wall Street sentiment that outlasted Pecora. The 1937 panic was followed by the setting up of the larger Temporary National Economic Committee Inquiry, which produced thirty-seven volumes of testimony. Public unease and anger against Wall Street were to last, surviving World War II and the post-war prosperity. In 1947 in the hope of bringing the offending Wall Street to its knees, the Department of Justice sued seventeen investment banks for anti-trust violations. When six years later the case was dismissed, it was the siren that told everyone Wall Street was back. As Robert Sloan put it in his recall of this history, "Animus against Wall Street lasted twenty years, and it took another forty six years for it to swing the pendulum back its way." So we have been there before and there is no reason to think we will not be there again. The repeal of the Glass-Steagal Act in 1999 completed the circle of Wall Street's rebirth. As Robert Sloan stated, any hope that the public will soon forget the present transgressions of Wall Street is unrealistic, if history is anything to go by. He was wrong. The Occupy Wall Street movement has melted away. Sloan suggested that Wall Street needs to respond forcefully with vision and passion and set out why its function is central to America's capitalism, democracy, and philosophical heritage. He asserted that Wall Street is the cause why:

> "A country with 5 percent of the world's population con-
> trols 20 percent of its wealth: one reason is that major
> capital sources, from petro-dollars, through Chinese trade
> dollars to Japanese savings head to New York, where their
> owners can buy and sell financial instruments and find
> liquidity."[165]

You can bet that this kind of talk is the way Wall Street wants to rehabilitate itself which it has already done. We are going to be told, as it is already being claimed by G.W. Bush, Paulson and Obama, that without Wall Street the US will lose its world economic and financial dominance and that the US economy cannot exist without capital from Wall Street, that Wall Street is not going away is the determination of its leaders. They instead feel that it is their job to once again explain to Americans what good Wall Street is doing for America.

Jes Staley, head of J.P. Morgan Investment Bank at the time, said, "It is incumbent upon Wall Street to articulate what it does in a fashion that convinces the average person of the value of what we do."[166] He was of the view that we, in Wall Street, have "to be much better at explaining the innovation that takes place in our industry because you cannot stop innovation in the industry". We used to have deposits, loans, and stock exchange. Now we have credit market that is four times larger than the equity market, and it is immensely complex and idiosyncratic. It is akin to having lived all your life with arithmetic and all of sudden being shown calculators. I agree with Paul Volcker that what the economy does not need from Wall Street is not the innovation that Staley is talking about. Volcker told us that we just want simple arithmetic with which to produce the goods and services ordinary Americans need.

I worry that, as part of US long-term economic decline, the US is in for many more recessions. But as, we see, nothing has been done to stop future recessions as that is outside the field of conventional (financial) economics. Insofar as recessions are not stopped, Dodd-Frank cannot stop future financial crisis. Dodd-Frank in truth is therefore only an attempt to limit the damages of future financial crises, not to stop future recessions.

In Wall Street, you, therefore, find different attitudes to the 2008 crisis. At the height of the crisis, the stock market latched to the TARP as if it was the last hope of redemption. Traders who previously were repelled by any hint of government meddling now were asking for bigger bank rescues in the belief that without it stocks would continue to flounder. Warren Buffett declared that the US faced an economic Pearl Harbor that required action by Congress.

Many in Wall Street banks today themselves do not necessarily feel indebted to government for the rescue but feel it is the job of government to deal with the financial crisis and in any case they have repaid the government what it spent at a profit to the taxpayer. Others think that what happened is an accident, which can happen to anyone. But many forget that past financial crises have always depended on the Fed's assistance.

Much economic theorizing has been done to buttress the mysticism of financial market in order to reinforce its eminent position over the economy. Bernanke, however, tried to use Adam Smith's invisible hand to buttress his claims about the supremacy of the financial market over everything else because Adam Smith's invisible hand statement is a highly respected hand. But like so many people, Bernanke was making a mistaken use of Adam Smith. Price stability, according to Bernanke, is supposed to arise from the invisible hand, which, according to him, arranges for a dynamic equilibrium ensuring efficient use of resources at which point the economy is performing at maximum efficiency and economic growth and employment are at a peak. When the most serious recession since the 1933 depression occurred in 2007 and a crash of the financial market followed in 2008, it was concluded that Adam Smith's invisible hand failed going by the fact that Friedman had told us that the invisible hand could have prevented the Great Depression and so could easily have stopped that recession. What failed in 2007 was not Adam Smith's invisible hand, as Bernanke wanted to claim nor Friedman's monetarism.

For Smith, the invisible hand was the self-regulation of an economy not of finance. In Smith's day, there was no financial market. There was no Wall Street. Smith was talking of people freely trading in goods that were produced with free competition. Smith's self-regulation is about dynamic economic equilibrium or balance, the same dynamic equilibrium that is at the center of my theory of factor proportions. Freely trading, in Smith's language, refers to free competition, certainly not the monopolistic US economy maintained and organized by Wall Street. Individual trading in Smith's language means equality of factor proportion.

Professor Phelps the 2006 economics Nobel Prize winner re-emphasized this concept of balance in a 2013 book, *How Grassroot's Innovation Created Jobs: Challenger and Change.* He worried whether the West "will recommit to modern, grass root dynamism, indigenous innovation, widespread personal fulfillment or will we go on with a narrowed innovation that limits flourishing to a few." Bernanke's transplanting claims of Smith's invisible hand into the financial market is a botched attempt to prove and claim the efficiency of the financial market because (a) Smith was not talking of the financial market but was talking of an economy (b) Smith was not talking of the present financial market or the current US economy where factor proportions are so disruptive as in figure 1 of chapter 1 of this book.

The rational market theory was another financial market false construct intended to elevate the financial market (Wall Street) and give it scientific status. The theory claims that the decisions of millions of investors in the market will always lead to the best judgment of values. The rational market theory, like the claim of invisible hand, is driven by a basic acknowledgment that a dynamic economic balance is the ideal state for the achievement of economic efficiency. Reference to millions of investors in the theory is another way of describing equality because no one is boss. In his book, *The Myth of the Rational Market*, Justin Fox told us that behaviorists and other critics who poked holes in the edifice of rational market have not been willing to dispense with the equilibrium framework that the originators of rational market imposed on the field a century ago. He told us that while people who believed in rational market theory spent time studying disturbances and biases, they still held firm to a rational theory in which they still believed that (unknown to them) pervasive forces (hidden hand) are out there somewhere pushing prices at least in the general direction of where they belong.[167] Just like the attempt of financial experts like Bernanke, to steal Smith's hidden hand, the myth of the rational market was based on the attempt of some of its proponents to define a non-existent (scientific) finanancial dynamic equi librium in the financial market in their further attempt to cleverly move the theory from finance to economic growth. It was a failed attempt to equate finance as a science with scientific economic growth. They wanted scientific dynamic equilibrium which they were trying to ascribe to finance to be seen as the motivator for US economic growth.

When instead the 2007 recession occurred, the worst in over sixty years, the foly of the promoters of rational theory was exposed. Fox told us in his book that those within and outside the financial discipline who ventured to think that may be, because the theory of rationality failed, that even though equilibrium has been part of economics that may be they (the promoters) were wrong to rely on equilibrium as part of economics.[168] The error in the claim of a dynamic equilibrium of the financial market is because financial theorists were trying to steal the magic word "equilibrium" from structural economics to finance. Next time anyone presents you with any science sounding rules or theories on finance or monetarism or other finance-related matter, do not believe them because finance is not a science.

Wall Street's Po werful Publicity Machine

The Wall Street machine does a lot to sustain the American public belief that Wall Street represents the economy. Publicity for Dow Jones Industrial, NASDAQ, and S&P 500 are part of Wall Street's publicity machine, intended to make the ordinary American believe that these indexes are telling us about the changing state of the real US economy. No main news on television and radio in the US today is complete without numbers for Dow Jones NASDAQ and S&P 500 claiming to tell us whether the economy is up or down. The charade is that sometimes even as the US economy was slowing, the Dow Jones and the NASDAQ have hit record highs because of some happenings have nothing to do with the real economy. The overpowering influence of these indices is they have manged to make ordinary Americans believe that Wall Street is the US economy. A lot of Washington's actions and policies are determed by these Wall Street published indices.

Another related way in which the financial market and Wall Street want to make people believe that Wall Street is the economy is the way they employ people called economists. Economists employed by Wall Street do a lot to promote the financial market as if it is the real economy. They are regularly called on television, radio, and press to analyze all the problems of the economy and give advice and opinions. Naturally they give economic news, with a Wall Street/financial bias. Wall Street journalists and financial economists dominate the elite group that writes learned articles and books dissecting American economic ills and analyzing economic data. Indeed one stipulation in the contract of some Wall Street economists is that they should secure a certain minimum amount of media time and coverage. They help to reinforce the false idea that US economics is all about finance and Wall Street.

Summary

My intention in this chapter is to demonstrate the extent to which the US economy is held hostage by Wall Street with its very diverse interests, which have also taken deeper control of the technology industry ever since the dot.com revolution of the 1990s. The dot.com revolution of the New Economy was taken over by Wall Street that led to the dot.com bubble. The dot. com gave the US the sense of mastery of the world and initially transformed American industry and services. The dot.com bubble that followed accelerated the structural imbalance of the US economy. As Wall Street expands and our capitalist economy expands, we are continually increasing the structural imbalance of the economy, reducing economic growth and increasing income inequality, and heading to a future of increasing conflict between democracy and capitalism.

Chapter 10

Dark Clouds over the US Economy

I am concluding this book by stating simply that there are dark clouds hanging over the US economy. What worries me most is the fact that most people in the United States including our political and economic leaders are not aware of the seriousness and depth of the US coming economic decline. There is a clear attempt by the political class to play it that there is no crisis. What we have is a mixture of ignorance, arrogance, and incompetence, as I highlighted in chapter 3. America's economic problems, as I have said, are structural. The structural nature of the US economicproblems means that like all structural problems the US economic structure is quietly rotting away in its foundations.

I have shown that the US structural economic problems are very old. They started from the end of the nineteenth century, immediately after the United States achieved world economic leadership but have been getting worse in Fig. 10.1 because economists have all along not developed the economics that will enable them understand what structurally is going on with their economy.

**US Average Annual Per-Capita
G.D.P. Growth Over the Preceding 10 Years**

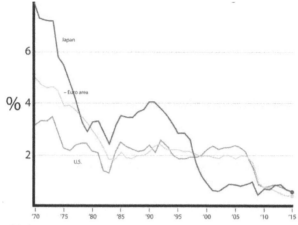

Fig.10.1

Increasing structured imbalance: lower growth rates
Source: World Bank

While we all know of the Great Depression, it is less well-known, as I previously mentioned, that the US economy had a number of recessions before the Great Depression. For over a century, the US suffered depressions and recessions. American economists have no way to stop recessions but claim credit each time they recovered from a recession. They however forget that all recessions will eventually end after the economic cycle has run its course not because of their expertise of the Fed.

US long-term economic decline in growth rate as in Fig. 10.2 is therefore coming at a time when the country has no strategies for dealing with it. Ever since the year 2009 when the economics profession in the United States finally accepted that it has failed (as I detailed in chapter 1), and that it is unable to provide a solution to the country's economic crisis, no one has come out with an alternative economic approach to the issues yet. It means that the US increasing economic terminal sickness is coming at a time when the doctors say that they are not equipped to provide a cure and don't understand the full nature of the illness.

I have attempted in chapter 9 to point out that, despite claims by Americans that they have a free enterprise economy, the US economy is highly monopolistic and uncompetitive, controlled by large corporations working in cooperation with a powerful Wall Street, operating in cohort with a Fed that plays financial games and tricks with the real economy. In the midst of a declining economy, US large corporations are largely doing fine with large profits, a good portion of which is externally generated supported by a bouncing Wall Street. Those that claim that US has a free economy are mainly those who benefit from the present economic system.

I pointed out that Wall Street and the financial market go out of their way to make all of us believe they are the economy. It has the huge publicity machine to support it. All this has reinforced the Fed's false claim that it controls the economy of the United States. The Fed, in turn, is owned by Wall Street and is the agent of the financial market. The Fed, as I have shown, has neither the science nor knowledge of the economy to bring sustainable economic growth to the US economy.

The freewheeling American economy (the free enterprise system) has put those who control money in the country in a position to direct, control, and gamble with the economy. The basic worry which some of the early Presidents of the US like Hoover had about the country's growing monopolistic tendency—as I described in chapter 6—has not been solved and we now have legally and constitutionally accepted a monopolistic institutions as the norm.

The solution to the US economic problems, as I emphasized in chapter 7, does not lie with the Fed because in some ways the Fed is part of the problem because it does not have the knowledge or expertise to ensure how to deal with US structural economics.

One major obstacle that further may make it difficult is that, as things are presently, America will resolve its structurally unbalanced economy is that Americans don't have a scientific approach to economics. Economic science needs discipline and planning. Our free enterprise economy goes against national planning and economic discipline. For many Americans economic freedom is also freedom from government. Americans have from time have not agreed on the role of their government in economic management and will like government to be kept out. During the two world wars, Presidents Wilson and Roosevelt had full powers on the economy. The war emergency set-up enabled the country to mobilize its resources and each time the economy that resulted at war was structurally balanced because of the structure of a War Economy had the economic disciplines needed. War did not provide for capital-intensive use of factors. The economy however immediately went back to imbalance after each war because the war type economic institutions and discipline were disbanded immediately after and uncontrolled free enterprise once more took over. The recent bungling of the economy and enrichment of Wall Street in 2008–2009 by the US government has regrettably tarnished any trust Americans will have for government in economic management/direction. Worse still is that, as I have stated in chapter 9, any attempt to tackle the structural imbalance of the US economy will be highly resisted by the enormous political power of Wall Street and those who will say that it runs against our freedom/democracy and free enterprise system. President Obama in his last State of the Union speech in 2016 twice berated those whom he said were saying that the US economy was declining. He said that they were "peddling fiction" and that such a claim was a "political hot air."

The basic issue of the role of government in economic strategy is, as today, not resolved despite the existence of many regulatory agencies in the economy. Thomas Friedman once enthused in an article in New York Times titled *"Capitalism, Version 2012"* that the thing other people have most admired and tried to emulate about American capitalism is that American success for over 200 years was largely due to its healthy, balanced *public-private* partnership—where government provided the institutions, rules, safety-nets, education, research, and infrastructure to empower the private sector to innovate, invest, and take the risks that promote growth and jobs.[169] But if America's economy is in decline, it may be that the existing partnership Friedman is talking about has outlived its usefulness. President Clinton has in his book, *Back to Work,* advocated for stronger government to move the country economically forward. If the structural weakness of the US economy can be addressed, it needs the government to step in much further than Clinton suggested, in some ways similar to the Chinese. At the moment, in my view, using Friedman's partnership analysis and seeing what I said in chapter 9 on, I will say that the private sector (Wall Street) in the US has overwhelmed the public sector. Advocates of small government have continued to grow into the majority especially after the G. W. Bush and Obama's governments' ineptitude of their sellout to Wall Street 2007 to 2009 to which I have already referred.

There is great falsehood in the claim that the private sector in the US knows best how to organize the economy. US Presidents over time have tended to seek out the chief executives of major corporations to tell them how to move the US economy forwards. These people are simply experts on how to make money for their corporations but are often ill-equipped on conceptual concepts of economic structuring and strategy. Some of today's major US economic structural problems are in fact the makings of these CEOs. They are closely tied to Wall Street. A good example that CEOs and high level industry gurus are not necessarily the ones that can teach the country how to run the economy is the Council of Jobs and Competitiveness, which was set up in 2011 by President Obama with the Chairman/ CEO of GE as chairman. In a summary of the report of the council, the chief executives claimed that their report laid out an agenda for investing in US future through education and innovation, build on America's strengths in the critical sectors of energy and manufacturing, and play to win by making overdue tax and regulatory reforms.

In another instance, the Council thought that infrastructure projects and energy will help create employment. It called for an overhaul of the processing of business and tourist visa system. They called for a National Investment Initiative *that will help regain America's place as the destination for foreign and domestic investment*. They called for means to help start-up businesses. What the Council had was a shopping list of what it *thought* were needed to increase jobs and competitiveness. Any pressure group in the US (as these CEOs were) will easily produce its own shopping list, which will likely have many of the same items as the Council had. There was therefore nothing structurally strategic in the council's offerings. Professor Stiglitz put this problem this way: "Too much power (to CEOs), too much deference to their supposed wisdom, is given to corporate executives" in his book, *The Price of Inequality,* as he was trying to analyze the economy's poor performance.[170] The Professor is right. A new set of people with the necessary expertise need to be brought in for the new economic science approach which we need.

Reading the car industry's application/proposals for government bailout in 2008, it was clear, for example, that there was no structural strategic thinking in the industry nor was the one appointed by the government to study and appraise the car proposals for government bailout any better equipped. The evidence of the top executives of the three car companies before Congress when they applied for bailout in 2008 was disturbing for its lack of structural substance and strategy. Everybody was mainly concerned with the capital investment for a sector which has major structural, effects on the US economy.

Since Chrysler was acquired by a private fund in 2007, it emerged from the evidence that in the process of rescuing itself, Chrysler had reduced its capacity by 30 percent by eliminating 1.2 million units of capacity. This meant mothballing capital intensity that should not have been there in the first place. The Chief Executive told Congress he now wanted *a lean and agile* company—depending on what he calls lean and agile. Why was the company not lean and agile all along? General Motors said they had cut fixed cost by 23 percent, about $9 billion of plant and hoped by 2011 to have cut fixed capital cost by up to 35 percent, a staggering $14 billion to $15 billion. It was also hoping, as a result, to be *more nimble.* I have all along in this book complained that our industries have excessive capital intensity in the erroneous pride that productivity in the United States is one of the highest in the world as the evidence at the Congress hearing on the car industry confirmed in 2008. One will recall that at one time the Big 3 in Detroit claimed falsely in the 1980s that the Japanese who introduced lean production methods were outcompeting them because of the yen/dollar exchange rates.

Many people in the US recognize that the country's economic problems are structural. David Brooks in a *New York Times* Opinion Page of May 7, 2012 stated that he believed that the core (economic) problems of the US are structural, not cyclical. He believed that: Fixing these structural problems should be the order of the day...[171] In a *New York Times* article of March 31, 2013, Jeffrey Sachs stated that "It's time to move beyond transitory and piecemeal policies. Our underlying economic problems are chronic, not temporary, structural not cyclical."[172] The problem is that people like David Brooks and Jeffrey Sachs were not talking of technical structural problems. They only talk of structural in the context that each problem in the US economy is part of a set of interrelated and interconnected problems.

If US economic problems are structural, which is the theme of this book, then it is unfortunate that there many people who display economic arrogance and/or ignorance by giving the impression that the solutions to the country's economic problems can simply be found by producing a shopping list of what they believe needs to be done to save the US economy just as the Council on Jobs and Competitiveness tried to do. Bill Clinton's book *Back to Work* with his deep experience as President had a checklist of forty-six things that needed to be done to make the US competitive. The Obama administration listed innovation, education, energy, and infrastructure as its key to US economic revival. These do not constitute a structural economic strategy. Equally problematic in dealing with the country's chronic economic problems are instances where many important people: Wall Street executives, journalist, and politicians believe they have one unlocking solution or the other for the economy. They are all mostly financial solutions. R. Glenn Hubbard, George W. Bush's tax-cutting guru who had been expected to be the Treasury secretary in a Romney government is an example. To him entitlement programs are an *autopilot* for the US economy.

Hubbard argued that the important priority at the moment for the US economy is the rolling back of the Federal benefits for the wealthier and middle class Americans. He argued that the challenge facing the US economy is the steady rise in entitlement spending, as the population ages and health care costs rise faster than inflation. These payments, he argued, will be a major problem. Rolling back, according to him, if undertaken, will cause taxes to fall and more entrepreneurs will start business. Corporate investment would rise. Individuals will work harder and earn more. The country would therefore have a faster growth, according to him. On the other hand, Larry Summers, Obama's economic guru, said that what the country needed is to *start playing offense at the long-time unemployment.* He believed that the US is poorer without the contribution of millions of Americans with long-time unemployment. He believed that US government can address this problem in several ways by committing to more government spending notably on infrastructure.[173] Where was Larry when the US unemployment plunged below 4%?

Considering that these two men reached the top of economic advising in the US within the Republican and Democrat settings, it is clear that the Presidents hearing from them didn't receive any strategic structural economic advice from either of them. Each adviser was intent or was only trained on focusing on financial microeconomic issues in his attempt at solving the country's macroeconomic problems. They were not aware that each of the problems on which they focused was the result of the structural imbalance of the US economy and could not be solved unless the structural imbalance of the economy is removed.

Arthur Laffer and Stephen Moore—representatives of "one topic" solutions—thought the answer was America's return to prosperity was to re-order the tax system to a flat tax regime.[174] The prospects of solving the US structural economic problems are further compounded because even if the government acquires the powers to restructure the US economy, it is going to be a very long journey to change the mental mode in the US government system about economic strategy. Inside the American government system there is a pervading capitalist ideology, even among policy level public servants who will be required to implement a new government control of the economy.

For example, the American Enterprise Institute set up to defend American freedom and democratic capitalism and private enterprise boasted that during the G. W. Bush era, it had more than twenty of its scholars and fellows who served in Bush's policy posts or served in one or more of the government panels and commissions. The structure of government in the United States may, therefore, itself be resistant and impervious to new ideas about the economy as I described in chapter 2.

Wall Street also dominates *economic* thinking in the governments of the United States through the Treasury Department (which sometimes claims it is in charge of economic policy), and which maintains a revolving door with Wall Street while White House economic advisers are largely disciples of Keynes or Friedman with fiscal tendencies attuned to their president's political party and with no industrial experience. Even given their economic limitations, the present brand of present and former economic advisers forget that Keynes and Friedman were pragmatists and empiricist intellectuals and that each of them was carefully aware of the limits in their claims. It was their followers, the present economic leaders that took the financial ideas of the two men beyond where the two wanted them and have made futile attempts to turn these ideas into a science.

With the economic decline facing the US, one will have thoughts that it is the economic profession that will take the lead in solving the country's structural problems. But as I showed in many instances in this book, the state of the profession is not good. While there are noises about the need for economics to be a science, the bulk of the profession is steeped in conventional financial based economics intent on achieving a particular social or political agenda. For example, I showed in chapter 2 how Obama's economic advisers tried purely for of political reasons to establish what they thought was a scientific link/economic formula between the quantum of Obama's stimulus and growth and claimed the employment created by it in their political attempt to prove that Obama's stimulus improved the economy.

There were those who sought (politically) in the days of G.W. Bush to show that Bush's tax cuts accelerated the economy. In chapter 5, we heard from the Peterson Institute experts on how many billions of dollars they falsely claimed that the United States gains a year from international trade. There are, in chapter 6, faulty claims and theories about globalization by some of the most well-known economists in the United States at the time. I am therefore pessimistic about the state of economics in the United States because of the very diverse sometimes purely selfish interests at play preying on conventional economics.

Overnight 9/11 turned terrorism, defence, intelligence and security into the top urgent national priority of the United States accounting for over \$600 billion a year when we take into account our financial and military commitments in Europe. Only with a strong growing economy can America sustain this rising level of external funding and expedition. US economy needs to be given the same highest priority by creating a cabinet level professional agency to reconstruct the US economy because economic power is in the end the source of all US power. That is why the Chinese wisely have affirmed in their Constitution that their economy has their highest national priority.

"Recovery" and After: Future Economic Despondency

Since 2009 when the 2007–2009 recession was supposed to have ended and expected to be followed by *recovery,* US economists and leaders and the Fed routinely poured over published weekly data on items like employment, consumer confidence, housing, retail trade, and so on to detect signs of *recovery.* Janet Yellen in her QE outing declared that if unemployment reduced to 5 percent, she will take it that recovery was completed waiting for interest rates to be increased. In his 2016 State of the Union Speech, Obama claimed that with with 14 million new jobs, that the US was "in the middle of the longest streak of private-sector job creation history." Obama was claiming that the recovery had been achieved adding that the auto industry had its best year ever. The end of the recession was the center of attention. The fact that US faces the possibility of more recessions/depressions did not at the time concern Janet Yellen and President Obama. This is why I talked about American short-termism in chapter 3. The cyclical nature of the US economy, however, *guarantees* that after each recession, there will be some kind of recovery. Just as the 2007–2009 recession came without notice, another will come. Looking at the cloud hanging over the US economy, most forecasts about the long-term GDP growth of the US economy are bleak showing an economy depicting an economy unable grow above 3.0 percent for some time indefinite. The problem is that even these bleakforecasts do not take account of possible future recessions/depressions.

Some Americans have long accepted the prospects of American economic decline. In his book: *The Crash of 2016*, Thomas Hartman is sure America will have a depression in 2016. Hartman's main message is not the literal year 2016, but is intended to draw attention to an economy that is in serious urgent decline. Earlier, the 2013 Economic Report to the President commented as follows about US economy: "From 1960 to 2007, the US economy had seven recessions. The economy contracted by an average of 4.7 percent during the 2207-2009 recession about double in the earlier seven recessions and the annual rate of growth of real GDP during the 12 quarters following those recessions was 4.2 percent nearly double that of the 2007–2009 recession. After three years of recovery, the cumulative growth of real GDP was 6.3 percentage points lower than its average for earlier post 1960 recessions…For each of the three recent business cycles, the recovery in real GDP has been slower than the 1960–2007."[176]

In a New York Times article of November 18, 2013 titled *"A Permanent Slump,"* Paul Krugman feared that the present "depression-like conditions (in the US)"—were on track to persist, not for another one or two years *but for decades."* He called it a situation of *secular stagnation*—a persisting state in which a depressed economy is the norm, with episodes of full employment few and far between. He confessed that a number of economists had flirted with the thought of permanent slump for a while. And now, according to him, such thoughts had moved into mainstream. Krugman referred to the fact that Larry Summers made a similar case for possible persistence of secular stagnation in the 2013 IMF annual research conference. Summers told the conference that the financial crisis of 2008 which he said caused the Great Recession was far behind us and yet more than four years after (in 2013), the depressed economy persists. Summers's talk at the conference, which Krugman called part of mainstream, was a clear affirmation of despondency. Larry Summers followed up on this despondency with an FT article of December 15, 2013 titled "Why stagnation might prove to be the new normal." The surprise and disappointing thing about the article is that it did not hint or consider the need for the profession to improve or change its know-how so as to understand the economy better. Krugman, in a New York Times article of June 19, 2015, titled *"Voodoo, Jeb! Style"* confirmed this failure when he admitted that economists don't know much about how to raise the long-run rate of economic growth. Janet Yellen in her Mid-Year Economic Policy Report to Congress June 2016 commented: "Well, growth has been disappointing. I am not sure of the reason! Professor Stiglitz had earlier in his 2010 book *Freefall* stated that "The system is broken, and we can only fix it by examining the underlying theories that have led us into this new "bubble capitalism." CBO (Congress Budget Office) had earlier thrown in the towel. In *New York Times* of March 2014, Lloyd Morris in an article titled "A Dire Economic Forecast Based on New Assumptions" reported that the CBO economists essentially decided that they will treat recent years of poor performance as a sort of norm. They have seen enough of slow economy to know that we should get used to sluggishness, even though, according to the CBO, *Wall Street and its banks are doing very* well. The CBO forecasted that the actual US economy will settle into a prolonged period in which it grows at an average of 2.1 percent from 2019 through 2024, job growth will average less than 70,000 a month."

A mood of despondency has taken control over the future of the US economy. Our reigning economists don't kow how to revive growth of a fledgling economy. Conventional economists now seem to acknowledge that since the death of development economics in the 1980's they don't know how to grow the economy. As Frank Bruni confirmed in an article in New York Times May 4, 2014, Americans are now "walking small" and that a shift in our gait and our gumption have been possible for many years, during our sustained period of frustration that has the feel of something more than temporary dive: a turned corner, the downward arc of a diminished enterprise.... At the core of American anger and alienation is the belief that the American dream is no longer attainable." Mr. J. Young, formally of the Treasury and GMB, in a December 2014 *Forbes* publication stated that after the worst four years of US economic down-turn in decades, it has become necessary to ask if there are inescapable facts on US short- and long-term growth figures. He concluded "Something is very different and seemingly worrisome. This is clear in the current post-crisis period, but it really stretches back much further, and could be far more serious than a temporary economic slowdown." All the conventional economists I have quoted accept that the US economy is in decline and that its future is poor and uncertain unware that there is a structural problem to be solved.

Paths to US Economic Decline

The 1930 US economy is in GDP terms about 6 percent the size of the post 2010 US economy. The roaring 20s was a period of what Maury Klein called "insatiable appetite for stocks in which promoters happily pushed forward mergers creating new shares and still more investment trusts."[177] In August 1929, the *New York Times* noted that *hardly a week passes but a new investment trust appears*. By end of 1929, 265 new investments trusts had produced $3 billion in new shares, 14 of them with assets exceeding $100 million. The Founders Group had evolved into a pyramided system of investment trusts and holding companies with paid in capital exceeding $686 million. There were mergers in banks, chemical company mergers, gas mergers, power mergers, aviation mergers, food company mergers, asbestos-gypsum mergers, etc.[178] For the relatively small size of the economy at the time in the 1920s–1930s, these trusts and mergers were structural factors that were still strong enough to have contributed to the depression. The mathematical imbalance factor that caused the depression in 1930 could not, by any structural reasoning, cause a murmur in the current United States post-2010 economy considering the current size of the present US economy as compared to the economy then. Since the 1970s, however, the structure of the American economy has (apart from the current phenomenal growth of its ever enlarging capital intensive monopoly sector) seriously deteriorated and become more and more uncompetitive as its trade imbalance and deficit have steadily grown.

America's failure in its globalization adventures since the 1990s has all added to its sharply worsened and exacerbated the state of its structural economic imbalance. All these have contributed to US worsening recessions. That is why the latest 2007–2009 recession was the worst since the depression. Going forward, the US will face more recessions/depressions in the future as I have continued to emphasize. The US economy, as I hinted earlier, in recessions is like a man who has had a long history of constant heart attacks without seeking treatment. It is only to be expected that such a man's heart attacks will be progressively worse with time. US structural sickness, as I have shown, is over one hundred years old *without treatment*. The financial experts and Feds had thought they had eliminated recession only to get the worst recession since the Depression.

With all the information I presented, I don't think it will be fair to accuse me that I am presenting a pessimistic picture of the US future economy. A depression, when it occurs again in the US, will be the end of the American economy as an economy to be reckoned with in the world and will spell the eclipse of US economic influence in the world. With America's recession- prone economy—China does not have recessions—the simplistic thought among some Americans is that if Chinese economy overtakes theAmerican economy—which it has—, a new era in which the world will be controlled by the United States and China co-operating with each other may be wishful thinking.

The End of Western Civilization

I am suggesting that a reason why the United States needs to solve its economic problem is that the people who are taking over the world's economic leadership from the United States will be people who will probably turn our world into what we as American don't like or want. It may be the end of western civilization as we know it. I find it difficult to understand that, in view of what is at stake and as facts emerge about America's increasing economic subservience to China, some people especially in the United States busy themselves saying that America is not in danger because China's economic growth will soon stall.

I have dealt in some details about the Chinese economy in chapter 4 and what is driving it. A most recent and important example of Western complacency and ignorance, which needs to be mentioned here is

Professor Michael Pettis's 2013 old book titled, *The Great Rebalancing*. The professor, a Westerner, is a professor of finance and economics at Peking University. That places him in a position that anything he says about China will be believed. The Professor's viewpoint is that the Chinese economic growth is unsustainable. He believes that China is the cause of the present global economic imbalance because while other regions of the world, particularly American and the European Union are in economic crisis, the China was able, by what he described as a massive bank-financed increase in investment of over 30 percent of GDP, to *barge through the global crisis* with GDP growth rate of 9 percent and over while keeping consumption in China at a very low level. He argued that the global crisis will be over when the Chinese are unable to maintain their growth rate and when they are forced to rebalance their economy by creating more domestic demands instead of a blind pursuit of growth. The result, according to him, will be a drastic fall in Chinese exports that will force a global rebalancing from which the United States will be an automatic winner and beneficiary with its economy restored in strength. He concluded that "Only when China is importing capital and exporting demand will it be a net contributor to growth abroad."[179] In effect, Professor Pettis is asking the United States to do nothing and that the US economic crisis is not its fault and that China's contradictions, when China is forced to confront them, will bring the United States out of its economic problems. There are many similar comforting messages to the US in chapter 4.

What baffles me is that all the Western *experts* on China's economy like Professor Pettis and others mentioned in chapter 4 of this book do not have any in-depth knowledge of Chinese economic structure. Professor Pettis concluded that Chinese economy is unbalanced just because Premier Wen in 2007 said, in answer to a question, that China has maintained fast yet steady growth in recent years. The Premier, on that occasion, cautioned against China being complacent in the past, present, and future. He stated that his mind was focused on the pressing challenges facing China. This to me was modest encouragement for the Chinese economy by the Premier at the time. He was speaking as a deeply knowledgeable professional should, which he was. Chen described Chinese development as *unsteady, unbalanced, uncoordinated and unstable*. He then explained what he meant by these words as the Professor admitted:

> "Unsteady development means overheated investment as well as excessive credit supply and liquidity, and surplus in foreign trade and international payments. Unbalanced development means uneven development between urban and rural areas, between different regions and between economic and social development. Uncoordinated development means that there is lack of proper balance between primary, secondary, and tertiary sectors and between investment and consumption. Economic growth is mainly driven by investment and export. Unsustainable development means that we have not done well in saving energy and resources and protecting the environment. All these are pressing problems facing us, which require long-term efforts to resolve."

Professor Pettis pointed out that in 2009, the same Premier said that China's economic rebound was not yet solid and that in June 2010 the then vice premier, now premier, said that China's *past* development had created irrational economic structure and uncoordinated and unsustainable development that is increasingly apparent. Pettis never said that nothing was being done about these problems by the Chinese. The two Chinese leaders expressed an in-depth critical structural appraisal and criticism of their economy, an in-depth knowledge of the economy I will hardly expect any Western political leader to have. Is he saying that because no leader in America has pointed out the vast structural imbalance in the US that the US is balanced? The Chinese leaders were expressing unhappiness at the speed of transformation they wanted in the Chinese economy and also from their statement it was clear they acknowledged that progress was being made. It however seems naïve for Professor Pettis to use these statements as his sole proof of the instability of the Chinese economy in his book.

The Professor and many of the West's *experts* on Chinese economy like him are committing sweeping errors about the Chinese economy because they are ignorant about its structural system. In chapter 4, I showed and demonstrated the Chinese scientific structural economic strategy is based on their adoption of scientific factor proportions strategy, which no other country to date is either aware of or practicing, which means that China stands out among all countries in the world and is growing economically and scientifically on its own merit, no matter what economic crises there are elsewhere. Its export to GDP ratio of 40 percent is not outlandish compared with Germany of 50 percent, United Kingdom 32 percent, Sweden 50 percent because of false claims that China's economic success is built on exports. In chapter 4, I also discussed in some detail the history of the Chinese development of balanced development strategy and how the Chinese through their Five-Year Plans maintain constant structural experimentation and adjustment, constant balancing and rebalancing of the economy. I showed how the country has rebalanced the economy by reducing heavy industries and high energy consumption activities in an attempt to continually rebalance their economy and that substantial progress has been made in the past few years to bring development in Chinese rural areas and decrease in migrant labor in further spatial balancing the economy.

I have earlier wondered why all the Western experts who comment on Chinese economy have not wondered why China has not had a recession since 1978 when recessions are today part and parcel of Western economies. A number of Western economists have instead tried to fault or doubt Chinese long-term economic sustainability on the claim that Chinese growth is fixed investment led, which I disproved in chapter 4.

Paul Krugman wrote a NY Times opinion essay January 8, 2016 titled, *"When China Stumbles."* For those just starting to pay attention (according to Krugman): "It has been obvious for a while that China's economy is in trouble." The basic problem, he claimed, is that China's economic model—which I am sure he doesn't understand because he has no knowledge of economic science—involves very high saving and very low consumption. He claimed that China now faces transitioning to much lower growth without stumbling into a recession. Here is his advice to China—to buy time with credit expansion and infrastructure spending in ways that put purchasing power into families' hands! The advice is based on the unproven claim that money in the hands of people creates demand that produces growth." Considering Krugman earlier statement that (Western) macro-economics of the past 30 years had been useless and dangerous, he is the last person to advise on China's economy.

Projections about Chinese soft or hard landing featured frequently over the past two decades in Western media but the planned landings never came. From its balanced economy of fig 1.1 and from chapter 4, it is clear that the Chinese have *scientifically* continued to rebalance and readjust their economy. A balanced economy structurally means assured long-term sustainable growth. It means no reces sions. With its large population, China has since 1978 attained a steady and continuing sustainable economic growth that thrives even when the US economy is going through recessions.

How China wants to use its growing economic power and advantage is, in the last resort, up to China. It is to be expected that other people will complain if China does not play it the way they want. In order not to disrupt its structural economic balancing and maintain and increase its economic power, China has done and is doing everything to protect its structurally balanced economy from outside disruptive forces. In a well-researched old 2011 book titled, *Eclipse: Living in the Shadow of China's Economic Dominance*, Arvind Subramanian of the Peterson Institute for International Economics correctly stated Chinese (economic) dominance is more imminent and more broad-based and in greater magnitude than is currently anticipated or contemplated. He stated that reasonable projections suggest that the relative economic dominance of China by 2030 could resemble that of the United Kingdom around 1870 or the United States in the aftermath of World War II. In the end the Chinese economy overtaking the US (PPP) occurred in 2014. The Chinese renminbi will rival or overtake the dollar as primary world currency as soon as the early years of the next decade having now become an international currency. China is determined to replace the US dollar as the key international currency. Not a day passes without some company or some transaction in the world getting greater access to China's currency. China's internationalization of renminbi is going ahead in typical Chinese fashion: micromanaged, discretionary, selective, gradual, and "enclave-based" as Subramanian described it.[180] Countries are now having the Chinese currency in their reserves. China has continued to use the renminbi in many bilateral trade arrangements. One restricting factor in accelerating its currency plan is Chinese restriction of foreign capital entry into China. China does not want to create a Wall Street in China because it is fully aware what damage Wall Street had done and is doing to America's structural economic imbalance. But it plans to use Hong Kong and Shanghai as islands where it will try to open capital account and internationalizing the renminbi. China's US Treasury appetite, a cornerstone of global economy for more than a decade is waning.

China's economic power is already on display. For example, despite threats to China from the United States over its exchange rate for years, the United States did not get anywhere. Despite recent exchange rate adjustments China has made, there is still a core in Capitol Hill that still wants to threaten and punish China, but America is now powerless to do anything unilaterallyon exchange ratesagainst China in that respect. The United States used such threats during the Japanese short-lived economic emergence to get the Japanese to adjust their exchange rate. With its huge market as a dangling carrot and with a good number of major US corporations given presence in China, many of the major US corporations in China have somewhat divided loyalty to the United States. China has used trade and investment in Africa, Latin America, and Asia to circumvent the United States as it champions its Silk Road project. At one time, China wanted to buy the debt of Greece, Ireland, Portugal, and Spain, all intended to demonstrate its economic power and influence.

The US Export-Import Bank, recently disabled, over its 80 year life has extended $590 billion in loans, guarantees, and insurance. Chinese institutions have provided an estimated $900 billion just for its Silk Road Project. This is intended to usher in Chinese era and control to replace the West and its financial institutions and systems, as China establishes its own "World Bank". In 2015, China established the Asian Infrastructure Investment Bank—its World Bank. Despite

American objection, the bulk of Western countries have joined the new institution. Many Western countries participate in Chinese Silk Road Project. China is therefore on its way to put the West and its world influence under the shadow. In 2015, the IMF accepted the Chinese currency as an international currency—the IMF Special Drawing Rights Basket of currencies. This is part of the Chinese long term objective to reduce/eliminate the US and Western influence in the world.

It is clear that the open, cooperative world economic system which the United States has sought since its own economic decline in its new one-worldist stance is not in the Chinese menu. China is building up its growing military and space power. While the United States prides itself that Chinese military is not up that of the United States for the time being, we are talking of the next decade or two, with a United States reducing its military budget if and when its economy declines and China increasing its military budget and capability. We are dealing with a country that is angry and feels the West destroyed its empire in the past and which has focused on restoring its past empire through economic power by stating in its constitution that economic development is its single most important priority.

As Martin Jacques stated in his book, *When China Rules the World,* "The Chinese, who are constantly making reference to what they describe as their 5,000–year history, are aware that what defines them is not a sense of nation state but rather as a civilization state."[181] American hopes that China will in time be more democratic and be part of a growing open-rules based world economic system are not realistic in the context of Chinese ambitions which I have just described. China will never be a democracy.

India is another possible country to could overtake the United States if it gets its act together. Its economic system is presently a mix of capitalism and socialism/democracy with its recent change to encourage FDI but has, unlike China not embraced any economic science.

US economy's prospects are with food. The economy will slow to below 20% growth from 2020 with prospects of recessions. Professor Summers thought there is nearly 50% chance for a recession in 2020.

Ordinary Americans Are Hurting

Even aside from the concerns about its economic future, America has a duty to do well with its citizens, to increase welfare, long term prosperity and stop our growing long-term drift into poverty and divisiveness through increasing inequality. Increasing economic strains which leads to poverty and inequality are things that can increase divisiveness in America. I have stressed that the basic cause is structural which cannot go away with present conventional economic theories.

I hope I have in this book made the reader realize the almost unavoidable prospects of American economic long-run decline and the need for action. It is clear that the following sample statements by important Americans are misleading and illustrate the depth of economic arrogance and complacency and unconcern among Americans about the state of our US economy:

a. Larry Summers, as he was leaving the Obama administration: (Speech at the National Economic Council Washington December 13, 2010): "Predictions of America's decline are as old as the republic. They perform a crucial function in driving the kind of renewal that is required of each generation of Americans. We have our challenges. But we also have the most flexible, dynamic, entrepreneurial society the world has ever seen. If we can make the right choices, our best days as competitive and prosperous citizens still lie ahead."

b. Thomas Friedman and Michael Mandelbaum in their book, *That Used to be US:* "In order to sustain its remarkable economic progress, we believe, China will ultimately have to adopt more features of the American system."

c. Bill Clinton in his book *Back to Work:* "No one can take the future away from us... critics have been betting on America's demise for more than two hundred years now and that they have been always proved wrong."

d. Ed Whitacre in his book, *America Turnaround—Reinventing AT&T and GM and the Way We Do Business in the USA*: "We can do anything. We're the best. We're the most enthused. We're the most capable."

Notes

Chapter One

[1] B. Bernanke, *Semi-annual Monetary Policy Report Testimony to the Committee on Financial Services of the House,* July 18, 2007.

[2] Citi Group Study, *The top Eight Resource-Rich Countries; Central Intelligence Agency: The World Fact book: Country Comparison Oil Proven Reserve; Congressional Research Service Fossil Reserves/ Coal reserves.*

[3] Paul Krugman, "The Great Wealth Transfer," *The New York Times,* June 22, 2006.

[4] G. Walton and H. Rockoff, "History of the American Economy," *The Dryden Press* (New York: London, 1998), 502.

[5] Charles Holt, *Who benefited from the Prosperity of the twenties?: Exploration in Economic History,* 14 (1977), 277–289.

[6] Brookings Institute, *What Caused the Depression?* 1934.

[7] Michael Spence, *The Next Convergence: The future of Economic Growth in a Multispeed World,* (New York: Farr, Straus and Giroux), 229.

[8] McKinsey Global Institute, *Growth and Renewal in the United States: Retooling America's economic engine.*

[9] *Economic Report to the President,* 2013, 25.

[10] US Department of Labor, *Bureau of Labor: Overview of Labor Statistics.*

[11] Ibid.

[12] Martin Wolf, "How unruly economists can agree," *Financial Times,* February 25, 2010.

[13] Gregg Jarrell, *En-Nobelling Financial Economics,* March 24, 2007.

14   "The Other-worldly Philosophers," *The Economist*, July 18, 2009.

15   Brad DeLong, "But Economic Profession Right Now Useless," *Financial Times*, July 17, 2009.

16   "Making sense of Modern Economy," *The Economist*, July 16, 2009, 281.

17   Paul De Grauwe, Warring Economists Are Carried Along by the Crowd, *Financial Times*, July 22, 2009.

18   P. Krugman, *End this Recession Now*, (New York: W.W. Norton, 2012), 19.

19   P. Krugman, *The Return of Depression Economics and the Crisis of 2008*, (New York: W.W. Norton, 2009), 182.

20   Maury Klein, *Rainbow's End: The Crash of 1929*, (Oxford: Oxford University Press, 2011), 237.

21   Liquat Ahamad, *The Bankers who Broke the World*, (Penguin Books, 2009).

22   A. Greenspan, "Human's propensity to sway from fear to despair," *Financial Times*, August 4, 2008.

23   Iron Age, "End of the Road," March 31, 1931.

24   A. A. Adams, *Monopoly of Power in R. Himmelberg ed: The Great Depression and American Capitalism*, (Boston Heath, 1968), p.19.

25   Peter Temin, *Did Monetary Forces Cause the Great Depression?* (W.W. Norton, 1976), p.172.

26   J. Atack and P. Passell, *A New Economic History: From Colonial Times to 1940*, 2nd ed., (New York: W.W. Norton, 1994).

27   C. Henderson, *Asia falling: Making Sense of the Asian Crisis and its Aftermath*, (McGraw–Hill, 1998), 94-95.

28   World Bank, *The East Asian Miracle: Economic Growth and Public Policy. World Bank Policy Research Report 1020-0851*, (New York: Oxford University Press, 1996).

29   A.A. Adams, *Ibid.*

30   Robert McElvaine, *The Great Depression: America 1929- 1941*, (Time Books/Random House-Three Rivers, 1984), 102.

31   Gary Walton and Hugh Rockoff, *History of the American Economy*, (New York: The Druden Press, 1983), 515.

Chapter Two

[32] Wall Street Journal, *Paulson Expects Markets to Slow, Not Stall Growth,* August 16, 2007.

[33] *Populist,* December 31, 2008.

[34] Joseph Stiglitz, *Globalization and its discontents,* (W.W. Norton & Co NY, London 2002), 99.

[35] Alan Greenspan, *The Age of Turbulence,* (New York, Penguin Press, 2007), 395.

[36] A. Greenspan, "Technology and the Economy," Speech to Economic Club of New York, Jan 13, 2000.

[37] A. Greenspan, Technology and *I*nnovation and the *E*conomy, (White House Conference on the new Economy. Washington D, C April 5, 2000.

[38] R. Bootle, *The Death of Inflation: Surviving and Thriving in Zero Areas,* (Nicholas Brealey 1977), 216.

[39] Paul Krugman, T*he Return of Depression Economics and the Crisis of 2008,* (W.W. Norton NY. London 2009), 144.

[40] J. Chamberlin, *The Enterprising Americans: A Business History of the United States,* (New Edition) (New York: Harper and Raw 1974), 1–2.

[41] "Economic View by Daniel Altman," *New York Times,* December 10, 2006.

[42] The Big Picture, July 16, 2008.

[43] Henry Paulson in remarks before the Economic Club of Washington, March 1, 2007.

[44] Spiegel Special, Interview with Henry Paulson: We should expect upheavals, November 21, 2005.

[45] *The Per Jacobson Lecture,* Washington DC, 2007.

[46] Michael Oxley, *America on the Rebound: The Resilience of the US Economy,* Ashbrook Center at Ashland University, April 2004.

[47] Gerald M. Loeb, *The battle for investment Survival,* (New York: John Wiley &Sons, 2007), 51.

[48] Joseph Stiglitz, *The Roaring Nineties,* (New York: W.W. Norton & Co., London), xviii.

[49] *What goes up must come down: What goes up must come down*, March 4, 2007.

[50] Dave Maney, Forbes–Why who's President Matters so much for our economic future and why you should be worried, May 28, 2013.

[51] Economic Report to the President 2008, 1.

[52] Thomas Friedman, "Future of Capitalism," *New York Times*, June 9, 2010.

[53] Economic Report to the President, 2013, 33.

[54] Dave Maney, *Forbes,* Ibid May 28, 2013.

[55] A. Greenspan, Remarks: At the Haas Business Faculty Research Dialogue University of California Berkeley Cal., September 4, 1998.

[56] H. Paulson, Press release on the eve of visit to China, September 14, 2006.

Chapter Three

[57] Brookings Institute, *The Polarization of the US Labor Market,* (Brookings Papers on Economic Activity), Jan 2010, 1-69.

[58] John Schitt, *Is the "Real" US Unemployment Rate 13%?* Center for Economic and Policy Research: Issue Brief, June 2007.

[59] B. Bernanke, Before the Greater Omaha Chamber of Commerce, Omaha, Nebraska: The Level and distribution of Economic Well-Being.

[60] US Minimum Wage History, US Bureau of Census. US Dept. of Labor: Bureau of Labor Statistics; Statistical Abstracts of the United States 2007.

[61] Public Papers of US President B. Johnson 1963–1964, (Washington G.P.O. 1965, 1. 375.

[62] J. Stiglitz, *The Price of Inequality,* (New York: W. W. Norton & Company, 2012), 287.

[63] B. Bernanke, Before the Greater Omaha Chamber of Commerce Omaha Nebraska: The level and distribution of Economic Well-being, February 6, 2008.

[64] Sir. Keith Joseph, Center for Policy Studies Stockton England: "Monetarism is not enough" with foreword by Margaret Thatcher, April 5, 1976.

[65] National Commission on Fiscal Responsibility and Reform: Moment of Truth, December 2010.

[66] James Bacon, "What the IMF's Slow-growth Forecast Means for Bulky US Fiscal Deficit," *The Examiner,* July 10, 2010.

Chapter Four

[67] Professor Wu Jinglian: Does China need to change its industrialization Plan? (Conference Edition), Beijing.

[68] Wu Xiaobo, *China Emerging 1978-2008,* translated by Martha Avery (China International Press 2008) 159.

[69] Jinglian Wu: *Understanding and Interpreting Chinese Economic Reform,* Thompson-South–Western. Australian, United States, 2005 191.

[70] Document of the 17th National Congress of the Communist Party of China (2007) (Foreign language Press Beijing China 2007), 19.

[71] Document of the 17th Congress Ibid, 20.

[72] Document of the 17th Congress Ibid, 21.

[73] Documents of the 17th Congress Ibid, 88.

[74] Andrew Wilson, *China's Early Encounter with the West: A History in Reverse,* A Newsletter of FPRI's Watch Center, April 2008.

[75] David Roberts, *Obama's Stimulus Package was a Ginormous Energy Bill Says Michael Grunwald,* (Grist, August 14, 2012).

[76] I need to differentiate from proliferate waste of materials arising from deliberate replacement of labor by material in senseless pursuit of productivity.

[77] Vivek Wadha, "The End of Chinese Manufacturing and Rebirth of the US Industry," *Forbes,* July 23, 2012

[78] Martin Jacques, *When China Rules the World (End of the Western World and the Birth of a New Global Order),* (New York: Penguin Press 2009), 214.

Chapter Five

[79] Paul Krugman: "Is Free Trade Passé/" Economic Perspective 1, No. 2 1987, 131.

[80] Paul Krugman and Maurice Obstefeld, International Trade, 4th ed. (New York: Addison-Wesley, 1907, 57.

[81] Paul Krugman and Maurice Obstefeld, Ibid, 51.

[82] D. Appleyard and A. Field, *International Economics,* (New York: McGraw Hill, 1998), 43.

83 R. Carbaugh, International Economics, (International Thomas Publishing, 1995), 22.

84 R. Carbaugh, International Economics, Ibid, 89,

85 D. Appleyard and A. Field, (New York: Irwin McGraw- Hill, 1998), 160–161.

86 Professor D. Irwin, *Free Trade under fire,* (New York: Princeton University Press, 2002), 32-33.

87 H. Bowen, A. Hollander, and J. Vianne:*Applied International Trade Analysis,* (Ann Arbor: The University of Michigan Press, 2001), 228.

88 Paul Krugman:"Is Free Passe?" *Jounal of Economic Perspective* 1, 2, (1987), 132–41.

89 Robert C. Carbaugh: *International Economics,* (Ohio: South–Western College Publishing Co., 1995), 74.

90 Harry P. Bowen et al, (Ann Arbor: The University of Michigan Press, 2001), 329.

91 Paul R. Krugman et al, (New York: Addison–Wesley, 1997), p.132.

92 Womack, Jones, and Roos: *The Machine that changed the World.* (New York: Rawson Associates, 1990), 126.

93 H. Bowen et al: Ibid, 382.

94 P. Aghion and P. Howitt: *Endogenous Growth Theory,* (Cambridge: MIT Press, 1998), 389.

95 P. Aghion and P. Howitt: Ibid, 369.

96 P. Aghion et al: Ibid, 389–90.

97 P. N. Weerrasinghe, Trade policy: Openness and Economic performance: (Conference on Policy Options and Challenges for Developing Asia: Perspectives from the IMF and Asia. Organized by IMF and Japan Bank for International Cooperation (jbIC), Tokyo, Japan, April 19–20, 2007.

98 Daniel Griswold, Free Trade Bulletin no 27 Cato Institute, March 12, 2007.

99 Heritage Foundation: The Economy Hits Home: International Trade: Why Free Trade is the Fairest Trade of all by Jay Wesley Richards, June 10, 2013.

100 Economic Report to the President, 2013, 209.

Chapter Six

[101] H. M. McCracken, *Technological Change, Monopolistic Competition and Unemployment in Edward Chamberlain: The Theory of Monopolistic Competition 1933*, (Harvard University Press. 1933).

[102] Economic Report to the President 2006, 15.

[103] Roy Jenkin, *Frank Delano Roosevelt*, (New York Time Books 2003), 67

[104] Economic Report to the President 2006: Ibid150.

[106] R. Higgs, "Wartime prosperity? A Re-Assessment of the US economy in the 1940s." *Journal of Economic History*, 52 (1992), 56.

[106] D. Norick, M. Anshen, and W. Trupper, *Wartime Production Controls:* (New York Columbia University Press 1949).15.

[107] D. Wilson, *Wartime Construction and Expansion Survey of Business*, October 18, 1944.

[108] *New York Times*, Editorial June 24, 1944.

[109] *New York Times*, July 4, 1944.

[110] V. A. Canto, US Trade Policy: History and Evidence, *Cato Journal*, Vol 13 No 3, (Winter 1983/84).

Chapter Seven

[111] J. Stiglitz, *Making Globalization Work*, (W.W. Norton & Co. 2006), 188.

[112] Andrei Markovits: *Uncouth Nation: Why Europe dislikes America.* (Princeton University Press, 1997)

[113] Thomas D. Schoonover: *Uncle Sam's War of 1898 and the Origin of Globalization.* (University of Kentucky Press, 2003) 77.

[114] Maurice Obstefeld and Alan M. Taylor, *Capital Market Integraton, Crisis and Growth*, (Cambridge University Press, 2005), 5/6.

[115] J. Bhagwatti, *In Defense of Globalization*, (New York: Oxford University Press, 2004), 67.

[116] R. Rubin and J. Weisberg, *In an Uncertain World*, (New York: Random House Paperback, 2004), 54.

[117] Lawrence Summers, "America needs to make a new case for trade," *Financial Times*, Monday, April 28, 2008 and also *Financial Times*, May 5, 2008.

[118] Outlook for Global Economy, Business Inside, May 29, 2012.

119 J. E. Stiglitz, *Making Globalization Work,* (New York: W.W. Norton, 2006, 30–35.

120 Allan Greenspan, "American Economy in a world context," 35ᵗʰ Annual Conference on Bank Structure and Competition of the Federal Reserve Bank of Chicago, May 6, 1999.

121 Gov. Donald Kohn, The effects of globalization and their implications for monetary policy: Federal Reserve Bank of Boston's 51ˢᵗ Economic Conference Chatham, Mass., Jan 16, 2006.

122 A. Greenspan, 35ᵗʰ Annual Conference, Chicago, May 6, 1999, Ibid.

123 Gordon Brown, *Financial Times,* January 20, 2008.

124 Gordon Brown, *Financial Times,* "Ways to Fix the World's Financial System, February 25, 2008.

125 Gordon Brown, *Financial Times,* Friday, February 26, 2008.

126 Krishna Guha, *Financial Times,* IMF Must Reform to Remain Relevant, February 26, 2008.

Chapter Eight

127 Ben Bernanke, Speech at the Center for Economic Policy Studies on the occasion of the 75ᵗʰ anniversary of Woodrow Wilson School of Public and International Affairs, Princeton University, NJ, February 24, 2006.

128 Ben Bernanke, "Constrained Discretion and Monetary Policy," Remarks by Ben S. Bernanke before the Money Marketers of New York University, February 3, 2003.

129 Zhou Xiachuan, Avoid misreading history and objectively sum up lessons and experiences, Speech to the 'Forum of 50 Chinese Economists.' July 2009 in Peking.

130 Gov. Randall S. Krosner, Speech at the Bankers Association for Finance and Trade, *New York Times,* June 15, 2006.

131 A debate in the open on Fed, *New York Times,* April 2, 2013.

132 Donald L. Kohn, Comment on "Understanding the Evolving Inflation Process" by Cecchint, Hooper, Kaeman, Schehotz, Watson, March 9, 2007.

133 Governor Frederic S. Mishkin, At the Annual Macro Conference, Federal Bank of San Fransico CA., March 23, 2007.

[134]   Ivan O'Kitov, "Inflation, unemployment, labor force in the US" Russia Academy of Sciences ECINEC, October 28, 2006.

[135]   *New York Times,* Epitaph to NAIRU, July 20, 2000.

[136]   Donald Kohn, Commenting on paper: Understanding the Evolving Inflation, Ibid, March 9, 2007.

[137]   Bernanke, Inflation Expectation and Inflation Forecasting: At the Monetary Economics Workshop of the National Bureau of Economic Research Summer Institute. Cambridge Mass., July 10, 2007.

[138]   Samuel Brittan, "Headroom for Economic Recovery," *Financial Times,* March 19, 2010.

[139]   Kevin J. Lansing, FRBSF: Economic Letter 2002–2009, October 4, 2008.

[140]   Roger Bootle, *The death of Inflation,* London: Nicholas Brealey Publishing, 1996.

Chapter Nine

[141]   Ernst 2011 USIM/2012 Investment Monitor.

[142]   US International Trade/Commerce: Machinery Manufacturing: A major component of US exports, March 25, 2012.

[143]   Global Industries Analysts Inc., PRweB, February 13, 2012.

[144]   Ars. Technica, January 8, 2009.

[145]   Kevin Phillips, *Bad Money,* (Viking Penguin Group), 2008, 79.

[146]   Private Equity Growth Capital Council.

[147]   Michael Hirsh, *Capital Offense,* (John Wiley & Sons Inc., 2010, 9/12.

[148]   Nomura Securities Research May 2007 predicted housing slump with 8% price decline over 4 to 4 years.

[149]   Kevin Phillips, *Bad Money,* (New York: Free Press, 2012), 124.

[150]   J. Stiglitz, *The Price of Inequality,* (New York: W. W. Norton & Company, 2012), 238.

[151]   Henry Paulson, *On the Brink,* (New York: Business, 2009), 225.

[152]   Sheila Bair, *Bull by the Horns,* (New York: Free Press,), 120.

[153]   Henry Paulson, Prepared Remarks on the Growth and Future of China's Financial Markets (Shanghai China).

[154]   Simon Johnson and James Kwaki, *Their Wall Street Takeover and the Next Financial Meltdown,* (New York: Panthen Books, 2010), 221.

[155] Robert Barbera, *The Cost of Capitalism,* (The McGraw Hill Companies, 2009), 165.
[156] Newt Gingrich, *Real Change,* (New York: Regency Publishing Inc., 2008), 43.
[157] J. Michael Hirsh, Ibid, 147.
[158] J. Michael Hirsh, Ibid, 149.
[159] R. E. Rubin and J. Weisberg, *In An Uncertain World,* (New York: Random House Paperback, 2003), 122.
[160] Simon Johnson and James Kwaki, *13 Bankers: Their Wall Street Takeover and the Next Financial Meltdown,* (New York: Panthen Books, 2010), 221.
[161] K. Warsh and S. Dams. W. J. S. com. The Retreat of Globalization, October 14, 2012.
[162] Andrew R. Sorkin, *Too Big to Fail,* (New York: Viking, 2009), 442.
[163] Simon Johnson and James Kwaki, Ibid, 219.
[164] Bill Moyer Journal, February 13, 2009.
[165] Robert Sloan,"The Banker's Need to Fight Back." *Financial Times,* April 14, 2010.
[166] Jes Staley, "A Wider Divide," *Financial Times,* May 25, 2010.
[167] Justin Fox, *The Myth of the Rational Market (A History of Risk, Reward and Delusion on Wall Street,* (New York: Harp Business, 2009), 301.
[168] Justin Fox, Ibid, 305.

Chapter Ten

[169] *New York Times,* Capitalism Version 2012, March 132012
[170] Joseph E. Stiglitz, *The Price of Inequality,* (New York: W. W. Norton & Company, 2012), 271.
[171] "The Structural Revolution," *New York Times,* May 7, 2012.
[172] "On Economy, Think Long-term," *New York Times,* March 31, 2013.
[173] "Boom, Bust or what (Larry Summers and Glenn Hubbard Square off on our economic future)," *New York Times* Magazine, May 2, 2013.
[174] Arthur Laffer and Stephen Moore, *Return to Prosperity,* (New York: Threshhold Editions, London 2010).
[175] The 2013 Economic Report to the President, 29.
[176] The 2013 Economic Report to the President, 72.

[177] Maury Klein, *Rainbows. The Crash of 1929,* (Oxford: Oxford University Press, 2001), 191.

[178] Maury Klen, *Rainbow End,* Ibid, 191.

[179] Michael Pettis, The Great Rebalancing, (Oxford: Princeton University Press, 2013), 182.

[180] Arvind Subramanian Eclipse, Living in the shadow of China's Economic Dominance, (Peterson Institute for International Economics. Washington, 2011), 124.

[181] Martin Jacques, When China rules the world: The end of Western World and the Birth of a New Global Order, (New York: The Penguin Press, 2009), 13.

Index